THE LIFE AND LETTERS OF
MARTIN LUTHER

THE LIFE AND LETTERS OF
MARTIN LUTHER

BY

PRESERVED SMITH, Ph.D.

WITH ILLUSTRATIONS

" Nothing extenuate,
Nor set down aught in malice."

TOVT
BIEN OV
RIEN

BOSTON AND NEW YORK
HOUGHTON MIFFLIN COMPANY
The Riverside Press Cambridge
1911

Published May 1911

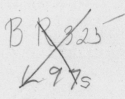

TO MY PARENTS

PREFACE

IT can hardly be denied that the men who have most changed history have been the great religious leaders. " Priest, Teacher," says Carlyle, "whatsoever we can fancy to reside in man, embodies itself here, to command over us, to furnish us with constant practical teaching, to tell us for the day and hour what we are to do." Among the great prophets, and, with the possible exception of Calvin, the last of world-wide importance, Martin Luther has taken his place. His career marks the beginning of the present epoch, for it is safe to say that every man in western Europe and in America is leading a different life to-day from what he would have led, and is another person altogether from what he would have been, had Martin Luther not lived. For the most important fact in modern history is undoubtedly the great schism of which he was the author, the consequences of which are still unfolding and will continue to unfold for many a century to come. In saying this we do not attribute to him the sole responsibility for the revolt from Rome. The study of history, as of evolution in other forms, has shown that there are no abrupt changes, — appearances to the contrary, — and that one epoch follows another as naturally and with as gradual a development as one season follows another in the year. In a sense the Protestant revolt, and the larger movement of which it was but the chief symptom, the expansion of the human mind, was inevitable. In another sense, equally true, it was the courage and genius of a great man which made it possible. If some such crisis was inevitable, he at least determined its time and to a large extent its direction. Granting, as axiomatic, that essential factors of the movement are to be found in the social, political, and cultural conditions of the age, and in the work of predecessors and followers, in short, in the environment which alone made Luther's lifework possible, there must still remain a very large element due directly and solely to his personality.

The present work aims to explain that personality; to show
him in the setting of his age; to indicate what part of his work
is to be attributed to his inheritance and to the events of the
time, but especially to reveal that part of the man which seems,
at least, to be explicable by neither heredity nor environment,
and to be more important than either, the character, or individ-
uality.

A new biography of Luther, however, requires more apology
than is to be found merely in the intrinsic interest of the subject. A glance at the catalogue of almost any great library —
that of the British Museum for instance — will show that more
has been written about Luther than about any man, save one,
who ever lived. Why bring another coal to this Newcastle?

One main reason is to be found in the extraordinarily rapid
advance of recent research, which, within the last ten, and still
more, of course, within the last twenty years, has greatly
changed our knowledge of the man. For example, the publication, in 1908, of the long lost Commentary on the Epistle to
the Romans has revolutionized our conception of the Reformer's
early development; the opening of the Vatican Archives by the
late Pope, by which many important documents were first
(1904) brought to light, has at last revealed the true history of
the legal process taken against the heretic by the Curia; the
researches of Dr. Kroker have but lately (1906) enabled us to
speak with precision of the early life of Catharine von Bora;
those of Dr. Rockwell (1904) have performed a similar service
for an important incident in Luther's life. Again, the great
edition of Luther's Works published at Weimar, and of the
letters by Dr. Enders and Professor Kawerau, both of which
are still in progress, have now made possible a more scientific
study of his most important works. A few random instances,
however, can give no adequate idea of the number of details,
not to mention larger matters, which have first been revealed
within the last decade. I have aimed to gather up, correlate,
and present the results of recent research now scattered through
a host of monographs. This has seemed to me the most pressing
need of the present, and I have, therefore, only to a limited
extent used unpublished material. In several points, however,

my own studies have led me to different conclusions from those commonly held, and I venture to hope that this feature of the book will not be without value to specialists.

In another respect the present work undertakes to present Luther to English readers from a standpoint different to that from which he is usually approached. I have endeavored to reveal him as a great character rather than as a great theologian. In order to do this I have given copious extracts from his table-talk and letters, those pregnant documents in which he unlocks his heart. No such self-revelation as is found in them exists elsewhere. Neither Pepys, nor Cellini, nor Rousseau has told us as much about his real self as has Luther about himself. Every trait of character is revealed: the indomitable will, "and courage never to submit or yield," the loyalty to conscience, the warm heart, the overflowing humor, the wonderful gift of seeing the essence of things and of expressing what he saw, and also the vehement temper and occasional coarseness of a rugged peasant nature. In the tremulous tone of the first epistles is reflected the anguish of a soul tortured by doubt and despair; later the writer tells with graphic force of the momentous debate at Leipsic; again, in the same hour in which he stood before the Emperor and Diet at Worms, asked to recant and expecting death if he did not, he writes a friend that he will never take back one jot or tittle. The letters from the Wartburg and Feste Coburg breathe the author's fresh, almost idyllic communion with nature; in the table-talk it is now the warm family affection which charms, now the irrepressible, rollicking joviality which bursts forth. The man's faults, too, stand in his unconscious autobiography, neither dissembled nor attenuated. Two blunders, his incitement to bloody reprisals against the rebellious peasants and his acquiescence in the bigamy of Philip of Hesse, blunders which his enemies called crimes, are frankly told in all the hideousness of their conception and consequences. It is, moreover, plain to the reader of the letters and table-talk that Luther was often in language and sometimes in thought the child of a coarse age. But of him it is especially true that to understand all is to pardon all. Through all his mistakes, and worse, he emerges a good and conscientious as well as a very great man: a son of thunder calling down fire from heaven; a Titan hurling Pelion upon Ossa against the hostile gods.

It is a pleasure to acknowledge the help I have received from many quarters. Professor Adolph Harnack has personally assisted my researches in the Berlin Royal Library. To Dr. Cowley and Professor Reginald Lane Poole I am indebted for special facilities in the use of the Bodleian Library at Oxford. Dr. Ernest Kroker, of Leipsic, has given me several valuable suggestions. Principal J. Estlin Carpenter, of Manchester College, Oxford, has kindly placed at my disposal the excellent collection of Lutherana made by the late Dr. Beard, whose History of the Reformation to the Diet of Worms, unfortunately left unfinished at his death (1888), is a well-known contribution to the subject. My friend Dr. David Saville Muzzy, of New York, has kindly revised the chapter on the Peasants' Revolt; Professor R. L. Poole, and Mr. Percy S. Allen, Fellow of Merton College, Oxford, have done the same for the chapter on Luther and Henry VIII as it originally appeared in the *English Historical Review*. My friend, Professor Herbert P. Gallinger, of Amherst, has read the proofs. I feel under especial obligations to Professor Gustav Kawerau, of Berlin, who, during my long stay at the Prussian capital, with the greatest possible kindness placed at my disposal his rare books and manuscripts and his more valuable time. To all these gentlemen I tender my warmest thanks. Last, but not least in love, I must acknowledge the help received in my own family. My father, the Rev. Dr. Henry Preserved Smith, has read the whole manuscript, and thus given me the benefit of his lifelong studies in divinity and experience as a writer. My sister, Miss Winifred Smith, and my wife have also aided me with criticism and suggestion.

P. S.

Paris, May 16, 1910.

LIST OF LIBRARIES AND ARCHIVES USED IN THE PREPARATION OF THIS WORK

ENGLAND

LONDON: British Museum, and Dr. Williams's Library.

OXFORD: Bodleian Library.

GERMANY

BERLIN: Königliche Bibliothek, Universitätsbibliothek, and private library of Professor Gustav Kawerau.

LEIPSIC: Universitätsbibliothek and Stadtbibliothek.

MARBURG: State Archives and Universitätsbibliothek.

FRANCE

PARIS: Bibliothèque Nationale, Bibliothèque de Sainte-Geneviève, Bibliothèque Mazarine, Bibliothèque de la Sorbonne, Bibliothèque de la Faculté Protestante.

UNITED STATES

BOSTON: Public Library.

CAMBRIDGE: Harvard University Library.

NEW YORK: Columbia University, Union Seminary, Astor and Lenox Libraries.

WASHINGTON: Congressional Library.

CONTENTS

ILLUSTRATIONS

THE LIFE AND LETTERS OF
MARTIN LUTHER

THE LIFE AND LETTERS OF
MARTIN LUTHER

CHAPTER I

CHILDHOOD AND STUDENT LIFE. 1483-1505

THE hills and forests of Thuringia, in the very heart of
Germany, unite great natural loveliness with the romantic
attractions of ancient historical association. If the traveller
stopping at Eisenach, the tiny metropolis of this favored region,
will walk south for about fifteen miles through the fairy forest,
he may visit the hamlet of Möhra, famous as the home of the
Luther family, still flourishing here in several branches. Here
lived Martin Luther's great-grandfather and grandfather as
peasants — for it is with them that the family pedigree begins.
Attempts to connect the name with that of the Emperor Lo-
thaire, as well as with other noble though less remote personages, have failed.

In the old days when Columbus was meditating his momentous voyage, and Richard III was about to murder his nephews
in the Tower, Hans Luther married Margaret Ziegler of Eisenach. Following the ancient peasant custom, by which the
older sons were sent out into the world to make their way,
while the youngest inherited the farm, Hans was forced to take
his wife away from home. He was attracted to the county of
Mansfeld, about sixty miles northeast of Eisenach, then as
now a mining district.

The first stop of the young couple was at Eisleben, and here,
on November 10, 1483, their oldest son was born, and the next
day baptized by the parish priest, Bartholomew Rennebrecher,
with the name Martin, after the saint whose day it was. The
little room under the tower of the church of St. Peter and St.
Paul where the baptism took place is shown, with part of the

antique font, exactly as it was then; the house exhibited as the birthplace is not, on the other hand, well authenticated.

While Martin was still a wee baby, the Luthers moved to the town of Mansfeld near by, where they were to spend the rest of their days. It is a pretty little village in the midst of its hills, on one of which stands the red sandstone castle of the Counts of Mansfeld.

The boy's life here was one of grinding, squalid poverty. The comely little cottage going by the name of the Luther house was bought or built by his father long after Martin had left home.

Hans Luther was a sturdy, frugal, hardworking man; that admirable type of character, who, having small natural gifts and no advantages, by sheer industry and will-power makes his way in the world. Starting as a stranger and a common miner, he gradually won a small competence and a place of honor among his fellow citizens, who eventually elected him to the highest office in the town. A man of natural shrewdness, his pointed and pithy sayings more than once made a lasting impression upon his son. He was ambitious to give this promising child the education he himself had lacked, and but for the wisdom and self-sacrifice with which he pursued this aim, Martin's career would have been impossible.

The mother, Margaret, was a quiet woman, bowed a little by poverty and toil. The son remembered seeing her carry on her back wood gathered from the forest. Both parents were strict, and even harsh. "My father," Luther said many years later, "once whipped me so severely that I fled from him, and it was hard for him to win me back. . . . My mother once beat me until the blood flowed, for having stolen a miserable nut. It was this strict discipline which finally forced me into the monastery, although they meant heartily well by it."

Martin had at least one brother and three sisters. He rarely saw them and never wrote to them after he left home, at the age of thirteen. Late in life his relations with them were disturbed by a quarrel about the division of his father's estate; but this was smoothed over, and the Reformer did his duty by the family nobly in caring for several of his orphan nephews and nieces.

The natural question, What were the first religious influences experienced by Martin Luther? can be briefly answered. He was taught a few simple prayers and hymns at his mother's knee. God the Father and Jesus were represented to him as stern, nay, cruel judges, to appease whose just wrath the intercession of the saints must be secured. No doubt was entertained by the humble peasants of the effectiveness of the ministrations of the Church; the ecclesiastical hierarchy, and especially the Pope, were regarded with reverent awe.

One prominent element of the popular religion of the time was superstition. The gloomy old Northern mythology, full of witches and kobolds, good spirits and evil spirits, survived from heathen times. It is hard to imagine now how gross and vivid was the belief in the supernatural in Hans Luther's house. Martin never freed himself from it, and many are his reminiscences of the witches who plagued his mother. Even his barelegged rambles through the hills were haunted by the dread of surrounding demons. " In my native country," he once said, " there is a high hill called the Pubelsberg, on top of which is a lake; if one throws a stone into the water a great tempest will arise over the whole region, for it is the habitation of captive devils. Prussia is full of them, and Lapland full of witches."

The boy's education began very early in the village school, which may still be seen by the traveller. Latin was the principal subject taught; the boys were required to speak as well as read it. Martin's recollections of the ignorance and brutality of his first teachers were very unhappy indeed. He was flogged repeatedly on the same morning for faltering in a declension. " Ah! " he exclaims, " what a time we had with the *lupus* [1] and Donatus! [2] My teachers made us parse everything, and made obscene jokes. The examination was like a trial for murder."

When Luther was only thirteen years old, he was sent to the school of a religious brotherhood — the " Nüllbrudern " — at

---

[1] The *lupus*, or wolf, was the monitor who punished the pupils for speaking German.

[2] The Latin grammar then and long after in use; Luther once said it was the best.

Magdeburg. Here he began to contribute to his own support by begging, in those days one of the recognized means by which a poor lad might get an education. No more stigma attached to it than attaches to the acceptance of a scholarship by a student nowadays. One of the few things known of this year is that the miserable life brought on a fever, which might have proved fatal had not the patient drunk some water in disobedience to the doctor's orders.

It may have been at Magdeburg that Martin's thoughts first turned in the direction of the monastic life. Erasmus, who attended one of the schools of the same order, relates graphically how hard the brothers tried to guide their pupils into the cloister.[1] One incident, at any rate, made so deep an impression on Luther's mind, that thirty-five years later he wrote of it thus:[2]

When, in my fourteenth year, I went to school at Magdeburg, I saw with my own eyes a prince of Anhalt . . . who went in a friar's cowl on the highways to beg bread, and carried a sack like a donkey, so heavy that he bent under it, but his companion walked by him without a burden; this prince alone might serve as an example of the grisly, shorn holiness of the world. They had so stunned him that he did all the works of the cloister like any other brother, and he had so fasted, watched, and mortified his flesh that he looked like a death's head, mere skin and bones; indeed he soon after died, for he could not long bear such a severe life. In short, whoever looked at him had to gasp for pity and must needs be ashamed of his own worldly position.

After one year at Magdeburg, Martin was transferred to Eisenach to attend the school of St. George the dragon-killer. His mother had, in this her native town, a relative named Conrad Hutter[3] on whose help she counted for her son. Hutter was sexton of St. Nicholas' Church, and it may have been through him that Luther learned to know and love the parish priest, John Braun. It was not with his kinsman that he lodged, however, but with a certain family identified by most biographers with the Cottas. Luther sometimes speaks in later years of "his

---

[1] *Erasmi opera*, ed. Clericus, Leyden, 1701, vol. iii, col. 1822.

[2] *Defence before Duke George*, 1533, Erlangen edition, xxxi, 239 ff.

[3] O. Clemen: *Beiträge zur Reformationsgeschichte*, ii, 1.

hostess of Eisenach," but never by name, assuming her to have been well known to his audience. She took him in, according to tradition, "for his hearty singing," and under her charitable and pious roof the boy for the first time tasted modest comfort. Frau Cotta was by birth a Schalbe ; this wealthy family had founded a little Franciscan monastery at the foot of the Wartburg,[1] with whose inmates young Luther, serious and pious beyond his years, became friendly. So priestly indeed was his circle of friends that he heard with astonishment from his hostess a little verse to the effect that nothing was dearer on earth than the love of woman to him who could win it.

The promise of the industrious, bright boy induced his father, whose circumstances, though not easy, were improving, to continue his liberal education. Accordingly at the beginning of the summer semester (about May, 1501) "Martinus Ludher ex Mansfeld" matriculated at the old and famous University of Erfurt. It was the custom of students who did not board with one of the professors to live at a "Burse," a combination of dormitory and eating-club. Luther lived at the "Burse" of St. George, which once stood on Lehmann's bridge, but is now no longer in existence.

The course of studies began with logic, dialectic, grammar, and rhetoric, followed by arithmetic, various natural sciences, ethics, and metaphysics. All the studies were sicklied o'er with a pale cast of scholasticism. Mediæval thought had progressed little, if at all, beyond Aristotle, who was regarded as an inerrant authority, but it had elaborated his rules of argumentation into fantastic extremes, at once dry and ridiculous. The two most celebrated professors at Erfurt in the early sixteenth century, Trutvetter and Usingen, were entirely under the sway of the Stagirite, and one may well believe Melanchthon's testimony "that a particularly thorny kind of dialectic" prevailed there. The natural sciences were studied absolutely without experiment or original research, in perfect reliance on Aristotle's ancient works. The philosophy, too, was founded

---

[1] Not now preserved, probably it was on or near the Barfüsser Strasse. The house shown as the Luther house, i. e., Frau Cotta's, is of very doubtful authenticity.

on his essays, though in this case some changes in his system had been made by the great thinkers of the Middle Ages in their endeavors to harmonize it with Christianity. The great question which agitated mediæval thought was whether the individual or the class was the reality ; *e. g.*, in the word " horse," is the essential thing each particular horse, or the abstract of all the qualities which make up the conception? The realists, who decided in favor of the latter, flourished in the heyday of scholasticism, but the nominalists, who maintained the former, had now supplanted them, and Erfurt philosophy was therefore of this school.

The universities in the sixteenth century were undergoing a change somewhat similar to that which they are experiencing in the twentieth. The old mediæval course, which has just been sketched, no longer prevailed without opposition. Some rays of the "new learning," the glorious rebirth of classical antiquity, had penetrated Erfurt. Indeed there were several courses in the classics, and a circle of students devoted to the humanities. The inclinations of the miner's son, however, did not lead him that way. His serious, religious mind preferred the rough road of scholasticism to the primrose path of poetry and oratory. He later regretted that he had read no more history and poems, and added that the study of scholastic philosophy prevented his reading any verse except Baptista Mantuan,[1] Ovid's Heroides, and Virgil.

Of the student's life little is known. That it was pure and godly may be inferred from the fact that his enemies never found any reproach in it and because of the absence of self-accusation. He sometimes suffered from ill-health and depression. One day he found a Bible in the library, and began to read the passage about Hannah and Samuel, but a lecture called him away, and he apparently did not pursue his reading farther at this time.[2]

After taking, with high rank, the degrees of bachelor of arts

[1] This late poet (1448–1516), Shakespeare's " good old Mantuan," was a great favorite of the Renaissance.

[2] Kroker: Rörers Tischreden, in *Archiv. f. Reformationsgeschichte*, no. 20 (1908), p. 345.

in 1502 and of master in 1505, Luther just began the study of jurisprudence. This was in accordance with the wishes of his ambitious father, who bought him an expensive Corpus Juris. He had worked in law only two months, however, when he abruptly decided to enter the monastery.

CHAPTER II

THE MONK. 1505-1512

VARIOUS reasons have been assigned for the sudden decision of Luther to become a monk. The real cause lay in a torturing sense of sin and a longing for reconciliation with God, experienced by many deeply spiritual Christians at one time or another in their lives. The cloister had been the refuge of such persons for a thousand years; to it the Saxon student naturally turned to find rest for his soul. After all, the seemingly abrupt vow is only the natural culmination of previous experiences. The strict discipline of a stern and pious home, the terrible vision of the begging prince, the priestly circle of friends at Eisenach, had all pointed the boy to the career then regarded as the perfection of Christianity.

The influences in the same direction at Erfurt were also very strong. This flourishing but by no means large town boasted twenty cloisters, twenty-three churches, thirty-six chapels, and in all more than one hundred buildings devoted to religious uses. Among the numerous orders represented by chapters at "little Rome," as the devout city was called, the strongest were those of the begging friars, the Franciscans, Dominicans, and Augustinians.

This last order could not claim, like the others, a great saint as founder, for Augustine had not written their rule. Since their first incorporation by Innocent IV in 1243, confirmed by Alexander IV in 1256, the Augustinian Hermits, as they were officially called, flourished mightily. By the middle of the fifteenth century, there were two thousand chapters, and the order, like most of the older ones, had begun to show some signs of degeneracy. A reform had been carried through many of the chapters by Proles, for the last quarter of the fifteenth century Vicar of the German province. Erfurt had joined "the congregation of the observants," as the reform movement was called, in 1475. What made Luther choose this monastery cannot be certainly told; perhaps some personal ties and the good fame of the Hermits attracted him.

The spring and early summer of 1505 was a terrible time at Erfurt. The plague broke out, some of the students died of it, and most of the others left town in a panic. It is at such time, that men's thoughts turn to the other world, and Luther, who had already been asking himself the question, "When will you be righteous and do enough to win a gracious God?" seriously considered abandoning a worldly for a spiritual calling. The faculty of law began lecturing on May 19, but the young student had hardly attended their courses for a month before he became thoroughly disgusted with a profession which, to his mind, had no relish of salvation in it. Towards the last of June he returned to his father's house, perhaps to get permission to drop his juristic studies.

As he was coming back to the university, on July 2, he was overtaken at Stotterheim, near Erfurt, by a terrible thunderstorm, and, in a fright, vowed to St. Anna to be a monk. If it may seem strange that a young man of twenty-two should be panic-stricken by a clap of thunder, it must be remembered that the miner's son regarded such phenomena as frequently occasioned by the direct interposition of the devil. Moreover, it has been shown that he probably had the more than half-formed intention already in his mind. He later speaks of being warned to enter the cloister by a heavenly vision. What this was, whether connected with the storm or not, is entirely unknown.

Old Hans Luther was bitterly opposed to his son's step, which he believed destroyed all chance of a successful career. Martin also cast some longing, lingering looks behind, but dared not turn back, and hastened the day of his entrance to shorten this temptation. On July 16 he invited some friends, including "honorable matrons and maidens," to a farewell supper. The evening was spent in music and good cheer; the next day he entered the monastery.

The reception of a would-be brother was a solemn occasion. The young man fell down before the feet of the prior and was asked what he wanted, to which he replied, " God's mercy and yours." The superior instructed him in the hardships, the duties, the sacrifices, and also in the blessedness of the life he had chosen. He was then put under the care of an older brother, and obliged to fulfil a year of probation. During this period he not only learned the rules of the order — such as the prayers five times a day — but he was instructed in the higher spiritual life. At the same time he was obliged to do the humblest menial service, such as sweeping and cleaning. Luther's novitiate ended in September, 1506, when he took the irrevocable vows of poverty, chastity, and obedience, through which he was supposed to die to the world and be " rebaptized " to a higher life.

Brother Martin was ordained priest in February, 1507. The celebration of the first mass was a great occasion, to which he invited his father, his kinsman Conrad Hutter of Eisenach, and the parish priest of that town, whom he had learned to love while at school. Luther's first extant letter is the invitation to this friend to attend the mass: —

TO JOHN BRAUN AT EISENACH

ERFURT, April 22, 1507.

. . . God, glorious and holy in all his works, has deigned to exalt me, wretched and unworthy sinner, and to call me into his sublime ministry only for his mercy's sake. I ought to be thankful for the glory of such divine goodness (as much as dust may be) and to fulfil the duty laid upon me.

Wherefore the fathers have set aside Sunday, May 2, for my first mass, God willing. That day I shall officiate before God for the first time, the day being chosen for the convenience of my father. . . . Dearest father, as you are in age and care for me, master in merit and brother in religion, if private business will permit you, deign to come and help me with your gracious presence and prayers, that my sacrifice may be acceptable in God's sight. . . .

Whether Braun accepted the invitation is not known. Luther's father, however, who seems to have been partially reconciled, came, bringing a number of friends, and gave his son a handsome present. The two had an earnest talk, the son urging that he was warned to become a monk by a terrible heavenly vision, to which his father replied that he hoped it was not an apparition of the devil. Again, when Martin tried to justify himself, and gently reproached his father for his anger, the old man replied, "Have you never heard that a man should honor his parents?"

Luther's studies were not long interrupted by his vow. On the contrary, he continued philosophy and took up divinity, a nearly allied science. He applied himself with such zeal and success that about eighteen months after his first mass he was called to the recently founded University of Wittenberg to teach Aristotle's Ethics. He spent a year in this position, at the same time continuing his own studies. He took his first theological degree (*baccalaureus ad biblia*) on March 9, 1509, about the same time writing his second extant letter to Braun, apologizing for leaving Erfurt without bidding him farewell. The letter, which is hastily written, and somewhat faltering, has one extremely interesting passage : —

Now I am at Wittenberg, by God's command or permission. If you wish to know my condition I am well, thank God, but my studies are very severe, especially philosophy, which from the first I would willingly have changed for theology, I mean that theology which searches out the meat of the nut, the kernel of the grain and the marrow of the bones. But God is God; man is often, if not always, at fault in his judgment. He is our God, he will sweetly govern us forever.

In the fall of 1509 Luther was sent back to Erfurt "because he had not satisfied the Wittenberg faculty." This sentence in the Dean's book, with Luther's own later addition, "because he had no means : — Erfurt must pay," is usually taken to mean that he had not the money to pay the academic fees. It is also probable that there was some trouble about the lectures he was to give; he wishing to discontinue philosophy and take up the Bible. It was the academic rule that before lecturing on the Scriptures a young professor should devote three semesters to expounding Peter Lombard's Sentences, the common textbook in theology. This Luther did at Erfurt, where he remained for about twenty-one months, until he was called back to a permanent position at Wittenberg in the summer of 1511. This stay at Erfurt was interrupted by the journey to Rome.

Such is the bare history of the outward events of the seven years in the cloister. Far more interesting, though more difficult to trace, is the record of his inward life during the same time. What did the young monk experience which fitted him for the great duties which lay before him? What, in short, was his development?

Instead of finding peace within the monastic cell, at first doubt and despair only increased. His table-talk, taken down late in life, is full of statements of the utter depth of the sufferings of the doubter of his own salvation. God appeared to him as a cruel judge; he felt that he could never do enough to win his favor and deserve free pardon. Though there is some reason to believe that in looking back he painted his past even darker than it really was, there can be no doubt that he went through agonies before he attained strength and peace of mind. His course of thought can be followed by studying the books he read, with his own notes on them.

The theologians he read belonged to what was then called "the modern" school — "the modernists" of the sixteenth century. Thomas Aquinas, perhaps the greatest of the schoolmen, was not much regarded; he belonged to the old-fashioned, superseded faction. The philosopher most studied was William Occam; next to him Gabriel Biel, the Parisian doctors Ailly and Gerson, Bernard of Clairvaux, Bonaventura, John Mauburn, and Gerhard of Zütphen. The fundamental thesis of the Occamists was that man can do anything he will — fulfil the Ten Commandments to the letter or persuade his reason that white is black. The cloister adopted this view and held that by a man's own acts, asceticism, prayer, and meditation, he could prepare his soul for union with God. Biel especially emphasized the possibility and duty of a man hating his own sins; — fear, said he, is not enough to make repentance acceptable to God.

Luther took this all in and tried to act accordingly. He fulfilled all the monastic duties with punctuality; he buffeted his body with zeal to keep it under; he froze in his unheated cell, he starved himself until he was a skeleton "so that one could almost count his bones," he underwent such austerities that he was found fainting by his brothers. But all this did not bring him peace. After each access of devotion came a fresh access of despair.

A second doctrine that Luther imbibed from the theologians was that God is pure, arbitrary will. He had created the world solely for his own pleasure; his will made right and wrong; and finally his arbitrary choice alone conditioned man's salvation. But in this latter particular, having promised to consider certain actions as meritorious, he has put in each man's power to obtain his favor by performing these acts, and his acceptance of man is sealed by the sacraments of the Church. The young monk could not bring himself to love a God like that; he feared, he even hated him. "When I looked for Christ," he said, "it seemed to me as if I saw the devil."

Luther's development is largely a history of his enfranchisement from the Occamist theology. But even after he had freed himself from the oppressive doctrines he bore lasting marks of the apprenticeship in Occam's school. In 1515 we find him calling these scholastics the "hog-doctors," but throughout life he carried certain of their teachings with him. Occam — the "modernist" — was the sharpest critic of the mediæval Church, and especially of the hierarchy. He said flatly that popes and councils could err, and remembering this doubtless made the break with Rome easier for Luther.

But taken as a whole the reading of scholastic philosophy only deepened his perplexity and anguish of soul. He had to win his own way to light, which came at last. Several of his fellow monks helped him with counsel and comfort, especially his spiritual director who sought to combat his doubts by giving him orthodox literature. Of this man Luther speaks long afterwards: —

I remember with what ardor and pleasure I read Athanasius' dialogue on the Trinity during my first year in the cloister when my monastic pedagogue at Erfurt, an excellent man and a true Christian under the cursed cowl, gave me a copy of it made by himself.

This same wise old man pointed out to him that God was not

angry with him, but he with God, and emphasized the *duty* of believing in the forgiveness of sins. This was the first comfort he received.

Most of all he was helped by John Staupitz, since 1503 the Vicar of the German province of Augustinians, and dean of the faculty of theology at Wittenberg. With statesmanlike breadth combining energy and tact, he constantly sought to purify, consolidate, and enlarge his order, but while prosecuting these comprehensive plans never forgot small chapters and young brothers in need of help. His relations with Luther were so special that some have proposed to regard his influence as the decisive factor in the Reformer's development, but this view is hardly justified by the known facts. With many expresssons of gratitude from the young man to the elder we have his own sorrowful statement that even Staupitz did not rightly understand him. His superior, a mystic in doctrine, helped him not so much by teaching as by loving him. The vicar was a man who understood men, and it was due to his recommendation that Luther received the call to Wittenberg.

The young monk was chiefly illumined by the perusal of the Bible. The book was a very common one, there having been no less than one hundred editions of the Latin Vulgate published before 1500, as well as a number of German translations. The rule of the Augustinians prescribed diligent reading of the Scriptures, and Luther obeyed this regulation with joyous zeal, in spite of the astonishment of Staupitz and discouragement on the part of Dr. Usingen.

Next to the Bible, St. Augustine was the most helpful of all the writers read by Luther. He began to know him at latest in 1508 ; a recent find has given us the very copy of Augustine's works that he used, with the margins crammed full of notes. According to these indications what impressed him most was the saint's mysticism — his philosophy of God, the world, the soul, the worthlessness of earthly life and the blessedness of the life hid with God. These thoughts so cheered him that at times he felt as if he was "among choirs of angels."

With all the helps that he received, it was years before he found even the key of his solution. The letter to Braun of 1507 witnesses the downcast, trembling posture of his soul. At the first mass he experienced torturing doubts: "When I came to the words 'thee, most merciful Father,'" he says, "the thought that I had to speak to God without a mediator almost made me flee like another Judas."

It was one day at Wittenberg in 1508 or 1509, as he was sitting in his cell in a little tower, that his life message came to him, and with it the first assurance of permanent comfort and peace. He was reading Paul's Epistle to the Romans, and came to the verse (i, 17) "The just shall live by faith." Pondering over this it came to him that it was not, as he had been taught, by man's own works that he was redeemed, but by faith in God and the Saviour. Justification by faith has been rightly selected as the cardinal doctrine of the Lutheran theology; he himself recognized in it the corner-stone of his whole life.

Of course Luther's development was not completed at once. Even after the master-key had been found, the long struggle continued, and other factors entered in to modify and enrich his character. He entered the monastery to save his soul, and the struggle for peace took twelve long years before the monk was ripe for the great deeds he was called on to perform. No one can get even an idea of what the struggle cost him save by reading after him the folios and quartos he perused, and trying to follow him in all that tangled labyrinth. And yet his development was perfectly normal and even. That his health suffered somewhat from asceticism is undoubtedly true, but there were no morbid symptoms in his conversion. Comparing it to that of other famous Christians, there were no visions such as Loyola saw, and no moral breakdown such as that of Augustine. In those years of hardship, meditation, study, and thought, he laid the foundations of that adamantine character which stood unshaken amidst a tempest that rocked Europe to its base.

CHAPTER III

WORK at Erfurt was interrupted by one of the most important and interesting events in Luther's early career, the journey to Rome. As nearly all known about this trip comes from reminiscences, of many years afterwards, there is a good deal that is obscure. Scholars are divided on a number of points connected with the event, among others on the time at which it took place. The probability points to the date given at the head of this chapter, but this is far from certain; many students think the trip to Rome was at the same season a year later, and a few find still other dates. The Reformer in his table-talk places it now in one year, now in another, though the majority of references give 1510. Many other points are also unsettled; the account in this chapter follows what seems to me the greatest probability and the best authority.

The cause of the trip is connected with the history of the Augustinian order. As previously stated, when Proles carried through his reform of 1473–1475 all the cloisters did not adhere to the movement. Staupitz was anxious to complete the work of his predecessor by uniting all the chapters again, and some years after he was elected vicar of the Augustinian Observants, in 1503, the opportunity arrived. Securing the interest of the general of the order at Rome, and of the Curia, on June 26, 1510, he was appointed provincial of the whole Saxon province, with authority to force the non-observant cloisters into the reformed congregation. Several of these chapters, who felt themselves aggrieved, decided to appeal to Rome, and their motion was supported by some of the cloisters under Staupitz's jurisdiction, including Erfurt. The disaffected chose as their agent John von Mecheln of Nuremberg, and with him went Martin Luther.

It is probable that the latter had little or nothing to do with the business in hand. At any rate he never mentions it. Moreover, his warm relations with Staupitz make it unlikely that he would be willing to take a decided part against him. The laws of the order required that the brothers should always travel two and two, and he was simply the *socius itinerarius* of John von Mecheln. He grasped eagerly at the opportunity to visit the Eternal City; indeed, he once stated that the purpose of his going was to make a general confession of all his sins and to receive absolution.

The brothers set out in October, not cheerfully talking side by side, but walking silently in single file. Their itinerary is not known; there were various routes used by pilgrims, and it is impossible to judge much from Luther's own vague mention of places. When they arrived in Italy, they discovered the insidious quality of the climate, as the following incident relates: —

On the journey to Rome the brother with whom I was travelling and I were very tired one night and slept with open windows until about six o'clock. When we awoke, our heads were full of vapors, so that we could only go four or five miles that day, tormented by thirst and yet sickened by the wine and desiring only the water which is deadly there. At length we were refreshed by two pomegranates with which excellent fruit God saved our lives.

The journey took the brothers through Florence, rich then as now with the art treasures which are the delight and wonder of the world. It is characteristic of Luther, who says very little about the painting and sculpture he saw, that he should have carefully visited the hospitals. The principal one was the Spedale di Santa Maria Nuova, just back of the cathedral, founded by Portinari, the father of Dante's Beatrice. Not far from it is the foundling hospital, the Spedale degli Innocenti, founded in the fifteenth century and richly decorated with medallions by Andrea della Robbia. The pilgrim related his experience thus: —

The hospitals of the Italians are built like the palaces, supplied with the best food and drink, and tended by diligent servants and skilful physicians. The painted bedsteads are covered with clean linen. When a patient is brought in, his clothes are taken off and given to a notary to keep honestly. Then they put a white bed-gown on him and lay him between the clean sheets of the beautifully painted bed, and two physicians are brought at once. Servants fetch food and drink in clean glass vessels, and do not touch the food even with a finger, but offer it to the patient on a tray. Honorable matrons, veiled, serve the poor all day long without making their names known, and at evening return home. These carefully tended hospitals I saw at Florence. They also have foundling asylums, where children are well sheltered and nourished and taught ; they are all dressed in uniform and most paternally provided for.

Continuing the trip south, the brothers finally caught sight of Rome. The emotions of the young man were overpowering; he fell on his face and cried: "Hail, holy Rome!"

The month of December was spent here. While his companion did the business of the order, Luther spent the time seeing the sights. There was then a guide-book, the so-called Mirabilia Romae, which had been published as a block-book before the days of movable types. That Luther used it is probable from parallels found in the table-talk, and Professor Hausrath has constructed his whole visit from this hint, just as one might imagine what a modern tourist saw by consulting Baedeker. What impressed him most of all the sights were the remains of classical antiquity, the Coliseum, the baths, the Pantheon. He also speaks of the catacombs of Calixtus and of some of the churches.

"I was a foolish pilgrim," says he, "and believed all that I was told." He visited all the shrines to take advantage of the indulgences granted to pious worshippers, and even went so far as to wish that his parents were dead that he might get their souls out of purgatory, for which charitable work so many opportunities offered. One of the most celebrated shrines of the Holy City is the chapel Sancta Sanctorum at the eastern end of the Piazza di San Giovanni, in which was, and still is, the flight of twenty-eight steps, taken, as the Romans fabled, from the judgment hall of Pilate in Jerusalem. Leo IV had granted an indulgence of nine years for every step climbed by the pilgrim on his knees while saying the appointed prayers.

If one may trust the story which Luther's son Paul remembered hearing his father tell,[1] he started climbing these stairs and praying, but suddenly remembered the verse in Romans, " The just shall live by faith," arose and descended.

Luther could not fail to be shocked by many things he saw. At the time they did not shake his faith in the Church, nor his allegiance to the Pope, but when the breach came in after years his heart was hardened by the remembrance of the visit. He could never have attacked Rome so vigorously and successfully in 1520 had it not been for what he saw in 1510. He often refers to it in words like these : —

Rome is a harlot. I would not take a thousand gulden not to have seen it, for I never would have believed the true state of affairs from what other people told me, had I not seen it myself. The Italians mocked us for being pious monks, for they hold Christians fools. They say six or seven masses in the time it takes me to say one, for they take money for it and I do not. The only crime in Italy is poverty. They still punish homicide and theft a little, for they have to, but no other sin is too gross for them. . . .

So great and bold is Roman impiety that neither God nor man, neither sin nor shame, is feared. All good men who have seen Rome bear witness to this; all bad ones come back worse than before.

The return journey took about seven weeks. Passing through Milan, Luther was surprised to find priests who claimed not to acknowledge the supremacy of the Pope, for they followed St. Ambrose. His eyes were open to the beauty and fertility of the Lombard plains. He arrived at Erfurt in February.

It is not without interest to note another trip, though one of infinitely less importance than the Italian journey, taken by Luther in his monastic days. This was to Cologne, where he saw the relics of the three kings. He never forgot the wine he drank in this city, which he said was the best he ever tasted.[2]

[1] This celebrated story was first published in its original form in 1903. Köstlin-Kawerau, i, 749. Paul was only eleven years old when the story was told (in 1544) and he wrote it down thirty-eight years later.

[2] Weimar edition, xxxiv, i, 22, and note at end of volume.

CHAPTER IV

THE PROFESSOR. 1512-1517

WITTENBERG is situated on the banks of the Elbe about halfway between Leipsic and Berlin. The broad and winding river is not at this point navigable. The country is flat, the soil sandy and poor. Toward the end of the fifteenth century Wittenberg was a mere hamlet, containing about three hundred and fifty low, ugly wooden houses, with an old church and a town hall. To explain its rise to prominence as a university town and military post a short digression on contemporary history is necessary — an explanation which will also serve to clear up the matter of the two Saxonys, a standing puzzle to foreigners who read German history.

The treaty of Leipsic, August, 1485, divided the lands of the house of Wettin forever into two parts. The so-called "Electoral District" (Kurkreis) of which Wittenberg was the centre, together with some territory to the southward including Eisenach, Weimar, and Coburg, was given to the elder brother, Ernest, with the title of Elector of Saxony. The younger, Albert, who was called Duke of Saxony, obtained the smaller but better portion of the land, including the two cities of Leipsic and Dresden with the surrounding country.

Frederic, surnamed the Wise, who became Elector of Saxony in 1486, at once started to replenish his diminished resources. He chose Wittenberg as a sort of capital of his northern territory — usually himself residing at Altenburg in the south. He began immediately to ornament the town with public buildings, including a castle and a church, for the decoration of which he employed Albert Dürer, the Nuremberg painter. In 1502 he founded a university, in order that his subjects might not have to go to Leipsic, belonging to his cousin, or to Erfurt, under the jurisdiction of the Elector of Mayence. He appointed Staupitz first dean of the faculty of theology, intending that most of the professors should be monks of the Augustinian order, which had a chapter at Wittenberg. Staupitz entered into the work with zeal; he rebuilt and enlarged the Black Cloister (as the monastery was called, from the popular name of the Augustinians as Black Monks), began to lecture on the Bible, and gathered around him some young men whom he intended to train to fill positions as teachers.

The one in whom he had most confidence was Martin Luther. It was at his recommendation that the young brother had been made instructor in philosophy during the year 1508–09, and it was also at his recommendation that Martin was again called in the summer of 1511 to be professor of divinity. The vicar was anxious to retire and wished the younger man to take his own place. In order to do this a degree of doctor was considered necessary, to which, at first, Luther was averse. Many years later he told the following story, so characteristic of the vicar's gentle humor : —

Dr. Staupitz said to me one day as we were sitting under the pear-tree still standing in the court, "You should take the degree of doctor so as to have something to do." . . . I objected that my strength was already used up, and that I could not long survive the duties imposed on me by a professorship. He answered: "Do you not know that the Lord has a great deal of business to attend to, in which he needs the assistance of clever people? If you should die, you might be his counsellor."

Such argument could not be withstood, and accordingly October 18, 1512, was set aside for Luther to take the highest degree in theology, that of doctor in divinity. His invitation to his brothers at Erfurt to attend the ceremony is interesting, both because of the matter it contains, and because of its perfect self-possession in contrast to the previous letters.

TO THE PRIOR ANDREW LOHR AND THE CONVENT OF
AUGUSTINIANS AT ERFURT

WITTENBERG, September 22, 1512.

Greeting in the Lord! Reverend, venerable and dear Fathers! Behold the day of St. Luke is at hand, on which, in obedience to you and to our reverend Vicar Staupitz, I shall take my examination in theology in the hall of the university. . . . I do not now accuse my-self of unworthiness, lest I should seem to seek praise and honor by my humility; God and my conscience know how worthy and how grateful I am for this public honor. . . . I beg that you will deign to come and be present at the celebration, if convenient, for the glory and honor of religion and especially of our chapter. . . .

After taking the degree, to which he seems to have been thoroughly reconciled, Luther began to lecture on the Bible, a practice which he kept up all his life. The recent publication of the marginal notes (1509–10) in some of the books he used, and of his lectures on the Psalms (1513–15), on the Epistle to the Romans (1515–16), and on the Book of Judges (1516), together with the Commentary on Galatians, printed by Luther himself in 1519 (from lectures given in 1516–17), gives us a deep insight into his methods and results.

Glancing first at the more external qualities, these lectures and notes evince extreme thoroughness — not a bad quality in a professor, and one for which German professors have ever been justly famous. He not only turned the pages of his books, he read, marked, learned, and inwardly digested them. He criticised his authors and with such acumen that two works attributed to Augustine, the genuineness of which he first disputed, have been proved by modern criticism to be spurious. He sought diligently for the best authorities and the most recent books. In his Commentary on the Psalms he used the edition of the French humanist Lefèvre d'Étaples, published in 1509. This author, "a little Luther," as Michelet called him, is a chief guide in the exegesis of the text. Next to him, or perhaps one should say, ahead of him, the influence of Augustine, and through him of the Neoplatonic school, is the most important element. Comparing these lectures with the notes on Lombard (1509–10), a considerable advance in freedom and power is noticeable. The early work is stiff, formal, and timid; in the later, though the text and authorities are still followed fairly closely, there is more freedom of treatment and more of the subjective element. The new religious ideas, especially that of justification by faith, can be plainly made out, and several opinions which could find no room in the Catholic Church come forward. In fact, as far as we can judge, it was in these lectures, his first on the Bible, that Luther began to formulate his peculiar theology.

In the summer semester of 1515, about May, Luther began to lecture on Romans, continuing the course for about three semesters. His principal guide, at first, was again the humanist Lefèvre, whose text of St. Paul's epistles had appeared in 1512. While Luther was still lecturing, in March, 1516, Erasmus' edition of the New Testament with a new Latin translation and notes came out, and was immediately procured by the Wittenberg professor. From this time on, beginning, namely, with the ninth chapter of Romans, Erasmus took the lead as an exegetical authority. Not that the lecturer follows him slavishly; he balances authorities, and occasionally disagrees with all of them. Nevertheless we can hardly overestimate the importance of the Greek Testament on the Reformer's thought; from this time on almost all of his important theological work is founded on it, and of course on the material supplied by its editor.

The Commentary on Romans is a great human document, priceless for its biographical interest. So important is it in the history of the author's thought that Father Denifle, who first called attention to it,[1] was inclined to date the commencement of the Reformation from it. Though we cannot agree with him in this, for, according to our reading of the sources, Luther had attained his fundamental convictions in previous years, we must assign immense importance to these lectures for the development and perfection of these ideas. The care with which he prepared the lectures is plain; he laboriously annotated almost every word of the text, and then wrote out, in a fair, legible copy, the whole discourse. There is still some remnant of mediævalism in the manner in which he explains the text in two or three different ways, but through the old dress the modern spirit shines forth. Luther was one of the first to show what

[1] He knew it in some notes taken by students now in the Vatican archives. The original manuscript, long supposed to be lost, was discovered but a few years ago in the show-cases of the Royal Library at Berlin, and first published in 1908. I have read a portion of it in manuscript.

Paul really felt, thought, and taught, though some others, like Lefèvre and Colet, had preceded him by a few years in applying the new learning to the elucidation of Scripture. These commentaries were and are valuable contributions to exegesis.

But they are far more; they are living epistles from Brother Martin's heart. His lofty ideas are taking shape, and what an insight into his deep ponderings do such sentences as these give: "We are partly sinners and partly just, but nothing if not penitent, for repentance is the mean between sin and righteousness"; and again, "We are not called to ease but to labor against our passions." Throughout the whole, the theological, practical, and moral interest is the dominant one. The lecturer is even more interested in his own day than in Paul's. With what solemn words does he arraign the princes and prelates who oppress the poor and live only for luxury and pride! How often does he refer to the events of the day, the Reuchlin trial, the wars of Pope Julius, or of Duke George, or of the Bishop of Brandenburg! Again, in words which have a double meaning for us who know their sequel, he blames the sellers of indulgences who deceive the poor people, and "are cruel beyond all cruelty, not freeing souls for charity, though they do for money."

In this commentary can first be seen how far Luther is from the doctrine taught him by his professors Trutvetter and Usingen, the old philosophy of Aristotle and the schoolmen. Of them he says: —

Wherefore it is mere madness for them to say that a man of his own powers is able to love God above all things and to do the works of the law in substance, if not literally, without grace. Fools! Theologians for swine! According to them grace would not be necessary save for a new requirement above the law. For if the law is fulfilled by our own powers, as they say, then grace would not be necessary for the fulfilment of the law, but only for a new exaction beyond the law. Who can bear these sacrilegious opinions?

It is from this high opinion of the function of grace that Luther deduced the doctrine of determinism, which he carried to the utmost lengths of logic.

These lectures also give a vivid idea of the author's reading at the time. The humanists, especially Erasmus, are his favorites. He often quotes, however, from the Fathers, either directly or as he had learned to know them through textbooks and compendiums. Moreover, he is interesting. Similes, illustrations, examples from current events, apt translation into German, with careful summaries at the end of each subject, made the lectures a wide departure from the ordinary. The students flocked to them with enthusiasm.

Luther's work at the university was so successful that within a few years he was able to carry through a complete reform of the whole curriculum. The bondage of the old-fashioned professors to Aristotle has already been described in connection with Martin's education at Erfurt. The humanists, eager for the cultivation of the classics, rebelled against the reign of the Stagirite, and had been partly successful in dethroning him. Luther was in thorough sympathy with them, but his motive was different; he objected to the study of that "cursed heathen" (verdammter Heide), because his ethics were not Christian and his philosophy not Pauline. This dislike, noticeable as early as 1510, grew until, on September 4, 1517, Luther published ninety-seven theses calling into question the value of Aristotle's works as textbooks. Every one is familiar with the Ninety-five Theses against indulgences published the following month, but only specialists know of this Disputation against Scholastic Theology. And yet Luther, who did not think the theses on indulgences worth publishing, printed this protest against Aristotle and his followers, and sent it around to numerous friends for opinions. Among the theses the forty-first calls Aristotle's Ethics bad and inimical to grace, the fifty-first expresses the well-founded suspicion that the Latin translations used in the university do not give his exact sense, and the fifty-second states that it would be a good thing if he who first started the question of nominalism and realism had never been born. Luther was especially anxious to have his opinions known to his old professors at Erfurt, who were strong adherents of the Greek philosopher, and accordingly sent the theses with this letter.

TO JOHN LANG AT ERFURT

WITTENBERG, February 8, 1517.

Greeting. I enclose a letter, dear Father, for the excellent Trutvetter, containing propositions directed against logic, philosophy, and theology, *i. e.*, slander and malediction of Aristotle, Porphyry,[1] and the *Sentences*, the wretched studies of our age. The men who interpret them are bound to keep silence, not for five years, as did the Pythagoreans, but for ever and ever, like the dead ;[2] they must believe all, obey always ; nor may they ever, even for practice in argument, skirmish with their master, nor mutter a syllable against him. What will they not believe who have credited that ridiculous and injurious blasphemer Aristotle ? His propositions are so absurd that an ass or a stone would cry out at them. . . . My soul longs for nothing so ardently as to expose and publicly shame that Greek buffoon, who like a spectre has befooled the Church. . . . If Aristotle had not lived in the flesh I should not hesitate to call him a devil. The greatest part of my cross is to be forced to see brothers with brilliant minds, born for useful studies, compelled to spend their lives and waste their labor in these follies. The universities do not cease to condemn good books and publish bad ones, or rather talk in their sleep about those already published. . . .

BROTHER MARTIN LUTHER, Augustinian.

The professor's efforts to rid his own university of Aristotle were completely successful, as on May 18, 1517, he wrote Lang : —

Our theology and St. Augustine prosper and reign here, by God's help. Aristotle is gradually tottering to a fall from which he will hardly rise again, and the lectures on the Sentences are wonderfully disrelished. No professor can hope for students unless he offers courses in the new theology, that is on the Bible or St. Augustine or some other ecclesiastical authority.

While teaching, Luther continued his own studies. Hebrew he had already begun to learn at Erfurt, with the help of

---

[1] Porphyry, born 233 A.D., started the debate on the reality of individuals and species which divided the Middle Ages. Cf. p. 6.

[2] An oath never to contradict Aristotle was actually administered in the Italian universities. P. Monnier: *Le Quattrocento* (Paris, 1908), ii, 76.

Reuchlin's new grammar-dictionary. There were no courses in Greek at either Erfurt or Wittenberg, but he began to study it under the private tuition of his friend Lang, who taught at Wittenberg for three years from 1513 to 1516. Besides these linguistic pursuits he continued his reading in mediæval theologians, — Bernard of Clairvaux, Bonaventura, Gerson, and Gerhard Zerbolt of Zütphen.

Toward the end of 1515 or early in 1516 he became acquainted with a school of German mystics which had an important influence on his development. The leader of this movement had been Tauler, whose sermons, in an edition of 1508, Luther bought and annotated in his own careful way. He was still more impressed by a manuscript of one of this school known as " the Frankfürter," a work to which the young professor gave the name of " A German Theology," when he edited it in an incomplete form in 1516 (his first publication) and fully in 1518. In the preface he says there is no better book, after the Bible and Augustine, and none in which one may better learn the nature of "God, Christ, man, and all things." He warns the reader not to be repelled by the archaic German, and the influence of this rough, but pure old speech, has been noted on his own style.

What attracted Luther to the mystics was their doctrine of the necessity of a spiritual rebirth of anguish and despair before a man could approach the felicity of union with God. Just as Christ had gone through pain to blessedness, so, they taught, man must experience woe before he can appreciate happiness. A person who seeks God with all his heart is left by him for a time in doubt and distraction, that God may thereby teach him his absolute dependence on him. This was balm to the soul of one who had been at a loss to explain the long period of suffering through which he had just come; now he felt sure that he had not gone astray, but that even *in profundis* God had loved and watched over him.

The young professor's work was not confined to the classroom. Soon after his transfer to Wittenberg he began to preach, at first to the brothers in the convent, and then in the tiny, barnlike chapel at that time standing near the cloister. He was at first very timid about it, but gradually developed a wonderful

homiletic gift. Even his earliest addresses are full of fresh
earnestness and have some touches of uncommon power. The
first extant sermon, probably preached on Whitsunday, 1514,
takes the text from the golden rule (Matthew vii, 12). The
preacher begins by classifying goods as wholly external, — such
as money, houses, and wives; partly external and partly internal, — health and beauty; and wholly internal, — wisdom,
virtue, charity, and faith. He then shows how a man may help
or hurt his neighbor in any of these goods. He asks if it is
enough to abstain from hurting our fellow men, and answers by
inquiring if we should be satisfied if all that they ever did for
us was to let us alone. We must give to others, teach them,
incite them, and help them to do right even as we want them to
do unto us. Christ judged the wicked servant, not for wasting
his talent, but for letting it lie idle; he condemned the persons
at his tribunal, not for despoiling him, but because when he
was hungry they gave him no meat. Thus it will be with us if
we do not help each other to the utmost of our ability.

So I might go on with other sermons, and show how simple,
direct, interesting, moral, and saintly they are. They reveal the
heart of young Luther striving with all his might to be the best
and do the best that was in him. What flashes of revelation there
are now and then, as in the comment on John iii, 16 (God so
loved the world that he gave his only begotten Son) — "There
is a wonderful emphasis and propriety in these words, as is the
wont of the Holy Spirit!"

In both sermons and lectures many a trenchant word against
spiritual wickedness in high places remind one that the monk
was already a reformer. Many of the abuses he later attacked
are scored or glanced at in these early years. He says, for
example, that the Canon Law needs a thorough cleansing; he
speaks against fasts, ceremonies, and pilgrimages. He criticizes
the hardness and tyranny of the princes, the coarseness of the
priests, the arrogance of the monks, the ignorance of indulgence-
preachers, the superstition of religious foundations, the laziness
of workmen, and the irreligion and greed of lawyers. Sometimes
he rebukes by name or clearly indicates persons in high stations,
among them the late Pope Julius II, the Bishop of Strassburg,

Duke George of Albertine Saxony, and his own sovereign, the Elector.

Of more than common interest, as showing Luther's general attitude toward the Church, is his opinion on a *cause célèbre* of that day, the trial for heresy of John Reuchlin. This learned man's refusal to participate in the scheme of a converted Jew to burn all Hebrew books except the Old Testament was made the ground of an action against him by the Dominicans of Cologne, among whom the most conspicuous was Hochstratten, aided by the humanist Ortuin Gratius. The trial, which lasted from 1510 to 1516, excited the interest of the whole of Europe. The monks and obscurantists sided with the inquisitors, the humanists, all but Ortuin, with Reuchlin. The contest was carried on by a hundred pens, and gave rise to a great satire — the Epistles of Obscure Men. This work, most of which was written by Crotus Rubeanus, in the form of a series of letters addressed to Ortuin Gratius by poor monks, ridicules the bad Latin, ignorance, gullibility, and superstition of the theologians.

Luther, though a monk, sided with the progressive party against the inquisitors. His letters on the subject are written to a man who was, throughout life, one of his best friends, George Burkhardt of Spalt. Spalatin, as he was always called, was of the same age as his friend, whom he probably came to know first in 1512, when he was tutor to some young princes at Wittenberg. About 1514 he was appointed chaplain and private secretary to Frederic the Wise, after which he was rarely at Wittenberg. Of the voluminous correspondence of the two friends about four hundred and fifty of Luther's letters to him have survived. Among the first of these are two on the Reuchlin trial : —

TO GEORGE SPALATIN AT ALTENBURG

WITTENBERG (February, 1514).

Peace be with you, reverend Spalatin! Brother John Lang has asked me what I think of the innocent and learned Reuchlin and whether he is, as his prosecutors of Cologne allege, in danger of heresy. You know that I greatly esteem and like the man, and perhaps my judgment will therefore be suspected, but my opinion is that in all his writings there is absolutely nothing dangerous.

I greatly wonder at the men of Cologne ferreting out such an obscure point, worse tangled than the Gordian knot, though the case is really as plain as day. . . . What shall I say? That they are trying to cast out Beelzebub but not by the finger of God. I often regret and deplore that we Christians are wise abroad and fools at home. A hundred times worse blasphemies than this exist in the very streets of Jerusalem, and the high places are filled with spiritual idols. We ought to show our superabundant zeal in removing these offences, which are our real, intestine enemies, instead of abandoning all that is really urgent and turning to foreign matters, under the inspiration of the devil, who intends that we shall neglect our own business without helping others. . . .

Your brother,

MARTIN LUTHER.

TO GEORGE SPALATIN AT ALTENBURG

WITTENBERG, August 5, 1514.

Greeting. Hitherto, most learned Spalatin, I considered that poetaster of Cologne, Ortuin Gratius, simply an ass. But you see he has turned out a dog, or rather a ravening wolf in sheep's clothing, if not indeed a crocodile, as you quite properly suggest. I really believe he has felt his own asininity (if you allow the word) since our Reuchlin has pointed it out, but that he thinks he can shake it off and put on the lion's majesty. The change is too much for him; presto! he remains a wolf or crocodile, for to turn into a lion is beyond his power.

Good Heavens! How can I express my feelings? From the example of this fellow alone we may form the truest, sanest, and justest estimate possible of all who have ever written or now write, or will write from envy. The most insane of all passions is that envy which ardently desires to hurt but has not the power. . . .

This little Ortuin gets together a lot of ridiculous, contradictory, painful, pitiful propositions, twisting the words and meaning of innocent Reuchlin, only to increase the penalty of his own blindness and obstinacy of heart. . . .

In addition to preaching and teaching, Luther had numerous duties connected with his order, in which he was rapidly rising to a leading position. In May, 1515, he was elected vicar of the district, a responsible position involving the superintendence of eleven cloisters. How seriously he took his duties is shown by his letters to priors of monasteries under his charge. Two of them especially reveal the writer's deep spiritual life at the time when he was most under the influence of the mystics. The first is conceived in the spirit of Paul's epistle to Philemon.

TO JOHN BERCKEN, AUGUSTINIAN PRIOR AT MAYENCE

DRESDEN, May 1, 1516.

Greeting in the Lord! Reverend and excellent Father Prior! — I am grieved to learn that there is with your Reverence one of my brothers, a certain George Baumgartner, of our convent at Dresden, and that, alas! he sought refuge with you in a shameful manner, and for a shameful cause. I thank your faith and duty for receiving him and thus bringing his shame to an end. That lost sheep is mine, he belongs to me; it is mine to seek him, and, if it please the Lord Jesus, to bring him back. Wherefore I pray your Reverence, by our common faith in Christ and by our common Augustinian vow, to send him to me in dutiful charity either at Dresden or at Wittenberg, or rather to persuade him lovingly and gently to come of his own accord. I shall receive him with open arms; only let him come; he has no cause to fear my displeasure.

I know, I know that scandals must arise. It is no miracle that a man should fall, but it is a miracle that he should rise and stand. Peter fell, that he might know that he was a man; to-day the cedars of Lebanon, touching the sky with their tops, fall down. Wonder of wonders, even an angel fell from heaven and man in paradise! What wonder is it, then, that a reed be shaken by the wind and a smoking flax be quenched? May the Lord Jesus teach you and use you and perfect you in every good work. Amen. Farewell.

BROTHER MARTIN LUTHER,
Professor of theology and Augustinian Vicar of the
district of Meissen and Thuringia.

TO MICHAEL DRESSEL, AUGUSTINIAN PRIOR AT NEUSTADT

WITTENBERG, June 22, 1516.

. . . You seek peace and ensue it, but in the wrong way, for you look to what the world gives, not to what Christ gives. Know you not, dear Father, that God is so wonderful among his people that he has placed his peace in the midst of no peace, that is, in the midst of all trial, as he says: Rule thou in the midst of thine enemies? It is not *that* man, therefore, whom no one disturbs, who has peace, — which is, indeed, the peace of the world, — but he whom all men and all things harass and who yet bears all quietly with joy. You say with Israel: "Peace, peace," and there is no peace; say rather with Christ, "Cross, cross," and there is no cross. For the cross ceases to be a cross as soon as you say joyfully: "Blessed cross, there is no tree like you." . . .

Seek peace and you will find it, but seek only to bear trials with joy as if they were holy relics. . . .

It may be imagined that such varied occupations kept Luther busy. Of his work he gives a lively account in a letter to his recent colleague and instructor in Greek: —

TO JOHN LANG AT ERFURT

(WITTENBERG,) October 26, 1516.

Greeting. I need a couple of amanuenses or secretaries, as I do almost nothing the live-long day but write letters. I do not know whether on that account I am always repeating myself, but you can judge. I am convent preacher, the reader at meals, am asked to deliver a sermon daily in the parish church, am district vicar (that is eleven times prior), business manager of our fish-farm at Litzkau, attorney in our case versus the Herzbergers now pending at Torgau,[1] lecturer on St. Paul, assistant lecturer on the Psalter, besides having my correspondence, which, as I said, occupies most of my time. I seldom have leisure to discharge the canonical services, to say nothing of attending to my own temptations with the world, the flesh and the devil. You see how idle I am!

I think you must already have my answer about Brother John Metzel, but I will see what I can do. How in the world do you think I can get places for your epicures and sybarites? If you have brought them up in this pernicious way of life you ought to support them in the same pernicious style. I have enough useless brothers on all sides — if, indeed, any can be called useless to a patient soul. I have persuaded myself that the useless are the most useful of all — so you can have them a while longer. . . .

You write me that yesterday you began to lecture on the second

---

[1] On the incorporation of the parish church at Herzberg with the local Augustinian chapter.

book of Sentences. I begin to-morrow to lecture on Galatians, though I fear the plague will not allow me to finish the course. The plague takes off two or at most three in one day, and that not every day. A son of the smith who lives opposite was well yesterday and is buried to-day, and another son lies ill. The epidemic began rather severely and suddenly in the latter part of the summer. You would persuade Bernhardi and me to flee to you, but shall I flee? I hope the world will not come to an end when Brother Martin does. I shall send the brothers away if the plague gets worse; I am stationed here and may not flee because of my vow of obedience, until the same authority which now commands me to stay shall command me to go. Not that I do not fear the plague (for I am not the Apostle Paul, but only a lecturer on him), but I hope the Lord will deliver me from my fear.

How great is the contrast between this letter and that written ten years before! The shy boy has become a man of unusual power, universally respected and trusted. Indeed, he had already attracted the notice of his sovereign, the Elector Frederic. This prince, who enjoyed a great and deserved reputation for wisdom, was a pious man according to mediæval standards. He had made a pilgrimage to the Holy Land, and brought back a large collection of relics to which he kept adding from time to time. He built the Castle Church at Wittenberg, 1493-1499, to keep these sacred objects of which by 1505 he had accumulated 5005, graced with enormous indulgences, reckoned, according to the scale of measurement adopted, as equivalent to 1443 years of purgatory. In addition to this provision for his future life, Frederic had ten thousand masses said yearly in Saxon churches for the benefit of his soul.

Luther had now come to regard such things as superfluous and wrong, and consequently judged his sovereign severely for superstition, as is shown in the next letter written to answer Spalatin's request for his advice about the proposed appointment of Staupitz to a bishopric : —

TO GEORGE SPALATIN AT ALTENBURG

WITTENBERG, June 8, 1516.

. . . I by no means wish that the reverend father should receive the appointment simply because it pleases the Elector to give it him. Many things please your elector, and appear glorious in his eyes, which displease God and are base. I do not deny that the Prince is of all most wise in worldly matters, but in those which pertain to God and salvation I think he is seven times blind, as is your friend Pfeffinger.[1] I do not say this privily as a slanderer, nor do I wish that you should in any way conceal it; when the opportunity comes I am ready to say it to both of them.

Dear Spalatin, these are not such happy times that it is blessed, or even not most miserable to be a bishop — that is to carouse and practise the vices of Sodom and Rome. You will clearly understand this if you compare the bishops of our age with those of ancient times. The best of modern prelates wage foreign wars with all the power of artillery, or build up their private fortunes, a hell of avarice. And although Staupitz is most averse from such wickedness, yet would you, with your confidence in him, force him to become involved in the whirlpools and racking tempests of episcopal cares, when chance, or rather fate, urges him on any way? . . .

Staupitz did not get the appointment, and about a year later fell into such disfavor with his sovereign that Luther had to intercede for him. The letter in which he does so has an uncommon interest as indicating how free the Wittenberg professor felt to remonstrate with his prince on matters of state: —

TO THE ELECTOR FREDERIC OF SAXONY AT ALTENBURG

WITTENBERG, November, 1517.

Most gracious Lord and Prince! As your Grace promised me a gown some time ago, I beg to remind your Grace of the same. Please let Pfeffinger settle it with a deed and not with promises — he can spin mighty good yarns but no cloth comes from them.

I have learned that your Grace is offended at Dr. Staupitz, our dear and worthy father, for some reason or other. When he was here on the way to see your Grace at Torgau, I talked with him and showed him that I was sorry your Grace should take umbrage, and after a long conversation could only find that he held your Grace in his heart. . . . Wherefore, most gracious Lord, I beg you, as he several times asked me to do, that you would consider all the love and loyalty you have so often found in him.

My gracious Lord, let me now show my devotion to you and deserve

---

[1] State treasurer and receiver-general of taxes.

· CHRISTO · SACRVM ·

ILLe · DEI · VERBO · MAGNA · PIETATE · FAVEBAT ·
· PERPETVA · DIGNVS · POSTERITATE · COLI ·

· D · FRIDR · DVCI · SAXON · S · R · IMP ·
· ARCHIM · ELECTORI ·
ALBERTVS · DVRER · NVR · FACIEBAT ·
· B · M · F · V · V ·
· M · D · XXIIII ·

FREDERIC THE WISE, ELECTOR OF SAXONY, 1524

After an etching by Albrecht Dürer

my new gown. I have heard that at the expiration of the present impost your Grace intends to collect another and perhaps a heavier one. If you will not despise the prayer of a poor beggar, I ask you for God's sake not to do this. For it heartily distresses me and many who love you, that this tax has of late robbed you of much good fame and favor. God has blessed you with high intelligence in these matters, to see further than I or perhaps any of your subjects, but it may well be that God ordains it so that at times a great mind may be directed by a lesser one, so that no one may trust himself but only God our Lord. May he keep your Grace in health to govern us well and afterwards may he grant your soul salvation. Amen.

Your Grace's obedient chaplain,

DR. MARTIN LUTHER.

CHAPTER V

THE INDULGENCE CONTROVERSY. 1517-1519

NOTWITHSTANDING Luther's severe criticism of the Elector for venerating relics; and notwithstanding his despondent estimate of spiritual wickedness in high places, he was, as yet, a true son of the Church. In attacking a flagrant ecclesiastical abuse, the indulgence trade, he did not intend to raise the standard of revolt, nor did he do so until forced, gradually if rapidly, by the authorities of the Church herself, into irreconcilable opposition. In order to understand his protest against indulgences, it is necessary to glance at the history of this institution.

According to the theory of the Roman Catholic Church, forgiveness is imparted to sinners in absolution after confession, by which the penitent is freed from guilt and eternal punishment in hell, but still remains liable to a milder punishment to be undergone in this life as penance, or in purgatory. The practice had arisen in the early Church of commuting this penance (not the pains of purgatory) in consideration of a good work such as a pilgrimage or a contribution to pious purpose. This was the seed of the indulgence which would never have grown to its later enormous proportions had it not been for the crusades. Mohammed promised his followers paradise if they fell in battle against unbelievers, but Christian warriors were at first without this comforting assurance. Their faith was not long left in doubt, however, for as early as 855 Leo IV promised heaven to the Franks who died fighting the Moslems. A quarter of a century later John VIII proclaimed absolution for all sins and remission of all penalties to soldiers in the holy war, and from this time on the "crusade indulgence" became a regular means of recruiting, used, for example, by Leo IX in 1052 and by Urban II in 1095. By this time the practice had grown up of regarding an indulgence as a remission not only of penance but of the pains of purgatory. The means which had proved successful in getting soldiers for the crusade were first used in 1145 or 1146 to get money for the same end — pardon being assured to those who gave enough to fit out one soldier on the same terms as if they had gone themselves.

When the crusades ceased, in the thirteenth century, indulgences did not fall into desuetude. At the jubilee of Pope Boniface VIII in 1300 a plenary indulgence was granted to all who made a pilgrimage to Rome. The Pope reaped such an enormous harvest from the gifts of these pilgrims that he saw fit to employ similar means at frequent intervals, and soon extended the same privileges as were granted to pilgrims to all who contributed for some pious purpose at their own homes. Agents were sent out to sell these pardons, and were given power to confess and absolve, so that by 1393 Boniface IX was able to announce complete remission of both guilt and penalty to the purchasers of his letters.

Having assumed the right to free living men from future punishment, it was but a step for the popes to proclaim that they had the power to deliver the souls of the dead from purgatory. The existence of this power was an open question until decided by Calixtus III in 1457, but full use of the faculty was not made until twenty years later, after which it became of all branches of the indulgence trade the most profitable.

The practice of the Church had become well established before a theory was framed to justify it. This was done most successfully by Alexander of Hales in the thirteenth century, who discovered the treasury of the Church (*thesaurus meritorum* or *thesaurus indulgentiarum*) consisting of the merits of Christ and the saints which the Pope, as head of the Church, could apply as a sort of a credit to whom he chose. This doctrine, so far as it applied to living men, received the sanction of Clement VII in 1343 and became a part of the Canon Law, but the popes usually claimed to free the souls of the dead from purgatory simply by prayer. The mere dictum of the Supreme Pontiff did not at that time absolutely establish a dogma. A powerful party in the Church held that a council was the supreme authority in matters of faith, and it will be remembered that the infallibility of the Pope was not made a dogma until 1870. Luther was therefore not accused of heresy for his assertions regarding indulgences for the dead.

It was not so much the theory of the Church that excited his indignation as it was the practices of some of her agents. They encouraged the common man to believe that the purchase of a papal pardon would assure him impunity without any real repentance on his part. Moreover, whatever the theoretical worth of indulgences, the motive of their sale was notoriously the greed of unscrupulous ecclesiastics. The " holy trade " as it was called had become so thoroughly commercialized by 1500 that a banking house, the Fuggers of Augsburg, were the direct agents of the Curia in Germany. In return for their services in forwarding the Pope's bulls, and in hiring sellers of pardons, this wealthy house made a secret agreement in 1507 by which it received one third of the total profits of the trade, and in 1514 formally took over the whole management of the business in return for the modest commission of one half the net receipts. Naturally not a word was said by the preachers to the people as to the destination of so large a portion of their money, but enough was known to make many men regard indulgences as an open scandal.

The history of the particular trade attacked by Luther is one of special infamy. Albert of Brandenburg, a prince of the enterprising house of Hohenzollern, was bred to the Church and rapidly rose by political influence to the highest ecclesiastical position in Germany. In 1513 he was elected, at the age of twenty-three, Archbishop of Magdeburg and administrator of the bishopric of Halberstadt, — an uncanonical accumulation of sees confirmed by the Pope in return for a large payment. Hardly had Albert paid this before he was elected Archbishop and Elector of Mayence and Primate of Germany (March 9, 1514). As he was not yet of canonical age to possess even one bishopric, not to mention three of the greatest in the Empire, the Pope refused to confirm his nomination except for an enormous sum. The Curia at first demanded twelve thousand ducats for the twelve apostles, Albert offered seven for the seven deadly sins. The average between apostles and sins was struck at ten thousand ducats, or fifty thousand dollars, a sum equal in purchasing power to near a million to-day. Albert borrowed this, too, from the Fuggers, and was accordingly confirmed on August 15, 1514.

In order to allow the new prelate to recoup himself, Leo obligingly declared an indulgence for the benefit of St. Peter's Church, to run eight years from March 31, 1515. By this transaction, one of the most disgraceful in the history of the papacy, as well as in that of the house of Brandenburg, the Curia made a vast sum. Albert did not come off so well. First, a number of princes, including the rulers of both Saxonys, forbade the trade in their dominions, and the profits of what remained were deeply cut by the unexpected attack of a young monk.

Albert did his best to put his holy wares in the most attractive light. A short quotation from his public advertisement will substantiate what has just been said about the popular representation of the indulgence as an easy road to atonement : —

" The first grace is a plenary remission of all sins, than which one might say no grace could be greater, because a sinner deprived of grace through it achieves perfect remission of sin and the grace of God anew. By which grace . . . the pains of purgatory are completely wiped out." The second grace for sale is a confessional letter allowing the penitent to choose his own confessor ; the third is the participation in the merits of the saints. The fourth grace is for the souls in purgatory, a plenary remission of all sins. . . . Nor is it necessary for those who contribute to the fund for this purpose to be contrite or to confess.

Albert's principal agent was a certain Dominican named Tetzel, a bold, popular preacher already expert in the business. He did all in his power to impress the people with the value of his commodities. When he entered a town, there was a solemn procession, bells were rung, and everything possible done to attract attention. Some of his sermons have survived, painting in the most lively colors the agonies of purgatory and the ease with which any one might free himself or his dead relatives from the torturing flames by the simple payment of a gulden.

Though forbidden to enter Saxony, Tetzel approached sufficiently near her borders to attract a number of her people. In

January, 1517, he was at Eisleben, and in the spring came to Jüterbog, so near Wittenberg that Luther could see the bad effects of indulgences in his own parish. After preaching against the abuse several times in 1516 and 1517, the earnest monk finally decided to bring matters to a head by holding a debate on the subject. He announced his intention in a rather dramatic way. On the Feast of All Saints (November 1), the Elector's relics kept in the Castle Church were solemnly displayed and the special graces attached to them publicly announced. This festival drew crowds to Wittenberg, both from curiosity and from desire to participate in the spiritual benefits then obtainable. It was to give notice to these people that on October 31, 1517, Martin Luther posted up on the door of the church an announcement of his intention to hold a debate on the value of indulgences, "for the love and zeal for elucidating the truth," ninety-five theses or heads for debate being proposed.

The Theses are a good specimen of much of Luther's work. Their chief defect is lack of perfect logical order. They evince a tolerably deep acquaintance with mediæval theology, but their main interest is not theoretical but practical. Each proposition is a blow at some popular error or some flagrant abuse. Though occasionally qualifying, they deal trenchantly with the nature of repentance, the power of the Pope to release souls from purgatory, the virtue of indulgences for living sinners, the outrageous practices of the preachers of pardons, the treasury of the Church, and other matters.

The first thesis cannot be understood without a slight knowledge of Latin. This language, singularly enough, has but one word (penitentia) for the two very distinct ideas of penance and penitence. Consequently the words of Christ translated in the Vulgate "Penitentiam agite" might equally well mean, "Repent ye," or "Do penance." They were taken in the latter sense by the average priest, but Erasmus in his Paraphrases to the New Testament had seen the real significance of the words, and so had some other doctors known to Luther. Accordingly, in the first two theses he says : —

1. Our Lord and master Jesus Christ in saying "Penitentiam agite" meant that the whole life of the faithful should be repentance.

2. And these words cannot refer to penance — that is confession and satisfaction.

Among the other propositions the following are the most important : —

5. The Pope does not wish, nor is he able, to remit any penalty except what he or the Canon Law has imposed.

6. The Pope is not able to remit guilt except by declaring it forgiven by God — or in cases reserved to himself. . . .

11. The erroneous opinion that canonical penance and punishment in purgatory are the same assuredly seems to be a tare sown while the bishops were asleep.

21. Therefore those preachers of indulgences err who say that a papal pardon frees a man from all penalty and assures his salvation.

22. The greater part of the people will be deceived by this undistinguishing and pretentious promise of pardon which cannot be fulfilled.

26. The Pope does well to say that he frees souls from purgatory not by the power of the keys (for he has no such power) but by the method of prayer.

28. It is certain that avarice is fostered by the money chinking in the chest, but to answer the prayers of the Church is in the power of God alone.

29. Who knows whether all the souls in purgatory want to be freed? . . .

30. None is sure of the sincerity of his contrition, much less of his full pardon.

31. They who believe themselves made sure of salvation by papal letters will be eternally damned along with their teachers.

33. One should beware of them who say that those pardons are an inestimable gift of the Pope by which man is reconciled to God.

36. Every Christian truly repentant has full remission of guilt and penalty even without letters of pardon.

37. Every true Christian, alive or dead, participates in all the goods of Christ and the Church without letters of pardon. . . .

38. Nevertheless papal pardons are not to be despised.

40. True contrition seeks and loves punishment, and makes relaxations of it hateful, at least at times.

43. Christians are to be taught that he who gives to the poor or lends to one in need does better than he who buys indulgences.

50. Christians are to be taught that if the Pope knew the exactions of

the preachers of indulgences he would rather have St. Peter's church in ashes than have it built with the flesh and bones of his sheep.

60. The treasury of the Church is the power of the keys given by Christ's merit.

62. The true treasure of the Church is the holy gospel of the glory and grace of God.

71. Who speaks against the apostolic truth of indulgences, let him be anathema.

72. But who opposes the lust and license of the preachers of pardons, let him be blessed.

The scandalous practices of those preachers will induce the laity to ask inconvenient questions, as: —

82. Why does not the Pope empty purgatory from charity ?

92. Let all those prophets depart who say to the people of Christ, Peace, peace, where there is no peace.

93. But all those prophets do well who say to the people of Christ, Cross, cross, and there is no cross.

On the same day that he posted his Theses Luther wrote a letter of remonstrance to the prelate under whose sanction the indulgences had appeared, which still further explains his position.

TO ALBERT, ARCHBISHOP OF MAYENCE

WITTENBERG, October 31, 1517.

Grace and the mercy of God and whatever else may be and is !

Forgive me, Very Reverend Father in Christ, and illustrious Lord, that I, the offscouring of men, have the temerity to think of a letter to your high mightiness. . . .

Papal indulgences for the building of St. Peter's are hawked about under your illustrious sanction. I do not now accuse the sermons of the preachers who advertise them, for I have not seen the same, but I regret that the people have conceived about them the most erroneous ideas. Forsooth these unhappy souls believe that if they buy letters of pardon they are sure of their salvation; likewise that souls fly out of purgatory as soon as money is cast into the chest; in short, that the grace conferred is so great that there is no sin whatever which cannot be absolved thereby, even if, as they say, taking an impossible example, a man should violate the mother of God. They also believe that indulgences free them from all penalty and guilt.

My God! thus are the souls committed, Father, to your charge, instructed unto death, for which you have a fearful and growing reckoning to pay. . . .

What else could I do, excellent Bishop and illustrious Prince, except pray your Reverence for the sake of the Lord Jesus Christ to take away your Instructions to the Commissioners altogether and impose some other form of preaching on the proclaimers of pardons, lest perchance some one should at length arise and confute them and their Instructions publicly, to the great blame of your Highness. This I vehemently deprecate, yet I fear it may happen unless the grievance is quickly redressed. . . .

Your unworthy son,

MARTIN LUTHER, Augustinian, Dr. Theol.

On receipt of this letter, with the Theses enclosed, Albert began an "inhibitory process" against the "presumptuous monk," which was soon dropped on account of the action taken at Rome. The archbishop promptly sent an account of the matter, with several of the Wittenberg professor's works, to the Curia.

The attack on indulgences was like a match touched to gunpowder. Every one had been thinking what Luther alone was bold and clear-sighted enough to say, and almost every one applauded him to the echo. Certain persons wrote exhorting him to stand fast and congratulating him on what he had done. The Theses had an immediate and enormous popularity. Luther himself was astonished at their reception, and before he knew it they were printed at Nuremberg both in Latin and German. The circle of humanists in this wealthy town received them warmly, the famous painter, Albert Dürer, sending the author a present of his own wood-cuts as a token of appreciation. These were forwarded to him by his friend Scheurl, who enclosed copies of the printed Theses. The answer explains the writer's position: —

TO CHRISTOPHER SCHEURL AT NUREMBERG

WITTENBERG, March 5, 1518.

Greeting. I received both your German and Latin letters, good and learned Scheurl, together with the distinguished Albert Dürer's gift, and my Theses in the original and in the vernacular. As you are surprised that I did not send them to you, I reply that my purpose was not to publish them, but first to consult a few of my neighbors about them, that thus I might either destroy them if condemned or edit them with the approbation of others. But now that they are printed and circulated far beyond my expectation, I feel anxious about what they may bring forth; not that I am unfavorable to spreading known truth abroad — rather this is what I seek — but because this method is not that best adapted to instruct the public. I have certain doubts about them myself, and should have spoken far differently and more distinctly had I known what was going to happen. I have learned from their publication what is the general opinion about indulgences entertained everywhere by all, although they conceal it "for fear of the Jews." I have felt it necessary to write a defence of my Theses which I have not yet been able to print because my Lord Bishop of Brandenburg, to whom I referred it, has long kept me waiting for his opinion. If the Lord give me leisure I should like to publish a work in German on the virtue of indulgences to supersede my desultory Theses. For I have no doubt that people are deceived not by indulgences but by the use made of them. . . .

The defence of which Luther has just spoken was returned to him by the Bishop of Brandenburg with the advice not to print it. He did so, however, but the slowness of the printers prevented the appearance of the Resolutions, as the book was called, until September. In this he takes up the Theses one by one, explains and supports them by argument — in the case of the first, for example, citing the Greek to prove his statement. He dedicated the work to Pope Leo X in a letter written about the last of May, in which, while speaking as a submissive son of the Church, he shows his opinions have only been confirmed by the attacks of enemies. The letter is well adapted to the man to whom it is addressed, a humanist, perhaps a freethinker, who would despise the writer more as an uncultured German than condemn him as a heretic. There is a fine irony in the words about the wonderful literary attainments of the age.

TO POPE LEO X

(WITTENBERG, May 30?) 1518.

I have heard a very evil report of myself, Most Blessed Father, by which I understand that certain persons have made my name loathsome to you and yours, saying that I have tried to diminish the power of the keys and the authority of the Supreme Pontiff, and therefore accusing me of being a heretic, an apostate and a traitor, besides branding me with an hundred other calumnious epithets. My ears are horrified and my eyes amazed, but my conscience, sole bulwark of confidence, remains innocent and at peace. . . .

In these latter days a jubilee of papal indulgences began to be preached, and the preachers, thinking everything allowed them under the protection of your name, dared to teach impiety and heresy openly, to the grave scandal and mockery of ecclesiastical powers, totally disregarding the provisions of the Canon Law about the misconduct of officials. . . . They met with great success, the people were sucked dry on false pretences . . . but the oppressors lived on the fat and sweetness of the land. They avoided scandals only by the terror of your name, the threat of the stake and the brand of heresy . . . if, indeed, this can be called avoiding scandals and not rather exciting schisms and revolt by crass tyranny: . . .

I privately warned some of the dignitaries of the Church. By some the admonition was well received, by others ridiculed, by others treated in various ways, for the terror of your name and the dread of censure are strong. At length, when I could do nothing else, I determined to stop their mad career if only for a moment; I resolved to call their assertions in question. So I published some propositions for debate, inviting only the more learned to discuss them with me, as ought to be plain to my opponents from the preface to my Theses. Yet this is the flame with which they seek to set the world on fire! . . .

Now what shall I do? I cannot recall my Theses and yet I see that great hatred is kindled against me by their popularity. I come unwillingly before the precarious and divided judgment of the public, I, who am untaught, stupid and destitute of learning, before an age so fertile in literary genius that it would force into a corner even Cicero, no mean follower of fame and popularity in his day.

So in order to fulfil the desire of many and appease my opponents, I am now publishing a little treatise to explain my Theses. To protect myself, I publish it under the guardianship of your name and the shadow of your protection. . . .

And now, Most Blessed Father, I cast myself and all my possessions at your feet; raise me up or slay me, summon me hither or thither, approve me or reprove me as you please. I shall recognize your words as the words of Christ, speaking in you. If I have deserved death, I shall not refuse to die. For the earth is the Lord's and the fulness thereof; blessed be he forever. Amen. May he always preserve you. Amen.

Long before this letter was published, energetic steps had been taken against Luther in Rome. As previously stated, the Archbishop of Mayence, early in December, 1517, had forwarded to the Pope the monk's Theses on Indulgences, those on scholastic philosophy, with other documents. Leo read the Theses, which he judged clever though animated by envy. At another time he professed to think they had been composed by a drunken German who would see the error of his ways when sober. It was, therefore, with no great apprehension that he ordered Gabriel della Volta, General of the Augustinians, " to quiet that man, for newly kindled flames are easily quenched."

Accordingly Volta instructed Staupitz to force the presumptuous brother to recant. The matter was brought before the general chapter of the Saxon province, held at Heidelberg, April and May, 1518. Luther refused to recant, but resigned his office of district vicar, to which his friend Lang was elected, Staupitz being again chosen provincial vicar. Far from recanting, the heretic expounded his fundamental ideas in a public debate on justification by faith and free will. " The doctors," he writes Spalatin on May 18, " willingly heard my disputation and rebutted it with such moderation that I felt much obliged to them. My theology, indeed, seemed foreign to them, yet they skirmished with it effectively and courteously, all except one young doctor who moved the laughter of the audience by saying, ' If the peasants heard you they would stone you to death.' " Among the converts won by the new leader at this time was Martin Bucer, later one of the most prominent of the Protestant divines.

While at Heidelberg, Luther was received by the brother of the Elector Palatine in the splendid old castle, and shown all the armor and precious objects there collected.[1]

---

[1] The castle, which Luther describes as " almost royal," was imposing. Some authorities believe that it is reproduced, as it was about 1495, in the background of a picture of Frederic Count Palatine, sometimes attributed to Dürer. Reproduced in Mrs. H. Cust: *Gentlemen Errant* (London, 1909), p. 248. *Klassiker der Künst*, iv. Dürer (Stuttgart and Leipsic, 1908), p. 87. Cf. note, p. 396.

Soon after his return to Wittenberg, Luther wrote the letter to the Pope last translated, which may have been forwarded to his Holiness by Staupitz.

In the mean time the Dominicans, wounded in the person of Tetzel, sent urgent denunciations of the Wittenberg monk for heresy to the fiscal procurator (we should say attorney-general) of the Curia. Leo waited to see what would be the result of the efforts of Volta, but when it was known that these had entirely failed, he empowered the procurator to begin a formal action "for suspicion of heresy." At the desire of this official, Perusco by name, the general auditor (supreme justice of the Curia), Jerome Ghinnucci, was charged with the conduct of the process, and Silvester Prierias, Master of the Sacred Palace, was requested to give an expert opinion on the Theses. As a Dominican and a Thomist he discharged his task thoroughly. His memorial, which he proudly printed with the title The Dialogue, takes the strongest ground of papal supremacy, and asserts that whoever denies that the infallible Church has a right to do what she actually does is a heretic. On this advice Ghinnucci summoned Luther to appear at Rome within sixty days, sending the citation together with the Dialogue, which were received by the professor early in August. He answered the latter by a pamphlet asserting that both popes and councils could err, and this he sent to Prierias with a scornful letter:—

Your refutation seemed so trifling [he wrote] that I have answered it *ex tempore*, whatever came uppermost in my mind. If you wish to hit back, be careful to bring your Aquinas better armed into the arena, lest you be not treated so gently again.

Before Luther had time to decide whether to obey the summons to Rome or not, the Curia suddenly altered the method of procedure. On August 23 the Pope wrote his agent in Germany, Cardinal Thomas de Vio of Gaeta, thence called Cajetan, to cite Luther to Augsburg at once, hear him, and if he did not recant, send him bound to Rome, or failing that to put him and his followers under the ban. This step was so surprising that many Germans believed it a breach of the Canon Law, which provides a much slower process against a *suspected* heretic. Such, however, was not the case. The Pope's action in expediting matters was due to Cajetan himself. This nuncio had been sent to Germany to attend the Diet of Augsburg (1518) and urge the cause of the Turkish war on the Empire. From this vantage-point he had observed the immense commotion caused by the Theses and Resolutions, and was still more unfavorably impressed by a sermon on the ban published by the Wittenberg professor. Bans, said he, flew about like bats, and were not much more to be regarded than those blind little pests. Cajetan thought he would teach the scoffing preacher what a terrible thing a ban really was, and wrote to Rome warning Leo of the danger of allowing Luther at large any longer, and pointing out the advantage of dealing with him at once at Augsburg. His letter was enforced by one from the Emperor Maximilian, — who disliked and feared the Elector Frederic, — promising his help in quelling the schismatic.

These missives had their desired effect. Ghinnucci, especially shocked by the flippant reference to the apostolic thunders as "bats," concluded that Luther was already a *notorious* heretic, and that he was justified in using the summary process provided by the Canon Law against criminals of this class. The moment seemed favorable for a decisive blow, for Maximilian had promised his help. Consequently the letter of August 23 written to Cajetan, and accompanied by one from Volta to the Augustinian Provincial of South Germany, Hecker, urging him to coöperate in securing the heretic's arrest.

At this critical juncture Luther was not left in the lurch by his powerful friends. The Elector of Saxony refused to allow him to appear without a safe-conduct from the Emperor, which was secured late and with difficulty. Staupitz and Link also went to Augsburg, where the interview was held, in order to use their influence against the employment of force. Fortified by this support, Luther went to Augsburg, where he arrived on October 7, but waited three days until the safe-conduct of Maximilian had reached him. During the interval he had a visit from an Italian, Urban de Serralonga, with whom he had the following conversation : —

Urban — Your business here may be summed up in one word of six letters : Recant !

Luther — But may I not defend my position, or at least be instructed on it ?

Urban — Do you think this is a game of running in a ring ? Don't you know that it is all right to deceive the people a little — as you say the preachers of indulgence do — to get their money ? Do you think the Elector Frederic will take arms to protect *you* ?

Luther — I hope not.

Urban — If not, where will you live ?

Luther — Under heaven.

Urban — What would *you* do if you had the Pope and cardinals in your power ?

Luther — I would show them all reverence and honor.

Urban — (with a scornful gesture) Hem !

Luther had three separate interviews with Cajetan, on October 12, 13, and 14 respectively. On the first day, having studied the etiquette of the occasion, he fell down on his face before his judge. Much pleased with this humility, the legate complimented him on his learning and bade him recant his errors. Asked what errors he meant, the prelate, who had been studying theology for two months, named two: first, the statement in the Theses that the treasury of the Church (thesaurus indulgentiarum) consisted of the merits of Christ, and second, the assertion in the Resolutions that the efficacy of the sacrament depended on the faith of the recipient. The selection was a clever one, both because on these two points there was most unanimity at Rome, and also because it was supposed that the accused would more readily retract these purely speculative points than others of a more practical bearing. That Luther did not recant, however, and that the altercation with his judge at times became hot and furious, he himself tells, in his own vivid way, in a letter to a friend at court : —

TO GEORGE SPALATIN

AUGSBURG, October 14, 1518.

Greeting. As I do not care to write directly to the Elector, dear Spalatin, do you, as his intimate friend, communicate the purport of my letter to him. This is now the fourth day that my lord the legate negotiates with me, or rather against me. He fairly promises, indeed, that he will do all mercifully and paternally, for the sake of the most illustrious Elector, but in reality he wishes to carry all before him with mere stubborn brute force. He would neither allow me to answer him in a public debate nor would he dispute with me privately. The one thing which he repeated over and over was: " Recant. Admit your error; the Pope wishes it so, and not otherwise; you must willy, nilly," with other words to the same effect. He drew his most powerful argument against me from the decretal of Clement VI Unigenitus.[1] " Here," said he, " here you see that the Pope decides that the merits of Christ are the treasury of the Church; do you believe or do you not believe ? " He allowed no statement nor answer, but tried to carry his point with force of words and with clamor.

At length he was with difficulty persuaded by the prayers of many to allow me to present a written argument. This I have done to-day, having taken with me Philip von Feilitzsch to represent the Elector, of whose request he again reminded the legate. After some time he threw aside my paper with contempt, and again clamored for recantation. With a long and wordy argument, drawn from the foolish books of Aquinas, he thought to have conquered and put me to silence. I tried to speak nine or ten times, but every time he thundered at me, and continued the monologue. At length I, too, began to shout, saying that if he could show me that that decretal asserted that the merits of Christ was the treasury of the Church, I would recant as he wished. Good Heavens, what gesticulation and rude laughter this remark caused ! He suddenly seized the book, read from it with breathless rapidity, until he came to the place where it is written that Christ by his passion acquired a treasure. Then I: " O most reverend Father, consider this word ' acquire.' If Christ by his merits acquired a treasure, then his merits are not the treasure, but that which the merits merited, namely, the keys of the Church, are the treasure. Therefore my conclusion[2] was correct." At this he was suddenly confused, but not wishing to appear so, suddenly jumped to another place, thinking it prudent not to notice what I had said. But I was hot and burst forth, certainly without much reverence: " Do not think, most reverend Father, that we Germans understand no grammar; it is a different thing to *acquire* a

---

[1] Canon Law, Extravagant, lib. 5, tit. 9, cap. 6. Not to be confused with the bull *Unigenitus* of Clement IX.

[2] In the Fifty-eighth Thesis, to the effect that the power of the keys is the treasury of the Church.

treasure and to *be* a treasure." Having thus broken his self-confidence, as he still clamored for recantation, I went away. He said : " Do not return to me again unless you wish to recant."

But lo! as soon as he had finished dinner he called our reverend vicar, Father Staupitz, and used his blandishments on him to try to get him to persuade me to recant. The legate even asserted, as I was absent, that I had no better friend than he. When Staupitz answered that he had always advised me, and still did so, to submit humbly to the Church, and that I had declared publicly that I would do so, Cajetan even confessed that he was, in his own opinion, inferior to me in theological learning and in talent, but that, as the representative of the Pope and of the prelates, it was his duty to persuade me to recant. At length they agreed that he should suggest articles for me to revoke.

Thus the business stands. I have no hope nor confidence in him. I am preparing an appeal, resolved not to recant a syllable. If he proceeds as he has begun, by force, I shall publish my answer to him, that he may be confounded throughout the whole world.

Farewell in haste,
BROTHER MARTIN LUTHER, Augustinian.

As indicated in this letter, Staupitz and Link were far more amenable to pressure than was Luther. They hoped that all might be settled peaceably, in a way which would satisfy the legate without compromising their brother. Finding that he was immovable, Staupitz absolved him from the vow of obedience, partly to relieve himself from responsibility, and partly, no doubt, to guard him against molestation from Hecker and Volta. Staupitz and Link then judged it best to retire from the city without giving the nuncio notice of their intention.

On October 16, Luther drew up an appeal from the Pope badly informed to the Pope to be better informed, and the next day wrote Cajetan a courteous but firm letter. Notwithstanding all precautions, the accused man stood in considerable danger, for safe-conducts to heretics had been broken before. The moment was almost as decisive as the later one at Worms, and here, as there, the heroic monk stood like iron against the threats of foes and the supplication of friends alike, resolved to do nothing against his conscience.

TO CARDINAL CAJETAN AT AUGSBURG

(AUGSBURG, October 17, 1518.)

Very Reverend Father in Christ, I come again, not personally but in writing; deign to hear me mercifully.

My reverend and beloved father in Christ, our Vicar John Staupitz, has pleaded with me to think humbly of my own opinion and to submit, and has persuaded me that your Reverence is favorably disposed towards me. . . . So that my fear has gradually passed away, or rather changed into a singular love and true, filial veneration for your Reverence.

Now, Most Reverend Father in Christ, I confess, as I have before confessed, that I was assuredly unwise and too bitter, and too irreverent to the name of the Pope. And although I had the greatest provocation, I know I should have acted with more moderation and humility, and not have answered a fool according to his folly. For so doing I am most sincerely sorry, and ask pardon, and will say so from the pulpit, as I have already done several times, and I shall take care in future to act differently and speak otherwise by God's mercy. Moreover I am quite ready to promise never to speak of indulgences again and to maintain silence, provided only the same rule, either of speaking or of keeping silence, be imposed on those men who have led me into this tragic business.

For the rest, most reverend and now beloved Father in Christ, as to the truth of my opinion, I would most readily recant, both by your command and the advice of my vicar, if my conscience in any way allowed it. But I know that neither the command nor the advice nor the influence of any one ought to make me do anything against conscience or can do so. For the arguments [you cite] from Aquinas and others are not convincing to me, although I have read them over in preparation for my debates and have thoroughly understood them. I do not think their conclusions are drawn from correct premises. The only thing left is to overcome me with better reasons, in which I may hear the voice of the Bride which is also the voice of the Bridegroom.

I humbly implore your Reverence to deign to refer this case to our Most Holy Lord Leo X, that these doubts may be settled by the Church, so that he may either compel a just withdrawal of my propositions or else their just affirmation. I wish only to follow the Church, and I know not what effect my recantation of doubtful and unsettled opinions might have, but I fear that I might be reproached, and with reason, for not knowing either what I asserted or what I withdrew. May your Reverence deign to receive my humble and suppliant petition, and to treat me with mercy as a son.

Your Reverence's devoted son,

BROTHER MARTIN LUTHER, Augustinian.

After waiting in vain for three days for an answer, Luther left Augsburg secretly at night and returned to Wittenberg. The first thing he did there was to write out the account of the interview of which he had spoken to Spalatin, and to publish it as the Acta Augustana. In the preface to the reader he says : —

They vexed Reuchlin a long time for some advice he gave them, now they vex me for proposing questions for debate. Who is safe from the teeth of this Behemoth ? . . .

I see that books are published and various rumors scattered abroad about what I did at Augsburg, although truly I did nothing there but lose the time and expense of the journey . . . for I was instructed there that to teach the truth is the same as to disturb the Church, but to flatter men and deny Christ is considered the same as pacifying and exalting the Church of Christ.

Foiled of his purpose, Cajetan wrote the Elector Frederic asking him to arrest Luther and send him to Rome. The peace-loving prince may have wavered for an instant. According to the story he summoned his counsellors and asked their advice. One of them, Fabian von Feilitzsch, related the fable of the sheep, who, at the advice of the wolves, sent away the watchdogs. If we give up Luther, he concluded, we shall have no one to write in our defence, but they will accuse us all of being heretics. It is probable that Frederic never seriously considered the surrender of his subject, but he did ponder a plan to hide him in a castle, as he later did in the Wartburg. Early in December Spalatin and Luther had a meeting at Lichtenberg to discuss this project, which was not adopted. On December 8 the Elector wrote a diplomatic letter to the cardinal, saying that he was not convinced that the accused was a heretic, but had rather been informed by learned men that his doctrines were only objectionable to those whose pecuniary interests were involved. He wished only to act as a Christian prince, but could not com-

promise his university by sending an uncondemned man to
Rome.

Cajetan had been convinced by his interview that it would be
difficult to convict Luther of heresy. He therefore requested
Leo to settle the points in dispute once for all by an *ex cathedra*
declaration. This was done in a bull of November 9, which,
without mentioning names, condemned the errors of certain
monks on indulgences and other points. The claim could now
no longer be made that the matters in question were not decided
authoritatively.

Immediately upon the failure of Cajetan to arrest the heretic,
the Pope dispatched a special nuncio to Germany for this purpose, Charles von Miltitz. Hoping to win the Elector to his
side, Leo sent him a long-coveted honor, the anointed golden
rose, with flattering letters both to him and to his principal
counsellors. On the other hand, Miltitz was furnished with a
ban against Luther and power to declare the interdict (*i. e.*,
suspension of all ministrations of the Church except baptism
and supreme unction) against Saxony. Cajetan had not thought
it wise to excommunicate a man whom he had not been able
to convict, but now it was felt that there would be no more
excuse for delay, and that the disturber of the Church's peace
would be brought to terms at once.

The plan of Rome was wrecked partly by the resistance of
Frederic, partly by the conduct of Miltitz, a Saxon by birth,
and a vain, frivolous person, who forgot his instructions as
soon as he arrived in Germany, hoping that instead of using
force he could set everything right by gentle means. He accordingly arranged for a personal interview with the Augustinian friar, whom he expected to cajole into recantation; this
took place at Altenburg, the capital of Electoral Saxony, early
in January, 1519. The result of the first day's negotiations is
thus related in a letter: —

TO FREDERIC, ELECTOR OF SAXONY

(Altenburg, January 5 or 6, 1519.)

Most serene, highborn Prince, most gracious Lord! It overwhelms
me to think how far your Grace has been drawn into my affairs, but

as necessity and God so dispose it, I beg your Grace to be favorable still.

Charles von Miltitz yesterday pointed out with care the crimes I had committed against the Roman Church, and I humbly promised to make what amends I could. I beg your Grace to attend to the plan I proposed, for by it I meant to please your Grace.

First, I agreed to let the matter alone henceforth, until it bleeds to death of itself, provided my opponents also keep silence. . . .

Secondly, I agreed to write to his Holiness the Pope, humbly submitting and recognizing that I had been too hot and hasty, though I never meant to do aught against the Holy Roman Church, but only as her true son to attack the scandalous preaching whereby she is made a mockery, a byword, a stumbling-block, and an offence to the people.

Thirdly, I promised to send out a paper admonishing every one to follow the Roman Church, obey and honor her, and explaining that my writings were not to be understood in a sense damaging to her. . . .

Fourthly, Spalatin proposed, on the recommendation of Fabian von Feilitzsch, to leave the case to the Archbishop of Salzburg.[1] I should abide by his judgment, with that of other learned and impartial men, or else return to my appeal. Or perhaps the matter might remain undecided and things be allowed to take their natural course. But I fear the Pope will allow no other judge but himself, nor can I tolerate his judgment; if the present plan fails, we shall have to go through the farce of the Pope writing a text and my writing the commentary. That would do no good.

Miltitz thinks my propositions unsatisfactory, but does not demand recantation. . . .

> Your Grace's obedient chaplain,
> DOCTOR MARTIN.

In accordance with this plan Luther drew up a very humble letter to the Pope, but as it did not satisfy Miltitz he never sent it. On the second day of the conference for the agreement here proposed there was substituted a much simpler one.

---

[1] Mathew Lang, at this time coadjutor, though soon after Archbishop of Salzburg, is meant. He was a close friend of Staupitz.

TO FREDERIC, ELECTOR OF SAXONY

(ALTENBURG, January 6 or 7, 1519.)

Serene, highborn Prince, gracious Lord! Let me humbly inform your Grace that Charles von Miltitz and I have at last come to an agreement, and concluded our negotiations with two articles.

1. Both sides shall be inhibited from preaching, writing, and acting further in the matter.

2. Miltitz will write the Pope at once, informing him how things stand, and asking him to recommend the matter to some learned bishop, who will hear me and point out the errors I am to recant. For when I have learned my mistakes, I will gladly withdraw them, and do nothing to impair the honor and power of the Roman Church.

The letter of Miltitz to the Pope was couched in somewhat too sanguine terms. He represented that Luther was ready to recant everything. Leo was so pleased to hear it that he dispatched a right friendly missive to the Wittenberg monk (March 29, 1519) inviting him to Rome to make his confession, and even offering him money for the journey.

That he was able to take no further action for a time was due to the political situation. In January, 1519, the Emperor Maximilian died. Among the candidates for the position were King Charles of Spain, King Francis of France, and the Elector Frederic. The interest of the papacy in this election overshadowed all other matters for a time, and the cautious policy necessary prevented too much pressure being brought to bear on Frederic. The process for heresy was consequently suspended during fourteen months.

If Miltitz had been satisfied with his interview, Luther was not. When they parted with the kiss of peace he felt that it was a Judas kiss and that the envoy's tears were crocodile's tears. He tried, nevertheless, to live up to the spirit of the agreement. In fulfilment of the third proposition in the first day's interview, he published An Instruction on Certain Articles. In this he explains his position on a number of points. Prayers for the dead in purgatory he thinks are allowable. Of indulgences it is enough for the common man to know that indulgence is a relaxation of the satisfaction for sin, but is a much smaller thing than a work of charity, for it is free; no one sins in not buying a papal pardon, but if he buys one instead of giving to the poor or helping his neighbor, he sins, mocking himself and God. The Church's commands, he says, are to be obeyed, yet one should place God's commands higher. "Of good works I have said, and still say, that no one is good nor can any one do right, unless God's grace first makes him just; wherefore no one is justified by works, but good works come naturally from him who is just." In conclusion he adds that there is no doubt that God has honored the Roman Church above all others.

The first article of the agreement, that both sides should maintain silence, came to nothing, for neither party observed the truce, and the whole controversy was soon given an even wider publicity than it had yet attained, by an event of the first importance, the great debate with John Eck at Leipsic.

CHAPTER VI

THE LEIPSIC DEBATE. 1519.

THE ablest and most persistent opponent Luther ever had was John Eck. From 1517 to 1543 this champion of the Church met him at every turn and did everything in his power to foil the great heresiarch. Like the Wittenberger, Eck was a peasant by extraction and a monk by profession, a theologian of no mean ability and a man of energy and resource. Before 1517 he had distinguished himself in debates at Vienna and elsewhere, and burned to make himself still more famous in this line. Just before Luther crossed his path, he charged Erasmus — the foremost scholar of the day — with something very like heresy because the latter had said that the Greek of the New Testament was not as good as that of Demosthenes.[1]

The publication of the Ninety-five Theses gave him a more substantial object to attack, and he at once assailed them in a pamphlet called Obelisks (literally the small daggers with which notes are marked). Of it Luther wrote, on March 24, 1518, to his friend John Silvius Egranus of Zwickau : —

A man of signal and talented learning and of learned talent has recently written a book against my Theses. I mean John Eck, doctor of theology, chancellor of the university of Ingolstadt, canon of Eichstätt and preacher at Augsburg, a man already famous and widely known as an author. What cuts me most is that we had recently formed a great friendship. Did I not already know the machinations of Satan, I should be astonished at the fury with which Eck has broken that sweet amity without warning or letter of farewell.

In his Obelisks he calls me a fanatic Hussite, heretical, seditious, insolent and rash, not to mention such slight abuse as that I am dreaming, clumsy, unlearned, and a despiser of the Pope. In short the book is nothing but the foulest abuse, expressly mentioning my name and directed against my Theses. It is nothing less than the malice and

---

[1] *Erasmi opera.* Leyden, 1703, vol. iii, no. 303, February 2, 1518.

envy of a maniac. I would have swallowed this sop for Cerberus,[1] but my friends compelled me to answer it.

The answer was a pamphlet entitled Asterisks, circulated in manuscript.

Before the altercation had progressed any further, it was taken out of Luther's hands by another Wittenberg professor, John Bodenstein of Carlstadt, a man destined to play an important part in the Protestant revolt. Though careful to incur no great danger, he was by nature a revolutionary, and longed to out-Luther Luther. While the latter was away at Heidelberg in the spring of 1518, Carlstadt came forward with a set of theses, against Eck on free will and the authority of Scripture. The Ingolstadt professor answered these with some counter-theses, in which an extreme view of the papal supremacy was maintained. Carlstadt, who held a benefice directly from the Pope, was not prepared to answer this point, but Luther had no such scruples, and towards the end of the year he published twelve propositions directed against Eck. Of these the most important was the twelfth : —

The assertion that the Roman Church is superior to all other Churches is proved only by weak and vain (frigidis) papal decrees of the last four hundred years, against which militates the accredited history of eleven hundred years, the Bible, and the decree of the Nicene Council, the holiest of all councils.

This unheard-of attack on the power of the Roman See made an immense sensation. Eck could not leave it unnoticed, nor did he wish to, and therefore arranged that he should debate with both Wittenberg professors. A letter — according to modern notions a very rude one — written during the course of negotiations, is illuminating : [2] —

TO JOHN ECK AT INGOLSTADT

WITTENBERG, February 18, 1519.

I wish you salutation and that you may stop seducing Christian souls. I regret, Eck, to find so many reasons to believe that your pro-

[1] As Burke would have said, " this honeyed opiate compounded of treason and a murder."

[2] Enders, v, 6.

fessed friendship for me is hypocritical. You boast that you seek
God's glory, the truth, the salvation of souls, the increase of the faith,
and that you teach of indulgences and pardons for the same reasons.
You have such a thick head and cloudy brain that, as the apostle says,
you know not what you say. . . .

I wish you would fix the date for the disputation or tell me if you
wish me to fix it. More then. Farewell.

Leipsic was finally chosen as the ground for the debate.
The faculty of that university made some difficulties, fearing
to become involved, but Duke George of Albertine Saxony,
maintaining that the advancement of Christian truth was the
chief end of the university, forced them to yield. During the
next six months Luther's principal occupation was the preparation for the battle, for which he plunged eagerly into the study
of Church history and especially of the Canon Law. The results of these researches, which left a lasting influence on his
mind, are brilliantly portrayed in two letters written on the
same day to his best friend: —

TO GEORGE SPALATIN AT ALTENBURG

(WITTENBERG, about February 24, 1519. Letter no. 1.)

Greeting. I beseech you, dear Spalatin, be not fearful nor let your
heart be downcast with human cares. You know that if Christ did not
rule me, I should have perished long ago, either at the first controversy about indulgences, or when my sermon on them was published,
or when I promulgated my Resolutions, or when I answered Prierias,
or recently in the interview at Augsburg, especially as I went thither.
What mortal man was there who did not either fear or hope that I
would cause my death by one of these things? In fact Olsnitzer recently wrote from Rome to our honorary chancellor, the Duke of Pomerania, that my Resolutions and Answer to Prierias had so perturbed
the Roman Church that they were at a loss how to suppress them, but
that they intended to attack me not by law, but by Italian subtility
— these were his very words. I understand this to mean poison or
assassination.

I repress much for the sake of the Elector and university which
otherwise I should pour out against that spoiler of the Bible and the
Church, Rome, or rather Babylon. For the truth of the Scripture and
of the Church cannot be spoken, dear Spalatin, without offending that

beast. Do not therefore hope that I shall be quiet or safe in future unless you wish me to give up theology altogether. Let my friends think me mad. For the thing will not be ended (if it be of God) even should all my friends desert me as all Christ's disciples and friends deserted him, and the truth be left alone to save herself by her own might, not by mine nor by yours nor by any man's. I have expected this hour from the first.

My twelfth proposition was extorted from me by Eck, but, as the Pope has defenders enough, I do not think they ought to take it ill unless they forget the freedom of debate. At all events, even should I perish, nothing will be lost to the world. For my friends at Wittenberg have now progressed so far, by God's grace, that they do not need me at all. What will you? I fear I am not worthy to suffer and die for such a cause. That will be the blessed lot of better men, not of so foul a sinner. . . .

TO GEORGE SPALATIN AT ALTENBURG

(WITTENBERG, about February 24, 1519. Letter no. 2.)

Greeting. I had just finished my last letter, dear Spalatin, when Carlstadt gave me the letter which you sent him, full of such complaints that I was almost moved to anger. You urge me to tell my plan. I am not unwilling for you to know what I intend, but I know the best way to defeat a plan is to tell it, especially if the matter be of God, who does not like his plans to be laid bare before they are fulfilled. . . .

You know that I have to do with a crafty, arrogant, slippery, loud-mouthed sophist, whose one aim is to traduce me publicly and hand me over to the Pope devoted to all the furies. You will understand his iniquitous snares if you read his twelfth proposition.[1] Wherefore, considering his craft, and seeing that I was about to be ruined by his arts, I carefully prepared *my* twelfth proposition, that he may imagine that he has most certainly triumphed, and while singing a pæan of joy, shall forthwith expose himself to the scorn of all, God willing. For I know that at this stage of the debate he will burst forth passionately gesticulating and shouting that I cannot prove my assertion, but have made a mistake in reckoning time (as you also think), and that it is much more than four hundred years ago, more than a thousand, ever since the time of Pope Julius I, directly after the Nicene

[1] Asserting the universal supremacy of the Pope, opposed to Luther's twelfth proposition quoted above.

Council, that the Roman Church published decrees asserting that she was the superior of all and that no council could be called without her assent. Relying on these statements he will even laugh, I hope, at my incredible folly and rashness.

Then I shall say that these decrees were not then received, and that if Gregory IX, the first collector of the decretals (who in the time of Frederick II canonized St. Francis, St. Dominic, and our own St. Elizabeth, i. e., is not yet dead four hundred years), and if Boniface VIII, author of the sixth book of decretals, and Clement V, author of the Clementines, had not collected these decretals and published them, Germany would doubtless never have known them.[1] Therefore it is to be attributed to these three popes that the decretals of the Roman pontiffs were spread abroad and the Roman tyranny was established.

To what conclusion do these arguments lead? I deny that the Roman Church is superior to all Churches, but not that she is our superior, as she now is *de facto*. How will Eck prove that the Church of Constantinople, or any Greek Church, or that of Antioch or Alexandria or Africa or Egypt, was ever under the Roman Church or received bishops confirmed by her? . . .

We Germans established the authority of the popes as much as we could when the Empire was transferred to us, and in return we have borne them as a punishment of the furies, headsmen and tormentors and blood-suckers of archbishoprics and bishoprics.

I call the decretals "vain" because they twist scriptural texts to their own purposes, texts which speak nothing of government but only of spiritual food and faith. . . .

I count the papal power as a thing indifferent, like wealth or health or other temporal goods, and am very sorry that so much is made of temporal matters, which are insisted on as if by the command of God, though he always teaches that they should be despised. How can I bear with equanimity this perverse interpretation of God's Word and that wrong opinion, even if I allow the power of the Roman Church as a thing convenient?

Farewell.

BROTHER MARTIN LUTHER, Augustinian.

---

[1] The Canon Law is composed of several parts. The first, the *Decretum of Gratian* is a collection of ancient canons made in the twelfth century. To this Gregory IX added five books of decretals (*literæ decretales* 1243), and Boniface VIII a sixth book (*liber sextus*, 1298). Other additions, the *Clementines* and *Extravagantes*, were made at various times later until 1484. Many of the decretals in the Canon Law are forgeries, as Luther says.

Of the sojourn in Leipsic (June 27–July 18), the reception there and the debate itself, the best account is given by Luther in the letter next translated. The encounter was held in a richly decorated hall of the Pleissenburg, a castle only recently torn down to make way for the new Rathaus. A large and distinguished audience had gathered, including Duke George, later one of the most determined opponents of the new doctrine.

An eye-witness has left us the first description of Luther as he appeared on this occasion, and one which agrees well with Cranach's earliest portrait of him, the wood-cut of 1520. He was of middle height, so emaciated that one could almost count his bones, yet he seemed in the vigor of manhood. His voice was clear and distinct. Polite and cheerful in society, he affected no stoicism, but gave each hour its due. His serene countenance was never disturbed. The richness and fluency of his Latin diction was noticed, as was his careful preparation of the material.

Only contemporaries can appreciate the ability of the speakers in this debate, full notes of which have been preserved. In learning and force of argument the honors seem to be about equal. Eck manœuvred skilfully to make Luther's opinions appear identical with those of Huss. The latter took up the challenge, and on the second day of the combat boldly asserted: "It is certain that among the articles of John Huss and the Bohemians there are many which are most Christian and evangelic, which the universal Church is not able to condemn." These words sent a thrill through the audience: Duke George put his arms akimbo, shook his head, and said loudly, "That's the plague."

Eck had accomplished his point in driving Luther to a position of universally acknowledged heresy. He played his advantage with great skill, taxing his opponent over and over with being a Hussite, Luther often interrupting him with "It is false," or, "He lies impudently."

After the question of the papal supremacy was put aside for other points, the debate, which continued until July 14, was comparatively tame. Let us now hear what Luther has to say about it: —

TO GEORGE SPALATIN AT ALTENBURG

(WITTENBERG,) July 20, 1519.

. . . I should have written long ago about this famous debate of ours, but I had neither time nor place to do it. Certain men of Leipsic, neither candidly nor justly, triumph with Eck and babble of his fame, but you can judge of it from my account.

Almost the instant that we came, before we had descended from our wagons, the Inhibition[1] of the Bishop of Merseburg was fixed to the doors of the churches, alleging against the debate some new points, declaratory and other. This was disregarded, and he who had posted the notice was thrown into chains by the Town Council because he had done it without their knowledge.

Accomplishing nothing by this trick, they resorted to another. Having called Carlstadt aside, they urged him (at Eck's desire) to agree that the debate should not be reported in writing, for he hoped to get the better of us by shouting and gesticulating, in which points indeed he is our superior. Carlstadt said that the agreement had already been made and must be adhered to, and that the debate should be reported. At length, to obtain this point at all, he was forced to consent that the report of the debate should not be published prior to the decision of the judges. Then a new dispute arose about choosing them. At length they forced him to consent that the judges should be chosen after the disputation was finished, otherwise they would not debate at all. Thus they put us on the horns of a dilemma, so that in either case we should have the worst of it, whether we refused to debate on these terms, or recognized the necessity of submitting to unjust judges. See how plain is their guile by which they would filch the freedom we had agreed upon! For we know that the universities and the Pope will either never decide or will decide against us, which is just what they desire.

The next day they called me aside and proposed the same thing. I refused their conditions, fearing the Pope. Then they proposed the universities as judges without the Pope. I asked that the conditions agreed upon be observed, and when they refused I withdrew and declined to debate. At once an uncontradicted report went abroad that I dared not, and what was worse would allow no judges. The affair was bandied about and interpreted in the most odious and malignant light, so that they even won over our best friends and prepared a last-

---

[1] The bishop thought the matter of the debate had already been decided by the bull of November 9, 1518, mentioned above, p. 54.

AETHERNA IPSE SVAE MENTIS SIMVLACHRA LVTHERVS
EXPRIMIT·AT VVLTVS CERA LVCAE OCCIDVOS
· M·D·X·X ·

LUTHER AS MONK

After an etching by Cranach, 1520

ing shame for our university. So I went to them with conciliatory friends, and accepted their conditions, even though indignant at them. But I reserved my power of appeal and excluded the Roman Curia, so that there might be no prejudice to my case.

Eck and Carlstadt debated a week on free will. Carlstadt with God's help advanced splendid and copious arguments and citations and brought books to prove his points. A chance was thus given Eck to oppose Carlstadt; he refused to debate unless the books were left at home, because by them Carlstadt could prove the correctness of his own quotations from the Bible and the Fathers and the inaccuracy of Eck's. So another tumult arose. At length it was decided for Eck that the books should be left at home, but who cannot see that when a question of truth is at stake it is desirable to have the books at hand? Never did hatred and ambition show themselves more impudently than here.

At last the man of guile conceded all that Carlstadt argued for, although he had violently opposed it, and agreed with him in all, boasting that *he* had brought Carlstadt over to *his* opinion. He abandoned Scotus and the Scotists, Capreolus and the Thomists, saying that the schoolmen had thought and taught the same as Carlstadt. Then and there fell Scotus and Capreolus with their respective schools!

The next week he debated with me — at first sharply about the primacy of the Pope. His strength lay in the words, " thou art Peter," " feed my sheep," " follow thou me," and " strengthen thy brethren," together with a lot of quotations from the Fathers. (You will soon see what I answered.) Then, resting his whole weight on the Council of Constance, which had condemned the assertion of Huss that the papacy was dependent on the Emperor, he went to the extreme length of saying that it bore sway by divine right. Thereupon, as if entering the arena, he cast the Bohemians in my teeth, and charged me with being an open heretic and an ally of the Hussites. For the sophist is no less insolent than rash. These charges tickled the Leipsic audience more than the debate itself.

In rebuttal I pointed to the Greeks for a thousand years, and to the ancient Fathers who had not been under the sway of the Roman pontiff to whom I did not deny a precedence in honor. Then I discussed the authority of a council. I said openly that some articles had been wrongly condemned [*sc.* by the Council of Constance], as they had been taught in the plainest words by Paul, Augustine, and even Christ himself. At this point the reptile swelled up, painted my crime in the darkest colors, and almost drove the audience wild with his rhetoric.

At length I proved from the words of that council that not all the articles there condemned were heretical and erroneous, so that his mode of proof accomplished nothing. And thus the matter rested.

The third week we debated penance, purgatory, indulgences, and the power of a priest to absolve. For he did not care about his dispute with Carlstadt, but only that with me. Indulgences fell through completely and he agreed to almost all I said, so that their use was turned to scorn and mockery. He hoped this would be the subject of a future debate with me, as he said in public, that people might understand that he made no great matter of indulgences. He is said to have granted that had I not disputed the power of the Pope he would have agreed with me easily on all points. He even confessed to Carlstadt: "If I could only agree with Luther as much as I do with you, I would go home with him at once." The man is fickle and subtle, ready to do anything. He who once said to Carlstadt that the schoolmen taught the same as he, said to me that Gregory of Rimini was the only one who supported me against all others. Thus he thinks it no fault to assert and deny the same thing at different times. Nor do the men of Leipsic grasp this, so great is their stupidity. And what is still more monstrous, he asserts one thing in the academy and another in the church to the people. Asked by Carlstadt why he did this, the man shamelessly replied that the people ought not to be taught points on which there was doubt.

My part thus ended, he debated the last three days with Carlstadt, agreeing to and yielding all: that spontaneous action is sin; that free will without grace can do nothing but sin; that there is sin in every [natural] good work; that it is only grace which enables a man to do what he can for the Disposer of grace; — all of which the schoolmen deny. So in the whole debate he treated nothing as it deserved except my thirteenth [1] proposition. In the mean time he congratulates himself, triumphs and reigns, but only until we shall have published our side. As the debate turned out badly, I shall draw up additional propositions.

The citizens of Leipsic never greeted us nor visited us, but acted like the bitterest enemies; but Eck they followed and clung to and invited to dinners in their houses and gave him a robe and a chamois-hair gown. They escorted him around on horseback; in fact they tried everything they could think of to insult us. Moreover, they persuaded Cæsar Pflug and Duke George to let these things pass. They

[1] That about the supremacy of the Pope quoted above as the twelfth. The number had been changed by the interpolation of an additional proposition.

did give us one thing, the customary present of wine, which perhaps it would not have been safe for them to omit. The few who favored us came to us clandestinely, but Dr. Stromer of Auerbach, a man of upright mind, invited us and so did Professor Pistorius. Duke George himself invited three of us together. Likewise the most illustrious Duke summoned me by myself and talked much with me about my writings, especially that on the Lord's Prayer, and mentioned that the Hussites expected much from me, and that I had raised doubts in many consciences about the Lord's Prayer, so that many complained that they would not be able to say one paternoster in four days if they thought they ought to believe me, and much else to the same effect. Nor was I so stupid as not to know the difference between a fife and a f— ; I regretted that the excellent and pious prince should represent and comply with the feelings of others when I saw he was so clever in speaking like a prince about his own.

The last exhibition of hatred was this : when on the day of St. Peter and St. Paul [June 29] I was asked by our rector, the Duke of Pomerania, to read the gospel in the chapel of the castle, suddenly the report of my preaching filled the city, and such a vast concourse of men and women came to hear me that I was compelled to preach in the debating-hall, with all the professors and other hostile listeners sitting around. The gospel for the day [Matthew xvi, 13–19] clearly takes in the subject of both debates, and so I was forced to expound the substance of the disputations to all, to the great annoyance of Leipsic.

Stirred up by this, Eck preached four times thereafter in different churches, reviling me and attacking all I had said. Thus those would-be theologians bade him do. But *I* was not allowed to preach again, although many asked it. I was only to be accused and criminated without a chance to defend myself. They acted on the same principle in the debate, so that Eck, although in the negative, had the last word, which I could not refute.

When Cæsar Pflug heard that I had preached (for he was not then present), he said, "I wish Dr. Luther would save his sermons for Wittenberg." In short, I have known hatred before, but never more shameless nor more impudent.

Here you have the whole tragedy. Dr. Planitz will tell you the rest, for he was present in person. Because Eck and Leipsic sought their own glory and not the truth, it is no wonder that they began badly and ended worse. For whereas we hoped to make peace between Wittenberg and Leipsic, they acted so odiously that I fear it will rather seem that discord and mutual dislike are now first born. I, who try to bridle my impetuosity, am not able to banish all dislike of them, because I am flesh and their impudent hatred and malignant injustice were overbearing in so sacred and divine a cause.

Farewell and commend me to the most illustrious Elector. . . .

> Yours,
>
> MARTIN LUTHER.

It is plain from this letter that the writer was smarting under the sense of outrage. If he had not been defeated, he had been out-manœuvred. Such debates, of course, decide nothing. Each party remained strengthened in its own opinion. In this case, too, the universities, to whom the decision was submitted, put off giving it for one reason or another.

Yet the disputation at Leipsic was a turning-point. It showed that the Wittenberg monk was no longer in a position where reconciliation with the Church was possible. In the train of the combat followed a cloud of polemics, half the Germans who could write taking sides against the new leader, and the other half for him. As this bickering — for that is what most of it was — left little permanent result, it need not find a large place in the biography of Luther, even though he took an active part in the controversy.

As he has spoken in a recent letter of the danger of assassination, it is interesting to see what foundations his suspicions had. The peril was probably very slight, but was given some color by the visit of suspicious strangers, one of whom he described, many years later, as follows : —

A man came to me in 1519, with whom I shook hands, and whom I took home with me. He said : " Dear Doctor, it surprises me that you so readily shake hands with strangers ; are you not afraid of being shot ? I am alone with you." I replied : " If you killed me, you would die, too." "In that case," said he, " the Pope would make me a saint and you a heretic." When I heard that, I called in Sieberger [the monastery servant], after which he soon left town.

CHAPTER VII

THE PATRIOT. 1519-20

THE revolt from Rome was by no means a purely religious phenomenon. Its enormous and immediate success can only be explained by the great variety of motives to which it appealed. It promised to the Christian a purer faith; to the patriotic German a stronger country freed from the foreign yoke; to the lower classes a millennium of universal brotherhood, equality and freedom. The hopes of all parties were not destined to be realized, some of them suffered a bitter disappointment; but all were willing to join in the common movement for their special ends, and it was this union and interaction of forces which produced that great revolution usually known as the Reformation. And of these stirring times Luther was the heart and soul. During the years 1519-1523 especially, it almost seemed as if he were lifted above himself and transcended the limits of his own personality. Of this time Professor Harnack has well said : —

For a period — it was only for a few years — it seemed as if his spirit would attract to itself and mould into a wonderful unity all that the time had of living vigor in it; as if to him, as to no one before, the power had been given to make his personality the spiritual centre of the nation, and to summon his century into the lists, armed with every weapon.

Luther himself was astonished at the almost universal response to his appeal. The course of events reacted on him, hurrying him along from a position of humble protest to the leadership of all the revolutionary forces of the time. Every occurrence carried him on like a wave and left him far in advance of his previous station. Each book he read, each friend he made, offered a powerful stimulus to his development. His progress, accurately traceable in his letters and other writings, is a study of absorbing interest.

His best friend and ablest lieutenant, at this time as later, was Philip Melanchthon, whom he first learned to know in the summer of 1518. When called in this year to teach Greek at the University of Wittenberg, Melanchthon was not yet twenty-one. The precocious youth, who had entered Heidelberg at thirteen and had taken the degree of bachelor at fifteen, and of master one year later, began at once to lecture on and to edit the classics. These studies were his passion, though he later won greater distinction in the field of divinity. He was a perfect contrast to Luther, a scholar and pedagogue rather than a man of action, a peacemaker rather than a warrior. The relations of the two men were always uncommonly close. Though the younger occasionally found the support given him by the elder and more robust irksome, he leaned upon it, and more than once found that when deprived of it he was unable to stand alone. Melanchthon was the disciple whom Luther loved, and, as can be seen from this extract of a letter to Spalatin written a few days after the young scholar's advent (August 31, 1518), loved at first sight: —

Doubt not that we have done all and shall do all you recommend about Philip Melanchthon. He delivered an oration the fourth day after he came, in the purest and most learned style, by which he won the thanks and admiration of all, so that you need not worry about commending him to us. We have quickly abandoned the opinion we formed from his small stature and homeliness, and now rejoice and wonder at his real worth, and thank our most illustrious Elector and your good offices, too, for giving him to us. Indeed, it is you who must rather study to put his merits in a proper light to our sovereign. While Philip is alive, I desire no other Greek teacher. I only fear that perhaps his delicate health cannot well endure the life in our parts, and besides, I hear that his salary is so small that the boastful University of Leipsic hopes to get him away from us soon. Indeed he was called by them before he came to us. I suspect (and not I alone) that Pfeffinger[1] will prove true to his custom in this matter also, and be too faithful a guardian of the Elector's purse. And so, dear Spalatin, if I may speak frankly, as with a good friend, take care not to despise Melanchthon for his looks and his tender age, for the man is worthy of all honor. I would not have our university want-

[1] The treasurer of Electoral Saxony: cf. *supra*, p. 34.

ing in those humane studies, the lack of which gives our rivals some excuse for making us a byword.

From this time on Luther's letters are full of allusions to him " who has almost every virtue known to man and yet is my dear and intimate friend." Shortly after the Leipsic debate Melanchthon published some theses denying the doctrine of transubstantiation — an important contribution to the thought of Luther, who speaks of them and their author in a letter to Staupitz, October 3, 1519: —

You have seen Philip's theses by this time — somewhat bold, to be sure, but true. His solution of the problem naturally would excite our admiration as it has. If Christ please, Melanchthon will make many Luthers and a most powerful enemy of the devil and of scholasticism, for he knows both the trumpery of the world and the rock of Christ, therefore shall he be mighty.

Melanchthon's fundamental ideas were drawn from Luther's inexhaustible mine of thought, but he developed, clarified, and systematized them, and thus repaid the debt he had contracted. Another powerful influence towards the formation of the new system of theology in Luther's mind was found in the writings of John Huss. The German reformer had read one of them during the first years in the cloister, and had wondered how a heretic could speak so Christianly, but thinking that the particular book must have been composed before the apostasy, he shut it up and forgot it. Later in preparing for the Leipsic debate, he had read enough of the history of the Council of Constance, where Huss was condemned, to believe that many of the latter's propositions were evangelic and orthodox, and he had flatly declared his conviction of this at the encounter with Eck. Several Hussites, having formed hopes in the new reformer destined to be realized, had gathered at this great event, and two of the most distinguished of them had written him and sent one of Huss's works. Luther did not have time to read it until early in 1520. He then first recognized that in many things the Bohemian had been his predecessor, and he did not hesitate to proclaim himself the condemned heretic's disciple. How deep and fervent was his admiration can best be gathered from his own words: —

TO GEORGE SPALATIN AT ALTENBURG

(WITTENBERG, February, 1520.[1])

. . . Having consulted with friends about the Elector's advice, I find I cannot, without peril to my conscience, offer peace of my own accord. I have done enough that way hitherto, and met no response to my efforts ; I am always treated with force when it comes to negotiation, and cannot relax my whole strength as long as Eck is clamoring : I am obliged to commend the cause to God and follow him loyally, having committed my ship to the winds and waves. I can only pray for God's mercy. I have an idea that a revolution is about to take place unless God withhold Satan. I have seen the devil's artful plans for my perdition and for that of many. What will you? The Word of God can never be advanced without whirlwind, tumult, and danger. The Word is of infinite majesty, it is wonderful in the heights and in the depths; as the prophet says : "It slew the fattest of them and smote down the chosen men of Israel." One must either despair of peace and tranquillity or else deny the Word. War is of the Lord who did not come to send peace. Take care not to hope that the cause of Christ can be advanced in the world peacefully and sweetly, since you see the battle has been waged with his own blood and that of the martyrs. I have hitherto taught and held all the opinions of John Huss unawares; so did John Staupitz; in short, we are all Hussites without knowing it. Paul and Augustine are Hussites to a word. Behold the horror which I have discovered without any Bohemian teacher or leader : I know not what to think for astonishment when I see such terrible judgments of God on mankind that the plain gospel truth has been publicly burned and considered damnable for a hundred years, and no one to assert it! Woe to the land!

Farewell.

MARTIN LUTHER.

Next to his studies in Huss and in the Canon Law, Luther's eyes were opened to the iniquities of Rome by a work of Lorenzo Valla, one of the most brilliant of the fifteenth century humanists, the proof that the Donation of Constantine was a forgery. This celebrated document, composed in the ninth century, purported to be a deed drawn up by the Emperor

[1] For this date, cf. Enders, ii, 345. Köhler argues for a later date; cf. *Luther und die Kirchengeschichte* (Erlangen, 1900), i, 198.

Constantine in the fourth century, presenting the Pope with central Italy, and giving him a general overlordship of the Western world. The forgery had been received for six uncritical centuries as authentic and had become one of the corner-stones of the papal pretensions, and of the Canon Law. Luther wrote of it, February 24, 1520, to his friend Spalatin as follows : —

I have at hand Lorenzo Valla's proof (edited by Hutten) that the Donation of Constantine is a forgery. Good heavens! what darkness and wickedness is at Rome! You wonder at the judgment of God that such unauthentic, crass, impudent lies not only lived but prevailed for so many centuries, that they were incorporated in the Canon Law, and (that no degree of horror might be wanting) that they became as articles of faith. I am in such a passion that I scarcely doubt that the Pope is the Antichrist expected by the world, so closely do their acts, lives, sayings, and laws agree. But more of this when I see you. If you have not yet seen the book, I shall take care that you read it.

Ulrich von Hutten, first mentioned by Luther in the last letter, was soon to become one of his strongest supporters and allies. A knight of old Franconian family, combining considerable literary ability with fiery ambition, he devoted his life to the cause of patriotism and the resistance of ecclesiastical oppression. He and his friend Franz von Sickingen, whose large resources and wide connections made him feared even by the greater princes, were the leaders of the party of the knights whose programme was the restoration of German national prestige under the leadership of their order. At first the nationalists regarded Luther merely as a squabbling monk, but by 1520 they read the sign of the times more plainly, and saw what an immense impulse would be given to the cause of German freedom by uniting it with the cause of spiritual emancipation. Hutten had only one fear—that Luther would compromise with or else be crushed by the foreign oppressor, and wrote urging him to stand fast and promising support : —

ULRICH VON HUTTEN TO LUTHER AT WITTENBERG

MAYENCE, June 4, 1520.

Long live liberty! If anything hinders you from completing what you have begun I shall mourn as a spiritual kinsman and friend.

Christ be with us, as we bring his teachings again to light, you more happily, but I at least according to my powers. May all be like-minded with us or soon return to the right way. It is said that you are under the ban of the Church. If this is so, how great are you, Luther, how great! . . . But beware! You see that if you fall it will be a great injury to the State, but I know from your actions that you are resolved to die rather than merely live. . . . Be strong! But why should I admonish you when I have no need ? In any event you have a supporter in me and may confide your plans to me. Let us defend the common freedom and liberty of our long enslaved fatherland! We have God on our side ; if he be for us, who can be against us ? . . . Your letters will reach me in Brabant. Write me there and farewell in Christ. Salute Melanchthon and Fach and all our friends, and farewell again.

Shortly after the arrival of this letter came one from another leader of the party, Sylvester von Schaumburg, offering protection in case of need. It seemed to Luther that this support came in the nick of time. Hutten had been correctly informed that the bull against the heresiarch had been drawn up at Rome. Cardinal Riario, a friend of Erasmus and a moderate, had written the Elector from that city on May 20, urging him as he valued his safety to "make that man recant." The letter only reached the Elector on July 6, and was promptly forwarded to Wittenberg. Luther's answer is eloquent of his attitude : —

TO GEORGE SPALATIN AT ALTENBURG

WITTENBERG, July 10, 1520.

. . . I almost wish that famous bull would come from Rome to rage against my doctrine. . . .

I send the letter of the Franconian knight, Sylvester von Schaumburg, and unless it is too much trouble I wish the Elector would communicate its contents to Cardinal Riario, that they may know in Rome that even if they thrust me out of Wittenberg with their furies they will only make matters worse, since there are now some not only in Bohemia but in the heart of Germany who are able and willing to receive me in spite of the thunders of the hostile Curia.

In this lies their danger ; for were I saved by those protectors I should grow more terrible to the Romanists than I am now while publicly teaching under the Elector's government. Doubtless this will happen unless God interpose. For hitherto I have given in on many points, even when enraged, out of respect to my sovereign, but *then* there would surely be no need to consult his wishes. So let them know that they owe it neither to my moderation nor to the success of their own tyranny, but to the name and authority of the Elector, and to my respect for the University of Wittenberg, that I have proceeded no further against them.

My die is cast; I despise the fury and favor of Rome; I will never be reconciled to them nor commune with them. Let them condemn and burn my books. On my side, unless all the fire goes out, I will condemn and publicly burn the whole papal law, that slough of heresies. The humility I have hitherto shown all in vain shall have an end, lest it still further puff up the enemies of the Gospel.

The more I think of Cardinal Riario's letter the more I despise it. I see they write with cowardly fear and a bad conscience, trying to put on a ferocious mien with the last gasp. They try to protect their folly by force, but they fear they will not succeed as happily as they have in times past. But I doubt not that the Lord will accomplish his purpose through me (though I am a foul sinner) or through another.

Farewell.

MARTIN LUTHER, Augustinian.

CHAPTER VIII

THE ADDRESS TO THE GERMAN NOBILITY, THE BABYLONIAN
CAPTIVITY OF THE CHURCH, AND THE FREEDOM OF
A CHRISTIAN MAN. 1520.

THE art of printing with movable types was invented about
1470 at Mayence, and spread with such marvellous rapidity
that before the end of the century every European country
from Ireland to Turkey, east and west, and from Norway to
Italy, north and south, had its own presses. The powerful
stimulus to progress furnished by this discovery has often been
pointed out; this mighty engine for disseminating truth made
accessible to almost all what had before been the property of
comparatively few. The success of the Reformation, as of all
subsequent democratic and progressive movements, may be
largely attributed to it.

It is safe to say that Martin Luther was the first man to
make full use of the press as an agent for appealing to public
opinion. By means of it he won the support of a majority of his
countrymen as well as of many foreigners who could read Latin.
There were, of course, no newspapers, or other periodicals, but
to supply their want quantities of short pamphlets, and even of
letters, were poured forth from the printing-houses and eagerly
bought and read. A vast number of these were written by
Luther, a born pamphleteer, who may be said with some truth
to have created the German book trade, for before he began to
write, a majority of books printed in Germany were Latin, but
soon afterwards the scale turned rapidly and decisively in favor
of German. The exact figures will bring home the vivifying
effect of the new spirit. In 1518 there were only 150 German
works published, in 1519 the number rose to 260, in 1520 to
570, in 1521 to 620, in 1522 to 680, in 1523 to 935, and in 1524
to 990. In five years the output increased more than sixfold.

Luther was an extremely prolific author. His works, in num-

ber more than four hundred, fill more than a hundred volumes.
He was also an extremely popular author. On February 14,
1519, Froben, the great Basel publisher, wrote him that his
works were already exported to France, Spain, Italy, the Low
Countries, and England, as well as to all parts of the Empire.
The number of the editions was legion. The letters of the
time are full of references to the latest publications of the
Reformer. On November 1, 1520, for example, Glarean writes
Zwingli from Paris that no books are bought more quickly than
Luther's, and that at the last Frankfort fair (the great book
mart of Germany held in the spring of every year) fourteen
hundred copies of his works had been sold. This was before
Luther had written any of his greatest works.

At first, as we have seen, the Wittenberg professor devoted
himself chiefly to commentaries on Scriptures, of which the
lectures on Romans and Galatians have already been noticed.
During the years 1519–21 he again took up the Psalms and published in several parts a stout commentary on the first twenty-
one. These Operationes in Psalmos, as they were called, won
the admiration of Erasmus. They did not satisfy the author,
however, who feared that being in Latin they would not edify
the common people. While he was lecturing on them he wrote
a letter on the subject, from which, as it is almost unknown,
even to scholars, we will translate a portion, including the
observations on Melanchthon's work: [1]—

TO GERARD LISTRIUS AT ZWOLLE

WITTENBERG, July 30 (1520).

. . . Philip is theologizing most happily, lecturing, as a first attempt,
and yet with incredible success to almost five hundred auditors on
Paul's Epistle to the Romans. . . . I do not think that for a thousand
years Holy Scripture has been treated with the same simplicity and
clearness, for his talent is next that of the apostolic age. . . . I lose
these years of mine in unhappy wars and would like all my works to
perish, lest they should become obstacles to pure theology and better
geniuses, although to-day I expound my philosophy without slaughter
and blood. It is my fate that all evil beasts attack me alone, all seek-

[1] For text of this letter see Appendix II.

ing to win the laurel and palm from me. God grant that I may be David pouring out blood, but that Melanchthon may be Solomon reigning in peace. Amen. . . .

I have completed my bulky commentary on the Psalms to the XVIIIth, and have almost begun to be sorry for doing it, not on account of the labor, but because these works are so little popular and do not capture many, nor have I yet decided whether to publish any more (for it is the food of the perfect), and not rather treatises more easy to be understood. . . .

Luther's sermons were often published shortly after their delivery, especially if they had to do with some question of the day. Such was the sermon on the ban already mentioned (1518), and such was the sermon on the Lord's Supper advocating the participation of the laity in the cup. This excited an outcry from the preacher's enemies, especially Duke George and the Bishop of Merseburg. Consequently Luther published an explanation, which was considerably more radical than the original homily : —

I published a sermon on the venerable sacrament of the altar [he begins], in which I said that it seemed good that both bread and wine should be given to any one that desired it. Here upon my dear friends, who thirsted after my blood, thought they had me in a sack, and bawled out: "We have won!"

Another work of 1519 was the Tesseradecas, or Fourteen, written to console the sick elector. The author classifies all goods and ills in seven most original categories: those which are over, under, before, behind, on the right, on the left, and within one.

Not many months after completing this, Luther set his hand to a little treatise on ethics, entitled Good Works. These are taken up in the order of the Ten Commandments, the first and greatest duty being faith.

Of all Luther's works the most eminent, next to his translation of the Bible, are three pamphlets written in the latter half of 1520 : To the Christian Nobility of the German Nation on the Improvement of the Christian Estate, A Prelude on the Babylonian Captivity of the Church, and The Freedom of a Christian.

The first of these is a rousing appeal to his countrymen to right the many wrongs under which Germany suffers, especially such as she endures from Roman tyranny. It was written under the influence of the patriots, with whom the Reformer now made common cause. The inspiration to write came largely from them, and the sources of much in the work are found in the writings of Hutten and Crotus Rubeanus, as well as in Erasmus' Dialogue of St. Peter and Julius II.[1] Many things were also taken from private letters and personal conversations with friends who had been in Rome, especially a Dr. John van Wick, who stopped at Wittenberg in June, 1520, on his way from Italy to Hamburg. A far more important source is found in the Grievances of the German Nation presented at the Diet of Augsburg in 1518. But what Luther borrowed he made his own. He did not need Hutten to make him a patriot nor the Grievances to tell him what was rotten in the Empire. The book, like its author's character, in which so many influences had been at work, was not a mere aggregate of certain external elements, but something new and original, fused by genius into a living organism. It is a work of world-wide importance, at once prophesying and moulding the future.

Luther dedicated the book to his colleague in the university, Nicholas von Amsdorf, in a stirring preface dated June 23, 1520: —

God's grace and peace. Honorable, worthy, dear friend! The time to keep silence is past and the time to speak has come, as Ecclesiastes says. I have, according to our plan, brought together some propositions on the improvement of the Christian estate, and have addressed them to the Christian Nobility of the German Nation, to see whether God will help his Church through the laity, since the clergy, to whom such matters rather belong, has become entirely heedless of them. I am sending them to you, worthy sir, to correct, and, at need, to improve. I am well aware that people will not let me escape unblamed for having esteemed myself too highly, in that I, a poor, despised man, dare to address such great and noble persons on such important affairs, as though there were no one in the world except Dr. Luther who could

---

[1] Mentioned as a source of Knaake (Weimar), vi, 393, but wrongly attributed to Faustus Andrelinus. Cf. F. M. Nichols: *The Epistles of Erasmus* (London. 1901–1904), ii, 446.

take on himself the care of the Christian estate, and give counsel to such high and mighty persons. I do not excuse myself : let him blame me who will. Perhaps I owe my God and the world some folly, which I have now undertaken, as far as in me lies, to pay honestly, even if it be to become court fool. If I cannot pay it, at least no one will dare buy me a fool's cap or cut my comb, for he who fastens bells on his neighbor keeps some for himself. I must fulfil the proverb that whenever the world has some work to be done, a monk must do it even if he be ground to pieces by it. In times past fools have often spoken wisely and the wise have often been great fools, as St. Paul says : If any man would be wise, let him become a fool. As I am not only a fool, but a doctor sworn to defend Holy Scripture, I am glad that I now have a chance to discharge my oath, even if I do it in a foolish way. Please excuse me to those who have moderate understanding, for I know not how to deserve the favor of those who are wise beyond measure : I have often tried to do it with great pains, but from henceforth will not try nor care what they think. God help us to seek not our own but his glory. Amen.

After this dedication the author commences with a compliment to "the noble young blood Charles" and an appeal to him to reform the grievances which weigh so heavily on all men. He then goes on to show why it is that the laity have never been able to bring the clergy to account : —

"The Romanists have built three walls about themselves with great dexterity, with which they have hitherto protected themselves so that no one has been able to reform them, and the whole of Christendom has consequently declined. The first wall is that if the civil authority presses them, they affirm that civil government has no rights over them, but contrariwise spiritual over temporal. Secondly, if one would punish them by the Bible, they oppose it by saying that no one has a right to interpret the Bible except the Pope. Thirdly, if they are threatened with a general council, they pretend that only the Pope has the right to summon a council. So they have privily stolen three rods from us, to remain unpunished, and they have entrenched themselves in these three walls to do all rascality and evil. . . . May God now give us one of the trumpets by which the walls of Jericho were thrown down. . . .

"The first wall consists in the discovery that the Pope, bishops, priests, and monks are the spiritual estate, whereas princes, lords, laborers, and peasants are of the temporal estate. . . . But all Christians are really of the spiritual estate and there is no difference except of office, . . . for we were all made priests by baptism . . . a higher consecration than any that Pope or bishop gives. But handling God's Word and the sacrament is simply the work of the priest, bishop and Pope, as bearing the sword and punishing evil is the work of the civil magistrate. Even so cobblers, smiths and peasants — though consecrated priests and bishops — have their own work. Each one should help his neighbor's body and soul as the members of the body serve one another.

"Now one may see how Christian is their law that the temporal authority has no right to punish the spiritual. That is as much as to say that when the eye is suffering, the hand should do nothing for it. . . . Wherefore the temporal powers of Christendom should freely exercise their office, not regarding whether it is Pope, bishop, or priest that they punish, but only that the guilty suffer.

"The second wall is still frailer and poorer, the claim, namely, that they alone are masters of the Bible. Although their whole life long they learn nothing in it, yet they presume to say that they alone understand it, and juggle with such words as that the Pope cannot err: be he bad or good, one cannot teach him a letter! It is for this reason that so many heretical and unchristian, yes, unnatural laws stand in the Canon Law. . . .

"The third wall falls of itself when the first two are down, for when the Pope acts against Scripture, we are bound by Scripture to punish and compel him." There is no Scriptural proof that the Pope only can call a council: to assert this is like saying "if a fire break out in a city every one should stand still and let it go on and burn as it pleases, because the private citizens have not the power of the mayor, or because the fire started in the mayor's house. . . . No one in Christendom has the right to do harm."

Now we will examine the articles which should properly be treated by a council. If the Pope and bishops loved Christ, they would busy themselves with them day and night, but as they do not love Christ, let the temporal power attend to them, not regarding the bans and thunders of the clergy, for one unjust ban is better than ten just absolutions and one unjust absolution worse than ten just bans. . . .

1. It is horrible and terrible to see the Primate of all Christendom, who boasts he is Christ's Vicar and St. Peter's follower, should live in more worldly pomp than any king or emperor, and that he who is called "most holy and spiritual" is really more worldly than the

world itself. The Pope should therefore be forced to live more simply.

"2. What is the use of that people in Christendom who are called cardinals? I will tell you. Italy and Germany have many rich cloisters, foundations, livings, and benefices which people do not know how to turn to the profit of Rome better than by making cardinals and giving them abbacies and bishoprics, though in so doing they trample God's service under foot. . . . I advise that the cardinals be reduced in number, or else that the Pope support them from his own purse. Twelve would be enough, with one thousand gulden [1] a year."

3. The papal court should be reduced to one hundredth part of its present size. Germany gives more to the Pope than to the Emperor. The annates (one half the income of one year payable by all appointees of benefices) should be abolished, as well as raising money by the Pope under pretext of the Turkish war. The numerous reservations of the Pope to appointments in certain months and to certain livings should be curtailed. Palls should no longer be sold to archbishops, and the habit of appointing old and sickly men to offices in order to have a fresh vacancy soon should be stopped. Another crying abuse is plurality; Luther has heard of one man in Rome who holds twenty-two livings, seven provostships and forty-four canonries. Simony and the transfer of appointments under the fraudulent pretext of a "mental reservation" on the part of the Pope is a sin and a shame. In short, at Rome, "there is a buying and selling, a change and exchange, a crying and lying, fraud, robbery, theft, luxury, whoredom, rascality, and despite of God in every way, so that it would not be possible for Antichrist to outdo Rome in iniquity." There all things are sold and all laws can be abrogated for money. " Let no one think I exaggerate : it is public ; they cannot deny it." If I want to fight the Turks, the worst Turks are those in Italy.

" Now, though I am too little to propose articles for the reformation of such things, yet will I sing my fool's game to the end and say, as much as my reason is able, what might and should be done by the temporal power or a general council."

1. Each prince should forbid annates.

2. No foreigners should be allowed to take benefices.

3. An imperial law should be made that no ecclesiastic should go to Rome to get any dignity and that whoever appealed to Rome should lose his office.

[1] Five hundred dollars; in purchasing power worth about twenty times as much.

4. No legal cause should be appealed to Rome.[1]

5. There should be no more papal reservations.

6. There should be no more " casus reservati." (Legal actions which could only be heard in Rome.)

7. The Pope should abolish most offices and support the rest himself.

8. Bishops should be invested by the civil magistrate as in France and not obliged to swear allegiance to the Pope.

9. The Pope should claim no authority over the Emperor, whom he should crown only as a bishop does a king. It is ridiculous for the Pope to claim that when the Empire is vacant he inherits it. The Donation of Constantine is an unexampled lie.

10. The Pope should give up his pretensions to Naples and Sicily.

11. Kissing the Pope's foot and other silly signs of respect should be abolished.

12. There should be no more pilgrimages to Rome, especially in the years of jubilee. No one should undertake any pilgrimage without the consent of his pastor.

13. The begging friars are a curse. Many monasteries should be suppressed and no more founded. It would be an excellent thing if the inmates were allowed to leave when they pleased " as in the time of the apostles and long after."

" 14. We see how it has happened that many a poor priest is burdened with wife and child and wounded in his conscience and yet no one does aught to help him. . . . I advise that it be left free to every man to marry or not as he chooses. . . . Those who live together as man and wife are surely married before God."

15. It is a shame that in the cloisters abbots and abbesses make their brothers and sisters confess their secret sins and then persuade them that they are going to hell.

16. Vigils and private masses should be abolished or reduced in number.

" 17. Certain pains and penalties provided by the Canon Law must be done away, especially the interdict which was doubtless invented by the evil spirit. For is it not the devil's work to mend a sin by doing greater sin? And is it not an enormous sin to stop all divine services? "

18. All saints' days and holidays should be done away except Sundays, for now they are only spent in drunkenness, gaming, and idleness.

19. Marriages between distant relations should be allowed, as their

---

[1] Compare these provisions with the English statutes of Provisors and Præmunire.

prohibition is only a means of the Pope getting money. Fasts should be left free.

20. Shrines and chapels in fields and woods should be taken down. Pilgrimages to them cause all kinds of disorders. It makes no difference if miracles are performed at these shrines, "for were there no other sign that these are not of God, this would be enough, that men flock to them like cattle without reason." If the authorities refuse to abate these nuisances let every man resolve not to be deceived by them.

21. One of the greatest needs is that begging should be prohibited throughout Christendom. Each city should take care of its own poor, and nothing should be given to sturdy pilgrims, and friars. "There is no other trade in which there is so much rascality and cheating as mendicancy."

22. Foundations and canonries should be reduced to a small number in the cathedrals which would serve to support children of the nobility. Pluralities should be forbidden.

23. Religious brotherhoods and such things should be abolished. Papal commissaries ought to be chased out of the country.

24. It is high time that some effort be made to heal the Bohemian schism. It should be granted that Huss and Jerome of Prague were wrongly burned. "If I knew that the Beghards had no other error about the sacrament of the altar except the belief that it was natural bread and wine, though the flesh of Christ were in it, I would not cast them out, but let them live under the Bishop of Prague, for it is not an article of faith to believe that natural bread and wine are not in the sacrament — which is a delusion of Aquinas and the Pope — but merely to believe that true and natural flesh and blood is in the bread and wine. . . ."

"25. The universities need a good, stiff reform; I must say it, let it offend whom it may. . . . It is my advice that the books of Aristotle, — Physics, Metaphysics, The Soul, and Ethics, — which have hitherto been esteemed the best, be entirely removed from the curriculum, together with all others which boast that they teach natural science, although from them one learns neither natural nor spiritual things. No one has ever understood Aristotle's meaning, and yet this study is kept up to waste time and burden the soul. I venture to think that a potter has more natural science than is contained in all those books. It is a sorrow to my heart that that cursed (verdammte), arrogant, rascally heathen has made fools of so many of the best Christians. God has plagued us thus for our sins. In his best book, On the Soul, Aristotle teaches that the soul dies with the body. . . . There is no worse

book than his Ethics, which goes directly counter to God's grace and
Christian virtue. . . . But I would gladly allow Aristotle's books on
Logic, Rhetoric, and Poetics to be kept, at least in an abbreviated form
without elaborate commentaries. . . . Besides these studies I recommend Latin, Greek, Hebrew, mathematics, and history. . . .

"The schools of medicine I will allow to reform themselves, but
take the schools of law and theology to myself. To the former I say
that it were good that the whole Canon Law, from the first to the last
letter, especially the Decretals, were eradicated. More than enough
law is to be found in the Bible. . . . And moreover the law of the
Church nowadays is not what is written in the books, but whatever the
Pope or his followers want. . . . God help us! What a wilderness
the Civil Law has become! Although it is much better and wiser than
the Canon Law — in which, except God's name, there is nothing good
— yet there is far too much of it. . . . It seems to me that the laws
of each State of the Empire should have precedence over the Imperial
law, which should only be used in case of need. Would to God that
each land had its own short law as each has its special nature and
gifts."

In the schools of divinity the Bible should be supreme, and other
works be duly subordinated.

Each city should have schools for boys and girls, where the gospel
should be read to them either in Latin or German.

26. It should no more be taught that the Pope, having transferred
the Empire to the Germans, has superiority over the Emperor.[1]

27. It is now time to speak of some things amiss in the civil polity,
having thoroughly treated the abuses of the Church.

Sumptuary laws should be passed restraining extravagance in dress.
"But the greatest misfortune to Germany is usury. . . . A bridle
should be put in the mouth of the Fuggers and such companies, who
make from twenty to one hundred per cent on their money annu-
ally." It would be better to increase agriculture and diminish commerce.

It is shameful that Christians should allow brothels. The chief
sinners in these places are the clergy. No man should therefore be
allowed to vow celibacy before thirty.

This brief analysis of Luther's greatest work can give but
a faint idea of the cause of its tremendous and immediate pop-

---

[1] This article, which repeats the substance of the ninth, was not in the first
edition.

ular success. This lay in the seasonableness of the strong words, which expressed what every one was thinking and what all desired. In timeliness and popularity it might be compared with " Uncle Tom's Cabin," though in dignity of treatment and creative thought it is far above that excellent novel.

Luther's vehemence offended some even of his best friends. Lang went so far as suggesting that the work be recalled a few days after its appearance, early in August. His letter met with the following response : —

TO JOHN LANG AT ERFURT

WITTENBERG, August 18, 1520.

Greeting. Dear Father, is my pamphlet, which you term a trumpet-blast, really so fierce and cruel as you and all others seem to think ? I confess it is free and aggressive, and yet it pleases many and does not even much displease our court. I am not able to determine my own place in the present movement; perhaps I am the harbinger of Melanchthon, for whom I shall, like Elias, prepare a way in spirit and in power, troubling Israel and the followers of Ahab. But to return to my book — good or bad it is no longer in my power to recall it. Four thousand copies have already been printed and sent away, nor could I cause Lotther, the publisher, the loss he would sustain in recalling these. If I have sinned, we must remedy it by prayer.

We are here persuaded that the papacy is the seat of the true and genuine Antichrist, against whose deceit and iniquity we think all things are lawful unto us for the salvation of souls. For myself, I do not admit that I owe any obedience to the Pope, unless I also owe it to the Antichrist. Think of these things, do not judge us rashly, for we have reason for our opinion.

Melanchthon is going to marry Catharine Krapp, for which people blame me ; I do the best I can for the man, nothing moved by the clamor of all ; may God make all turn out well.

From my heart I hate that man of sin and son of perdition, with all his kingdom, which is nothing but sin and hypocrisy.

Yours,

BROTHER MARTIN LUTHER.

A letter, written the next day to another friend, is interesting, as giving Luther's justification for the vehemence of his language, which has given offence not only in his own day but later.[1]

TO WENZEL LINK AT NUREMBERG

(WITTENBERG,) August 19, 1520.

Greeting. I do not do it [speak violently], dear Father, to get praise and honor by my books and writings, for almost all condemn my acrimony; but I agree with you that perhaps God exposes the impostures of men in this way. I see that whatever is treated mildly in our age soon falls into oblivion, for no one minds it. But the womb of Rebecca must bear strife and infants contending with each other. The present judges badly; posterity will judge better. Even Paul calls his adversaries now dogs, now the concision, now babblers, false workers of miracles, ministers of Satan, and things of that sort, and curses a whited wall to his face. What prophet does not use the bitterest invective? Such language becomes so trite that it ceases to move. Our Reverend Father Vicar[2] wrote me yesterday from Erfurt asking me not to publish my work on the Improvement of the Christian Estate; I know not on what ground complaint was made to him, at any rate his letter came too late, after the book had appeared; pray try and appease him when you see him. Who knows if it be not the Spirit who moves me with this ardor, since it is certain that I am not carried away by

---

[1] It is instructive to compare Luther's defence with that made by Milton more than a century later, on the same charge. "If therefore the question were one of oratory, whether the vehement throwing out of scorn and indignation upon an object that merits it, were among the aptest ideas of speech to be allowed, it were my work, and that an easy one, to make clear both by the rules of the best rhetoricians and the famousest examples of Greek and Roman orators. But since the religion of it is disputed and not the art . . ." many examples of such language may be cited from the Bible. "Yet that ye may not think inspiration the only warrant thereof, but that it is as any other virtue, of moral and general observation, the example of Luther may stand for all . . . who writ so vehemently against the chief defenders of the old untruths in the Romish Church, that his own friends and favorers were offended with the fierceness of his spirit." Milton goes on to show that when Luther betook himself to moderation he got only despite from Cajetan and Eck, "and herewithal how useful and available God made this tart rhetoric in the Church's cause, he often found by his own experience. . . . And this I shall easily aver, though it may seem a hard saying, that the Spirit of God, who is purity itself, when he would reprove any fault severely, or but relate things said or done with indignation by others, abstains not from some words not civil at other times to be spoken." Various citations of indecent expressions used by God are given, among others, 1 Kings xiv, 10. Cf. *Apology for Smectymnuus.*

[2] Lang, who had been elected Vicar in Staupitz's place, 1520.

love of glory or of money or of pleasure, much less by vindictiveness?
I do not wish to stir up rebellion but only to assert the freedom of a
general council.

Farewell in the Lord.   Your brother,

MARTIN LUTHER.

Luther's second great reforming pamphlet, The Prelude to
the Babylonian Captivity of the Church, followed hard on the
first, appearing early in October. The former tract had been
directed against the practical abuses of the Church; this was
a blow at the base of her theology, the sacramental system.
The thoughts expressed in it were old ones to the writer, but
were put with fresh force, energy, and comprehensiveness. The
Address to the Nobility had been written in German as an appeal to the mass of that nation; the Babylonian Captivity was
composed in Latin, and translated against its author's will, for
it was meant primarily for theologians and scholars. A brief
analysis of its ninety pages, as nearly as possible in the original
words, will give the best idea of its contents: —

Willy nilly, I am daily forced to become more learned, with so
many and such able teachers pressing me on and giving me exercises.
I wrote of indulgences two years ago,[1] but in such a way that I now
greatly repent having published that book. For at that time I stuck
in a sort of superstitious reverence for the tyranny of Rome, wherefore
I did not think that indulgences should be altogether reprobated, since
they were approved by the common opinion of mankind. It was no
wonder that I thought so, for I alone rolled this rock away. But later,
by the kindness of Prierias and his brothers, who strenuously defended
indulgences, I understood that they were nothing but a mere imposture
of the Pope's flatterers, alike destructive to men's faith and fortunes.
Would that I could persuade all booksellers and all who have read
my books on them to burn what I then wrote and substitute this proposition: —

INDULGENCES ARE THE INIQUITIES OF THE POPE'S FLATTERERS

After this, Eck and Emser with their allies forced me to learn
the nature of the Pope's primacy. Not to be ungrateful to such learned
men, I acknowledge that their books have moved me a great ways

[1] The Resolutions.

forward. For previously, while denying that the papacy was of divine
right, I admitted it as a thing of human law. But now that I have
read the most subtle subtilties of those little coxcombs (Trossuli) by
which they ingeniously forged their idol, not being unteachable in such
matters I have learned and am certain that the papacy is the kingdom
of Babylon and the power of Nimrod the mighty hunter. Wherefore
in this case also I beg all my booksellers and readers that having
burned what I have hitherto written on this matter they should hold
to this proposition : —

THE PAPACY IS THE MIGHTY HUNTING OF THE ROMAN BISHOP

Giving the cup to the laity at communion is enjoined by the Bible
and forbidden by the Pope ; wherefore I shall proceed to show that
they are wicked who deny the sacrament in both kinds to laymen. In
order to do this more conveniently, I shall sing a prelude on the
captivity of the Roman Church.

In the first place I deny that the sacraments are seven in number, and assert that there are only three, baptism, penance, and the
Lord's Supper, and that all these three have been bound by the Roman
Curia in a miserable captivity and that the Church has been deprived
of all her freedom. Howbeit, should I wish to speak according to the
usage of Scripture, I should say that there was only one sacrament
and three sacramental signs. . . .

Before summarizing Luther's criticisms of the Roman sacramental system, it may conduce to clearness to give the briefest
possible account of that system. Sacramentum in Latin means
a sacred thing and by the early fathers was applied to a number of holy objects, for example, the cross of Christ. It soon
came to have the more special meaning that it now bears, that
of a rite of the Church to which a spiritual meaning is attached,
the two distinguishing characteristics of a sacrament being an
outward sign and a promise. Thus the rite of distributing the
bread and wine, with the promise of forgiveness, constituted
the eucharist, the immersion or sprinkling with water, with
the promise of salvation (Mark xvi, 16), is baptism. In like
manner confession and forgiveness (James v, 16) were made
the sacrament of penance, and the anointing of the sick with
oil for his recovery and forgiveness (James v, 14 and 15) became the sacrament of supreme unction. Confirmation and

orders had the same sign, the laying on of hands, but with a different purpose, the first to strengthen a layman in his faith, the other to impart the spiritual character to a priest (Acts vi, 6; xiii, 3; 1 Tim. iv, 14; 2 Tim. i, 6). Finally marriage was made a sacrament for two peculiar reasons. Peter Lombard, who first formulated the doctrine (circa 1100), was, like many ancient and mediæval philosophers, much under the obsession of sacred numbers. Having as yet but six sacraments, he wished to complete the sacred seven by the addition of another, and hit upon matrimony, which is not a specially Christian institution at all, but one common to all mankind. St. Paul compares the union of man and wife with that of Christ and the Church, which, says he, is a great mystery (*i. e.*, holy secret), a Greek word translated in the Latin Vulgate sacramentum (Eph. v, 31 and 32). It was this misunderstanding of Paul's meaning that induced Lombard to include wedlock among the holy rites of the Church. It is not necessary to go deeply into Luther's criticisms of this theology, but a brief summary of his most interesting remarks is valuable for the insight it gives into his doctrine : —

Eucharist. The first "captivity" (*i. e.*, abuse) of this sacrament is the denial of the cup to the laity. The second is the doctrine of transubstantiation. (On Luther's nearly allied theory "consubstantiation," compare above in the Address to the Nobility, article 24, and below, chapter xxi.) The third abuse is the theory that the mass is a good work, whereas it is really a commemoration.

Baptism. God has preserved this rite from abuse, but the glory of the freedom whereunto we are baptized has been captured by the Roman Church. All other vows are a disparagement of the baptismal vow.

Penance. The first and capital abuse of this sacrament is they have entirely abolished it (*i. e.*, repentance), denying that faith is necessary.

Luther adds that "strictly speaking" penance is not a sacrament, there being only two. The remaining four he thinks have no right to be considered sacraments in any sense. In discussing matrimony he makes several digressions, some of which are rather shocking to our ears. For example, he proposes that a woman married to an impotent man be allowed, under certain conditions, to cohabit with another. Again: " I so detest divorce that I prefer bigamy, but whether divorce is ever allowable or not I dare not say." More will be said of this peculiar view when on later occasions Luther advised two sovereigns to take second wives rather than put away their first ones.

Such is the second of the three great pamphlets, which, like its predecessor, created an enormous stir. Erasmus judged that it precluded all possibility of peace, and Henry VIII of England, as well as a host of less distinguished persons, answered it. On the other hand, the mass of the people welcomed it eagerly, and the doctrines it taught have become fundamental to all the reformed systems of theology.

The Address to the Nobility and the Babylonian Captivity had treated of external abuses, the one in the State, the other in the Church; the third pamphlet, On the Liberty of a Christian Man (or, in the first Latin edition, On Christian Liberty), went far deeper to the inner life of the spirit. The occasion for writing this work was an earnest request of the officious peacemaker, Charles von Miltitz, for Luther to send a letter to the Pope saying that " he had never meant to twit him personally." The Reformer complied; a few extracts from this missive, composed in the latter half of October, are interesting: —

Of your person, excellent Leo, I have heard only what is honorable and good . . . but of the Roman See, as you and all men must know, it is more scandalous and shameful than any Sodom or Babylon, and, as far as I can see, its wickedness is beyond all counsel and help, having become desperate and abysmal. It made me sick at heart to see that under your name and that of the Roman Church, the poor people in all the world are cheated and injured, against which thing I have set myself and will set myself as long as I have life, not that I hope to reform that horrible Roman Sodom, but that I know I am the debtor and servant of all Christians, and that it is my duty to counsel and warn them. . . .

Finally, that I come not before your Holiness without a gift, I offer you this little treatise, dedicated to you as an augury of peace and good hope; by this book you may see how fruitfully I might em-

ploy my time, as I should prefer to, if only those impious flatterers of
yours would let me. It is a little book as respects size, but if I mistake not, the whole sum of a Christian life is set down therein, in
respect to contents. I am poor and have nothing else to send you, nor
do you stand in need of any but my spiritual gifts.

The little pamphlet of thirty pages, published early in November in both Latin and German, begins with a paradox: —

"A Christian man is the most free lord of all, subject to none.

"A Christian man is the dutiful servant of all, subject to every one.

"These statements seem to conflict, but when they are found to
agree they will edify us. For both are contained in that saying of
Paul's (1 Cor. ix, 19), 'For though I be free from all men, yet have
I made myself servant unto all.' You owe nothing but to love one another, for true love, by its nature, is dutiful and obedient to what it
loves. Thus also Christ, although Lord of all, yet was made a man
under the law, free and a servant, at the same time in the form of
God and in that of a slave."

A man consists of a double nature, spiritual and corporal; and
these two are contrary, the spirit fighting the flesh and the flesh the
spirit. "But it is clear that external things have no effect on Christian liberty. . . . For what can it profit the soul if the body is well,
free and lively, eats, drinks, and does what it pleases, since even the
wickedest slaves of all vice often have these advantages? Again, how
can ill health or captivity or hunger or thirst hurt the soul, since the
best men and those of the purest conscience often suffer these things?
. . . Nor does it profit the soul to have the body clad in priestly garments, nor hurt her to have it clothed as a layman. . . .

"One thing only is needful to a good life and Christian liberty, the
gospel of Christ. . . . Perhaps you ask: What is this Word of God
and how is it to be used, since there are many words of God? . . ."
Faith is the sole salutary and efficacious use of God's Word, for the
Word is not to be grasped or nourished with any works, but with faith
only. One incomparable grace of faith is that it joins the soul to
Christ as the bride to the bridegroom, by which mystery, as the
apostle teaches, Christ and the soul are made one flesh. Who is able
to prize this royal marriage enough, or comprehend the riches of this
grace?

Not only are we most free kings of all, but we are priests forever,
by which priesthood we can appear before God, pray for one another
and teach one another. "Here you ask, 'If all Christians are priests,

by what name shall we distinguish those whom we call clergy from the laity?' I answer: By those words 'priest,' 'clergyman,' 'spiritual,' 'ecclesiastic' an injury is done, since they are transferred from all Christians to a few. Scripture makes no distinction but to call them ministers, servants, and stewards, who now boast that they are popes, bishops, and lords. But although it is true that all are priests, all are not equally able to teach publicly, nor ought all who are able so to do. . . ."

Now let us turn to the second part and see how the master of all must become the ministering servant to all. When the soul has been purified by faith, she greatly desires to purify all things and especially her own body, and thus naturally brings forth the good works by which without faith she could not be justified. " Good works do not make a good man, but a good man produces good works, and so with bad works." Let us not despise good works, but rather teach and encourage them, only guarding against the false opinion that they make a man just. We conclude, therefore, that a Christian does not live to himself, but to Christ and his neighbor, to Christ by faith, to his neighbor by love. By faith he is snatched above himself to God; by love he falls below himself to his neighbor, yet always dwelling in God and his love.

This is properly the close of the work, but a postscript is added on the course a Christian should pursue in regard to ceremonies. The rule is first obedience to God's command and then charity to his neighbor. He should take a middle course, not tolerating any real abuse but not over-hasty to do away with ceremonies innocent in themselves.

The three great reforming pamphlets not only had a great influence in their own day, rallying the whole of Germany to their author's side at the time of trial, but they have a lasting importance in literature and thought. In them the whole Lutheran movement is epitomized: the first in relation to the State, the second as bearing on the Church, and the third, the most fundamental of all, as laying down the new rule for the guidance of the individual.

Before closing this chapter it is interesting to note an item in the Reformer's personal life, recalled long afterwards: —

In 1520 our Lord God tore me forcibly from saying the canonical prayers, for I wrote so much that I often missed them for a week to-gether, and on Saturday frequently made up for lost time by saying them one after another, so that I could neither eat nor drink the whole day. Thus I weakened myself so that I could not sleep, and Dr. Esch had to give me a sleeping-powder, the effects of which I still feel in my head.

CHAPTER IX

THE BURNING OF THE CANON LAW AND OF THE POPE'S BULL. 1520

THE action against Luther for heresy at Rome had been allowed to sleep since the beginning of 1519 on account of the exigencies of politics. The death of the Emperor Maximilian in January of that year made necessary the election of a successor. Of the three principal candidates Leo X preferred the Elector of Saxony, who, it was thought, would make both the weakest and most docile Emperor. Frederic was so highly esteemed for his personal qualities that he might have stood a good chance of the election, but feeling that the position would be too great for his resources, he did not press his own cause, but threw his great weight into the scale for the Hapsburg candidate against the Valois. It was, perhaps, largely due to his efforts that on June 28, 1519, Charles of Spain was chosen.

After this event had wrecked the hopes of the Curia, and especially after the Leipsic debate had brought Luther's heresy into a stronger light than ever before, the process against the Saxon was renewed. Another effort was made to induce the Elector to give him up; indeed Saxony was threatened with the interdict in case he did not comply, though later events showed that the Pope hardly dared to use such a drastic measure. The threat did not succeed; Frederic replied in his usual courteous and procrastinating style that Miltitz had undertaken to bring Luther's case before the Archbishop of Trier for judgment, and that the Curia had no right to threaten the ban and interdict before the result of this attempt at reconciliation was known.

This letter worked like a declaration of war. A consistory was held at Rome on January 9, 1520, in which Ghinnucci, who had charge of Luther's case, thundered against the peaceful, pious prince as a raging tyrant, the enemy not only of the clergy but of the whole Christian religion.

The Pope at once appointed a commission, consisting of Cajetan, Accolti, the general and procurators of the Dominican and Franciscan orders, and others, to draw up a bull against the heretic. Except the first two they were all but poor theologians, but making up in zeal what they lacked in knowledge, they proceeded in short order to damn *all* Luther's propositions as rank heresy. Leo, being advised by the wiser heads among the cardinals that such a sweeping position would be untenable, dissolved the first commission in February and appointed a second, consisting of Cajetan, Accolti, the generals of the orders, and some of the best theologians in Rome. This body, proceeding more cautiously, drew up a report carefully distinguishing a number of propositions as "partly heretical, partly scandalous, and partly offensive to pious ears." They recommended that a bull be drawn up condemning these propositions without mentioning Luther's name, and that a final summons be sent him to come to Rome and recant. In other words, they held that a peaceful solution of the problem was still possible. Following their advice, Leo commanded Volta to write to Staupitz asking him to force his brother to recant. Whether Staupitz tried to obey this letter of March 15, 1520, is not known; but in the following August he resigned his office in the order and shortly after secured a dispensation to become a Dominican.

Towards the end of March a sudden and decisive change in the papal policy was caused by the arrival of Eck. Since the great debate this zealous Catholic had been busy going around to the universities trying to get them to decide in his favor and condemn Luther; two of them, Cologne and Louvain, did so. Eck then turned his steps to Rome, where he painted his enemy's heresy in such black colors that Leo decided there was nothing left but to condemn him, and accordingly appointed a third commission, of Cajetan, Eck, Accolti, and the Spanish Augustinian Johannes, with orders to draft a bull for this purpose. Accolti was the draftsman for the committee; the theological material was largely supplied by Eck from the condemnation of Luther's doctrines by the University of Louvain.

The bull was presented for ratification before a consistory held on May 21, which decided, before promulgating the document, to hear the theologians who had drawn it up. This was done in three sittings of May 23, May 25, and June 1. No record of debates in these consistories has been published, but the fact is recorded that there were long arguments before the bull received the assent of the College of Cardinals. It is possible that a peace party was against the use of force even at this late stage, but it is more probable that the opposition came from a Spanish cardinal, Carvajal, who belonged to the conciliar party in the Church and was offended by the designation of Luther's appeal to a council as heretical. Whatever opposition there was, however, was finally overcome, the bull was ratified and signed by Leo at his hunting-lodge at Magliana on June 15.

According to the provision of the Canon Law, that before a heretic is finally condemned he must be given a fatherly warning, this bull, Exsurge Domine, does not excommunicate Luther, but only threatens this penalty in case he does not recant within sixty days after its publication in Germany. Beginning with the words : "Arise, Lord, plead thine own cause, arise and protect the vineyard thou gavest Peter from the wild beast who is devouring it," the bull sets forth some of the professor's opinions, quoted apart from their context, designates them as "either heretical, or false, or scandalous, or offensive to pious ears, or misleading to the simple," and condemns them. If, after all the Pope's fatherly care and admonition, Luther does not recant within sixty days after the posting of the bull in Germany, he is to be declared a stiff-necked, notorious, damned heretic, and must expect the penalties due to his crime.

Before this document was ratified, Cardinal Raphael Riario had written the Elector, May 20, urging him to force the heretic to recant or expect the consequences. The letter only arrived on July 6, and, as we have seen (p. 74), made a great impression upon the Wittenberg professor. Frederic answered it quite promptly, enclosing An Offer or Protestation (Oblatio sive Protestatio), drawn up by Luther, proposing to leave his doctrine to the arbitrament of impartial judges. This arrived in Rome by the end of July.

Eck, who had been so instrumental in drawing up the bull,

was commissioned to post it in Germany. Before he had done so, however, the document had been published there (August) by Ulrich von Hutten, who judged that it would injure the Church more than her enemy. Eck posted it officially at Meissen, Merseburg, and Brandenburg near the end of September. He also tried to force it on the universities of Germany, many of whom declined to receive it on technical grounds. At Wittenberg the faculty would have nothing to do with it, and at Erfurt the students seized all the printed copies and threw them into the river.

Having threatened the heretic with excommunication, Rome left no stone unturned to secure his condemnation by the Empire. Charles was coming from Spain to be crowned in October, 1520, and to hold his first diet at Worms early in 1521. To him and to the nation Leo dispatched two nuncios, Aleander and Caracciola. Leaving Rome on July 27, 1520, Aleander arrived in Cologne, where he published the bull on September 22. Four days later he was in Antwerp, and on September 28, he had an audience with Charles and secured from him the first decree against Luther and his followers in the Netherlands. On October 8, the indefatigable legate published the bull at Louvain and solemnly burned the condemned books, at the same time making a speech violently attacking Erasmus, who lived there, for supporting the heretic. For this Aleander was scored in a bitter anonymous satire — the Acta Academiæ Lovaniensis — which may have come from the pen of the great humanist. On October 17, the nuncio did at Liège what he had done at Louvain.

Charles was crowned Emperor at Aix-la-Chapelle on October 23. The plague breaking out in the overcrowded town, the royal suite, including the legate, was forced to leave soon after, and went to Cologne, where they arrived on October 28. Here they found the Elector Frederic, who, having started to attend the coronation, had been detained by an attack of gout. He had posted up Luther's Offer and Protestation, and had with him a letter from the monk to the Emperor, written about August 31. It is a humble appeal: —

That I dare to approach your Most Serene Majesty with a letter, most excellent Emperor Charles, will rightly cause wonder to all. A single flea dares to address the king of kings. But the wonder will be less if the greatness of the cause is considered, for as truth is worthy to approach the cause of celestial Majesty, it cannot be unworthy to appear before an earthly prince. It is a fair thing for earthly princes, as images of the heavenly Prince, to imitate him, as they also sit on high, but must have respect for the humble things of the earth and raise up the poor and needy from the mire. Therefore I, poor and needy, the unworthy representative of a most worthy cause, prostrate myself before the feet of your Most Serene Majesty.

I have published certain books, which have kindled the hatred and indignation of great men against me, but I ought to be protected by you for two reasons: first, because I come unwillingly before the public, and only wrote when provoked by the violence and fraud of others, seeking nothing more earnestly than to hide in a corner, and secondly, because, as my conscience and the judgment of excellent men will testify, I studied only to proclaim the gospel truth against the superstitious traditions of men. Almost three years have elapsed, during which I have suffered infinite wrath, contumely, danger, and whatever injuries they can contrive against me. In vain I seek respite, in vain I offer silence, in vain propose conditions of peace, in vain beg to be better instructed; the only thing that will satisfy them is for me to perish utterly with the whole gospel.

When I had attempted all in vain, I hoped to follow the precedent of Athanasius and appeal to the Emperor. . . . So I commend myself, so I trust, so I hope in your Most Sacred Majesty, whom may our Lord Jesus preserve to us and magnify for the eternal glory of his gospel. Amen.

Again on October 3, 1520, Luther had written Spalatin : —

Many think I should ask the Elector to obtain an imperial edict in my favor, declaring that I should not be condemned nor my books prohibited except by warrant of Scripture. Please find out what is intended; I care little either way, because I rather dislike having my books so widely spread, and should prefer to have them all fall into oblivion together, for they are desultory and unpolished, and yet I do want the matters they treat of known to all. But not all can separate the gold from the dross in my works, nor is it necessary, since better books and Bibles are easily obtainable.

It was in accordance with the plan here indicated that on October 31 the Elector had a conference with the Emperor in the sacristy of the cathedral, and the latter promised that he would allow Luther the way of the law which the professor himself had proposed.

On Sunday, November 4, the legates also obtained an audience with Frederic. Aleander handed him a letter certifying that he was commissioned by the Pope, and demanded, first, that the heretic's books be burned, and second, that he be either punished by Frederic or delivered up bound. The next day the Elector sent for Erasmus, who happened to be in the city, and asked him if Luther had erred. For answer he received the winged word, which flew to the farthest ends of Germany: " Yes. He has erred in two points, in attacking the crown of the Pope and the bellies of the monks." The learned humanist drew up twenty-two short propositions which he called Axioms, stating the best solution of the difficulty would be for the Pope to recommend the decision of the matter to a tribunal of learned and impartial men. On a second interview with the nuncios on November 6, Frederic refused their requests and insisted on such a court as Erasmus had recommended.

The time given Luther to recant expired on one of the last days of November. Instead of doing so, however, he hit back at his oppressors with his usual spirit. He first published two short manifestoes, Against the New Bull forged by Eck, — for like Erasmus he doubted the genuineness of the document, — and Against the Execrable Bull of Antichrist. But his most dramatic answer was solemnly to burn the bull along with the whole Canon Law. The notice to the students, drawn up and posted by Melanchthon on the early morning of December 10, reads as follows : —

Let whosoever adheres to the truth of the gospel be present at nine o'clock at the church of the Holy Cross outside the walls, where the impious books of papal decrees and scholastic theology will be burnt according to ancient and apostolic usage, inasmuch as the boldness of the enemies of the gospel has waxed so great that they daily burn the evangelic books of Luther. Come, pious and zealous youth, to this pious and religious spectacle, for perchance now is the time when the Antichrist must be revealed!

At the set time a large crowd gathered just outside the Elster gate, near the Black Cloister, but beyond the walls; the students built a pyre, a certain "master," probably Melanchthon, lighted it, and Luther threw on the whole Canon Law with the last bull of Leo X, whom he apostrophized in these solemn words: "Because thou hast brought down the truth of God, he also brings thee down unto this fire to-day. Amen." [1] Others threw on works of the schoolmen and some of Eck and Emser. After the professors had gone home, the students sang funeral songs and disported themselves at the Pope's expense.

Luther now justified his act by publishing an Assertion of All the Articles Condemned by the Last Bull of Antichrist, which appeared in Latin in December, 1520, and in German in March, 1521. In this he states that his positions have not been refuted by Scripture in the bull — whether that document is genuine or not. But if one cannot found his creed on the Bible now, he adds, why did Augustine have the right to do it eleven hundred years ago? He then takes up, one by one, the forty-one articles condemned and proves that they are right. In view of later developments the most interesting of these proofs is that of the 36th article, on free will. Since the fall of man, says the Wittenberg professor, free will is simply a name; when a man does what is in him he sins mortally. He cites Augustine to the effect that free will without grace is able to do nothing but sin. He quotes many texts of the Bible to prove this point and argues it at length.

Nothing was now left to the Church but to excommunicate the rebel and fulfil the threat of the Exsurge Domine. The "holy curse" was drawn up and signed at Rome on January 3, 1521, and sent to Aleander to publish in Germany. It banned not only Luther but Hutten, Pirkheimer, and Spengler, and denounced the Elector Frederic. The wise legate received the terrible document at the Diet of Worms, and rightly fearing

---

[1] Quonian tu conturbasti veritatem dei, conturbat et te hodie in ignem istum, amen. — Cf. Joshua vii, 25.

that in this form "it would prove destructive to the cause of the Church," sent it back with a recommendation to modify it. This was done; in its final form the bull Decet Pontificem Romanum confined itself to excommunicating the heresiarch, and was then, May 6, published at Worms, three weeks after he had already been heard by the Diet.

CHAPTER X

THE DIET OF WORMS. 1521

FROM Cologne Charles V proceeded to Mayence and thence to Worms, where he was about to open his first diet. The varied programme of the national assembly included the drafting of a constitution for the Empire and the formulation of grievances against the tyranny of the Roman hierarchy. It could hardly hope to avoid the religious question then agitating the whole nation, but the unprecedented course of summoning the heretic to answer before the representatives of his nation was not decided on until after the estates had been sitting for a month.

Luther himself, in appealing to the Emperor, did not expect to be called before the Diet; he hoped to be allowed to defend his doctrines before a specially appointed tribunal of able and impartial theologians. This plan was pressed quietly but vigorously by Erasmus, the foremost living man of letters. Besides his action in urging Frederic to insist on such a trial for his subject, the great humanist had, at Cologne, handed to the counsellors of the Emperor a short memorial, Advice of One heartily wishing the Peace of the Church, proposing the appointment of such a commission. He partly won over the Emperor's confessor, Glapion, but Chièvres and Gattinara, the real powers behind the imperial throne, remained in opposition. A little later at Worms, John Faber, a Dominican friar, came forward with a similar plan, composed with the help of Erasmus.

Such a solution of the difficulty would have been most distasteful to the Curia. Regarding the Wittenberg professor's opinions as res *adjudicatæ*, the Romanists saw no reason for giving him a chance to defend them, and wished only to punish the man already condemned. This course was urged by Aleander, an extremely able and unscrupulous diplomat. His chief support was the young emperor, whose formal, backward mind

failed to comprehend and even detested any variation from the
faith in which he had been brought up. Though by no means
a fool, he was a dull man, slow to learn and slow to forget, but
possessed of two extremely valuable qualities, moderation and
persistence. Of the Lutheran affair he had no understanding
whatever. Not being able to speak German, he was unable to
sympathize with even the nationalist side of the formidable
movement. On May 12, 1520, Manuel, his ambassador at Rome,
suggested that he use Luther as a lever to wring concessions
from the Pope, but the idea found no root in his mind; from
the first his opposition to the schismatic was a foregone conclusion.

Aleander worked with admirable diligence and consummate
ability to win powerful supporters among the electors and great
men of Germany. By skilful negotiation and concession he
secured the adhesion of Joachim I of Brandenburg, for many
years the leader of the Catholic party in Germany. He tried
hard to get the unqualified backing of Albert of Mayence by
the same means, but failed, partly because of the counter negotiations of Erasmus and his friend Capito. The Elector of
Mayence therefore represented a mediating policy.

Aleander's strongest opponent was Frederic of Saxony,
"that fox and basilisk," as he called him, a crafty statesman who knew well how to protect his obnoxious subject
without too deeply involving himself. Among the other members of the college, the Elector Palatine was not unfavorable
to Luther.

The common people were strongly in favor of Luther. "Nine
tenths of the Germans," wrote Aleander, "shout 'Long live
Luther,' and the other tenth 'Death to Rome.'" Foremost
among his adherents was Hutten, who with his followers hung
like a cloud near Worms, threatening to burst and sweep
away the Papists should any harm come to the bold monk of
Saxony.

When the alternative plan of Aleander to summon Luther,
not before an impartial tribunal to discuss his doctrines, but
before the estates to recant, was announced to him in Wittenberg he wrote as follows : —

TO GEORGE SPALATIN AT ALLSTEDT

WITTENBERG, December 21, 1520.

Greeting. To-day I received copies of your letter from Allstedt and also of that from Kindelbrück asking me what I would do were I summoned before the Emperor Charles as my enemies wish, in case I could go without danger to the gospel and the public safety.

If I am summoned I will go if I possibly can; I will go ill if I cannot go well. For it is not right to doubt if I am summoned by the Emperor I am summoned by the Lord. He lives and reigns who saved the three Hebrew children in the furnace of the king of Babylon. If he does not wish to save me, my life is a little thing compared to that of Christ, who was slain in the most shameful way, to the scandal of all and the ruin of many. Here is no place to weigh risk and safety; rather we should take care not to abandon the gospel which we have begun to preach to be mocked by the wicked, lest we give cause to our enemies of boasting that we dare not confess what we teach and shed our blood for it. May Christ the merciful prevent such cowardice on our part and such a triumph on theirs. Amen. . . .

It is certainly not for us to determine how much danger to the gospel will accrue by my death. . . .

One duty is left for us: to pray that the Empire be saved from impiety and that Charles may not stain the first year of his reign with my blood or with that of any other. I should prefer, as I have quite often said, to perish only at the hands of the Romanists so that the Emperor may not be involved in my cause. You know what nemesis dogged Sigismund after the execution of Huss; he had no success after that and he died without heirs, for his daughter's son Ladislaus perished, so that his name was wiped out in one generation and moreover his queen Barbara became infamous as you know, together with the other misfortunes which befel him. Yet if it be the Lord's will that I must perish at the hands not of the priests but of the civil authorities, may his will be done. Amen.

Now you have my plan and purpose. You may expect me to do anything but flee or recant; I will not flee, much less will I recant. May the Lord Jesus strengthen me in this. For I can do neither without peril to religion and to the salvation of many. . . .

In similar tone Luther wrote a month later to his best patron.

TO THE ELECTOR FREDERIC OF SAXONY AT WORMS

WITTENBERG, January 25, 1521.

Most serene, highborn Prince, most gracious Lord! My poor prayers and humble obedience are always at your Grace's service.

I have received with humble thankfulness and pleasure your Grace's information about his Imperial and Royal Majesty's intentions regarding my affair, and I humbly thank his Imperial Majesty and your Grace for your favor. I rejoice from my heart that his Imperial Majesty proposes to take up this business, which is rather God's, Christendom's, and the German Nation's than mine or that of any individual.

I am humbly ready, as I always have been, and as I have often said I would be (especially in a pamphlet recently published of which I am sending your Grace a copy), to do and allow all that may be done with God and Christian honor, or all which I shall be convinced by honorable, Christian, and sufficient reasons of Holy Writ that I ought to do or allow.

Therefore I humbly pray your Grace to pray his Imperial Majesty to provide me with sufficient protection and a free safe-conduct for all emergencies, and that his Imperial Majesty should command the business to be recommended to pious, learned, impartial Christian men, both clerical and lay, who are well grounded in the Bible, and have understanding of the difference between human laws and ordinances. Let such men try me, and, for God's sake, use no force against me until I am proved unchristian and wrong. Let his Majesty, as the temporal head of Christendom, in the mean time restrain my adversaries, the papists, from accomplishing their raging, unchristian plans against me, such as burning my books and grimly laying snares for my body, honor, well-being, life, and salvation, although I am unheard and unconvicted. And if I, more for the protection of the divine, evangelic truth, than for the sake of my own little and unworthy person, have done aught against them, or shall be compelled to do aught, may his Majesty graciously excuse my necessary means of protection, and keep me in his gracious care to save the Divine Word. I now confidently commit myself to the virtue and grace of his Majesty, and of your Grace and all Christian princes, as to my most gracious lords.

And so I am, in humble obedience, ready, in case I obtain sufficient surety and a safe-conduct, to appear before the next Diet at Worms and before learned, pious, and impartial judges, to answer to them with the help of the Almighty, that all men may know in truth that I have hitherto done nothing from criminal, reckless, disordered motives, for the sake of worldly honor and profit, but that all which I have written and taught has been according to my conscience and sworn duty as a teacher of the Holy Bible, for the praise of God and for the profit and salvation of all Christendom and the advantage of the German nation, in order to extirpate dangerous abuses and superstitions and to free Christendom from so great, infinite, unchristian, damnable, tyrannical injury, molestation, and blasphemy.

Your Grace and his Majesty will have an eye and a care to the much troubled state of all Christendom; as your Grace's chaplain I am humbly and dutifully bound to pray God for his mercy and favor on you and his Imperial Majesty at all times.

Your Grace's obedient, humble chaplain,

MARTIN LUTHER.

Now, if ever, Luther's plain heroism showed itself. Daily expecting an awful crisis not only in his own life but in all that he held dearer, he went quietly about his business, teaching, preaching, and doing whatever his hand found to do. While writing polemics "against ten hydras" his deeply untroubled spiritual life found expression in a tract on the Magnificat, in which Mary's canticle became again the song of the triumph of the lowly and the meek. His determination to stand fast never wavered; he often quoted Christ's words that whoso denied his Lord before men would be denied by him before his Heavenly Father. While so firm himself, he was much saddened by the irresolution of some of his friends, especially of his still beloved and revered Staupitz. After laying down his office as Vicar of the Augustinians, the old man had retired to distant Salzburg, where the learned and orthodox archbishop, Cardinal Lang, received him warmly. But even here he could not escape the tumult of the battle; for Lang tried hard to get him to denounce Luther openly. On January 4, 1521, Staupitz wrote pathetically to Link, acknowledging that "Martin has undertaken a hard task and acts with great courage illuminated by God; I stammer and am a child needing milk." Nevertheless but a little later he wrote an open letter submitting himself to the judgment of the Pope, a document intended as a compromise and as non-committal, but one which was generally taken as a renunciation of the reformed teaching. On seeing the declaration, Luther wrote Staupitz a letter equally solemn and gentle; he does not judge his old friend, but it is impossible not to feel all the more strongly the contrast between the irresolution of the one man and the unyielding courage of the other.

TO JOHN STAUPITZ AT SALZBURG

WITTENBERG, February 9, 1521.

Greeting. I wonder, reverend Father, that my letters and pamphlets have not reached you, as I gather from your letter to Link that they have not. Intercourse with men takes so much of my time that preaching unto others I have myself become a castaway. . . .

At Worms they have as yet done nothing against me, although the papists contrive harm with extraordinary fury. Yet Spalatin writes the Evangelic cause has so much favor there that he does not expect I shall be condemned unheard. . . .

I have heard with no great pain that you are attacked by Pope Leo, for thus the cross you have preached to others you may exemplify yourself. I hope that wolf, for you honor him too much to call him a Lion (Leo), will not be satisfied with your declaration, which will be interpreted to mean that you deny me and mine, inasmuch as you submit to the Pope's judgment.

If Christ love you he will make you revoke that declaration, since the Pope's bull must condemn all you have hitherto taught and believed about the mercy of God. As you knew this would be the case, it seems to me that you offend Christ in proposing Leo for a judge, whom you see to be an enemy of Christ running wild (debacchari) against the Word of his grace. You should have stood up for Christ and have contradicted the Pope's impiety. This is not the time to tremble but to cry aloud, while our Lord Jesus is being condemned, burned, and blasphemed. Wherefore as much as you exhort me to humility I exhort you to pride. You are too yielding, I am too stiff-necked.

Indeed it is a solemn matter. We see Christ suffer. Should we keep silence and humble ourselves? Now that our dearest Saviour, who gave himself for us, is made a mock in the world, should we not fight and offer our lives for him? Dear father, the present crisis is graver than many think. Now applies the gospel text: "Whosoever shall confess me before men, him shall the Son of man also confess before the angels of God, but whosoever shall be ashamed of me and my words, of him shall the Son of man be ashamed when he shall come in his glory."

May I be found guilty of pride, avarice, adultery, murder, opposition to the Pope, and all other sins rather than be silent when the Lord suffers and says: "I looked on my right hand and beheld, but there was no man that would know me: refuge failed me; no man cared for my soul." By confessing him I hope to be absolved from all my sins. Wherefore I have raised my horns with confidence against the Roman idol, and the true Antichrist. The word of Christ is not the word of peace but the word of the sword. But why should I, a fool, teach a wise man?

I write this more confidently because I fear you will take a middle course between Christ and the Pope, who are now, you see, in bitter strife. But let us pray that the Lord Jesus with the breath of his mouth will destroy this son of perdition. If you do not wish to, at least let me go and be bound. With Christ's aid I will not keep still about this monster's crimes before his face.

Truly your submission has saddened me not a little, and has shown me that you are different from that Staupitz who was the herald of grace and of the cross. If you had said what you did, before you knew of the bull and of the shame of Christ, you would not have saddened me.

Hutten and many others write strongly for me and daily those songs are sung which delight not that Babylon. Our elector acts as constantly as prudently and faithfully, and at his command I am publishing my Defence [1] in both languages. . . .

In the mean time Luther's enemies were not idle. Aleander addressed the Diet on February 18, painting the new heresy in the blackest colors, touching lightly on the points with which the Germans would sympathize, but bearing his whole weight on certain opinions relative to the sacrament which would shock most of them, and demanding, in conclusion, that proper steps be taken to extirpate the impending schism and its author. After a stormy debate the Estates decided to summon Luther to recant the objectionable heresies, and to be questioned on certain other points, those, namely, relative to the power of the Pope and the grievances of the German nation. The Emperor accordingly drew up a formal summons, addressing the excommunicated man as "honorable, dear, and pious," giving as the

[1] The Articles Wrongly Condemned by the Bull appeared in Latin in January and in German in March.

purpose of the citation " to obtain information about certain doctrines originating with you and certain books written by you," and assuring certain safe-conduct to and from the Diet. Charles also endeavored to get the Diet to pass a decree for the burning of the heretic's books, but failing in this, he issued a mandate on his own responsibility directing that they be delivered up to the magistrate and no more copies be printed.

Even now an attempt was made by the party of mediation to obtain a declaration from Luther which would obviate the necessity of his appearance before the Diet. Glapion, the Emperor's confessor, possibly acting at the suggestion of Erasmus, held a friendly interview with Spalatin in which he pointed out that all might be amicably settled if Luther would repudiate a few articles. These he had drawn from the Assertion of all the Articles Wrongly Condemned, and from the Babylonian Captivity; the latter he thought might be the more easily given up, as the book had appeared anonymously. When these articles were forwarded by Spalatin, the Wittenberg professor replied as follows: —

TO GEORGE SPALATIN AT WORMS

WITTENBERG, March 19, 1521.

Greeting. I have received the articles they ask me to recant, with the list of things they want me to do. Doubt not that I shall recant nothing, as I see that they rely on no other argument than that I have written (as they pretend) against the usages and customs of the Church. I shall answer the Emperor Charles that if I am summoned solely for the sake of recantation I shall not come, seeing that it is all the same as if I had gone thither and returned here. For I can recant just as well here if that is their only business. But if he wishes to summon me to my death, holding me an enemy of the Empire, I shall offer to go. I will not flee, Christ helping me, nor abandon his Word in the battle. I am assuredly convinced that those bloody men will never rest until they slay me. I wish if it were possible that only the Pope's followers should be guilty of my blood. We are turned heathen again as we were before Christ, so firmly does Antichrist hold the kingdoms of this world captive in his hand. The Lord's will be done. Use your influence, where you can, not to take part in this council of the ungodly. . . .

MARTIN LUTHER, Augustinian.

The expected summons and safe-conduct reached Luther on March 26. After quietly finishing some literary work, he set out, on April 2, accompanied by his colleague Amsdorf, a brother monk, and a talented young student named Swaven. Horses and wagon were provided by the town, and the university voted twenty gulden to cover the necessary expenses. The journey was a triumphal progress; the people thronged to see the bold asserter of the rights of conscience. At Erfurt, where Luther preached, he was given a rousing reception by the students and their professor, the humanist Eoban Hess. Notwithstanding popular sympathy, there was considerable danger in going to Worms: in spite of an imperial safe-conduct, Huss had been burned. When Spalatin wrote reminding his friend of this precedent, he received the following answer: —

TO GEORGE SPALATIN AT WORMS

FRANKFORT ON THE MAIN (April 14), 1521.

I am coming, dear Spalatin, even if Satan tries to prevent me by a worse disease than that from which I am now suffering, for I have been ill all the way from Eisenach, and am yet ill, in a way I have not hitherto experienced.

I know that the mandate of Charles has been published to terrify me. Truly Christ lives and I shall enter Worms in the face of the gates of hell and the princes of the air. I send copies of the Emperor's summons. I think better not to write more until I can see on the spot what is to be done, lest perchance I should puff up Satan, whom I propose rather to terrify and despise. Therefore prepare a lodging.

MARTIN LUTHER.[1]

Finding that Luther was not to be intimidated, the Catholics, who were more frightened than he was, tried by a stratagem to prevent his appearance or at least to delay it until the time granted had expired. The Emperor's confessor, Glapion,

---

[1] Spalatin says in his *Annalen* (edition of Cyprian, 1718, p. 38) that Luther wrote him from Oppenheim, where he arrived April 15, that he would enter Worms if there were as many devils there as tiles on the roofs. It is probable that Spalatin was thinking of this letter, or some expression used at another time (cf. *Tischreden*, ed. by Förstemann and Bindseil, iv, 348), as it is almost inconceivable that he, who preserved so many of his friend's letters, should have lost this important one.

in an interview with Sickingen, Hutten, and Bucer, assumed a friendly attitude, and proposed that instead of exposing himself to the danger of an appearance the heretic should hold a private conference with himself in a neighboring castle. Bucer was dispatched with this proposition. Luther knew no way but the direct one, however, and proceeded.

On the morning of April 16 he arrived at his destination, greeted by a vast concourse of people, and took up his abode in the hostel of the Knights of St. John. He was summoned to the Diet the next day at four o'clock, though he was not admitted until nearly six.

Few moments in history have been at once so dramatic and so decisive as that in which Luther appeared before the Emperor and Diet at Worms. In the greatness of the tribunal, of the accused, and of the issues involved, nothing is lacking to impress a thoughtful mind. In the foreground of the assembly sat the young Emperor, on whose brows were united the vast, if shadowy, pretensions to Roman dominion and the weight of actual sovereignty over a large congeries of powerful states. Around him were the great princes of the realm, spiritual and temporal, and the representatives of the Free Cities of Germany. The nuncios, representing the supreme power of the Church, were conspicuous by their absence; the Pope would not even hear the rebel in his own defence.

The son of peasants now stood before the son of Cæsars: the poor and till lately obscure monk before a body professing to represent the official voice of united Christendom. To challenge an infamous death was the least part of his courage: to set up his own individual belief and conscience against the deliberate, ancient, almost universal opinion of mankind required an audacity no less than sublime.

And how much depended on his answer! The stake he played for was not his own life, nor even the triumph of this religion or of that: it was the cause of human progress. The system against which he protested had become the enemy of progress and of reason: the Church had become hopelessly corrupt and had sought to bind the human mind in fetters, stamping out in blood all struggles for freedom and light. Hitherto her efforts

had been successful: the Waldenses had perished; Wicliffe had
spoken and Huss had died in vain. But now the times were ripe
for a revolution; men only needed the leader to show them the
way.

The proceedings were short and simple. An officer first warned
the prisoner at the bar that he must say nothing except in
answer to the questions asked him. Then John Eck, Official of
Trier (not to be confounded with the debater of the same name),
asked him if the books lying on the table were his and whether
he wished to hold to all that he had said in them or to recant
some part. At this point Jerome Schurf, a jurist friendly to
the Wittenberg monk, cried out: "Let the titles of the books
be read." When this had been done, Luther replied:—

His Imperial Majesty asks me two things, first, whether these books
are mine, and secondly, whether I will stand by them or recant part of
what I have published. First, the books are mine, I deny none of them.
The second question, whether I will reassert all or recant what is said
to have been written without warrant of Scripture, concerns faith and
the salvation of souls and the Divine Word, than which nothing is
greater in heaven or on earth, and which we all ought to reverence;
therefore it would be rash and dangerous to say anything without
due consideration, since I might say more than the thing demands or
less than the truth, either of which would bring me in danger of the
sentence of Christ. "Whoso shall deny me before men, him will I also
deny before my Father in heaven." Wherefore I humbly beg your
Imperial Majesty to grant me time for deliberation, that I may answer
without injury to the Divine Word or peril to my soul.

After consulting the Emperor and his advisers, Eck replied:

Although, Martin, you knew from the imperial mandate why you
were summoned, and therefore do not deserve to have a longer time
given you, yet his Imperial Majesty of his great clemency grants you
one day more, commanding that you appear to-morrow at this time and
deliver your answer orally and not in writing.

Though Luther knew the general reason of his summons, he
had been surprised by the form in which the question was put
to him. He had expected that certain articles would be brought
forward and that he would have an opportunity to state the

reasons why he held them and to defend them in debate. When he was required to recant point-blank, without any chance to present his case and without hearing what particular things he was to recant, he was taken unprepared. Seeing how necessary it was to have his answer in exact form, he had only done the wisest thing. Some, however, inferred from his request and from the low tone in which it was uttered, that his spirit was broken. How little this was the case may be seen by a letter written the same evening to an imperial counsellor and humanist at Vienna, John Cuspinian. After leaving the assembly hall, Luther went to his lodgings, where he was visited by nobles and others who wished him well. Among them was George Cuspinian, a canon of Würzburg, who had followed his bishop to the Diet. He gave such warm assurances of good-will from his cousin, the more noted John, that the Reformer found time to acknowledge them: —

TO JOHN CUSPINIAN AT VIENNA [1]

WORMS, April 17, 1521.

Greeting. Your brother,[2] most famous Cuspinian, has easily persuaded me to write to you from the midst of this tumult, since I have long wished to become personally acquainted with you on account of your celebrity. Take me, therefore, into the register of your friends, that I may prove the truth of what your brother has so generously told me of you.

This hour I have stood before the Emperor and Diet, asked whether I would revoke my books. To which I answered that the books were indeed mine, but that I would give them my reply about recanting to-morrow, having asked and obtained no longer time for consideration. Truly, with Christ's aid, I shall never recant one jot or tittle. Farewell, my dear Cuspinian.

[1] The text of this letter is full of mistakes in all the printed editions, including Enders, iii, 122. A facsimile of the original in the archives of Vienna was published by T. Haase in the *Leipziger Illustrierte Zeitung* for August 31, 1889, and the text printed by me in *American Journal of Theology*, April, 1910.

[2] Frater carnis tuæ. I follow Haase in identifying this brother with Cuspinian's cousin. Professor G. Kawerau suggested to me in conversation that Luther's words would naturally mean "brother-in-law." Cuspinian had a brother-in-law (brother of his first wife) named Ulrich Putch, and a brother, Niklas Spiessheimer. Cf. H. Ankwicz: "Das Tagebuch Cuspinians," *Archiv für oestterreichische Geschichtsforschung*, xxx (1909), 304 and 325.

The following day he appeared at the same hour before the august assembly. Eck addressed him in an oration of which the following summary is given by one present, probably Spalatin : —

His Imperial Majesty has assigned this time to you, Martin Luther, to answer for the books which you yesterday openly acknowledged to be yours. You asked time to deliberate on the question whether you would take back part of what you had said or would stand by all of it. You did not deserve this respite, which has now come to an end, for you knew long before why you were summoned. And every one — especially a professor of theology — ought to be so certain of his faith that whenever questioned about it he can give a sure and positive answer. Now at last reply to the demand of his Majesty, whose clemency you have experienced in obtaining time to deliberate. Do you wish to defend all of your books or to retract part of them ?

Luther, now certain of what to say, made a great oration, at first in German and then in Latin, the substance of which, as written down by himself immediately afterwards, is here translated : —

Most Serene Emperor, Most Illustrious Princes, Most Clement Lords ! At the time fixed yesterday I obediently appear, begging for the mercy of God, that your Most Serene Majesty and your Illustrious Lordships may deign to hear this cause, which I hope may be called the cause of justice and truth, with clemency ; and if, by my inexperience, I should fail to give any one the titles due him, or should sin against the etiquette of the court, please forgive me, as a man who has lived not in courts but in monastic nooks, one who can say nothing for himself but that he has hitherto tried to teach and to write with a sincere mind and single eye to the glory of God and the edification of Christians.

Most Serene Emperor, Most Illustrious Princes ! Two questions were asked me yesterday. To the first, whether I would recognize that the books published under my name were mine, I gave a plain answer, to which I hold and will hold forever, namely, that the books are mine, as I published them, unless perchance it may have happened that the guile or meddlesome wisdom of my opponents has changed something in them. For I only recognize what has been written by myself alone, and not the interpretation added by another.

In reply to the second question I beg your Most Sacred Majesty and your lordships to be pleased to consider that all my books are not of the same kind.

In some I have treated piety, faith, and morals so simply and evangelically that my adversaries themselves are forced to confess that these books are useful, innocent, and worthy to be read by Christians. Even the bull, though fierce and cruel, states that some things in my books are harmless, although it condemns them by a judgment simply monstrous. If, therefore, I should undertake to recant these, would it not happen that I alone of all men should damn the truth which all, friends and enemies alike, confess?

The second class of my works inveighs against the papacy as against that which both by precept and example has laid waste all Christendom, body and soul. No one can deny or dissemble this fact, since general complaints witness that the consciences of all believers are snared, harassed, and tormented by the laws of the Pope and the doctrines of men, and especially that the goods of this famous German nation have been and are devoured in numerous and ignoble ways. Yet the Canon Law provides (*e. g.*, distinctions IX and XXV, quaestiones 1 and 2) that the laws and doctrines of the Pope contrary to the Gospel and the Fathers are to be held erroneous and rejected. If, therefore, I should withdraw these books, I would add strength to tyranny and open windows and doors to their impiety, which would then flourish and burgeon more freely than it ever dared before. It would come to pass that their wickedness would go unpunished, and therefore would become more licentious on account of my recantation, and their government of the people, thus confirmed and established, would become intolerable, especially if they could boast that I had recanted with the full authority of your Sacred and Most Serene Majesty and of the whole Roman Empire. Good God! In that case I would be the tool of iniquity and tyranny.

In a third sort of books I have written against some private individuals who tried to defend the Roman tyranny and tear down my pious doctrine. In these I confess I was more bitter than is becoming to a minister of religion. For I do not pose as a saint, nor do I discuss my life but the doctrine of Christ. Yet neither is it right for me to recant what I have said in these, for then tyranny and impiety would rage and reign against the people of God more violently than ever by reason of my acquiescence.

As I am a man and not God, I wish to claim no other defence for my doctrine than that which the Lord Jesus put forward when he was questioned before Annas and smitten by a servant: he then said: If I have spoken evil, bear witness of the evil. If the Lord himself, who knew that he could not err, did not scorn to hear testimony against his doctrine from a miserable servant, how much more should I, the dregs of men, who can do nothing but err, seek and hope that some one should bear witness against my doctrine. I therefore beg by God's mercy that if your Majesty or your illustrious Lordships, from the highest to the lowest, can do it, you should bear witness and convict me of error and conquer me by proofs drawn from the gospels or the prophets, for I am most ready to be instructed and when convinced will be the first to throw my books into the fire.

From this I think it is sufficiently clear that I have carefully considered and weighed the discords, perils, emulation, and dissension excited by my teaching, concerning which I was gravely and urgently admonished yesterday. To me the happiest side of the whole affair is that the Word of God is made the object of emulation and dissent. For this is the course, the fate, and the result of the Word of God, as Christ says: "I am come not to send peace but a sword, to set a man against his father and a daughter against her mother." We must consider that our God is wonderful and terrible in his counsels. If we should begin to heal our dissensions by damning the Word of God, we should only turn loose an intolerable deluge of woes. Let us take care that the rule of this excellent youth, Prince Charles (in whom, next God, there is much hope), does not begin inauspiciously. For I could show by many examples drawn from Scripture that when Pharaoh and the king of Babylon and the kings of Israel thought to pacify and strengthen their kingdoms by their own wisdom, they really only ruined themselves. For he taketh the wise in their own craftiness and removeth mountains and they know it not. We must fear God. I do not say this as though your lordships needed either my teaching or my admonition, but because I could not shirk the duty I owed Germany. With these words I commend myself to your Majesty and your Lordships, humbly begging that you will not let my enemies make me hateful to you without cause. I have spoken.

Eck replied with threatening mien: —

Luther, you have not answered to the point. You ought not to call in question what has been decided and condemned by councils. Therefore I beg you to give a simple, unsophisticated answer without horns (non cornutum). Will you recant or not?

Luther retorted : —

Since your Majesty and your Lordships ask for a plain answer, I will give you one without either horns or teeth.[1] Unless I am convicted by Scripture or by right reason (for I trust neither in popes nor in councils, since they have often erred and contradicted themselves) — unless I am thus convinced, I am bound by the texts of the Bible, my conscience is captive to the Word of God, I neither can nor will recant anything, since it is neither right nor safe to act against conscience. God help me. Amen.

The Spaniards in the audience broke into groans and hisses, the Germans into applause, and Luther was conducted from the hall amid an incipient tumult. When he reached his lodgings, he joyfully exclaimed: " I am through! I am through!" He had indeed done the great deed he had set out to do and spoken the words which will ring through ages.

But his business at Worms was not yet over. The moderate Catholics, hoping that something could yet be accomplished, held a series of conferences with him. Their representatives were Cochlæus, later one of the bitterest enemies of the Evangelic Church, Dr. Vehus, chancellor of the Margrave of Baden, and the Archbishop Elector of Trier. But nothing came of these negotiations. Luther hardened himself, as one of his opponents expressed it, like a rock.

On April 26 he left Worms. Two days later he reached Frankfort where he wrote an interesting letter to Lucas Cranach, his warm friend, the Wittenberg artist. In 1520 the monk had stood godfather to the painter's little daughter, and in return Cranach made two woodcuts of him, the one in 1520, the other in March, 1521.[2] This last, giving so plain an impression of iron will and strength of character that all who run may read, is perhaps the best portrait of the Reformer in existence.

[1] Neque cornutum neque dentatum. These words, which have puzzled historians from the day they were said till the present, have been the subject of a very thorough investigation by R. Meissner. He comes to the conclusion that the dentatum was suggested by the cornutum (without sophistry) of the official, but had no special sense, being merely an " overtrumping," or improvement on his metaphor.

[2] Referred to by Luther in a letter to Spalatin March 7. Enders, iii, 106. On Luther's portraits see Appendix, pp. 453, 454.

LUTHER IN MARCH, 1521

After an etching by Cranach

TO LUCAS CRANACH AT WITTENBERG

FRANKFORT ON THE MAIN, April 28, 1521.

My service to you, dear friend Lucas. I bless and commend you to God. I am going somewhere to hide, though I myself do not yet know where. I should indeed suffer death at the hands of the tyrants, especially at those of furious Duke George, but I must not despise the advice of good men nor die before the Lord's time.

They did not expect me to come to Worms, and what my safe-conduct was worth you all know from the mandate that went out against me. I thought his Majesty the Emperor would have brought together some fifty doctors to refute the monk in argument, but in fact all they said was: "Are these books yours?" — "Yes." — "Will you recant?" — "No!" — "Then get out." O we blind Germans, we act so childishly and let ourselves be fooled by the Romanists.

Give my friend your wife my greeting and say that I hope she is well.

The Jews must needs sing at times in triumph, "Ho, ho, ho!" But Easter will come to us, too, and then we shall sing Hallelujah. We must suffer and keep silence a little time. A little while and ye shall not see me, and again a little while and ye shall see me. At least I hope so, but God's will, which is best, be done, as in heaven, so on earth. Amen.

Greet Christian Döring and his wife. Please thank the town council for providing the carriage. You must get Amsdorf to preach, as he would be glad to do, if John Doltsch is not enough. Good-bye! God bless you and keep your mind and faith in Christ against the Roman wolves and serpents and their adherents. Amen.

DR. MARTIN LUTHER.

On May 1 he reached Hersfeld, where he was royally welcomed by the abbot of the Benedictine monastery and where he preached. On May 2 he entered his dear old Eisenach, where he also delivered a sermon the next day. On the third he drove through the beautiful forests to Möhra, his father's early home, and visited his uncle Heinz Luther. On the morning of May 4 he preached in the open air, and after dinner set out in the direction of Schloss Altenstein with Amsdorf and a brother monk. In the heart of the forest, in a place now marked by a monument, according to a preconcerted plan some masked riders appeared, captured the banned heretic, and rode with him back in the direction of Eisenach to the Wartburg, the castle in which the Elector had decided to keep him.

In the mean time great events were happening at Worms. Charles had been sincerely shocked at the audacity of the rebel monk. The usually reserved young man immediately drew up a paper, perhaps the one frank and spontaneous action of his whole career, stating that he had resolved to stake life, lands, and all on the maintenance of the Catholic faith of his fathers. Aleander, thinking that all was settled, was delighted. After waiting until the Elector of Saxony and other supporters of the new leader had left Worms, Charles drafted an edict, submitted it for approval to four electors and a few remaining members of the Diet, and signed it May 26 — although it was officially dated May 8. The Edict of Worms described Luther's doctrine in the strongest terms as a cesspool of heresies old and new, put him under the ban of the Empire, forbade any to shelter him and commanded all, under strong penalties, to give him up to the authorities. It was also forbidden to print, sell, or read his books.

When the news of Luther's disappearance spread throughout Europe a cry of dismay arose from all who had his cause at heart. Albert Dürer, the painter of Nuremberg, an ardent admirer of the Reformer, then on a visit to Antwerp, heard the news on May 17.

I know not whether he yet lives or is murdered [wrote he in his diary], but in any case he has suffered for the Christian truth. . . . If we lose this man who has written more clearly than any one who has lived for one hundred and forty years, may God grant his spirit to another. . . . His books are to be held in great honor and not burned as the Emperor commands, but rather the books of his enemies. O God, if Luther is dead, who will henceforth expound to us the gospel? What might he not have written for us in the next ten or twenty years?

Another glimpse of the temper of the people is given in an obscure letter of Albert Burer, at Kemberg, near Wittenberg, to Basil Amorbach, written June 30, 1521. The rustics, he says, if they meet others on the road, inquire of them : " Bistu gutt Marteinisch ? " and beat any one who answers in the negative.

CHAPTER XI

THE WARTBURG. MAY 4, 1521 — MARCH 1, 1522

THE Wartburg, about a mile south of Eisenach, is one of the finest old Gothic castles in Germany. Majestically crowning a steep hill, it commands a superb view of the lovely Thuringian forest. Surrounded by a moat and guarded by drawbridge and portcullis, the several buildings which unite to make up the pile are grouped around two courts. The largest hall, already old in Luther's day, is famous as having been, in the twelfth century, the meeting-place where the German bards, since immortalized in Wagner's opera, met to contend the palm. The fortress had been for generations the abode of the powerful, ostentatious landgraves of Thuringia, and was hallowed by the memory of St. Elizabeth of Marburg, the wife of one of them.

In this charming spot Luther remained hidden almost a year, obeying the command of his wary sovereign. The room assigned him was not in the main building, but in a small one. It was reached by a narrow flight of stairs which led immediately from the entrance to the chamber. It has been preserved as it was in his day, with the old stove, bedstead, table, and stump which served as a stool. As he sat by the leaded glass window, his eye swept the wild landscape for many miles towards the west.

Shortly after his arrival, he wrote Spalatin a long and interesting letter describing his journey, his capture, and his life and work. The two former have been related in the last chapter, but some other interesting items may well be given in his own words: —

TO GEORGE SPALATIN AT WORMS

THE MOUNTAIN, May 14, 1521.

Greeting. I received your letter, dear Spalatin, and those of Gerbel and Sapidus last Sunday, but have not written before for fear lest the notoriety of my recent capture should cause some one to intercept the letters. Various opinions of my disappearance are held in this region, the most popular being that I was captured by friends from Franconia.

To-morrow the Emperor's safe-conduct expires. I regret what you write about their savage edict [1] for trying consciences, not so much for my own sake as because they are inviting evil on their own heads and will only succeed in making themselves odious. Such indecent violence will only arouse deep hatred. But let it pass, perhaps the time of their visitation is at hand. . . . We see that the people are neither able nor willing — as Erasmus also wrote in his Advice [2] — to bear the yoke of the Pope and the papists; therefore let us not cease to press upon it and to pull it down, especially as we have already lost name and fame by so doing. Now the light reveals all things and their show of piety is no longer valuable and cannot rule as hitherto. We have grown by violence and driven them back by violence; we must see if they can be driven back any more.

I sit here lazy and drunken the whole day.

I am reading the Greek and Hebrew Bible. . . .

Now I have put off my old garments and dress like a knight, letting hair and beard grow so that you would not know me — indeed I have hardly become acquainted with myself. Now I am in Christian liberty, free from all tyrannical laws, though I should have preferred that that Dresden hog [3] had killed me publicly while preaching, had God pleased that I should suffer for his Word. The Lord's will be done! Farewell and pray for me. Salute all the court.

MARTIN LUTHER.

Life at the castle was indeed a change from the routine of Wittenberg. The disguised prisoner was attended by two pages of gentle blood and by an armed guard. The warden, John von Berlepsch, entertained him with distinguished courtesy. The strict incognito did not prevent constant intercourse with friends, not only by letters privately forwarded but by personal visits also. He strolled through the woods searching for strawberries and even hunted a little. Pity for the poor animals is an unex-

---

[1] On April 30 the Emperor called the electors and princes together to consult about an edict against Luther, which was not, however, signed until May 26.

[2] Luther is probably referring to the Consilium cujusdam ex animo cupientis, etc., though such strong views as these are hardly expressed therein.

[3] Duke George of Albertine Saxony. Both here and in the letter to Cranach, Luther does him wrong, for he advised observing the safe-conduct.

THE WARTBURG

pected and amiable trait in the sturdy peasant; it is a matter of course that St. Francis of Assisi should save a hare from the trap,[1] but it is almost surprising that Luther should do the same.

Most of his time, however, was spent in the little cell studying the Bible and writing. His letters are full of his experiences, and it is perhaps some of those translated below of which Coleridge was thinking when he said he could hardly imagine a more delightful book than Luther's letters, especially those written from the Wartburg.[2] His metaphysical tastes, however, may have led him to prefer the discussions of knotty points in theology. His reference to "the hearty mother tongue of the original" and (in his table-talk) to "the racy old German" are hardly happy, as most of the epistles are written in Latin: —

TO GEORGE SPALATIN AT COBURG

ISLE OF PATMOS, June 10, 1521.

. . . I am both very idle and very busy here, I study Hebrew and Greek and write without cessation. The warden treats me far better than I deserve. The trouble with which I suffered at Worms has not left me but increased, for I am more constipated than I ever was and despair of a remedy. The Lord thus visits me, that I may never be without a relic of the cross. Blessed be he. Amen.

I wonder that the imperial edict is so delayed. In my retreat I have read the letters against me sent to the estates of the Empire, but I find them faulty.

It is rumored that Chièvres[3] has died and left Charles a million gulden. How brave is Christ not to fear these mountains of gold! Would that they might learn once for all that he is the Lord our God.

I have not yet answered the young prince[4] for fear of revealing my hiding-place, nor, for the same reason, do I think it expedient to do so now.

Pray for me diligently. This is all I need, as other things abound. Now that I am at rest I care not what they do with me in public. Farewell in the Lord and greet all those whom you think it safe to greet.

HENRICUS NESICUS.[5]

---

[1] Sabatier: *Vie de St. François d'Assise*, 9th ed., Paris, 1894, p. 204.

[2] S. T. Coleridge: *The Friend.*

[3] Guillaume de Croy, Señor de Chièvres, one of the Emperor's counsellors.

[4] John Frederic, nephew of the Elector and later Elector.

[5] This signature is an unexplained bit of humor.

TO GEORGE SPALATIN AT ALTENBURG

(WARTBURG,) August 15, 1521.

Greeting. Dear Spalatin, I have received the second and third parts of my Sermon on Confession from you and the first part from Melanchthon. I cannot say how sorry and disgusted I am with the printing. I wish I had sent nothing in German, because they print it so poorly, carelessly, and confusedly, to say nothing of bad types and paper. John the printer is always the same old Johnny. Please do not let him print any of my German Homilies, but return them for me to send elsewhere. What is the use of my working so hard if the errors in the printed books give occasion to other publishers to make them still worse? I would not sin so against the gospels and epistles; better let them remain hidden than bring them out in such form. Therefore I send you nothing now, although I have a good deal of manuscript ready. I shall forward no more until I learn that these sordid mercenaries care less for their profits than for the public. Such printers seem to think: "It is enough for me to get the money; let the readers look out for the matter." . . .

Do not be anxious about my exile. It makes no difference to me where I am. But I fear I may at length become burdensome to the men here. I wish to cause expense to no one. I think I am living at the bounty of the Elector, and could not stay another hour if I thought I was consuming the substance of the warden, who serves me in all things cheerfully and freely. You know if any one's wealth must be wasted it should be that of a prince, for to be a prince and not a robber is hardly possible, and the greater the prince the harder it is. Please inform me on this point. I cannot understand this gentleman's liberality unless he supports me from the Elector's purse. It is my nature to be afraid of burdening people when perchance I do not, but such a scruple becomes an honorable man.

Last week I hunted two days to see what that bitter-sweet[1] pleasure of heroes was like. We took two hares and a few poor partridges — a worthy occupation indeed for men with nothing to do. I even moralized among the snares and dogs, and the superficial pleasure I may have derived from the hunt was equalled by the pity and pain which are a necessary part of it. It is an image of the devil hunting innocent little creatures with his gins and his hounds, the impious

---

[1] "γλυκύπικρον" one of the Greek words inserted as the author progressed in his study of that language.

magistrates, bishops and theologians. I deeply felt this parable of the simple and faithful soul. A still more cruel parable followed. With great pains I saved a little live rabbit, and rolled it up in the sleeve of my cloak, but when I left it and went a little way off the dogs found the poor rabbit and killed it by biting its right leg and throat through the cloth. Thus do the Pope and Satan rage to kill souls and are not stopped by my labor. I am sick of this kind of hunting and prefer to chase bears, wolves, foxes, and that sort of wicked magistrate with spear and arrow. It consoles me to think that the mystery of salvation is near, when hares and innocent creatures will be captured rather by men than by bears, wolves, and hawks, i. e., the bishops and theologians. I mean that now they are snared into hell, then they will be captured for heaven. Thus I joke with you. You know that your nobles would be beasts of prey even in paradise. Even Christ the greatest hunter could hardly capture and keep them. I jest with you because I know you like hunting.

I have changed my mind and have decided to send the rest of the Homilies, thinking that as they are begun they had better be finished. . . .

The writer's ill health was due partly to the rich fare and generally sedentary life, and partly, perhaps, to a reaction after the terrible strain of the preceding weeks. It caused the temptations and especially the depression of which he often speaks. Some have thought that it was also at the bottom of those visions of the devil which are popularly supposed to have been frequent at the Wartburg. The fact is, however, that not only the legend of the inkstand hurled at the fiend, but every other story about such visions receives not a particle of support from contemporary sources. In all his letters from the Wartburg, Luther never once mentions any supernatural experience, nor even in his work On the Abuse of the Mass, where he makes special mention of such apparitions in general, does he say one word of his ever having seen any himself. That he occasionally spoke of them long afterwards is due rather to an hallucination of memory than of the senses at the time. He heard some noises in the old spooky castle, so slight that he hardly noticed them, but they gradually grew in memory, so that he could say, just ten years later: —

Satan has often vexed me with visions, especially at the Wartburg. One night while I was there he took some walnuts from the table and kept snapping them at the ceiling all night.

As he told this story over and over, it gradually expanded with the years, until, in its final form, it assumed enormous proportions. It is a striking illustration of the fallibility of human memory and of the origin of ghost-stories, and demonstrates once for all the worthlessness of the table-talk as an historical source for events of long antecedent date. Indeed only as an illustration of these points the story has interest. It is so hopelessly confused, either by Luther or by the note-taker, that John von Berlepsch, a bachelor, is given a wife, and two rooms are spoken of, where there was, in reality, but one. This was at the head of one flight of stairs, with no other chamber near by. Thus it is that the story appears twenty-five years after the visions it records:—

When I left Worms in 1521, I was captured near Eisenach, and dwelt in the Wartburg, my Patmos. I was far from people, in a room where no one could come to me but two boys of good family, who brought me food and drink twice a day. Once they brought me a sack of hazel nuts, which I ate from time to time. I kept them in a box. When it was bedtime, I undressed in my study, put out the light, went into my chamber, and lay down in bed. Then the hazel nuts began, rose up one after another, hit the rafters hard and rattled on the bed, but I did nothing. If I only began to drop off to sleep such a noise started on the steps as if some one were rolling sixty barrels down the stairs, yet I knew that the steps were closed with iron bars so that no one could get to them. I got up, went to the stairs to see what the matter was, and there they were locked up! . . .
Later the wife of John von Berlepsch, who had heard that I was in the castle, wanted to see me, came, but they would not let her see me. But they took me to another room and the lady slept in my chamber. There she heard such a racket in the room hard-by that she thought a thousand devils were in it. The best way to drive out the fiend is to despise him and call on Christ, for he cannot bear that. You should say to him: "If you are lord over Christ, so be it!" That is what I said at Eisenach.

Whatever may have been at the base of this astonishing tale,

It is certain that at the Wartburg apparitions from the next
world did not interfere with an active participation in the business of the present one. A lively interest in public affairs was
maintained by means of letters forwarded by Spalatin. Luther
did not feel called upon to set all the wrongs in the world right,
but he was strongly inclined to intervene when he heard of the
deeds of his old enemy, Albert of Mayence. During the summer
following the Diet of Worms, Carlstadt had carried on reform
measures at Wittenberg, especially insisting that the clergy
should take wives. Luther soon wrote in favor of this, but even
before his tract was published a number of priests accepted
Carlstadt's invitation to marry. Some of them in the jurisdiction of Mayence were arrested by Archbishop Albert, though
that notoriously immoral prelate did not scruple to derive an
income from licenses to the clergy to keep concubines. At the
same time, thinking that there was no longer any danger, he
ventured to recommence the trade in indulgences in his capital,
Halle. When the Reformer heard of these things he wrote
a fierce and reckless tract, Against the Idol of Halle, which he
sent Spalatin to have printed. The Elector refused to allow
its publication for reasons of state, and after an angry protest,
Luther was forced to agree to postpone printing the obnoxious
tract until he had remonstrated privately with the offending
prelate : —

TO ALBERT, ARCHBISHOP AND ELECTOR OF MAYENCE

(THE WARTBURG,) December 1, 1521.

My humble service to your Electoral Grace, my honorable and gracious Lord. Your Grace doubtless remembers vividly that I have
written you twice before, the first time at the beginning of the indulgence fraud [1] protected by your Grace's name. In that letter I faithfully warned your Grace and from Christian love set myself against
those deceitful, seducing, greedy preachers thereof, and against their
heretical, infidel books. Had I not preferred to act with moderation
I might have driven the whole storm on your Grace as the one who
aided and abetted the traders, and I might have written expressly
against their heretical books, but instead I spared your Grace and the
house of Brandenburg, thinking that your Grace might have acted

[1] October 31, 1517, p. 42.

through ignorance, led astray by false whisperers, so I only attacked them, and with how much trouble and danger your Grace knows.

But as this my true admonition was mocked by your Grace, obtaining ingratitude instead of thanks, I wrote you a second time,[1] humbly asking for information. To this I got a hard, improper, unepiscopal, unchristian answer,[2] referring me to higher powers for information. As these two letters did no good, I am now sending your Grace a third warning, according to the gospel, this time in German, hoping that such admonition and prayer, which ought to be superfluous and unnecessary, may help.

Your Grace has again erected at Halle that idol which robs poor simple Christians of their money and their souls. You have thus shown that the criminal blunder for which Tetzel was blamed was not due to him alone, but also to the Archbishop of Mayence, who, not regarding my gentleness to him, insists on taking all the blame on himself. Perhaps your Grace thinks I am no more to be reckoned with, but am looking out for my own safety, and that his Imperial Majesty has extinguished the poor monk. On the contrary, I wish your Grace to know that I will do what Christian love demands without fearing the gates of hell, much less unlearned popes, bishops, and cardinals. I will not suffer it nor keep silence when the Archbishop of Mayence gives out that it is none of his business to give information to a poor man who asks for it. The truth is that your ignorance is wilful, as long as the thing ignored brings you in money. I am not to blame, but your own conduct.

I humbly pray your Grace, therefore, to leave poor people undeceived and unrobbed, and show yourself a bishop rather than a wolf. It has been made clear enough that indulgences are only knavery and fraud, and that only Christ should be preached to the people, so that your Grace has not the excuse of ignorance. Your Grace will please remember the beginning, and what a terrible fire was kindled from a little despised spark, and how all the world was surely of the opinion that a single poor beggar was immeasurably too weak for the Pope, and was undertaking an impossible task. But God willed to give the Pope and his followers more than enough to do, and to play a game contrary to the expectation of the world and in spite of it, so that the Pope will hardly recover, growing daily worse and one may see God's work therein. Let no one doubt that the same God yet lives and knows how to withstand a cardinal of Mayence even if four emperors support him. . . .

[1] February 4, 1520.   [2] February 26, 1520.

Wherefore I write to tell your Grace that if the idol is not taken down, my duty to godly doctrine and Christian salvation will absolutely force me to attack your Grace publicly as I did the Pope, and oppose your undertaking, and lay all the odium which Tetzel once had on the Archbishop of Mayence, and show all the world the difference between a bishop and a wolf. . . .

Moreover I beg your Grace to leave in peace the priests who, to avoid inchastity, have betaken themselves to marriage. Do not deprive them of their God-given rights. Your Grace has no authority, reason, nor right to persecute them, and arbitrary crime does not become a bishop. . . . So your Grace can see that if you do not take care, the Evangelic party will raise an outcry and point out that it would become a bishop first to cast the beam out of his own eye and put away his harlots before he separates pious wives from their husbands. . . .

I will not keep silence, for, though I do not expect it, I hope to make the bishops leave off singing their lively little song. . . .

I beg and expect a right speedy answer from your Grace within the next fortnight, for at the expiration of that time my pamphlet against the Idol of Halle will be published unless a proper answer comes. And if this letter is received by your Grace's secretaries and does not come into your own hands, I will not hold off for that reason. Secretaries should be true and a bishop should so order his court that that reaches him which should reach him. God give your Grace his grace unto a right mind and will.

Your Grace's obedient, humble servant,
MARTIN LUTHER.

The desired answer came. It is a proof of the great power wielded by Luther, that, after the presentation of an ultimatum, the primate of all Germany should reply with abject submission to the outlawed heretic. Albert was, indeed, in a difficult situation, for, notwithstanding a rather non-committal attitude at Worms he had been accused of having had Luther assassinated, and stood in mortal terror of popular vengeance. Both now and later, moreover, the Macchiavellian prelate sought to run with the hare and hunt with the hounds. While continuing to cultivate the friendship of Rome he anxiously avoided a breach with Wittenberg. He accordingly induced Capito, a humanist in his employ, to intercede with the Reformer, to whom he himself indited this astonishing missive : —

TO MARTIN LUTHER, IN CARE OF SPALATIN

HALLE, December 21, 1521.

My dear doctor, I have received your letter and I take it in good part and graciously, and will see to it that the thing that moved you so be done away, and I will act, God willing, as becomes a pious, spiritual, and Christian prince, as far as God gives me grace and strength, for which I earnestly pray and have prayers said for me, for I can do nothing of myself and know well that without God's grace there is no good in me, but that I am as much foul mud as any other, if not more. I do not wish to conceal this, for I am more than willing to show you grace and favor for Christ's sake, and I can well bear fraternal and Christian punishment. I hope the merciful, kind God will give me herein more grace, strength and patience to live in this matter and in others by his will.

ALBERT, with his own hand.

No wonder that the recipient was nonplussed by this letter, doubting whether it showed more godly contrition or devilish hypocrisy. The soft answer turned away his wrath, or rather suspended it for a year, when the polemic against the Idol of Halle came out in a revised form under the title, Against the Estate of the Pope and Bishops falsely called Spiritual. This bitter pamphlet attacks the "idol-worship" and vices of the higher clergy without mercy.

Luther accomplished an enormous amount of literary work during his year of hiding. One of his largest tasks was the composition of the Postilla, or homilies on the gospel and epistle for each Sunday.

More important in abiding results was the work on the celibacy of the clergy. When Carlstadt, the Wittenberg radical, came forward as the champion of marriage of priests, monks, and nuns, Luther was by no means clear in his own mind about the expediency of this practice. On August 6, 1521, he wrote Spalatin : —

I have received Carlstadt's pamphlets. Good Heavens! will our Wittenbergers give wives even to monks? They won't force one on me. . . . Farewell, pray for me and take care not to get married for fear of tribulation of the flesh.

And again on August 15 : —

How I wish that Carlstadt in attacking sacerdotal celibacy would quote more applicable texts. I fear he will excite a prejudice against it. . . . It is a noble cause he has taken up, I wish he were more equal to it. For you see how clear and cogent we are forced to be on account of our enemies, who calumniate even what is most perspicuous and convincing in our arguments. Wherefore we, who are a spectacle to the world, must take care that our words be above reproach, as Paul teaches. Perhaps I am meddling with matters which are none of my business, and yet they are my business, especially if he succeeds. For what is more dangerous than to invite so many monks and nuns to marry and urge it with unconvincing texts of Scripture, by complying with which invitation the consciences of the parties may be burdened with an eternal cross worse than they now bear. I wish that celibacy might be left free, as the gospel requires, but how to add to that principle I know not. But my warnings are in vain; Carlstadt's career will not be checked and therefore must be endured.

Having convinced himself that the cause was noble, Luther undertook to find adequate arguments in support of it. His first essay in this direction was a mere sketch (Themata de votis), a series of propositions on vows sent to Wittenberg for debate. The thesis here presented is that all that is not done by faith is sin, and that monastic vows are taken in reliance on good works and not on faith, and therefore are wrong. Indeed it is tantamount to vowing a life of impiety, and moreover it destroys Christian liberty.

These thoughts took form in a treatise On Monastic Vows, which the author dedicated to his father in the following letter : —

TO HANS LUTHER AT MANSFELD

THE WILDERNESS, November 21, 1521.

This book, dear father, I wish to dedicate to you, not to make your name famous in the world, for fame puffeth up the flesh, according to the doctrine of St. Paul, but that I might have occasion in a short preface as it were between you and me to point out to the Christian reader the argument and contents of the book, together with an illustrative example. . . .

It is now sixteen years since I became a monk, having taken the vow without your knowledge and against your will. You were anxious and fearful about my weakness, because I was a young blood of twenty-two, that is, to use St. Augustine's words, it was still hot youth with me, and you had learned from numerous examples that monkery made many unblessed and so were determined to marry me honorably and tie me down. This fear, this anxiety, this non-consent of yours were for a time simply irreconcilable. . . . .

And indeed, my vow was not worth a fig, since it was taken without the consent of the parents God gave me. Moreover it was a godless vow both because taken against your will and without my whole heart. In short, it was simple doctrine of men, that is of the spiritual estate of hypocrites, a doctrine not commanded by God. . . .

Dear father, will you still take me out of the cloister? If so, do not boast of it, for God has anticipated you and taken me out himself. What difference does it make whether I retain or lay aside the cowl and the tonsure. Do they make the monk? . . . My conscience is free and redeemed; therefore I am still a monk but not a monk, and a new creature not of the Pope but of Christ, for the Pope also has creatures and is a creator of puppets and idols and masks and straw men, of which I was formerly one, but now have escaped by the Word. . . .

The Pope may strangle me and condemn me and bid me go to hell, but he will not be able to rouse me after death to strangle me again. To be banned and damned is according to my own heart and will. May he never absolve me more! I hope the great day is at hand when the kingdom of abomination and horror will be broken and thrust down. Would to God that I had been worthy to be burned by the Pope! . . .

The Lord bless you, dear father, with mother, your Margaret, and all our family. Farewell in the Lord Christ.

The work itself is an elaborate inquiry into the nature of monasticism. Some vows are allowed, but one must distinguish between the good and the bad, for the more holy a thing is the more likely it is to be perverted. " What is more holy than worship which is the first commandment? But what is more common than superstition, that is, false and perverted worship?" No vow is to be taken except according to the Bible, — the very opposite of monastic rules. If the Bible allows virginity it rather deters men from it than invites them to it. Secondly, vows are the enemies of faith, for monastic life is a good work, and hence outside of faith, without faith and sinful. Thirdly, vows are hostile to Christian liberty. Fourthly, they are repugnant to God's commands. If there have been saints in the cloister, it has not been because of the cloister. Monks forget that they are Christians in remembering that they are Dominicans, Franciscans, or Benedictines. Vows are also hostile to charity. Finally, they are inimical to reason.

This book, which the author himself judged to be among his most important, had an enormous sale and great influence in its own day. Needless to say, for us it has only an historical interest, though, indeed, an eminent Catholic scholar thought it necessary, only a few years ago, to refute it point by point. But most of us will concur in the judgment of Erasmus when it came out that "it is very garrulous."

Far greater than this treatise was the work next undertaken by the Reformer, namely, the translation of the Bible, which from this time on was the constant labor of his life. He began with the New Testament, of which he speaks in the letter next given : —

TO JOHN LANG AT ERFURT

THE WILDERNESS, December 18, 1521.

I do not approve of that tumultuous exodus from the cloister, for the monks should have separated peaceably and in charity. At the next general chapter you must defend and cherish the Evangelic cause, for I shall lie hidden until Easter. In the mean time I shall continue to write my Homilies and shall translate the New Testament into German, a thing which my friends demand and at which I hear that you also labor. Would that every town had its interpreter, and that this book alone might be on the tongues and in the hands, the eyes, the ears, and the hearts of all men. Ask for other news at Wittenberg. I am well in body and well cared for, but am buffeted with sin and temptation. Pray for me and farewell.

MARTIN LUTHER.

The work, though carefully done, was prosecuted with such zeal that it was completed within three months. Of the methods, results, and peculiarities of this translation more will be said in a separate chapter. Suffice it here to note that Luther used the

Greek text edited by Erasmus in 1516 and supplied with a new Latin translation in parallel columns. It is possible that he also had by him one or more of the older German translations, of which there were at least fourteen, but the great originality of his work would suggest that he used them but little.

CHAPTER XII

THE WITTENBERG REVOLUTION AND THE RETURN FROM THE WARTBURG. 1521-1522

WHILE Luther was in retirement at the beautiful old castle near Eisenach, the movement started by him was carried on with accelerated velocity at Wittenberg. Carlstadt's attack on sacerdotal celibacy was only the first step in a revolution. In this movement two distinct factors combined, the one of constructive reform, the other of popular tumult; the best elements of the first were due to Luther, who, while absent, kept up a constant correspondence with Wittenberg; for the second element other leaders were responsible, Carlstadt, Zwilling, and the Zwickau prophets.

The constructive reform was embodied in two city ordinances, the first of November, 1521, the second of January 24, 1522. The earlier bit of legislation provided for "a common purse," that is, for the public care of the worthy poor, on new principles, deduced from the Address to the Nobility and the larger Sermon on Usury. It will be remembered how in his great pamphlet the author proposes that begging be prohibited. This was now done by the town of Wittenberg, while the deserving poor, *i. e.*, those who could not support themselves, were provided for from funds voluntarily contributed to the parish church. That not only the ideas but the form of this ordinance proceeded from Luther has been proved from a first draft of the document in his hand recently discovered.

The second decree passed by the town council two months after the first was an extension of the other on more radical lines, doubtless due to the active influence of Zwilling and Carlstadt. It provided that to the common fund should be applied the income from the property of the twenty-one resident brotherhoods, and especially from endowed masses, now regarded as an abomination. The expenses of the common treasury were also

greatly enlarged; orphans were to be cared for, students at the
schools and university to be helped, poor girls to be supplied
with dowries, and workmen loaned capital at four per cent.
The laws against begging were reënacted with additional penalties. A police charged with the surveillance of morals and especially with the suppression of houses of ill fame was instituted.
Finally, a new form of divine service was introduced, by which
all pictures and superfluous altars were to be torn down, communion was to be administered in both kinds, and the government bound itself to see that ministers preached only the pure
gospel. All the provisions of this comprehensive decree, except
the last on public worship, were suggested by Luther.

These reforms, for the most part salutary, were accompanied
by others, which, even when unobjectionable in themselves,
were carried through with mob violence. The riots began
about the first of October, when Gabriel Zwilling, an Augustinian monk, began to preach against the mass and the canonical hours. At his instance these services were stopped by the
monks on October 6 or 7; he then began a campaign against
the monastic life itself, not only leaving it free to his brothers
to quit the cloister, but forcing them to do so with insults and
threats.

Carlstadt now began to attack the mass and with such success that the priests celebrating it in the parish church on
December 3 were stoned, and the day following an altar in
the Franciscan convent was destroyed by the students. The
arrest of the offenders was the occasion of a worse riot on
December 12, when the mob went to the town officers and demanded their release.

The agitation spread. The monks at Erfurt left the cloister
tumultuously. A plan was hatched to stop all masses, not only
at Wittenberg, but throughout the surrounding country, on
January 1, 1522. At Eilenberg a rectory was plundered.
On All Saints' Day (November 1) the citizens of Wittenberg
demonstrated in force against the Elector's relics in the Castle
Church.

Much disturbed by the progress of innovation, Luther made
a secret visit to his city early in December, lodging with Me-

LUTHER AS JUNKER GEORG

From the painting by Cranach, December, 1521, in the Stadtbibliothek at Leipsic

lanchthon and privately interviewing other friends, among them
Lucas Cranach, who painted his picture. He was rather reas-
sured than otherwise by this visit, deciding not to take too
tragically a disturbance in the monastery and a few student
riots. He accordingly contented himself with remaining a few
days, leaving behind him a Warning to all Christians to keep
from Uproar and Sedition. This manuscript he also sent to
Spalatin, who, however, prudently refused to have it printed
until three months later.

In this year [says Luther] by God's grace the holy light of Christian truth, formerly suppressed by the Pope and his followers, has been
rekindled, by which their manifold and noxious corruption and tyranny
has been laid bare and scotched. So that it looks as if tumults would
arise, and parsons, monks, bishops, and the whole spiritual estate
hunted out and smitten unless they apply themselves earnestly to their
improvement. For the common man, agitated and disgusted with the
harm done to his property, body and soul, means to do something, and
vows that he will never suffer such things more, and has reasons at his
tongue's end and threatens to smite with flail and cudgel.

The author adds that though the intimidation of the clergy
is a good thing, nevertheless tumult is the work of the devil,
and all Christians should keep aloof from it and labor only by
word of mouth. It may be doubted whether this pamphlet was
expressed in really prudent terms, and whether it would not be
more likely to excite discontent than to allay it. Nevertheless
things might have quieted down had it not been for the powerful reënforcement received by the party of revolution on
December 27 in the advent of the Zwickau prophets.

Among the cloth weavers of this little Saxon town Thomas
Münzer, a fanatic, had formed a sect animated with the desire
to renovate both State and Church by the readiest and roughest
means. When the civil authorities, fearing the openly threatened revolt, imprisoned some of the agitators, Münzer escaped
to Bohemia, and three of his followers, Nicholas Storch, Mark
Thomas Stübner, and Thomas Drechsel, went to Wittenberg.
They proclaimed themselves prophets who talked familiarly
with God and foresaw the future, revelation coming to them
directly from the Spirit. Their mystic quietism was strangely

mingled with an anarchist programme for overturning the civil
government and extirpating the priests. The most harmless of
the dogmas of the new sect, and the one from which they were
to derive the name of Anabaptists, was opposition to infant
baptism and insistence on rebaptizing their proselytes.

At Wittenberg the prophets, or " ranters," as they were also
called, found a soil prepared for the seed of their doctrine. According to their suggestions learning was discouraged, dreams
were cultivated, and a systematic propaganda of anarchy organ-
ized.

The Wittenberg leaders either succumbed to the ascendancy
of the prophets or actively joined them. Carlstadt met them
more than halfway : he married, retired to a farm, affected to
dress like a laborer, and courted popularity by extolling the
revelation vouchsafed to babes and sucklings while disparaging
the wisdom of the wise. Other Lutherans, like Amsdorf, though
they heartily disapproved of the course things were taking,
were powerless to stem the tide.

The most responsible and gifted of all the professors left at
Wittenberg was Philip Melanchthon. Luther's admiration for
this pious and precociously learned young man was so great
that he felt perfectly safe in leaving the guidance of the new
cause in the latter's hands. "They will not need me, dear brother," he said on departing for Worms, " while you still live."
When he first heard of the new prophets he modestly opined that
Melanchthon would be better able to deal with them than he
would be. In this he was destined to disappointment. With
much delicacy and refinement, Melanchthon possessed the defects of his qualities in a certain want of robustness. Both now,
and still more later, at the crises when he was deprived of the
other's strong influence, his life was made miserable and his
fame tarnished by the exigencies of a situation too large for
his powers. In the present instance he wavered, was inclined to
believe the arguments against infant baptism, was impressed by
the pretensions of the prophets, and hoped his friend Storch
might meet his friend Luther. The latter's directions to him
how to act, are interesting not only for their connection with the
prophets, but also as a revelation of the writer's inner life :—

TO PHILIP MELANCHTHON AT WITTENBERG

(WARTBURG,) January 13, 1522.

Greeting. Had the letter of the Archbishop of Mayence come alone it would have satisfied me, but now that Capito's letter is added it is evident that there is some plot. I am greatly disappointed in Capito. I wished to put a stop to that impious trade, but he pleads for it like an attorney, and by teaching the archbishop to confess his private sins thinks to impose on Luther beautifully. I shall restrain myself and not treat the man as he deserves, yet I shall show him that I am alive.

Coming now to the "prophets" let me first say that I do not approve your irresolution, especially as you are more richly endowed with the spirit and with learning than I am. In the first place, those who bear witness of themselves are not to be believed, but spirits must be proved. You act on Gamaliel's contrary advice. Hitherto I have heard of nothing said or done by them which Satan could not emulate. Do you, in my place, search out whether they approve their calling. For God never sent any one who was not either called by men or attested by miracles, not even his own son. . . . Do not receive them if they assert that they come by mere revelation. . . .

Pray search their innermost spirit and see whether they have experienced those spiritual straightenings, that divine birth, death and infernal torture. If you find their experiences have been smooth, bland, devout (as they say) and ceremonious, do not approve them, though they claim to have been snatched up to the third heaven. . . . Divine Majesty does not speak directly; rather no man shall see him and live. Nature bears no small stars and no insignificant words of God. . . . Try not to see even Jesus in glory until you have seen him crucified. (Here follows a long argument in favor of infant baptism.)

Keep my book against the Archbishop of Mayence to come out and rebuke others when they go mad. Prepare me a lodging because my translation of the Bible will require me to return to you, and pray the Lord that I may do so in accordance with his will. I wish to keep hidden as long as may be; in the mean time I shall proceed with what I have begun. Farewell.

Yours,

MARTIN LUTHER.

But Melanchthon was not the man to cope with the situation. Feeling his own weakness he besought the Elector to allow his friend to return and quiet the disturbances, but the cautious prince, fearing openly to acknowledge the outlaw, positively refused to do so.

The tumults continued. On January 11 the Augustinians solemnly burned all their pictures. On January 24 Carlstadt forced the town council against their will to pass the ordinance above mentioned. They disapproved in it especially of two things: first, the illegal appropriation of the endowments of masses, and secondly, the abolition of all images in the churches, though the innovators described the making of images as worse than theft, murder, and adultery, because it was forbidden in the first commandment, but the other sins were relegated to the following ones.

The disorders attracted the attention of neighboring princes. Duke George of Albertine Saxony made representations to his cousin and also laid a complaint before the Imperial Executive Council (Reichsregiment) at Nuremberg, on January 20. For a moment it looked as if not only sedition but civil war threatened Germany.

On February 1 there was another riot. The government at last took action. Carlstadt was politely requested not to preach and Zwilling judged it best to leave town. The situation was still extremely delicate, however, and, fearing another outbreak, on February 20 the town council, without consulting the Elector, sent an urgent request directly to Luther imploring him to return to his place at Wittenberg.

This letter was probably the earliest intimation the Reformer had had of the continuation of rioting. His first idea was to send another warning to the people, but the more he thought about it the more certain he became that his presence was necessary. He intimated his intention of returning in a letter to his sovereign, ironically referring to the doings at Wittenberg as a cross which would be a valuable addition to Frederic's famous collection of relics. The mild and pious prince answered at once in a letter to John Oswald, one of his officers at Eisenach, bidding him have a personal interview with the Reformer and communicate the contents of the missive. This relates the course of events at Wittenberg, but also emphasizes the complaints already made against them by Duke George and the danger of a new process against Luther, whom he advises to have patience and wait at least until after the next diet, to be called about the middle of Lent. The cross Frederic says he is willing to bear.

This letter arrived on February 28 and its contents were communicated to the refugee just as he had made all preparations to depart. Unhindered by it, he did so the next day, making the dangerous journey alone on horseback. Reaching Jena on March 3, he chanced to meet two Swiss students, John Kessler and Spengler, on their way to Wittenberg to study. One of them has left us, in an account of the evening at the Great Bear inn, a vivid picture of the Reformer and a little drama as well. The scene is the public room of the hostel, heated with the large German tile stove and lighted by candles. At a table sits a stalwart man, no longer thin and not yet stout; his beard, red cap, jerkin and hose, and a long sword, proclaim him a knight. Before him is a glass of beer; one hand rests on the hilt of his weapon, in the other he holds an open book. Enter two youths, who on account of their muddy boots sit down near the door.

Luther — Good evening, friends. Draw nearer and have a drink to warm you up. I see you are Swiss; from what part do you come and whither are you going?

Kessler — We come from St. Gall, sir, and we are going to Wittenberg.

Luther — To Wittenberg? Well, you will find good compatriots of yours there, the brothers Jerome and Augustine Schurf.

Kessler — We have letters to them. Can you tell us, sir, whether Luther is now at Wittenberg, or where he may be?

Luther — I have authentic information that he is not at Wittenberg, but that he will soon return. But Philip Melanchthon is there to teach Greek, and Aurogallus to teach you Hebrew, both of which languages you should study if you wish to understand the Bible.

Kessler — Thank God that Luther will soon be back; if God grant us life we will not rest until we see and hear that man. For it is on account of him that we are going there. We have heard that he wishes to overturn the priesthood and the mass, and as our parents have brought us up to be priests, we want to hear what he can tell us and on what authority he acts.

Luther — Where have you studied formerly?

Kessler — At Basel.

Luther — How goes it at Basel? Is Erasmus there and what is he doing?

Kessler — Erasmus is there, sir, but what he does no man knows, for he keeps it a secret. (Aside to his companion as Luther takes a drink) I never knew a knight before who used so much Latin, nor one who understood Greek and Hebrew as this one seems to.

Luther — Friends, what do they think of Luther in Switzerland?

Kessler — There are various opinions there, sir, as everywhere. Some cannot extol him enough, and thank God for having revealed truth and discovered error by him; others, especially the clergy, condemn him as an intolerable heretic.

Luther — One might expect as much from the preachers.

Spengler — (Raising book which he sees is a Hebrew Psalter) I would give a finger to understand this tongue.

Luther — You must work hard to learn it. I also am learning it, and practise some every day.

(It is getting dark. Host bustles up, lights more candles, stops before table.)

Host — I overheard you, gentlemen, talking of Luther. Pity you were not all here two days ago; he was here then at this table, sitting right there (points).

Spengler — If this cursed weather had not hindered us we should have been here then and should have seen him. Is it not a pity?

Kessler — At least we ought to be thankful that we are in the same house that he was and at the very table where he sat. (Host laughs, goes toward door; when out of sight of Luther turns and beckons Kessler, who rises anxiously thinking that he has done something amiss and goes to host.)

Host (aside to Kessler) — Now that I see that you really want to hear and see Luther, I may tell you that the man at your table is he.

Kessler — You're just gulling me because you think I want to see Luther.

Host — No, it is positively he, but don't let on that you know him. (Kessler returns to table, where Luther has begun to read again.)

Kessler (whispering to his companion) — The host tells me this man is Luther.

Spengler — What on earth? Perhaps he said "Hutten"; the two names sound alike, and he certainly looks more like a knight than a monk.

(Enter two merchants, who take off their cloaks. One of them lays a book on the table.)

Luther — May I ask, friend, what you are reading?

Merchant — Doctor Luther's sermons, just out; have you not seen them?

Luther — I shall soon, at any rate.

Host — Sit down, gentlemen, sit down; it is supper-time now.

Luther — Come here, gentlemen; I will stand treat. (The merchants sit down and supper is served.) These are bad times, gentlemen. I heard only recently of the princes and lords assembling at Nuremberg to settle the religious question and remedy the grievances of the German nation. What do they do? Nothing but waste their time in tournaments and all kinds of wicked diversions. They ought to pray earnestly to God. Fine princes they are! Let us hope that our children and posterity will be less poisoned by papal errors and more given to the truth than their parents, in whom error is so firmly implanted that it is hard to root out.

First Merchant — I am a plain, blunt man, look you, who understand little of this business, but I say to myself, as far as I can see, Luther must be either an angel from heaven or a devil from hell. I would give ten gulden to have the chance to confess to him; I believe he could give me good counsel for my conscience. (The merchants get up and go out to feed their horses.)

Host (to students) — You owe me nothing; Luther has paid it all.

Kessler — Thank you, sir, shall I say Hutten?

Luther — No, I am not he; (to host) I am made a noble to-night, for these Switzers take me for Ulrich von Hutten.

Host — You are not Hutten, but Martin Luther.

Luther (laughing) — They think I am Hutten; you that I am Luther; soon I'll be Prester John. (Raising his glass) Friends, I drink your health (putting down his glass), but wait a moment; host, bring us a measure of wine; the beer is not so good for me, as I am more accustomed to wine. (They drink.)

Luther (rising to say good-night and offering them his hand) — When you get to Wittenberg, remember me to Jerome Schurf.

Kessler — Whom shall we remember, sir?

Luther — Say only that he that will soon come sends his greetings. (Exit.)

The next morning Luther departed early. At Borna, where he arrived on March 5, he wrote his sovereign to apologize for his reference to the latter's hobby of relic-collecting, and to point out why he must go to Wittenberg even if Frederic could no longer protect him there: —

TO FREDERIC, ELECTOR OF SAXONY, AT LOCHAU

BORNA, March 5, 1522.

Favor and peace from God our Father and from the Lord Jesus Christ, and my humble service.

Most serene, highborn Prince, most gracious Lord! Your Grace's kind letter reached me Friday evening as I was about to depart the next day. I need not say that I know your Grace meant the best for me, for I am certain of it as far as a man can be of anything. Indeed my conviction of it is almost superhuman, but that makes no difference.

I take the liberty of supposing from your Grace's tone that my letter hurt you a little, but your Grace is wise enough to understand how I write. I have confidence that your Grace knows my heart better than to suppose I would insult your Grace's famous wisdom by unseemly words. I assure you with all my heart that I have always had a perfect and unaffected love for your Grace above all other princes and rulers. What I wrote was from anxiety to reassure your Grace, not for my own sake (of that I had no thought), but for the sake of the untoward movement at Wittenberg carried on by our friends to the detriment of the Evangelic cause. I feared that your Grace would suffer great inconvenience from it. The calamity also bore hard on me, so that, had I not been certain we had the pure gospel, I should have despaired. To my sorrow the movement has made a mockery of all the good that has been done and has brought it to naught. I would willingly buy the good cause with my life could I do so. Things are now done for which we can answer neither to God nor to man. They hang around my neck and offend the gospel and sadden my heart. My letter, most gracious Lord, was for those men, and not for myself, that your Grace might see the devil in the drama now enacting at Wittenberg. Although the admonition was unnecessary to your Grace, yet it was needful for me to write. As for myself, most gracious Lord, I answer thus: Your Grace knows (or, if you do not, I now inform you of the fact) that I have received my gospel not from men but from Heaven only, by our Lord Jesus Christ, so that I might well be able to boast and call myself a minister and evangelist, as I shall do in future. I offered to be tried and judged, not because I had doubts myself, but to convince others and from sheer humility. But now I see that my too great humility abases the gospel, and that if I yield a span the devil will take all. So I am conscientiously compelled to resist. I have obeyed your Grace this year [by staying at Wartburg] to please you. The devil knows I did not hide from cowardice, for he saw my heart when I entered Worms. Had I then believed that there were as many devils as tiles on the roof, I would have leaped into their midst with joy. Now Duke George is still far from being the equal of one devil. Since the Father of infinite mercy has by the gospel made us happy lords of all devils and of death, and has given us rich confidence to call him dearest Father, your Grace can see for yourself that it would be a deep insult to such a Father not to trust him, and that we are lords even of Duke George's wrath. I am fully persuaded that had I been called to Leipsic instead of Wittenberg, I should have gone there, even if (your Grace will excuse my foolish words) it had rained Duke Georges nine days and every duke nine times as furious as this one. He esteems my Lord Christ a man of straw, but my Lord and I can suffer that for a while. I will not conceal from your Grace that I have more than once wept and prayed for Duke George that God might enlighten him. I will pray and weep once more and then cease for ever. Will your Grace please pray, and have prayers said by others, that we may turn from him the judgment that (God knows) is always in wait for him. I could slay him with a single word.

I have written this to your Grace to inform you that I am going to Wittenberg under a far higher protection than that of the Elector. I do not intend to ask your Grace's protection. Indeed I think I shall protect you rather than you me. If I thought your Grace could and would defend me by force, I would not come. The sword ought not and cannot decide a matter of this kind. God alone must rule it without human care and coöperation. He who believes the most can protect the most, and as I see your Grace is yet weak in faith, I can by no means regard you as the man to protect and save me.

As your Grace desires to know what to do in this matter, and thinks you have done too little, I humbly answer that you have done too much and should do nothing. God will not and cannot suffer your interference nor mine. He wishes it left to himself; I say no more, your Grace can decide. If your Grace believes, you will be safe and have peace; if you do not believe, *I* do, and must leave your Grace's unbelief to its own torturing anxiety such as all unbelievers have to suffer. As I do not follow your advice and remain hidden, your Grace is excused before God if I am captured or put to death. Before men your Grace should act as a prince of the Empire and be obedient to your sovereign, and let his Imperial Majesty rule in your cities over both life and property, as is his right by the Imperial Constitution, and you should not offer any resistance in case he captures and puts me to death. No one should oppose authority save he who ordained it, otherwise it is rebellion and displeasing to God. But I hope they will have the good sense to recognize your Grace's lofty position and so not become my executioners themselves. If your Grace leaves them an open door and free passes, when they come you will have done enough for obedience. They can ask nothing more of your Grace than to inquire if Luther be with you, which will not put your Grace in peril or trouble. Christ has not taught me to be a Christian to injure others. If they are so unreasonable as to ask your Grace to lay hands upon me, I shall then tell your Grace what to do, always keeping your Grace safe from injury and peril in body, soul, or estate, as far as in me is — your Grace may then act as I advise or not as you please. . . .

Your Grace's humble subject,

MARTIN LUTHER.

Frederic answered this letter on March 7 with one to the Wittenberg jurist Schurf, bidding him request Luther to draw up a statement that he had only returned to quiet the tumults. The Reformer did as requested on March 9; the Elector was not quite satisfied and a new memorial was accordingly drawn up by Luther on March 12, which the Prince might submit to the Diet soon to assemble at Nuremberg. The reasons here given, and above all the immediate subsidence of tumult, completely satisfied that august body and prevented any measures being taken against the banned heretic or his protector.

CHAPTER XIII

CARLSTADT AND MÜNZER. 1522-1525

EVERY revolution has its extremists against whose unwise fanaticism the true reformer has to guard as carefully as he resists the abuses of hopeless reactionaries. Some revolutions fall under the sway of the radical party — Jacobins and Communists — and thus plunge into excesses which every true friend of progress must regret. The Reformation was no exception to the general rule ; it had its extreme left, — Anabaptists and ranters as they were then called, — and had it not been for the master brain in control, any one of several revolutionary parties claiming alliance with the Reformation might have obtained the ascendancy and swept it along to the ruin which overtook each in turn. Luther's insight, courage, and genius shone brighter in steering his ship clear of these rocks and shoals than they had when he first cut the ropes and set sail.

His task now was to restore order at Wittenberg. Arriving late on the afternoon of Thursday, March 6, he spent two days looking about and getting his bearings. The impression he made is faithfully recorded in a contemporary letter from Albert Burer to Beatus Rhenanus, Wittenberg, March 29 : —

Martin Luther returned to restore order clad as a knight and in the company of knights. . . . He is a man in whose face one may read benevolence, charity, and cheerfulness ; his voice is mild and mellow ; his delivery very graceful. Whoever has heard him once will desire to hear him again.

Luther lost no time in starting a vigorous campaign against the agitation. In eight sermons, on eight successive days, from March 9 to 16, risking his popularity as freely as he had his life, he exhorted the people to good sense, moderation, and above all to charity. In the first address, on the text, " All things are lawful unto me but all things are not expedient," he shows how much better it is to tolerate some usages which we regard as superfluous and unnecessary, for the sake of our brothers who are not so far advanced. Reform must begin with milk for babes, the pure doctrine of charity and faith, after which may come the strong meat of drastic law. True Christian liberty is not evinced by boasting how free we are from all law, but by showing how ready we are to serve our neighbors in love. On the second day he enunciated one of his fundamental principles with distinctness : —

Compel or force any one with power I will not, for faith must be gentle and unforced. Take an example by me. I opposed indulgences and all the papists, but not with force ; I only wrote, preached, and used God's Word, and nothing else. That Word, while I slept and drank beer with Melanchthon and Amsdorf, has broken the papacy more than any king or emperor ever broke it. Had I wished it, I might have brought Germany to civil war. Yes, at Worms I might have started a game which would not have been safe for the Emperor, but it would have been a fool's game. So I did nothing, but only let the Word act.

Having laid down his general principles, that mob violence is not the way to reform the Church, that sedition, even when provoked, is always wrong, and that the people in presuming to regulate spiritual matters usurp an office which does not belong to them, the preacher goes on in the following sermons to take up one by one the matters which have so much exercised the community — images, the monastic life, taking the sacrament in both kinds — and applies these principles to them. The eight sermons must be given a high place in the oratory not only of the pulpit but of the forum. They are filled with the spirit of the statesman as well as of the priest. They were completely successful. The lowering clouds before which his colleagues had stood gaping or which they had helped to raise vanished almost in a moment. Luther mentioned no names, but the leaders of the opposition were thoroughly discredited and left without a follower. Carlstadt sulked at home ; the prophets beat a hasty retreat.

On the day after his last sermon the Reformer wrote a letter to the parish priest at Zwickau, one of his most devoted followers, expounding his method of action clearly and concisely. The epistle is conceived in the spirit of Paul's advice to the Corinthians (1 Corinthians, viii) :

TO NICHOLAS HAUSMANN AT ZWICKAU

WITTENBERG, March 17, 1522.

Greeting. Dear Nicholas, although I am variously occupied by our great disturbances, I cannot omit writing to you. Your Zwickau prophets were about to bring forth monsters, which if born would have done no little damage. Their spirit is fair-seeming and very wily, but the Lord be with you. Amen.

Satan has attempted much evil here in my fold, and in such a manner that it is hard to oppose him without scandal. Be on your guard against all innovations made by public decree or popular agitation. What our friends attempt by force and violence must be resisted by word only, overcome by word and destroyed by word. It is Satan who urges us to extreme measures.

I condemn masses held as sacrifices and good works, but I would not lay hands on those who are unwilling to give them up or on those who are doubtful about them, nor would I prevent them by force. I condemn by word only ; whoso believes, let him believe and follow, whoso does not believe, let him not believe and depart. No one is to be compelled to the faith or to the things that are of faith, but to be drawn by word that he may believe and come of his own accord. I condemn images, but only by word, saying not that they should be burned, but that faith should not be placed in them, as hitherto has been done and is yet done. They will fall of themselves when the instructed people learn that they are nothing before God. In like manner I condemn the Pope's laws about confession, communion, prayer and fasting, but by word, that I may free consciences from them. While their consciences are freed, they may use such things for the sake of the weaker brethren who are entangled in them, and then may cease to use them as they wax strong, so that charity may be the rule in external usages and laws.

Nothing vexes me more than this multitude, which abandons Scripture, faith, and charity, and boasts that it is Christian only because in the presence of weaker brethren it is able to eat flesh on Fridays, commune in both kinds, and stop fasting and prayer. . . . But all things are to be proved by Scripture and hearts are to be helped little by little like Jacob's sheep, that they may first receive the word of their own accord and afterwards grow stronger. . . .

Yours,

MARTIN LUTHER.

Early in April Luther consented to hear the prophets in their own defence, of which he later gave the following report : —

In 1522 [1] Mark Storch [2] came to me with sweet, seductive words to lay his doctrine before me. As he presumed to teach things not in Scripture I said to him : "I will not agree with that part of your doctrine unsupported by Scripture unless you work miracles to prove it." . . . He said : "You shall see miracles in seven years." (These words were from Satan who soon after instigated the Peasants' Revolt.) He presumptuously continued : "God will not take away my power. I can tell whether a man will be saved or not." — But Satan cannot remain hidden : his speech bewrayeth him. Storch had wonderful phrases, "illumination, quietism," and the like.[3] I asked him what he meant by these words, but he said he would not preach to inept disciples. I asked him how he knew the inept from the apt. He replied : "I can tell what sort of a talent a man has." I asked : "My dear Mark, what sort of a talent have I ?" He answered : "You are in the first degree of mobility, but you will soon be in the first degree of immobility," — in which I am.

After pacifying Wittenberg, Luther visited Weimar, Erfurt, and other neighboring places, preaching with great success against fanaticism and sedition.

But the battle was not to be so easily won. The ranters, driven from the neighborhood of Wittenberg, fled to other places, where they propagated the same doctrines. Thomas Münzer, the great original agitator, after his expulsion from

---

[1] Text 1521 (Bindseil, ii, 21). This is a mistake. The prophets did not arrive in Wittenberg until December 27, 1521. Cf. Enders, iii, 331.

[2] The names of the prophets are confused : Nicholas Storch and Mark Thomae Stübner.

[3] *Langweiligkeit*, translated quietism, refers to the doctrine of the mystics that the way to know God was to wait for him in absolute vacancy of thought. These phrases of the mystics recall Sir Thomas Browne's description of the mystic doctrine in *Urn-Burial :* "Christian annihilation, extasis, exolution, liquefaction, transformation, the kisse of the Spouse, gustation of God, and ingression into the divine shadow."

Zwickau and visit to Bohemia, settled in the little Saxon town of Allstedt, where he soon won followers. Images were broken down, infant baptism abolished, dreams systematically cultivated as a means of communication with God, laws reducing the interest and providing for the periodical repudiation of the principal of debt were passed and the right to hold private property was questioned. Worse yet, a campaign of fire and sword against the "godless," including papists and Lutherans alike, was preached with all the violence of fanaticism. The peasants streamed in from the surrounding country, armed and on the verge of rebellion. Seeing that an appeal to reason could no longer be made, Luther wrote the following letter to the Elector and his brother, who were hesitating whether to attack the wolf of rebellion masquerading under the sheeps' clothing of religious reform : —

TO THE ELECTOR FREDERIC AND DUKE JOHN OF SAXONY

(WITTENBERG, July,) 1524.

Grace and peace in Christ Jesus our Saviour. God's holy Word, when it arises, always has the good fortune to excite Satan with all his might against itself. At first the devil rages with his fist and wicked power, then, if that does no good, he attacks with false tongues and extravagant spirits and doctrines, so that what he could not crush with power he may suffocate with venomous lies. . . . Now Satan knows that the rage of Pope and Emperor will accomplish nothing against us; yea, he feels that, as is the way with God's Word, the more it is pressed down the more it spreads and grows, and therefore he now attacks it with false spirits and sects. We must therefore consider and not err, for it must be so, as Paul says to the Corinthians: "There must also be heresies among you that they which are approved may be made manifest." And so, as Satan driven out has now wandered two or three years through dry places, seeking rest and finding none, he has at last settled in your Graces' electorate, and made himself a nest at Allstedt, and thinks under our peace, protection, and guardianship to fight against us. For Duke George's principality, although it is our next neighbor, is, as they themselves boast, too favorable and gentle for such a bold and dauntless spirit, so that the sectaries cannot there show their courage and confidence, wherefore the bad spirit cries out and complains terribly that he must suffer much, although no one has yet attacked him with sword or tongue or pen, and they only dream that they are bearing a cross. So frivolously and causelessly must Satan lie, though he can thereby deceive no one.

Now it is an especial joy that our followers did not begin this heresy, as the sectaries themselves boast that they did not learn it from us, but directly from Heaven and that they hear God speak to them immediately as to the angels. It is a simple fact that at Wittenberg only faith, love, and the cross of Christ are taught. God's voice, they say, you must hear yourself, and suffer and feel God's work in you to know your own weight; aye, they make nothing of the Scripture, which they call " Bible-bubble-Babel." To judge by what they say their cross and passion is greater than Christ's and more to be prized. . . .

The sole reason for my inditing this letter to your Graces is that I have gathered from the writings of these people, that this same spirit will not be satisfied to make converts by word only, but intends to betake himself to arms and set himself with power against the government, and forthwith raise a riot. Here Satan lets the cat out of the bag, that is, makes public too much. What will this spirit do, when he has won the support of the mob? Truly here at Wittenberg I have heard from the same spirit that his business must be carried through with the sword. I then marked that their plans would come out, namely, to overturn the civil government and themselves become lords of the world. But Christ says his kingdom is not of this world, and teaches the apostles not to be as the rulers of the earth. So although I am aware that your Graces will understand how to act in this matter better than I can advise you, nevertheless it is my humble duty to do my part, and humbly to pray and warn your Graces to fulfil your duty as civil governors by preventing mischief and by forestalling rebellion. Your Graces may rest assured in your consciences that your power and rule was given and commended to you by God, that you might preserve the peace and punish those who break it, as St. Paul teaches in Romans. Therefore your Graces should neither sleep nor be idle, for God will demand an answer and reckoning from you for a careless or spiritless use of the sword. Moreover your Graces could not excuse yourselves before the people and the world if you allowed rebellion and crimes of violence to make headway.

If they give out, as they are wont to do with their swelling words, that the spirit drives them on to attempt force, then I answer thus: It is a bad spirit which shows no other fruit than burning churches, cloisters, and images, for the worst rascals on earth can do as much.

... Secondly ... that it is a bad spirit which dares not give an answer. ... for I, poor, miserable man, did not so act in my doctrine. ... I went to Leipsic to debate before a hostile audience. At Augsburg I appeared without safe-conduct before my worst enemy. I went to Worms to answer to the Emperor and Diet, although I well knew that they had broken my safe-conduct, and planned all manner of evil against me. ...

If they will do more than propagate their doctrines by word, if they attempt force, your Graces should say: We gladly allow any one to teach by word, that the right doctrine may be preserved; but draw not the sword, which is ours; if you do, you must leave the country. ...

Now I will close for this time, having humbly prayed your Graces to act vigorously against their storming and ranting, that God's kingdom may be advanced by word only, as becomes Christians, and that all cause of sedition be taken from the multitude (Herr Omnes) which is more than enough inclined to it already. For they are not Christians who would go beyond the word and appeal to force, even if they boast that they are full of holy spirits. God's mercy eternally strengthen and preserve your Graces. Amen.

Yours Graces' obedient,

DR. MARTIN LUTHER.

This letter "against the Satan of Allstedt," as Luther called him, was published, and Münzer summoned by the Elector to a conference with its author at Weimar. The fanatic feared to obey, and fled to the city of Mühlhausen, continuing, always and everywhere, his revolutionary agitation, and breathing out slaughter and reviling against "that archheathen, archrascal, Wittenberg pope, snake, and basilisk."

Carlstadt, too, continued his iconoclastic career. Unable to bear the peaceful atmosphere of Wittenberg, he had himself elected to the church at Orlamünde. Here he advanced ideas similar to those of Münzer, except that he refused to appeal to arms, thereby winning the opinion of that ranter that he was a coward and a reprobate. His reforms included the introduction of polygamy and the advocacy of a new doctrine of the sacrament. Luther, who was inclined to condone the former, as not forbidden by the Bible, vehemently objected to the latter as heretical. Discussion of this doctrine is reserved for a later chapter.

Notwithstanding Carlstadt's errors, the Reformer was not ready to break with him as soon as he had with Münzer. On August 22, 1524, the two had a conference at Jena, and parted with a friendly agreement to differ. "The more ably you attack me," said Luther, "the better I shall like it," and gave his old colleague a gold gulden as a sign that he was free to advance what opinions he liked so long as they were supported by argument only and not by violence. In accordance with this invitation, the pastor of Orlamünde began a work on the sacrament, but soon the order came to him, September 18, to leave Saxony. He went to Basel, and early in November published several pamphlets against Luther, defending his doctrine of the sacrament, denying the expediency of infant baptism, asserting that he had direct communications from God, and charging his opponent with having been responsible for his exile. These tracts excited a good deal of attention. Zwingli, a far abler head than Carlstadt, adopted his doctrine of the eucharist, and Capito, a reformer of Strassburg, wrote a pamphlet trying to harmonize the two opponents, which was the cause of Luther's letter to the Christians of that city, warning them against false doctrine. His animus against his old colleague was increased both by his pamphlets and by an experience at Orlamünde described in this epistle : —

TO THE CHRISTIANS OF STRASSBURG

(WITTENBERG, December 14, 1524.)

. . . Certain of your clergy have written about the outcry made by Dr. Carlstadt with his ranting about images and the sacrament and baptism, and that he reviles me with having driven him from Saxony. Now, dear friends, I am not your preacher and no one is bound to believe me . . . but I hope you have seen in my writings how simply and certainly I treat the gospel, the grace of Christ, the law, faith, love, the cross, doctrines of men, the Pope, and monastic vows. . . . Of these main articles of faith Carlstadt has not rightly set forth one, nor can he. Now that I look into his writings I am simply shocked to find out, what I did not before suspect, that the man is still in such deep darkness. It looks to me as if he thought the whole of Christianity lay in breaking images and hindering the sacrament. . . . I might stand his raging iconoclasm, for I have been more iconoclastic by my writing than he by his raging, but what is not to be borne is his imputation that all who do not do as he bids are not Christians. . . .

I can bear the charge of Carlstadt that I drove him out of the land. Were it true I could answer to God for it. . . .

He himself persuaded me at Jena not to confound his spirit with the seditious, murderous spirit of Allstedt. But when, at the Elector's behest, I went to his "Christians" at Orlamünde, I saw what seed he had sown and was glad to escape safe, being driven away with stones and mud, the inhabitants giving me their blessing with the words: "Go hence in the name of a thousand devils, lest you have your neck broken before you leave." . . .

I beg your preachers, dear brethren, to leave Luther and Carlstadt and point only to Christ, and not as Carlstadt does only to the work of Christ, and the example of Christ, which was the least part of his mission, in which he was like other saints, but to Christ as the gift of God, or, as Paul says, the strength of God, wisdom, righteousness, sanctification, and redemption, given to us, which these "prophets" have not tasted nor understood. They juggle with "their living voice from Heaven," and their "ecstasy, illumination, mortification," and such bombastic words which they do not understand themselves, though by them they make consciences heavy while men wonder at their great art and forget Christ. . . .

Shortly after writing this letter Luther published a comprehensive work Against the Heavenly Prophets of Images and the Sacrament, the first part of which appeared late in December, the second half early in January, 1525. In the first part he says : —

We should be very careful to distinguish and widely to separate fundamentals concerning the conscience and things indifferent concerning outward works. . . . These ambitious prophets do nothing but smash images, break into churches, lord it over the sacrament, and seek new ways of mortification, that is, of self-inflicted death of the flesh. They have not yet learned nor preached the doctrine of faith and how to rule the conscience, which is the principal and most necessary Christian doctrine. Suppose that they succeeded in leaving no more images and no churches standing, and suppose that they persuaded every one in all the world not to believe that Christ's flesh and blood were in the sacrament, and suppose all dressed in gray, peasants' clothes, what would they gain by all this ? . . . Would

they be Christians thereby? Where would be faith and love?—
Pictures are defended as a help to the faith of the ignorant.

Luther denies Carlstadt's charge that he has been at the
bottom of the latter's exile. He brings against him the counter-
charges, first, of neglecting the duties of a professor for which
he was paid, and secondly, of exciting sedition, for either of
which he might justly have been sent away. "These prophets
teach that the reform of Christendom should start with a
slaughter of the godless, that they themselves may be lords of
the earth. I myself have heard this from them, and Dr. Carlstadt knows that they are ranting and murderous spirits. . . .
For those who preach murder can have no other origin than
the devil himself, even if they have all wisdom and know the
Bible, for the devil also knows the Bible well. Is it not a
plague that people should be moved by such spirits before the
princes know aught of it, and that the populace is thereby
made presumptuous and turbulent?"

The second part is on the doctrine of the Lord's Supper,
Carlstadt's arguments being answered one by one.

The work had great notoriety but little success. The Strass-
burgers were rather alienated by it and inclined to side with
the exile. Public attention was soon drawn from the quarrel
of Luther and the prophets to a far larger movement in which
it was swallowed up, the Peasants' Revolt.

Before describing that important event, let us glance at the
latter end of Carlstadt. The death of Münzer and other agitators, in the defeat of the peasants, made him fear for his life.
Not knowing where to turn, he went back to Wittenberg and
besought a refuge with the Reformer. From near the first of
July till late in September he was sheltered by his old colleague and opponent, who wrote a letter to the Elector, on September 12, asking him to allow Carlstadt to live peaceably at
Kemberg. This petition was refused; the fanatic had to leave,
and wandered long from place to place, until at last he became
professor in the University of Basel. He had learned his lesson
and never more was a political agitator.

CHAPTER XIV

PEASANT risings were not uncommon in Europe for more than a millennium. Such an insurrection had taken place in Gaul in Roman times. Such were the Jacquerie in France in 1358 and the gigantic strike of English laborers in 1381. The struggle for Swiss freedom also may be viewed as a social as well as a national conflict. The fifteenth and early sixteenth centuries saw many local revolts. To the old standing grievances of the lords' tyranny, the heavy taxes and tithes, the game laws, the corvée and serfdom, common causes of all these risings alike, new motives were added to make this last the most terrible, among them the prevalent intellectual unrest and the powerful leaven of the new religious teaching.

Luther, indeed, could honestly say that he had consistently preached the duty of obedience and the wickedness of sedition, nevertheless his democratic message of the brotherhood of man and the excellence of the humblest Christian worked in many ways undreamed of by himself. Moreover, he had mightily championed the cause of the oppressed commoner against his masters. " The people neither can nor will endure your tyranny any longer," said he to the nobles; " God will not endure it; the world is not what it once was when you drove and hunted men like wild beasts." Other preachers, among whom Carlstadt and Münzer were two conspicuous examples, took up the word and carried it to the wildest conclusions of communism and anarchy.

Beginning in the autumn of 1524, in the highlands between the sources of the Rhine and the Danube, the rebellion swept north through Franconia and Swabia. The demands of the insurgents were embodied in the Twelve Articles, drawn up not later than February, 1525, by a Swabian, Sebastian Lotzer, and tacitly adopted as the official programme by most of the bands of rustics. The fundamental principle of this document is the entire assimilation of civil and divine law; all claims are supported by an appeal to the gospel, under which rule the insurgents declare their intention to live. The articles propose the free election by each parish of its pastor, the reduction of taxes and tithes, the abolition of serfdom, freedom to hunt, fish, and cut wood in the forests, less forced labor, reopening of commons to the public, substitution of the old (German) for the new (Roman) law, and abolition of the heriot.

Continuing to spread, the insurrection reached Thuringia and Saxony about April, 1525. In this region all eyes were turned to Luther, the man of the people. In one pamphlet, dated March 7, the peasants requested him, together with Melanchthon, Bugenhagen, and the Elector Frederic to act as arbitrators between them and the lords. As yet Luther had not heard of the atrocities committed by some of the rebels. But there was danger in the air. At the invitation of his old lord, Count Albert of Mansfeld, he journeyed to Eisleben to investigate the situation. Here, while the guest of Chancellor Dürr, on April 19 and 20, he composed An Exhortation to Peace on the Twelve Articles of the Swabian Peasants. By this warning, which he states is written in answer to the request of the insurgents for instruction, he hoped to bring both sides to reason and prevent the effusion of blood. He addresses each party by turns, the lords and the commoners. To the former he says : —

" We need thank no one on earth for this foolish rebellion but you, my lords, and especially you blind bishops, parsons and monks, for you, even yet hardened, cease not to rage against the holy gospel, although you know that our cause is right and you cannot controvert it. Besides this, in civil government you do nothing but oppress and tax to maintain your pomp and pride, until the poor common man neither can nor will bear it any longer. The sword is at your throat, and yet you still think you sit so firm in the saddle that no one can hoist you out. You will find out that by such hardened presumption you will break your necks. . . . If these peasants don't do it, others will; God will appoint others, for he intends to smite you and will smite you."

Some say the rebellion has been caused by Luther's doctrine, but he avers that he has always taught obedience to the powers that be. " But the prophets of murder are hostile to you as to me, and they have gone among the people these three years and no one has withstood them but I."

Some of the peasants' articles are right, as the demand to choose their own pastors and the repudiation of the heriot.

To the peasantry he says : —

"It is my friendly and fraternal prayer, dearest brothers, to be very careful what you do. Believe not all spirits and preachers." Those who take the sword shall perish by the sword and every soul should be subject to the powers that be, in fear and honor. "If the government is bad and intolerable, that is no excuse for riot and insurrection, for to punish evil belongs not to every one, but to the civil authority which bears the sword." Suffering tyranny is a cross given by God. Luther will pray for them.

Coming to a consideration of the Twelve Articles he says that even if they were all just, the peasants would have no right to put them through by force. The first article, for the right to elect pastors, is right. The second demand, that the tithes be divided between the priest and the poor, is simple robbery, for the tithes belong to the government. The third, for the abolition of serfdom on the ground that Christ has freed all, makes Christian freedom a carnal thing and is therefore unjustified. The other eight articles (that on the heriot having been already approved) are referred to the lawyers.

The pamphlet closes with a solemn charge to each side to strive not for its own gain, but for the right, and a warning to keep the peace.

Excellent as were Luther's intentions, his exhortation was imprudently expressed. In any case, however, interference came too late. Already on April 16, the rebel bands had stormed Weinsberg and massacred the inhabitants; within the next two weeks cloisters and castles were burned to the ground, while violence, anarchy, and rapine followed with all the ferocity characteristic of class warfare. The nobles made what terms they could; the towns either capitulated or joined the rising in full force. At Mühlhausen, Münzer, thinking the hour of triumph had come, urged the divine duty of ruthless slaughter.

The princes were entirely unprepared. Old Frederic was lying mortally ill at his castle of Lochau. Without troops and unnerved by disease, he wrote his brother John that if it was God's will that the common man should rule he would not resist it. John, too, was without hope: " There are thirty-five thousand men in the field against us," he wrote; "we are but lost princes."

For one awful moment it looked as if the insurgents would carry all before them. Luther saw the whole of Germany threatened with anarchy, and the Evangelic cause with extinction. Never found wanting in the hour of danger, he continued his journey through the disaffected districts, preaching against the rising. According to the somewhat unreliable table-talk he met with a hostile reception at some places; at any rate his intervention did no good. He found himself, on May 4, at Seeburg, in Mansfeld. Not a single blow had yet been struck in the cause of order. Luther saw that the only means left to restore peace was force, and accordingly wrote the following stern letter to one of the councillors of the Count of Mansfeld : —

TO JOHN RÜHEL AT MANSFELD

SEEBURG, May 4, 1525.

Grace and peace in Christ. Honored and dear doctor and friend! I have been intending to answer your last tidings, recently shown me, here on my journey. First of all I beg you not to make our gracious lord, Count Albert, weak in this matter, but let him go on as he has begun, though it will only make the devil still angrier, so that he will rage more than ever through those limbs of Satan he has possessed. We have God's Word, which lies not but says, " He beareth not the sword in vain, etc.," so there is no doubt that his lordship has been ordained and commanded of God. His Grace will need the sword to punish the wicked as long as there are such sores in the body politic as now exist. Should the sword be struck out of his Grace's hand by force, we must suffer it, and give it back to God, who first gave it and can take it back how and when he will.

May his Grace also have a good conscience in case he should have to die for God's Word, for God has so ordered it, if he permits it ; no one should leave off the good work until he is prevented by force, just as in battle no one should forego an advantage or leave off fighting until he is overcome.

If there were thousands more peasants than there are they would all be robbers and murderers, who take the sword with criminal intent to drive out lords, princes, and all else, and make a new order in the world for which they have from God neither command, right, power, nor injunction, as the lords now have to suppress them. They are faithless and perjured, and still worse they bring the Divine Word and gospel to shame and dishonor, a most horrible sin. If God in his wrath really lets them accomplish their purpose, for which he has given them no command nor right, we must suffer it as we do other wickedness, but not acquiesce in it as if they did right.

I hope they will have no success nor staying power, although God at times plagues the world with desperate men as he has done and yet does with the Turks. It is the devil's mockery that the peasants give out that they will hurt no one and do no harm. No harm to drive out and kill their masters? If they mean no harm, why do they gather in hordes and demand that others surrender to them? To do no harm and yet to take all — that is what the devil, too, knows how to do. If we let him do what he likes, forsooth he harms no one.

Their only reason for driving out their lords is pure wickedness. Look at the government they have set up, the worst that ever was, without order or discipline in it but only pillage. If God wishes to chastize us in his wrath, he can find no fitter instrument than these enemies of his, criminals, robbers, murderers, faithless, perjured peasants. If it be God's will, let us suffer it and call them lords as the Scripture calls the devil prince and lord. May God keep all good Christians from honoring and worshipping them as the devil tried to make Christ worship him. Let us withstand them by word and deed as long as ever we can and then die for it in God's name.

They purpose to hurt no one if only we yield to them; and so we should yield to them, should we? Must we indeed acknowledge as our rulers these faithless, perjured, blasphemous robbers, who have no right from God, but only the support of the prince of this world, as he boasts in Matthew, chapter four, that he has dominion and honor over all the world to give it to whom he will? That is true enough when God punishes and does not protect.

This matter concerns me deeply, for the devil wishes to kill me. I see that he is angry that hitherto he has been able to accomplish nothing either by fraud or force; he thinks that if he were only free of

me he could do as he liked and confound the whole world together, so
I almost believe that I am the cause that the devil can do such things
in the world, whereby God punishes it. Well, if I ever get home I will
meet my death with God's aid, and await my new masters, the murderers and robbers who tell me they will harm no one. Highway robbers always say the same : "I will do you no harm, but give me all
you have or you shall die." Beautiful innocence ! How fairly the devil
decks himself and his murderers ! Before I would yield and say what
they want, I would lose my head a hundred times, God granting me
his grace. If I can do it before I die, I will yet take my Katie to wife
to spite the devil, when I hear that they are after me. I hope they
will not take away my joy and good spirits.

Some say the insurgents are not followers of Münzer — that let their
own god believe, for no one else will.

I write to strengthen you to strengthen others, especially my gracious
lord Count Albert. Encourage his Grace to go forth with good spirit,
and may God grant him success, and let him fulfil the divine injunction to bear the sword as long as ever he can ; conscience at least is
safe in case he fall. If God permit the peasants to extirpate the princes
to fulfil his wrath, he will give them hell fire for it as a reward. The
just judge will come shortly to judge both them and us — us with
grace, as we have suffered by their crimes of violence, them with wrath,
for they who take the sword must perish by the sword as Christ said.
Their work and success cannot long stand.

Greet your dear wife for me.

DR. MARTIN LUTHER.

Very soon after writing this letter, Luther published a short
tract Against the Thievish, Murderous Hordes of Peasants,
expressed in much the same tone : —

"In my former book" (Exhortation to Peace) he writes, "I dared
not judge the peasants, since they asked to be instructed, and Christ
says Judge not. But before I could look around they forget their request and betake themselves to violence, — rob, rage, and act like mad
dogs, whereby one may see what they had in their false minds, and
that their pretence to speak in the name of the gospel in the Twelve
Articles was a simple lie. They do mere devil's work, especially that
Satan of Mühlhausen does nothing but rob, murder, and pour out
blood."

The peasants have deserved death for three reasons : (1) because they have broken their oath of fealty; (2) for rioting and plundering; and (3) for having covered their terrible sins with the name of the gospel. " Wherefore, my lords, free, save, help, and pity the poor people; stab, smite, and slay, all ye that can. If you die in battle you could never have a more blessed end, for you die obedient to God's Word in Romans 13, and in the service of love to free your neighbor from the bands of hell and the devil. I implore every one who can to avoid the peasants as he would the devil himself. I pray God will enlighten them and turn their hearts. But if they do not turn, I wish them no happiness for ever more. . . . Let none think this too hard who considers how intolerable is rebellion."

Almost as Luther was writing, steps were taken to suppress the insurgents. On May 5 the Count of Mansfeld, with a few personal retainers, scattered a small band near Osterhausen, a success insignificant in itself but important as the first blow struck for order in central Germany.

The decisive battle followed not long after. Philip of Hesse, the ablest of the Evangelic princes after Frederic the Wise, having come to terms with his own peasants by negotiation, gathered an army and marched, in coöperation with other lords, against eight thousand rebels at Frankenhausen. Hoping to come to a peaceful agreement, Philip found the peasants ready to negotiate until on May 12 Münzer arrived with reënforcements from Mühlhausen and roused the poor men by his baleful eloquence to such a pitch of fanaticism, that, in reliance on divine help, they refused all terms. When the troops attacked them on May 15, the raw countrymen fled in the wildest panic, more than half of them perishing on the field. Münzer was captured and put to death.

Rühel sent the tidings to Luther on May 21, and received the following answer: —

TO JOHN RÜHEL AT MANSFELD

WITTENBERG, May 23, 1525.

God's grace and peace. I thank you, honored and dear sir, for your news. I am especially pleased at the fall of Thomas Münzer. Please let me have further details of his capture and of how he acted, for it is important to know how that proud spirit bore itself.

It is pitiful that we have to be so cruel to the poor people, but what can we do? It is necessary and God wills it that fear may be brought on the people. Otherwise Satan brings forth mischief. God said: Who hath taken the sword shall perish by the sword. It is gratifying that their spirit be at last so plainly revealed, so that henceforth the peasants will know how wrong they were and perhaps leave off rioting, or at least do it less. Do not be troubled about the severity of their suppression, for it will profit many souls. . . .

After the lords had the upper hand the insurrection was put down with the utmost cruelty. At Frankenhausen and elsewhere the soldiers far outdid the peasants in acts of violence and blood. It is estimated that one hundred thousand of the poor rustics perished, and the rest sank back into a more wretched state than before.

The danger past and the pity of the public aroused, Luther's enemies raised a great outcry against him, accusing him of betraying his allies and the men whom his teaching had misguided, and most of all for the cruelty of his pamphlet. Whatever foundation these charges may have, there is absolutely none in the accusation that he sided with the insurgents while they seemed likely to win and then turned to curry favor with the princes when *they* had triumphed. The direct opposite was the truth, and Luther, excited by these widespread charges, defends himself with spirit in a letter to an old colleague.

TO NICHOLAS AMSDORF AT MAGDEBURG

WITTENBERG, May 30, 1525.

Grace and peace. You write of a new honor for me, dear Amsdorf, namely that I am called the toady of the princes; Satan has conferred many such honors upon me during the past years. . . .

My opinion is that it is better that all the peasants be killed than that the princes and magistrates perish, because the rustics took the sword without divine authority. The only possible consequence of their satanic wickedness would be the diabolic devastation of the kingdom of God. Even if the princes abuse their power, yet they have it of God, and under their rule the kingdom of God at least has a chance to exist. Wherefore no pity, no tolerance should be shown to the peasants, but the fury and wrath of God should be visited upon those men who did not heed warning nor yield when just terms were offered them, but continued with satanic fury to confound every-thing. . . . To justify, pity, or favor them is to deny, blaspheme, and try to pull God from heaven. . . .

Thus also, in a note inviting John Rühel to his wedding feast, the Reformer says (June 15, 1526): "What an outcry of Harrow has been caused by my pamphlet against the peasants. All is now forgotten that God has done for the world through me. Now lords, priests, and peasants are all against me and threaten my death."

Rühel accepted the invitation and brought with him a letter from the Chancellor Caspar Müller suggesting that the Reformer should defend himself against the attacks made upon him. In answer to this Luther published in July an open letter to Müller, under the title: On the Hard Pamphlet against the Peasants. In this he has nothing to retract. "One cannot answer a rebel with reason," he argues, "but the best answer is to hit him with the fist until blood flows from his nose." (Mit der faust mus man solchen meulern antworten, das der schweys zur nasen ausgehe.) He never meant to urge slaughter after battle, "but neither did I undertake to instruct those mad, rag-ing, insane tyrants, who even after combat cannot satiate their thirst for blood and never in their whole life long ask after Christ, for it is all the same to such bloodhounds whether they are guilty or innocent, or whether they please God or the devil. They use the sword to satisfy their passions, so I leave them to their master the devil."

That Luther really pitied the poor people after their defeat is shown by an intercessory letter: —

TO ALBERT, ARCHBISHOP AND ELECTOR OF MAYENCE

(WITTENBERG,) July 21, 1525.

Grace and peace in Jesus Christ. Most venerable Father in God, most serene, highborn Prince, most gracious Lord. I am informed that one Asmus Günthel, the son of a citizen of Eisleben, has been arrested by your Grace on the charge of having stormed a barricade. His father is sore distressed and tells me he did not take part in the storming, but only ate and drank there at the time, and as he begged me piteously to intercede for his life I could not refuse him. I humbly pray your Grace to consider that this insurrection has been put down not by the hand of man but by the grace of God who pities us all, and especially those in authority, and that accordingly you treat the poor people graciously and mercifully as becomes a spiritual lord even more than a temporal one. . . .

Alas! there are too many who treat the people horribly and so act unthankfully to God as if they would recklessly awaken the wrath of Heaven and of the people again and provoke a new and worse rebellion. God has decreed that those who show no mercy should also perish without mercy.

It is not good for a lord to raise displeasure, ill-will and hostility among his subjects, and it is likewise foolish to do so. It is right to show sternness when the commonalty are seditious and stubborn, but now that they are beaten down they are a different people, worthy that mercy be shown them in judgment. Putting too much in a bag bursts it. Moderation is good in all things, and, as St. James says, mercy rejoiceth against judgment. I hope your Grace will act as a Christian in this matter. God bless you. Amen.

Your Grace's obedient servant,

MARTIN LUTHER.

The Peasants' War was the hardest storm weathered by the new Church. Had not an iron hand been at the helm it might well have foundered the ship of reform and scattered all that was hopeful and good in it in a thousand fragments. As it was, the cause suffered heavily, and the reputation of its leader suffered still more. In steering too far from the dread whirlpool which would have engulfed all his cause, he sailed too close to the Scylla on the other side and lost men thereby. From his own day to the present he has been reproached with cruelty to the poor people who were partly misguided by what they believed to be his voice. And yet, much as the admirers of Luther must and do regret his terrible violence of expression, the impartial historian can hardly doubt that in substance he was right. No government in the world could have allowed rebellion to go unpunished; no sane man could believe that any argument but arms would have availed. Luther first tried the way of peace, he then risked his life preaching against the rising; finally he urged the use of the sword as the ultima ratio. He was right to do so, though he put himself in the wrong by his immoderate zeal. It would have been more becoming for Luther, the peasant and the hero of the peasants, had he shown greater sympathy with their cause and more mercy. Had he done so his name would have escaped the charge of cruelty with which it is now stained.

CHAPTER XV

CATHARINE VON BORA

FROM fierce war Luther's thoughts were turned to faithful, if unromantic love. Although convinced while still at the Wartburg of the nullity of vows of celibacy, it was a long time, as Erasmus sneered, before he made use of the liberty he preached to others. After all the brothers save one, Brisger, had departed to take up a worldly career, he continued to reside at the Black Cloister, as the Augustinian monastery was called, not from its own color, a brick red, but from the popular designation of its dark-robed inmates as black monks. Having laid aside their cowls and assumed the simple garb of laymen, the two like-minded men dwelt here with one servant, a student of theology named Sieberger. The building was large, but as the revenues had been dissipated by the custom of giving a handsome present to each departing brother, the two remaining inhabitants dwelt in poverty, for the professor had a salary of but one hundred gulden. One of his reminiscences of this period paints a speaking picture of his manner of life: —

Before I was married, the bed was not made up for a whole year and became foul with sweat. But I worked all day and was so tired at night that I fell into bed without knowing that anything was amiss.

When at last he decided to marry, it was something of an accident that his choice fell upon Catharine von Bora. She had been born, on January 29, 1499, at Lippendorf, a hamlet some twenty miles south of Leipsic. The name Bora (cognate in form and meaning with our word *fir*) is, like that of Staupitz and other aristocratic families of the region, of Wendish or Slavonic origin, but the family, deriving its name from the village of Bora, was Teutonic. Catharine's father, Hans von Bora, held modest estates, a portion of which, the farm of Zulsdorf, later passed by purchase to his famous son-in-law. The mother,

Catharine von Haugwitz, died shortly after the birth of her little girl, and Hans, marrying again, sent his five-year-old daughter to the convent school of the Benedictine nuns near Brehna. About four years later he transferred her to a Cistercian cloister at Nimbschen near Grimma, intending that in due time she should become a nun. Nimbschen was a wealthy foundation in which the education of the girls and their taking of the veil were gratuitous; it was therefore largely patronized by gentlemen like Bora of more influence than means. At the time of her entrance, one of her relatives was abbess, and another, Auntie Lena, as she afterwards came to be known at Wittenberg, was a sister.

The quiet years at Nimbschen, hardly broken by Catharine's consecration as a nun at the age of sixteen (October 8, 1515), were spent in the round of devotion, learning and teaching, prayer and charity, which form the routine of monastic life. The girl was well educated; besides the elementary accomplishments of reading and writing her own tongue (not so common then as now), she knew some Latin. The cloister had large estates, tilled under the direct supervision of the nuns, so that she may have here gained that knowledge of practical farming which she later turned to good account.

In almost any other age and country, Catharine would have finished her life in the convent as quietly as she had begun it. But she lived in stirring times. Luther's proclamation of monastic emancipation was promptly followed by a general evacuation of the cloisters, especially those of his own order, one of which was situated at Grimma. Inspired by the example of these monks several of the sisters at Nimbschen tried to follow it. One who was caught writing to Luther was severely disciplined. This did not prevent the others from doing the same, and it was at his advice that, after vainly applying to their relatives to receive them, twelve of the younger nuns secured the aid of Leonard Coppe, a wealthy and honorable burger of Torgau who had long stood in business relations with Nimbschen. Though the attempt was not without danger, for the abduction of a nun was a capital offence, he, with the assistance of his nephew and another young man, helped them to escape on the night of April

4–5, 1523. Three of them went to their own homes, the other nine were conveyed by Coppe first to Torgau and then to Wittenberg.

The Reformer, who at once took up their cause, defending them in a publication, announces their arrival in these words: —

TO GEORGE SPALATIN AT ALTENBURG

WITTENBERG, April 10, 1523.

Grace and peace. Nine fugitive nuns, a wretched crowd, have been brought to me by honest citizens of Torgau. I mean Leonard Coppe and his nephew Wolf Tomitzsch; there is therefore no cause for suspicion. I pity them much, but most of all the others who are dying everywhere in such numbers in their cursed and impure celibacy. This sex so very, very weak, joined by nature or rather by God to the other, perishes when cruelly separated. O tyrants! O cruel parents and kinsmen in Germany! O Pope and bishops, who can curse you enough? Who can sufficiently execrate the blind fury which has taught and enforced such things? But this is not the place to do it.

You ask what I shall do with them? First I shall inform their relatives and ask them to support the girls; if they will not I shall have the girls otherwise provided for. Some of the families have already promised me to take them; for some I shall get husbands if I can. Their names are: Magdalene von Staupitz,[1] Elsa von Canitz, Ave Gross, Ave von Schönfeld and her sister Margaret, Laneta von Goltz, Margaret and Catharine Zeschau and Catharine von Bora. Here are they, who serve Christ, in need of true pity. They have escaped from the cloister in miserable condition. I pray you also to do the work of charity and beg some money for me from your rich courtiers, by which I can support the girls a week or two until their kinsmen or others provide for them. For my Capernaäns have no wealth but that of the Word, so that I myself could not find the loan of ten gulden for a poor citizen the other day. The poor, who would willingly give, have nothing; the rich either refuse or give so reluctantly that they lose the credit of the gift with God and take up my time begging from them. Nothing is too much for the world and its way. Of my annual salary I have only ten or fifteen gulden left, besides which not a penny has been given me by my brothers or by the city. But I ask them for nothing, to emulate the boast of Paul, despoiling other churches to serve my Corinthians free. . . .   Farewell and pray for me.

MARTIN LUTHER.

[1] A sister of Luther's friend John von Staupitz, but much younger than her brother.

Luther was as good as his word in providing for the fugitives. For Staupitz's sister he interceded so effectually with the clergy of Grimma that a little house was presented her in that town in remembrance of her brother. For another nun the Reformer secured the position of teacher, while most of the rest returned to their relatives or married. The three who remained longest at Wittenberg were Ave and Margaret von Schönfeld and Catharine von Bora. For Ave Luther felt a certain attraction, even love, but she, too, as well as her sister, married, and of all the Nimbschen runaways, Catharine, whose father was now dead, was left alone. She had been taken into the house of the rich and honorable Reichenbach, who at times held the office of burgomaster at Wittenberg. Here the girl lived about two years, during which time she learned housekeeping, and a marvellously apt pupil she was, to judge by her later ménage.

What a contrast was Wittenberg to Nimbschen! A good deal of the world could be seen in this little town, with its students from all parts of Germany and from foreign lands, too. Here Catharine learned to know many a great man, Lucas Cranach, the artist, and Philip Melanchthon, the preceptor of the fatherland. In October, 1523, she was presented to King Christian II of Denmark, on his visit to Wittenberg, and was given a gold ring by the lavish monarch. In all her new experiences the girl's piety and modesty, or perhaps something in her looks, won her the nickname of St. Catharine of Siena.

Then she had an unhappy love-affair, Jerome Baumgärtner, a promising youth who had graduated from the university in 1521, in the autumn of 1523 made a long visit to Melanchthon. When he returned to his native Nuremberg there was an understanding, though not a formal engagement, that he should come back and marry Katie. The young man, though his later career was highly honorable, was unable in this case to fulfil his intentions, and his failure to return was so taken to heart by the poor girl that she actually became ill over it. About a year after Baumgärtner's departure, Luther wrote him: "If you want your Katie you had best act quickly before she is given to some one else who wants her. She has not yet con-

quered her love for you and I would willingly see you married
to each other." (October 12, 1524.)

Jerome, however, stayed away and in January his betrothal to
a rich girl was announced.

The suitor who wanted Katie was a certain Dr. Glatz. The
Reformer himself had no intention of marriage: "Not that I
lack the feelings of a man," as he wrote Spalatin on November
30, "for I am neither wood nor stone, but my mind is averse
to matrimony because I daily expect the death decreed to the
heretic."

But a little more than a month after this, Luther preached
and published his sermon on marriage, highly extolling that
estate as the one honored by all the patriarchs and prophets,
and pointing out the duties both of those who wished to marry
and of husbands and wives. A little later he issued a regular
manifesto in the form of an open letter to a friend who was
considering wedlock. One can easily see that the arguments
here given apply equally well to the writer's position : —

TO WOLFGANG REISSENBUSCH AT LICHTENBERG

WITTENBERG, March 27, 1525.

God's grace and peace in Christ. Honored Sir! I am moved by
good friends and by the esteem I bear you to write you this epistle on
the estate of matrimony, as I have noticed you would like to marry,
or rather are forced to do so by God himself, who gave you a nature
requiring it.

I do not think you should be hindered by the rule of the Order or
by a vow, for no vow can bind or be valid except under two conditions. First, a vow must be possible of performance, for who would
vow an impossible thing, or who would demand it ? . . . Now chastity
is not in our power, as little as are God's other wonders and graces,
but we are made for marriage as the Scripture says : It is not good
for man to be alone : I will make an help meet for him.

Who, therefore, considers himself a man, should hear what God
decrees for him. . . . This is the Word of God, through whose power
seed is created in man's body and the burning desire for the woman
kindled and kept alight which cannot be restrained by vows nor
laws. . . .

Secondly, that a vow may be valid it must not be against God and the Christian faith, and everything is against that which relies on works and not on God's grace. . . .

It would be a fine, noble example if you married, that would help many feeble ones and give them more scope, so that they might escape the dangers of the flesh. What harm is it if people say: "So the Lichtenberg professor has taken a wife, has he?" Is it not a great glory that you should thereby become an example to others to do the same? Christ was an example to us all how to bear reproach for conscience' sake. Do I say reproach? Only fools and fanatics think marriage a reproach, men who do not mind fornication but forbid what God has commanded. If it is a shame to take a wife, why is it not a shame to eat and drink, for we have equal need of both and God wills both? . . .

Friend, let us not fly higher nor try to be better than Abraham, David, Isaiah, Peter, Paul, and all the patriarchs, prophets, and apostles, as well as many holy martyrs and bishops, who knew that God had made them men and were not ashamed to be and to be thought so and therefore considered that they should not remain alone. . . .

Luther was evidently intending to marry. In casting about for an eligible wife, his first choice did not fall upon Katie but one of the other nuns. In 1538 he spoke of this inclination in rather a tasteless and rather a heartless way: —

Had I wished to marry fourteen years ago, I should have chosen Ave von Schönfeld, now wife of Basil Axt. I never loved my wife but suspected her of being proud (as she is), but God willed me to take pity on the poor abandoned girl and he has made my marriage turn out most happily.

For another girl, perhaps Ave Alemann of Magdeburg, Luther also had a certain liking, but this yielded to circumstances and Katie became the sole object of his attentions. When he had tried to marry her to Dr. Glatz, Baumgärtner's rival, she absolutely refused, saying that she would take Amsdorf or Luther himself but Glatz never. This naturally brought her to the Reformer's attention. He speaks of his various love-affairs in a jocose letter to his confidant: —

TO GEORGE SPALATIN AT LOCHAU [1]

(WITTENBERG,) April 16, 1525.

I have commended everything to friend Cranach and have asked him to be sure to send a hundred copies of my letter to Reissenbusch.

. . . .

You write me about my marriage. Do not be surprised if I, so famous a lover, do not wed, though it is really wonderful that I who write so much about marriage and have so much intercourse with women should not turn into a woman, let alone marry one. If you wish for my example you already have it. For I have had three wives at once and loved them so hard that I drove two away to get other husbands. On the third I have a precarious hold, but she, too, may soon be torn from me. It is really you who are the timid lover, not daring to marry even one. But take care, lest I, the old bachelor, should get ahead of lusty young bridegrooms like you, for God is accustomed to do what we least expect. I say this seriously to encourage you. Farewell, dear Spalatin.

MARTIN LUTHER.

On the same day on which he wrote this letter Luther started on his trip to Mansfeld to preach against the peasants' rising. His already half-formed purpose of taking the frank nun at her word was increased by his father, whom he saw at this time and who urged him to marry. His first announcement of his intention is in the letter to Rühel of May 4, where he says he will take "his Katie" to wife "to spite the devil." The formal betrothal followed soon after, and the wedding, hastened on by malicious gossip about the pair, took place very privately at the Black Cloister on the evening of June 13. Owing to its suddenness the customary festivities had to be put off until two weeks later, June 27. Among the invitations sent far and wide, the following have an especial interest: —

TO JOHN RÜHEL, JOHN THUR AND CASPAR MÜLLER AT MANSFELD

WITTENBERG, June 15, 1525.

Grace and peace in Christ. What an outcry of Harrow, my dear sirs, has been caused by my pamphlet against the peasants! All is now forgotten that God has done for the world through me. Now lords, parsons, and peasants are all against me and threaten my death.

[1] Spalatin was now here with his dying master.

Well, since they are so silly and foolish, I shall take care that at my end I shall be found in the state for which God created me with nothing of my previous papal life about me. I will do my part even if they act still more foolishly up to the last farewell.

So now, according to the wish of my dear father, I have married. I did it quickly lest those praters should stop it. Thursday week, June 27, it is my intention to have a little celebration and house-warming, to which I beg that you will come and give your blessings. The land is in such a state that I hardly dare ask you to undertake the journey; however, if you can do so, pray come, along with my dear father and mother, for it would be a special pleasure to me. Bring any friends. If possible let me know beforehand, though I do not ask this if inconvenient.

I would have written my gracious lords Counts Gebhard and Albert of Mansfeld, but did not risk it, knowing that their Graces have other things to attend to. Please let me know if you think I ought to invite them. God bless you. Amen.

MARTIN LUTHER.

TO GEORGE SPALATIN

WITTENBERG, June 16, 1525.

Grace and peace. Dear Spalatin, I have stopped the mouths of my calumniators with Catharine von Bora. If we have a banquet to celebrate the wedding we wish you not only to be present but to help us in case we need game. Meantime give us your blessing and pray for us.

I have made myself so cheap and despised by this marriage that I expect the angels laugh and the devils weep thereat. The world and its wise men have not yet seen how pious and sacred is marriage, but they consider it impious and devilish in me. It pleases me, however, to have my marriage condemned by those who are ignorant of God. Farewell and pray for me.

MARTIN LUTHER.

To Katie's old acquaintance and rescuer he wrote, June 21:

God has suddenly and unexpectedly caught me in the bond of holy matrimony. I intend to celebrate with a wedding breakfast on Thursday. That my parents and all good friends may be merry, my Lord Catharine and I kindly beg you to send us, at my cost and as quickly as possible, a barrel of the best Torgau beer.

To Amsdorf the bridegroom confides that " I married to gratify my father, who asked me to marry and leave him descendants. . . . I was not carried away by passion, for I do not love my wife that way, but esteem her as a friend. (Non amo sed diligo)."

The proudest of the many guests on the great day were assuredly old Hans and Margaret Luther. Among the wedding presents the most prized came from the town, the university, the Elector, and Cranach. Rühel brought a surprise in the way of twenty gulden from Albert of Mayence, who was thinking of becoming Lutheran in order to turn his electorate into a temporal fief as his cousin Albert had done with Prussia. The bridegroom wanted to return this gift, but the thrifty bride managed to keep it.

At this time Martin and Katie sat for their pictures to the celebrated Lucas Cranach. The bridegroom is forty-two, well built and very pale. His face is at once good-humored and strong. And yet who can be satisfied with this picture? Dürer's criticism that the Wittenberg artist could depict the features but not the soul is extremely just.

The portrait of Katie does not bear out the conjecture of Erasmus that the monk had been led astray by a wonderfully charming girl (mire venusta). She was of a type not uncommon among Germans, in whose features shrewdness, good sense, and kindliness often give a pleasant expression to homely persons —though even this can hardly be seen in Cranach's picture. Her scant reddish hair is combed back over a high forehead; the brows over her dark blue eyes slant up from a rather flat nose; her ears and cheek-bones are prominent.

Katie was sometimes reproached with pride and avarice. But that an orphan, without friends, money, or beauty should have any pride left is rather a subject for praise than blame, and what is sometimes called her greed of money was only the necessary parsimony of a housewife in narrow circumstances whose husband was uncommonly generous. Without marked spirituality, she was a Martha busied with many things rather than a Mary sitting in devotion at her master's feet. If there was little passion and no romance in the courtship, there was deep devotion and friendship in the twenty years following marriage. Of

CATHARINE LUTHER IN 1526

From the painting by Cranach in possession of Frau Geheimregierungsrat Richard
von Kaufmann, in Berlin

his own thoughts, and his wife's affection during their first year together, the Reformer once spoke thus : —

In the first year of marriage one has strange thoughts. At table he thinks : "Formerly I was alone, now I am with some one. In bed when he wakes, he sees beside him a pair of pigtails which he did not see before. The first year after our marriage Katie sat beside me when I studied, and once, when she could think of nothing else to say, asked me : 'Doctor, is the Grand Master of Prussia the Margrave's brother ?'" [1]

A still more intimate view of the relations of man and wife is given in the next letter to Spalatin. Luther lived in a time when it was considered not at all indelicate to speak of what few refined men, not to say pious preachers, would mention in these days. Spalatin had now retired from his position at court, married, and taken the incumbency of the first church at Altenburg. Here he remained the trusted counsellor of Frederic's successor, John the Steadfast. Though the new elector was an open convert to the Evangelic faith, as his brother had not been, nevertheless there was a party at court so hostile to Luther, whom they regarded as the real author of the peasants' rising, that when Spalatin invited the Wittenberg professor to attend his wedding, the latter felt unable to do it.

TO GEORGE SPALATIN AT ALTENBURG

WITTENBERG, December 6, 1525.

I wish you grace and peace in the Lord, and also joy with your sweetest little wife, also in the Lord. Your marriage is as pleasing to me as it is displeasing to those priests of Baal.[2] Indeed God has given me no greater happiness, except the Gospel, than to see you married, though this, too, is a gift of the Gospel, and no small fruit of our Evangelic teaching. Why I am absent, and wherefore I could not come to your most pleasing wedding, Brisger [3] will tell you. All things are changed under the new elector, who right nobly confesses the Evangelic faith. I am less safe on the road than I was under an elector who dissimulated his faith, but now where one hopes for citadels of refuge

[1] The Grand Master was the Margrave !

[2] The canons of Altenburg, with whom Luther had had a hard fight.

[3] The brother who had hitherto lived with Luther; he was the bearer of this letter to Altenburg, where he was soon to become pastor.

one is forced to fear dens of robbers and traitors. I wish you great happiness and children, with Christ's blessing. Believe me, my mind exults in your marriage no less than yours did in mine. Poor as I am I would have sent you that Portuguese gold-piece [1] which you gave my wife, did I not fear that it would offend you. So I am sending you what is left over from my wedding, not knowing whether it will also be left over from yours or not. . . . Greet your wife kindly from me. When you have your Catharine in bed, sweetly embracing and kissing her, think : Lo this being, the best little creation of God, has been given me by Christ, to whom be glory and honor. I will guess the day on which you will receive this letter and that night my wife and I will particularly think of you. [2] My rib and I send greetings to you and your rib. Grace be with you. Amen.

Yours,

MARTIN LUTHER.

Luther's marriage excited the interest of all Europe. Henry VIII of England and many other enemies taunted him with it as if it were a crime. Erasmus sneered that what he had taken to be a tragedy had turned out a comedy. Even Melanchthon disliked the step. To his best pupil, Camerarius, he wrote a letter on June 16 in Greek, at that time almost a cipher, saying : —

On June 13 Luther unexpectedly married Mistress von Bora, having announced his intention to none of his friends, but in the evening only inviting Bugenhagen, Cranach, and Apel to supper, after which he completed the usual ceremonies. You may perhaps be surprised that at this unhappy time, when all good gentlemen are suffering, Luther does not sympathize with them, but, as it seems, prefers a life of pleasure and to lower his dignity, though Germany has now the greatest need of his wisdom and strength. I think it came about in this way. The man is very facile and the nuns tried every plan to inveigle him. Perhaps the much intercourse with the nuns softened and inflamed him, noble and magnanimous as he is. . . . I hope this manner of life will make him more reverend and especially that he will cast away the scurrility with which we have often reproached him.

The marriage did indeed turn out happily. After his hard experiences in the monastery, Luther's whole nature blossomed

---

[1] *Portugaliensis*, a coin worth about seven dollars.

[2] Ea nocte simili opere meam [uxorem] amabo in tui memoriam, et tibi par pari referam.

out in response to the warm sun of domestic life. A true instinct for the best side of the man has made artists love to portray him surrounded by wife and children.

Katie was a woman of enormous energy — the morning star of Wittenberg as her husband called her with reference to her early rising. Her superintendence of a large household and growing estate was masterly. She faithfully cared for her husband on the numerous occasions when he was ill, and of course much of her time was taken up with the children whom she nursed and tended in the unabashed publicity of her crowded home. She took a lively interest in her husband's affairs and was confided in by him. Her piety is more a matter of inference than record; Martin probably appealed to her weaker side when he offered her a large sum to read the Bible through. That her studies in this book were successful may be inferred from her husband's remark that "Katie understands the Bible better than any papists did twenty years ago." Her picture, like that of her husband, is drawn to the life in the table-talk. Among many sayings taken down during the last fifteen years of Luther's life (1531–1546) the following give a charming picture of his conjugal felicity:—

I would not change my Katie for France and Venice, because God has given her to me, and other women have much worse faults, and she is true to me and a good mother to my children. If a husband always kept such things in mind he would easily conquer the temptation to discord which Satan sows between married people.

The greatest happiness is to have a wife to whom you can trust your business and who is a good mother to your children. Katie, you have a husband who loves you; many an empress is not so well off.

I am rich, God has given me my nun and three children: what care I if I am in debt, Katie pays the bills.

Luther loved to poke good-natured fun at his wife, but she was usually able to hold her own:—

Luther: We shall yet see the day when a man will take several wives.

Katie: The devil thinks so.

Luther: The reason, dear Katie, is that a woman can have only one child a year, whereas a man can beget several.

Katie: Paul says, "Let each man have his own wife."

Luther: Aye, his own wife, but not only one; that is not in Paul. Thus the doctor joked a long time until Katie said: "Before I would stand that I would go back to the convent and leave you and your children."

Something struck Katie in the side and she cried out, *"Ave Maria!"* The doctor said: "Why don't you finish your prayer? Would it not be a comfort to say 'Jesus Christ' too?"

Speaking jocosely of Katie's loquacity he said: "Will you not preface your long sermons with a prayer? If you do, your prayer will doubtless be long enough to prevent your preaching at all."

While he was talking in an inspired way during dinner, his wife said: "Why do you keep talking all the time instead of eating?" He replied: "I must again wish that women would pray before they preach. Say the Lord's prayer before you speak."

"Women's sermons only make one tired. They are so tedious that one forgets what they are saying before they finish." By this name he called the long speeches of his wife with which she was always interrupting his best sayings.

November 4 (1538) a learned Englishman who did not know German came to table. Luther said: "I will let my wife be your teacher. She knows the tongue so thoroughly that she completely beats me. But eloquence is not to be praised in women; it becomes them better to stammer and lisp."

While Luther gladly devolved upon Katie the care of the household and property — tasks for which he had neither time, aptitude, nor inclination — he had no idea of letting himself be ruled by her — indulgence to wives he once described as "the vice of the age." At other times he said: —

My wife can persuade me anything she pleases, for she has the government of the house in her hands alone. I willingly yield the direction of domestic affairs, but wish my rights to be respected. Women's rule never did any good.

The inferior ought not to glory over the superior, but the superior over the inferior. Katie can rule the servants but not me. David gloried in his own righteousness before men, not before God.

George Karg has taken a rich wife and sold his freedom. I am luckier, for when Katie gets saucy she gets nothing but a box on the ear.

This is the only time corporal chastisement of the wife is ever

mentioned in respect to Katie, though the practice was not
unknown to the best society of the day. In spite of a little blus-
tering it is probable that Luther gave in as often as not: —

As we were sitting in the garden, Jonas remarked that the women
were becoming our masters, to which the town-councillor of Torgau
added that it was indeed, alas! true. Luther said: "But we have to
give in, otherwise we would have no peace."

A priest came to Luther complaining of misery and want. Melanchthon, who was present, said: "You have vowed poverty, obedience,
and chastity, now practise them"; and Luther added: "I, too, have
to be obedient to my wife and all kinds of desperate fools and knaves
and ingrates."

"I must have patience with the Pope, ranters, insolent nobles, my
household and Katie von Bora, so that my whole life is nothing else
but mere patience."

In general Katie seems to have enjoyed good health. In the
winter of 1539–40, however, she had a terrible illness resulting
from a miscarriage. For weeks she was prostrate. When the
crisis was past her energy returned faster than her strength, and
one of the most realistic accounts of her tells how she crawled
around the house with the aid of her hands before she was able
to walk upright. Her excellent constitution stood her in good
stead, however, and she recovered rapidly and thoroughly. Her
husband's piety attributed this to the prayers offered for her.

CHAPTER XVI

PRIVATE LIFE. 1522–31

ONE of Luther's oldest and best friends was his vicar, John von Staupitz. Though it is probable that the two never agreed as closely as is usually thought, there can be no doubt of the great debt of the younger man to the elder and of the sorrow he felt at their gradual estrangement, and at the death of his "father." Luther was sensible of the coming division as early as the Leipsic debate; not long after this (October 3, 1519), he wrote: —

I have been most sad for you to-day as a weaned child for its mother. . . . Last night I dreamed that you were leaving me while I wept bitterly, but you waved to me and bade me cease weeping, for you would come back to me.

But the elder man did not come back. Notwithstanding great spiritual insight and devotion, his character lacked something of the firmness required by the times. His attempt to avoid taking sides by entering the Benedictine order, his public submission to the Pope, and the solemn letter Luther wrote him on that occasion, just before the Diet of Worms, on the duty of standing by Christ in the hour of danger, have already been described.[1]

Staupitz was more than ever alienated from the new teaching by the innovations of the Wittenberg mob while Martin was at the Wartburg. Three months after his return, June 27, 1522, the younger man wrote an earnest defence of his doctrine to the elder: "I pray you by the bowels of Christ not to believe our detractors; all that I have done is to publish the pure Word without tumult: it is not our fault if good and bad alike take it up."

Staupitz did not answer this letter, but a year later, September 17, 1523, the Wittenberger wrote him to ask a favor for a

[1] Letter of February 9, 1521, p. 107 f.

fugitive monk. "Reverend Father in Christ," he remonstrated, "your silence is most unjust, and you know what we are obliged to think of it. But even if you are no longer pleased with me, it is not fitting that I should forget you, who first made the light of the gospel shine in my heart."

The answer to this, dated Salzburg April 1, 1524, is a remarkable tribute to the personality of the younger man. "My love to you," protests the writer, "is most constant, passing the love of women, always unbroken. . . . But as I do not grasp all your ideas, I keep silence about them. . . . It seems to me that you condemn many things which are merely indifferent . . . but we owe much to you, Martin, for having led us back from the husks which the swine did eat to the pastures of life and the words of salvation." The letter closes with a request that the bearer of it be given the degree of master at Wittenberg, which was promptly complied with. No other epistles were exchanged between the two friends, the elder of whom died of a stroke of apoplexy on December 28 of this same year. This disease was commonly regarded as a special visitation from Heaven, and Luther once opined that God had thus punished the vicar for entering the Benedictine order, but added that he was a noble-minded man.

The work of teaching in the university, interrupted by the momentous events of 1521, was taken up again in 1522, and continued, with a few short breaks, for the rest of the professor's life. During his absence Melanchthon had consented, rather against his will, to lecture on the Bible, and his work proved such a success that his friend begged him to continue it. Luther met his colleague's plea that he was paid to teach Greek by writing to the Elector Frederic, saying : —

Your Grace doubtless knows that there are fine youths here, hungry for the wholesome Word, coming from abroad and enduring poverty to study. . . . Now I have proposed that Melanchthon lecture on the Bible, for which he is more richly endowed by God's grace than am I. . . . But he alleges that he is appointed to teach Greek. . . . Wherefore I beg your Grace to see fit to pay him his salary for lecturing on the Bible, as there are plenty of young men who can teach Greek.

Frederic's answer, if he wrote any, is not extant: he was soon to be too much preoccupied with the rising of the rustics to be able to attend to his once cherished seat of learning. This civil war had a disastrous effect on the university: not only did funds run very short, but the number of students fell from five or six hundred to forty in the summer semester of 1525. Seriously alarmed at this state of affairs, Luther wrote, shortly after the death of Frederic, to his successor John, and to the latter's son: —

TO JOHN FREDERIC OF SAXONY

WITTENBERG, May 20, 1525.

I have previously written my gracious Lord, your Grace's father, about putting the university in order and appointing some one to take charge of it. It is true that your Grace is very busy about other things, but here, too, delay is dangerous, as the matter has hung fire long enough and become tangled; moreover, men whose places we cannot easily fill have left us, so that our neighbors are rejoicing as if it were already up with Wittenberg. If we are to have a university here at all we must act betimes. It would be a shame that such a university as this, from which the gospel has gone out over the whole world, should perish. We need men everywhere and must take the necessary means to train them. I humbly beg your Grace to act quickly and not be held back by the courtiers who speak scornfully of book learning. For your Grace knows that the world cannot be ruled by force alone, but that there must be learned men to help with God's work and keep a hold on the people with teaching and preaching, for if there were no teachers or preachers the civil power would not long stand, not to mention the fact that the kingdom of God would entirely leave us. . . .

Your Grace's obedient,

MARTIN LUTHER.

These appeals were effective. Spalatin was sent to reorganize the university. The professors' salaries were raised — Luther's from one to two hundred gulden — from funds provided by the appropriation of the income of the endowed masses of the Castle Church, which Frederic had been too conservative to touch. The curriculum, too, was reformed, according to the ideas expressed in the Address to the German Nobility. A professor of

Hebrew had been secured from Louvain in 1519, but soon proved unsatisfactory, and his place was taken by another, Aurogallus, who was a great help in the translation of the Old Testament now under way.

Luther's own lectures on the Bible were soon resumed and steadily continued; on 2 Peter, Jude, and Genesis, 1523–1524; on Deuteronomy, 1523–1525. In his commentary on the Minor Prophets, 1524–1526, he perhaps reached the height of his exegetical ability. He showed a real historical sense, expounding the messages of the prophets with reference to the circumstances of their own days. One can see that his translation of the Bible into German is always in his mind, for he is continually searching for apt German words and phrases. These lectures, compared even with those on Romans and Galatians, show that he had almost entirely emancipated himself from the old commentaries of Lyra and the scholastics. It is noticeable that he took Jonah, whale and all, literally. That even here, however, his historical sense and his humor were not dormant may be gathered from the remark, made at another time, that if Jonah were not in the Bible he would laugh at it.

He next took up Ecclesiastes, which he called "the hardest of all books." He noticed the peculiarities of the vocabulary and explained them by saying: "Solomon tried to be more elegant than his father David." Simultaneously he was lecturing on 1 John, which he called "a noble epistle, having John's style and manner, able to raise up afflicted hearts, so fairly and sweetly does it depict Christ for us." Courses on Titus, Philemon, and Isaiah were given in the years 1527–1529.

Luther's work for the education of his people did not stop with his own university. He perpetually and strenuously urged the extension and reformation of the schools. During the first quarter of the sixteenth century learning had fallen into contempt for a variety of causes. The principal reason was that the learning itself was contemptible; the age had long outgrown the lore of the schools which passed for erudition; the satire levelled against the sophistry of the monks by the Letters of the Obscure Men, had brought into disrepute all pretensions to any education whatever. Then came Carlstadt and the

mystics, who taught that as God had revealed to babes and
sucklings what he had concealed from the wise and prudent, it
was better to preserve innocence and ignorance together. Lastly
the time was, like our own, one of marked materialistic tendency, fostered by the rapid expansion of commerce and industry.

Luther stemmed the ebbing tide. Early in 1524 he produced
a Letter to the Aldermen and Cities of Germany on the Erection and Maintenance of Christian Schools. Ranke says: "This
work has the same significance for the development of learning
as the Address to the German Nobility for the temporal estate
in general." The book had a great success, and, followed up as
it was by unremitting efforts in the same direction, it undoubtedly had an incalculable effect in popularizing and raising the
standard of education in Germany.

"Now we learn," says the author, "that throughout all Germany
the schools are declining, the universities becoming weak, and the
cloisters are ruined. Such grass dries up, and the flowers fall, as
Isaiah says, when God does not move upon them by his Word. . . .
For the carnal multitude sees that they cannot turn their sons and
daughters out of house and home to live in cloisters and therefore they
will not let them study any more. 'For,' say they, 'why should any
one study who is not going to be a priest, monk, or nun? Rather let
them learn a trade to support themselves.'" . . .

Now I beg all my dear friends not to think of this matter so con-
temptuously as many do who do not see what the prince of this
world intends. It is an earnest and great matter, deeply concerning
Christ and all the world, that we should help and counsel the young
people.

The principal reason for education is, of course, in the writer's opinion, that men may read the Word of God. But other
reasons are adduced, the example of Rome being cited, " for
the Romans brought up their children so that by the time they
were fifteen, eighteen, or twenty they knew marvellously well
Latin, Greek, and all the liberal arts, so that they were straightway fitted for war or government, and were brilliant, reasoning,
able persons, polished in all the arts and sciences." Men must be
trained to govern, for ignorant governors are as bad as wolves.

The chief subjects taught should be Latin, Greek, and Hebrew, the last two for the sake of reading the Bible in the original, for the mistakes of all the fathers were due to their ignorance of these tongues. The people are congratulated on the introduction of humaner methods of instilling knowledge: —

Now by God's grace it has come to pass that children may learn with pleasure, be it a language or some other art or science or history. Our schools are no more the hell and purgatory in which we were martyred by declension and conjugation, although we learned nothing of value with all our whipping, trembling, anguish, and crying. If people now take so much time teaching their children to play cards and dance, why should they not take an equal amount to teach them to read and learn other things while they are young, idle, and curious? For my part, if I had children they would have to learn not only the languages and history but also singing, music, and the whole mathematics. . . . It is a sorrow to me that I was not taught to read more poetry and history.

Children should therefore go to school an hour or two every day, learning a trade at home the rest of the time. Girls should be sent to school as well as boys. Public libraries in each town, like those of the monasteries, but with better books, are recommended.

Notwithstanding his other occupations, Luther found time to preach constantly; indeed, during the frequent and long absences of Bugenhagen, the parish priest of Wittenberg, the Reformer regularly took his place in the pulpit. He often took up one book of the Bible and preached on it for long periods together. Thus during the years 1524–1527, he went through Deuteronomy. The following may serve as a specimen of his homiletic style: —

But the miracle of the manna helped the children of Israel little, for it became common and they did not regard it. So the sun rising daily on us, though a great miracle, has become so customary that we think it cannot be otherwise. Likewise we esteem it no wonder that corn and wine grow yearly, yet by these and other daily miracles — for the growth of corn from the seed is as great a miracle as the manna — our faith ought to be strengthened.

Luther did not confine himself to any strict order, however;

he often took other texts, and in these cases his sermons perhaps show more of his thought. For example, one Sunday in 1527, a terrible year of affliction, he preached on Matthew ii, 28 : " Come unto me all ye that are weary and heavy laden and I will give you rest."

Ah, what a rare invitation is this (he comments). Why does he not call the strong, rich, well, learned, kings and lords? Why does he want the sorrowful and laden? Only because it pleases him to do so, and where else can one go with his unbelief, hunger, poverty, shame, and trouble?

These busy and generally happy years were not entirely free from ill health. There are some indications that Luther suffered from a malady of the nerves even as a student at Erfurt and as a monk. By 1523 this took a more pronounced form, causing ringing in the ears, faintness, depression, and irritability. Indigestion with various complications had set in at the Wartburg, and in 1526 were discovered the first symptoms of the then common disease of the bladder and kidneys, known as the stone. These complaints were not allowed as a rule to interfere with work, but in the summer of 1527 a terrible attack of nervous prostration for a time interrupted the almost unexampled toil of the Reformer's life. On July 6, feeling unwell, he arose from the table and started to go to the bedroom next the dining-hall, but before he reached the door he fainted and fell. Though only two days in bed, the patient suffered from weakness and depression for months afterward. " Satan rages against me with his whole might," he wrote Agricola on August 21, " and the Lord has put me in his power like another Job. The devil tempts me with great infirmity of spirit."

Before he had recovered, the plague broke out at Wittenberg. The university moved to Jena and most of the clergy followed. Luther, while admitting that in some cases it was justifiable for them to do so, declined to imitate them himself, saying that a good shepherd laid down his life for his sheep, and only the hireling fled. One of the two who stayed with him, the young and talented deacon Rörer, who for several years had been a literary help to the Reformer, paid heavily for his

fidelity in the loss of his wife. Katie was in a situation causing anxiety, and her baby Hans fell ill. In the midst of these
fightings without and fears within he wrote as follows: —

TO JUSTUS JONAS, AT NORDHAUSEN

(WITTENBERG, November 11 ? 1527.)

Grace and peace in the Lord Jesus our Saviour. I thank you, dear
Jonas, for your prayers and occasional letters. I suppose my letter of
day before yesterday reached you. I have not yet read Erasmus or
the sacramentarians except about three quarters of Zwingli's book.
Judases as they are they do well to stamp on my wretched self, making
me feel as did Christ when he said: "He persecuted the poor and
needy man, that he might even slay the broken in heart." I bear God's
wrath because I have sinned against him. Pope, emperor, princes,
bishops, and the whole world hate and persecute me, nor is this enough,
but my brothers, too, must add to my sorrows, and my sins and death
and Satan with his angels rage without ceasing. What could save and
console me if even Christ should desert me on whose account they all
hate me? But he will not leave the poor sinner at the end, though I
believe that I am the least of all men. Would that Erasmus and the
sacramentarians might feel the anguish of my heart for a quarter of
an hour; I can safely say that they would be converted and saved
thereby. . . .

I am anxious about the delivery of my wife, so much has the example of Rörer's wife terrified me. . . . My little Hans cannot send
his greetings to you on account of illness, but he looks for your prayers
for him. It is twelve days since he has eaten any solid food, but now
he begins to eat a little. It is wonderful to see how the baby tries to
be strong and happy as usual, but cannot because he is so weak.

Margaret Moch was operated on yesterday, and having thus at last
thrown off the plague begins to convalesce. She is lodged in our usual
winter room; we live in the lecture hall; little Hans has my bedroom
and Schurf's wife his room. We hope the pestilence is passing. Good-
bye, with a kiss to your little daughter and warm greetings to her
mother. . . .

I am sorry Rome was sacked, for it is a great portent. I hope it
may yet be inhabited and have its pontiff before we die. . . .

MARTIN LUTHER, Christi lutum.[1]

[1] Christ's mud; one of Luther's frequent puns on his own name.

The terrible year passed, and the habitual round of work and domestic joys and sorrows was resumed. Among the latter the heaviest that Luther was called upon to bear was the death of his parents. In February, 1530, his brother James wrote him of their father's serious illness. Feeling unable to go to his parent's bedside, the Reformer wrote him a long, hearty letter. " I would have come to you personally with the greatest readiness," he says, " but good friends persuaded me not to, and I myself thought it best not to tempt God by putting myself in peril, for you know how lords and peasants feel towards me." After a long exhortation and much ghostly comfort drawn from Scripture, he closes: —

I hope that your pastor will point out such things to you faithfully, so that you will not need what I say at all, but yet I write to ask forgiveness for my bodily absence, which, God knows, causes me heartfelt sorrow. My Katie, little Hans and Magdalene and Aunt Lena and all my household send you greetings and pray for you faithfully. Greet my mother and all dear friends. God's grace and strength be and abide with you forever. Amen.

Your loving son,

MARTIN LUTHER.

The writer of this letter was fond of telling how, when the Mansfeld pastor read it to old Hans, and asked him if he believed all that it contained, the latter replied: " Aye; he would be a knave who did not."

The aged miner died on May 29. His son was then at the castle known as Feste Coburg. When he heard the sad news he wrote Wenzel Link, June 5, 1530: " Now I am sorrowful, for I have received tidings of the death of my father, that dear and gentle old man whose name I bear, and although I am glad for his sake that his journey to Christ was so easy and pious and that, freed from the monsters of this world he rests in peace, nevertheless my heart is moved to sorrow. For under God I owe my life and bringing up to him."

A year, a month and a day after the demise of her husband Margaret Luther followed him into the grave. At this time, too, Martin felt unable to attend his dying parent, although the trip to Mansfeld was only fifty miles. Instead he again wrote a Scriptural letter recalling Jesus' words, " I have overcome the world." He closes, " All my children and Katie pray for you. Some cry, some say while eating, ' Grandmother is very ill.' "

CHAPTER XVII

HENRY VIII

ONE of the most curious incidents in Luther's career was his intercourse with Henry VIII of England. Although perhaps it had little influence on the Reformer's career, it is worth tracing on account of its intrinsic interest, especially to English readers.

Within little more than a year after the posting of the Theses, Luther's works had been exported to England, and that they attracted the attention of the government may be inferred from a letter of Erasmus, who says that but for his intervention they would have been burned. It was from this "vigilant person" that Henry got his first definite impression of the Reformer. When he came to Calais in the summer of 1520 the humanist visited him, and they talked of Luther. Erasmus especially wished to get the coöperation of his powerful patron in a plan he had of making peace by referring the question of heresy to a board of impartial and learned judges.

It was Cardinal Wolsey, ambitious for the highest place in the Roman Church, who urged his master to take a decided part against the German monk. He burned the heretic's books (May 12, 1521), induced Henry to write to the Emperor in the interests of the Catholic Church (May 30, 1521), and, procuring a copy of the Babylonian Captivity, gave it to his master, who was proud of his attainments, with a suggestion that it would be a worthy act for him to refute it. Henry complied, and produced, in the summer of 1521, An Assertion of the Seven Sacraments, dedicated to Pope Leo, from whom it won for its author the title Defender of the Faith.

In tone the work is as violent as most of the invective of the day: "What pest so pernicious as Luther has ever attacked the flock of Christ? . . . What a wolf of hell is he! What a limb of Satan! How rotten is his mind! How execrable his purpose!"

In point of logic the polemic is occasionally faulty. For instance Luther had denied that the mass is a good work in the sense in which the Catholic Church always considered it a meritorious act on the part of all participating. Henry replies that he who makes an image out of wood does a work; Christ in making his flesh out of bread does a work; but what Christ does is good; therefore the mass is a good work!

Luther answered in July, 1522. In tone he is as angry as "that king of lies, King Heinz, by God's ungrace King of England." Henry has acted so little like a king that he does not think he need treat him like one: "For since with malice aforethought that damnable and rotten worm has lied against my king in heaven, it is right for me to bespatter this English monarch with his own filth and trample his blasphemous crown under feet." As to the arguments advanced, he ridicules them, feeling that God has smitten the papists with blindness so that the more he cries out "the gospel and Christ" the more they answer, "the fathers, customs, statutes." Little ability as the work shows, it is plain that Henry did not write it, but "Lee [1] or one of those snivelling, drivelling sophists bred by the Thomist swine."

When Henry heard of the unquelled violence of his opponent he moved every lever to revenge his royal honor. First he wrote to Frederic, John and George, Dukes of Saxony, whom he evidently thought of as ruling over the same territory. From the first two he received a diplomatic but evasive answer; George replied more satisfactorily, but was able to do nothing.

Then the King moved a number of theologians to attack Luther; the two prominent English scholars, Fisher, Bishop of Rochester, and Sir Thomas More did so, as well as Murner, and, most important of all, Erasmus.

If these efforts, diplomatic and literary, failed to crush his opponent, a few years later Henry had an extremely good chance to humiliate him. In the spring of 1525 King Christian II of Denmark, a personal friend of Luther, gave him the somewhat

[1] Edward Lee, prominent as an opponent of Erasmus. The spirit of the work was Henry's, but he probably received much help from Fisher and other learned divines.

premature information that England was becoming favorable
to the Evangelic faith. In May, therefore, the Reformer composed a letter to the King, which he sent to Spalatin for advice.
This friend wisely advised him to keep silence, but Luther
could not let slip the opportunity of winning so powerful an
adherent, especially, perhaps, as he felt his position somewhat
weakened by the Peasants' Revolt and the death of the Elector
Frederic, and therefore on September 1 he dispatched the following missive : —

TO HENRY VIII OF ENGLAND

WITTENBERG, September 1, 1525.

Grace and peace in Christ, our Lord and Saviour. Amen. Indeed,
Most Serene and Illustrious King, I ought greatly to fear to address
your Majesty in a letter, as I am fully aware that your Majesty is
deeply offended at my pamphlet, which I published foolishly and pre-
cipitately, not of my own motion but at the hest of certain men who
are not your Majesty's friends. But daily seeing your royal clemency,
I take hope and courage; I will not believe that a mortal can
cherish immortal hatred. I have learned from credible authority that
the book published over your Majesty's name was not written by your
Majesty, but by crafty men of guile who abused your name, especially
by that monster detested of God and man, that pest of your kingdom,
Cardinal Wolsey. They did not see the danger of humiliating their
king. I am ashamed to raise my eyes to your Majesty because I allowed myself to be moved by this despicable work of malignant in-
triguers, especially as I am the offscouring of the world, a mere worm
who ought only to live in contemptuous neglect.

What impels me to write, abject as I am, is that your Majesty has
begun to favor the Evangelic cause and to feel disgust at the abandoned men who oppose us. This news was a true gospel — *i. e.*, tidings
of great joy — to my heart. . . . If your Serene Majesty wishes me
to recant publicly and write in honor of your Majesty, will you graciously signify your wish to me and I will gladly do so. . . .

Your Majesty's most devoted,

MARTIN LUTHER, with his own hand.

This letter naturally did no good. Indeed, though Luther was
certainly sincere in his desire to conciliate, he never displayed
greater lack of tact than in dispraising the King's book and

favorite minister. After a long delay, Henry replied in a fiercer work than before, printing Luther's missive with mocking comments, and taunting him with having caused the Peasants' Revolt and with living in wantonness with a nun.

The King sent his epistle, which reached the proportions of a small book, to Duke George, and it was promptly published in Germany at his instigation under the title, Luther's Offer to Recant in a letter to the King of England. This twisting of his apology into a recantation excited the Reformer's ire again and he replied with a pamphlet, Against the Title of the King of England's Libel. In this he asserts that he will not recant his doctrine: "No, no, no, not while I live, let it irk king, prince, emperor, devil, and whom it may." He has tried hard to keep the peace both with Erasmus and with Henry: "but I am a sheep and must remain a sheep to think that I can pacify such men."

Henry did not continue the altercation further, but revenged himself by stamping out the Evangelic faith in England and by giving a play, representing "the heretic Luther like a party friar in russet damask and black taffety, and his wife like a frow of Almayn in red silk," St. Martin's Eve, November 9, 1527.

The rancor borne by the haughty monarch did not prevent his seeking the aid of his enemy when the latter might become useful to him. It is not necessary here to résumé the history of Henry's separation from Catharine of Aragon nor to probe his strangely mingled motives. After a long but vain effort to get from the Pope a divorce on the ground that the union with a brother's widow was forbidden by Leviticus xx, 21, the monarch decided to take matters into his own hands, and, in order to reassure both himself and his subjects, began, in 1529, to solicit the opinions of foreign universities and "strange doctors."

As early as 1529 he threatened to appeal from the Catholics to the Lutherans, introduced some Evangelic books into his court, and even praised the once hated heretic to Chapuys, the imperial ambassador. It is possible that he applied to the reformers in 1530; it is certain that he did so in 1531. Simon Grynaeus was the agent employed to deal with the Swiss and with Melanchthon, but a special messenger was sent to Luther.

This man, whose name is not mentioned in the sources, applied first to Robert Barnes, who, having been forced to flee from England on account of his faith, in 1528, had made his way to Wittenberg and in time became a warm friend of Luther and a guest at his house. The agent then went to Philip of Hesse and urged him to write the Reformer for an opinion on Henry's divorce, a request with which the Landgrave complied.

Luther gave his answer to Barnes in a long letter dated September 3, 1531. Emphatically denying the legitimacy of the divorce, he writes : —

I do not now question what a papal dispensation in such matters is worth, but I say that even if the King sinned in marrying his brother's widow it would be a much greater sin cruelly to put her away now. Rather let him take another queen, following the example of the patriarchs, who had many wives even before the law of Moses sanctioned the practice, but let him not thrust his present wife from her royal position. I pray with all my heart that Christ may prevent this divorce.

The proposal to commit bigamy, rather than to divorce, shocks an age accustomed to regard the latter as the preferable alternative. The general opinion of the sixteenth century was exactly opposite to that of the twentieth on this point, for the simple reason that polygamy, practised in the Old Testament, was never expressly forbidden by the New, which discountenances divorce. Luther's good conscience in giving this advice is shown by its disinterestedness — for by complying with the King's wish for divorce he might have won a powerful convert — as well as by the previous statement in the Babylonian Captivity of the same opinion. That his views were shared by a large number of his contemporary divines, both Protestant and Catholic, has been demonstrated in a very careful study by Doctor Rockwell.

Barnes left Wittenberg the day after this letter was written, and hastened, via Magdeburg and Lubeck, to London, where he was received by his royal master in December. The monarch was naturally displeased with his message and dismissed him "with much ill will."

Nevertheless the very next year he sent Paget to Germany to

persuade the Protestant doctors to write for the divorce. The emissary reached Wittenberg, August 12, 1532, but got no more satisfaction than had Barnes. On this occasion Luther says: " I advised the King that it would be better for him to take a concubine [1] than to ruin his people; nevertheless he craftily put away his queen."

In 1533 the King made another attempt to get a favorable opinion from the Wittenbergers, but presumably with the same result.

Undeterred by these rebuffs he dispatched Barnes, in March, 1535, on the same errand. Hardly had the ambassador returned before Henry heard that Francis I of France was seeking the alliance of the Schmalkaldic League, and, to counteract this move of his rival, he again sent Barnes posthaste with a gift of five hundred gulden to Melanchthon and an invitation to visit London, and with a smaller present of fifty gulden to Luther. In a letter of September 12, 1535, Luther strongly urged his government to allow Melanchthon to accept the invitation, and in the same letter adds: " Concerning the King's marriage it is agreed that the other ambassador shall treat with us. . . . I am curious to learn why they want to be so well satisfied on this point." This curiosity will be shared by others. The persistent efforts of the King remind one of Wolsey's saying that what he once took into his head no one could ever get out.

The expected ambassador — or rather two of them — arrived in December. They were no less personages than Edward Fox, Bishop of Hereford, and Archdeacon Nicholas Heath. Their special mission with Luther, apart from diplomatic business with the Elector, was to secure a favorable opinion of the divorce. For a time they had hopes of success, but their importunity finally wearied Luther, and when they returned they took with them a polite letter from the Reformer to Cromwell but an unfavorable judgment. According to this the Wittenberg theologians decided that though divine and moral law prohibit marriage with a brother's wife, after marriage had taken place no divorce is permissible.

[1] Luther uses this word to designate a second legitimate but subordinate wife. Cf. De Wette-Seidemann, vi, 276.

Soon after the return of the embassy to England, Henry executed Anne (May 19, 1536) and the next day married his third wife, Jane Seymour. He naturally did not apply to Luther any more. The Reformer was apprised of his act by a letter from Alesius, a Scotch Lutheran, and calls it " a monstrous tragedy." He seems, however, to have approved of the execution of his two old enemies, More and Fisher.

Intercourse with England was brisk during the next years, for it was the policy of Thomas Cromwell, the English minister, to ally himself to the Schmalkaldic League. In May, 1538, an Englishman came to Wittenberg and gave an interesting account of the visitation of the monasteries and of the images which were made to move by machinery. At the same time the German Protestants sent as envoys to Britain the Vice-Chancellor Burkhardt and the theologian Myconius. With them Luther sent a kind letter to Bishop Fox.

The alliance culminated in the marriage of Henry with Anne of Cleves, January, 1540. In the following July, however, she was divorced, and Cromwell paid with his life the penalty for the failure of his policy. A violent reaction against Lutheranism followed ; among its martyrs were Robert Barnes. The Reformer edited his English friend's confession of faith, drawn up just before his death, with a preface stating that he is forever done with Henry and such devils. Melanchthon only wished that God would free the world from such a monster at the hand of an able tyrannicide. Luther, though he never went so far as this, expressed his opinion with sufficient vigor : " This king wants to be God; he founds articles of faith which even the Pope never did. . . . I believe him to be an incarnate devil."

CHAPTER XVIII

ERASMUS

BEFORE Luther's fame had eclipsed that of all his contemporaries, the greatest figure in the republic of letters was Desiderius Erasmus of Rotterdam, who had attained to an acknowledged sovereignty like that later accorded to Voltaire. He combined great learning with a wonderful mastery of style, especially of the lighter kind, sparkling with wit. He was, moreover, inspired with a serious purpose of reform, in the service of which he used all his great and various talents. In his Praise of Folly (1511) he had written a cutting satire on the least admirable aspects of the mediæval Church, and by his edition of the Greek Testament (1516) he had given an immense stimulus along with necessary means to a fruitful study of the Bible. He was the deadly enemy of superstition and obscurantism, and the bold champion of sound learning and free thought. His true greatness would be proved, if by nothing else, by the fact that two such opposite and such large men as Martin Luther and François Rabelais [1] derived much of their inspiration from him.

Erasmus' idea of a reformation differed from that of Luther partly in aim but more in method. The humanist had a strong love of peace and a sincere horror of the "tumult." He judged that strong measures were *always* inexpedient, and, had he judged otherwise, he would not, by his own confession, have had the courage to adopt them.

The Wittenberg professor, who keenly sought the best and most recent books on divinity, learned to know many of Erasmus' commentaries and used them freely, along with the new edition of the Greek Testament, in preparing his lectures. With his usual independence of judgment he did not acquiesce

---

[1] L. Thuasne: *Études sur Rabelais*, Paris, 1904, pp. 27 ff. Förstemann und Günther: *Briefe an Erasmus*, Leipsic, 1904, p. 216.

in all the conclusions of the great scholar. On October 19, 1516, he wrote Spalatin that he had detected an unsound exegesis in the humanist's commentary on Romans, and begged his friend to communicate the objection to the author. Spalatin complied but received no answer. Luther continued to read Erasmus, and in the Commentary on Galatians referred with appreciation to his predecessor's work in this field. Indeed the first of the Ninety-five Theses may have been suggested by Erasmus' translation of Mark i, 15. That the monk also read the lighter works of the man of letters is proved by his reference in an epistle of November, 1517, to the Dialogue between Peter and Julius II : " It is written," said he, "so merrily, so learnedly and so ingeniously, — that is so, Erasmianly, — that it makes one laugh at the vices and miseries of the Church, at which every Christian ought rather to weep." Nevertheless he at one time had the intention of translating it into German, but gave it up, fearing that he could not do it justice.

That the young reformer expected to find an ally in the elder was perfectly natural. It was probably the influence of Melanchthon that first induced his friend to approach the great scholar definitely with this end. The first letter, somewhat condensed, is as follows : —

TO DESIDERIUS ERASMUS AT LOUVAIN

WITTENBERG, March 28, 1519.

Greeting. I chat much with you and you with me, O Erasmus, our glory and hope! — but yet we are not acquainted. Is not that monstrous? No, it is not monstrous, but a thing we see daily. For who is there whose innermost parts Erasmus has not penetrated, whom Erasmus does not teach and in whom he does not reign? I mean of those who love letters, for among the other gifts of Christ to you, this also must be mentioned, that you displease many, by which criterion I am wont to know what God gives in mercy from what he gives in wrath. I therefore congratulate you, that while you please good men to the last degree, you no less displease those who wish only to be highest and to please most. . . .

Now that I have learned from Fabritius Capito that my name is known to you on account of my little treatise on indulgences, and as I also learn from your preface to the new edition of your Handbook of

ERASMUS

From a painting by Holbein; at Basle

the Christian Knight, that my ideas are not only known to you but
approved by you, I am compelled to acknowledge my debt to you as
the enricher of my mind, even if I should have to do so in a barbarous style. . . .

And so, dear Erasmus, if it please you, learn to know this little
brother in Christ also : he is assuredly your very zealous friend, but
otherwise deserves, on account of his ignorance, only to be buried in
a corner, unknown even to your climate and sun. . . .

Erasmus, who had already praised the Theses (though he
denied the reference to them in the preface to the Handbook),
replied to this letter in a friendly way, assuring his correspondent
that he had many friends in the Netherlands and in England,
commending his Commentaries on the Psalms, but warning him
to guard against violence (May 30, 1519). About the same time
the humanist wrote to Frederic the Wise and to Melanchthon,
testifying his high esteem for the Saxon monk.

The letter of May 30, which the author had intended to be
private, was shortly printed at Leipsic. Partly to guard against
misapprehension, and partly to help the cause of reform, Erasmus wrote in November to Albert of Mayence, praising Luther's
character and urging that he be not condemned unheard, adding : " He wrote me a right Christian letter, to my own mind,
which I answered by warning him not to write anything seditious
or irreverent to the Pope or arrogantly or in anger. . . . I said
that thus could he conciliate the opinion of those who favor
him, which some have foolishly interpreted to mean that I
favor him." This letter, entrusted to the impetuous Ulrich von
Hutten, was by him forthwith published, with " Luther "
changed into " our Luther."

This indiscretion, to call it by its mildest name, was intended
to make Erasmus declare for the reform at once, but it had
rather the opposite effect. The humanist was already at swords'
points with the Dominicans, and now an enormous buzz arose
from this quarter that he of Rotterdam was in straight alliance
with him of Wittenberg and helped him to compose his
works. The theologians of Louvain, where Erasmus then lived,
published a condemnation of the heretic's doctrine ; the man
attacked struck back (1520), saying, " They have condemned

not only me, but Occam, Mirandola, Valla, Reuchlin, Wesel, Lefèvre d'Étaples, and Erasmus, that ram caught by the horns in the bushes." The humanist wrote in March to Melanchthon, saying that the Answer to the Condemnation of Louvain pleased him wonderfully, but at the same time wrote to the author a letter (now lost), probably asking him not to mention his name any more, to which Luther replied (if we may conjecture from other indications, for his letter, too, is lost) that he would not do so.

Throughout the year 1520 Erasmus did his best to secure the accused heretic a fair hearing. " They find it easier to burn his books than to refute them," he said, and set about writing and speaking, to Frederic the Wise, to Henry VIII of England, to Albert of Mayence, even to the Pope and cardinals, urging them not to proceed by force. When Aleander came to Louvain, on October 8, 1520, published the bull and burned Luther's books, Erasmus, who was attacked by him, replied in an anonymous polemic, The Acts of Louvain, discrediting the legate and declaring his belief that the bull was forged. His interview with the Elector of Saxony at Cologne on November 5, in which he urged him to insist that his subject have an impartial trial, has already been mentioned, as has his Counsel of One desiring the Peace of the Church, a memorial at this time pressed upon the Emperor's advisers, and the plan of arbitration composed by Erasmus and presented by Faber at the Diet of Worms.

Although these efforts immensely helped the Reformer, they did not accomplish all that the humanist hoped. Moreover he began, about 1521, to be alienated by the other's violence. The Babylonian Captivity he thought prevented the possibility of reconciliation, and he was especially incensed by the charge that this work, first published anonymously, was written by him.

When the news spread abroad of Luther's disappearance after the Diet of Worms, many expected that the humanist would take up the banner of reform. Albert Dürer, then travelling in the Netherlands where he had learned to know the great scholar, wrote in his diary: " O Erasmus of Rotterdam, where wilt thou abide? . . . O thou knight of Christ, seize the martyr's crown! . . ." But this was an honor the great scholar did not aspire to. A few days later he wrote Pace that the Germans were alienating him by trying to force him to declare for Luther, but that he feared, were a tumult to arise, that he would follow the example of Peter and deny his Lord.

Nevertheless he sought to remain neutral, although by so doing he brought on himself the suspicion of favoring the heretic. In numerous letters to his patrons and friends he excused himself from this charge. Some of these letters were published, and so Luther was kept posted on his quondam ally's change of attitude. In June, 1523, he wrote to Œcolampadius: —

I note the pricks that Erasmus gives me now and then, but as he does it without openly declaring himself my foe, I act as though I were unaware of his sly attacks, although I understand him better than he thinks. He has done what he was called to do; he has brought us from godless studies to a knowledge of the tongues; perhaps he will die in the land of Moab, for to enter the promised land he is unable.

That Erasmus finally came out as the opponent of the man he had once supported was due not only to the urging of his friends and patrons but also to the provocation given by the reformers. In the letter to Œcolampadius, Luther spoke slightingly of the humanist's theology, and this letter was shown Erasmus, who had, since 1521, removed from Louvain to Basel.

The fiery Hutten, who could bear no indecision, precipitated hostilities by publishing in June, 1523, an Expostulation with Erasmus, roundly rating him for duplicity and cowardice. Erasmus defended himself in the Sponge (August), in which he incidentally blames Luther for disturbing the peace, for scurrility, and especially for his recent unmeasured attack on Henry VIII. In a dedicatory letter to Zwingli he mentions as the chief errors of the Wittenberg professor: (1) Designation of all good works as mortal sin; (2) denial of Free Will; (3) justification by faith alone. Erasmus may have taken the idea from the letter of Henry VIII to Duke George (January 20, 1523), which mentioned these as the fundamental errors of the heretic. This letter with the Duke's answer was printed, and Erasmus read them both.

The reasons for Erasmus' choice of this subject, the freedom of the will, on which to attack Luther, have been much discussed. It has often been said that he chose the subject with the least practical interest, hoping in the first place not to put an obstacle in the way of reforms of which he really approved, and secondly not to antagonize the Reformer whose person he spared while criticising his doctrine. This motive probably had its weight with the humanist, but not the decisive weight. The matter was "in the air." Lorenzo Valla, always admired by Erasmus, had written a work on the freedom of the will in 1440, which had recently been edited by Vadian, 1518. The English Bishop Fisher had chosen this subject in his attack on Luther, the Refutation of Luther's Assertion, being a rebuttal of the Assertion of All the Articles Wrongly Condemned by the Last Bull of Leo X, in which, as we have seen (cf. *supra*, p. 101), Luther argues at length, in the thirty-sixth article, for his opinion that free will is but a name. The Reformer himself had selected this as the foundation of all his theology, being, in fact, no more than another form of the famous doctrine of justification by faith alone. His position was emphasized and clarified in Melanchthon's Common Places of Theology, appearing December, 1521.

The Diatribe on the Free Will was first mentioned by its author in a letter to Henry VIII of September 4, 1523, and it is possible that a first draft of it followed in this year. Finding that the printers at Basel were unwilling to publish anything against the popular hero of Germany, Erasmus had some thoughts of going to Rome to publish it.

The news of the impending attack soon spread. Luther himself, judging that the best way to prevent it was to threaten reprisals, wrote the following letter : —

TO DESIDERIUS ERASMUS AT BASEL

WITTENBERG (about April 15), 1524.

Grace and peace from our Lord Jesus Christ. I have been silent long enough, excellent Erasmus, having waited for you, as the greater and elder man, to speak first; but as you refuse to do so, I think that charity itself now compels me to begin. I say nothing about your

estrangement from us, by which you were made safer against my
enemies the papists. Nor do I especially resent your action, intended
to gain their favor or mitigate their hostility, in censuring and attacking us in various books. For since we see that the Lord has not given
you courage or sense to assail those monsters openly and confidently
with us, we are not the men to exact what is beyond your power and
measure. Rather we have tolerated and even respected the mediocrity
of God's gift in you. The whole world knows your services to letters
and how you have made them flourish and thus prepared a path for
the direct study of the Bible. For this glorious and splendid gift in
you we ought to thank God. I for one have never wished you to leave
your little sphere to join our camp, for although you might have profited the cause much by your ability, genius, and eloquence, yet as you
had not the courage it was safer for you to work at home. We only
fear that you might be induced by our enemies to fall upon our doctrine with some publication, in which case we should be obliged to
resist you to your face. We have restrained some who would have
drawn you into the arena, and have even suppressed books already
written against you. We should have preferred that Hutten's Expostulation had not been written, and still more that your Sponge had
not seen the light. Incidentally I may remark, that, unless I mistake,
when you wrote that book you felt how easy it is to write about moderation and blame Luther's excesses, but how hard or rather impossible it is to practise what you preach except by a special gift of the
Spirit. Believe it or not as you like, but Christ is witness that I
heartily regret that such zeal and hatred should be roused against
you. I cannot believe that you remain unmoved by it, for your forti-
tude is human and unequal to such trials. Perhaps a righteous zeal
moved them and they thought that you had provoked them in various
ways. Since they are admittedly too weak to bear your caustic but
dissembled sarcasm (which you would have pass for prudent moderation), they surely have a just cause for indignation, whereas if they
were stronger they would have none. I, too, am irritable, and quite
frequently am moved to write caustically, though I have only done
so against hardened men proof against milder forms of admonition.
Otherwise I think my gentleness and clemency toward sinners, no
matter how far they are gone in iniquity, is witnessed not only by my
own conscience but by the experience of many. Hitherto, accordingly,
I have controlled my pen as often as you prick me, and have written
in letters to friends which you have seen that I would control it until
you publish something openly. For although you will not side with

us and although you injure or make sceptical many pious persons by
your impiety and hypocrisy, yet I cannot and do not accuse you of
wilful obstinacy. What can I do? Each side is greatly exasperated.
Could my good offices prevail, I would wish my friends to cease
attacking you with so much animus and to allow your old age a peaceful death in the Lord. I think they would do so if they were reasonable
and considered your weakness and the greatness of the cause which
has long since outgrown your littleness, especially as the cause has now
progressed so far that it has little to fear from the might — or rather
the sting and bite — of Erasmus. You on your side, Erasmus, ought
to consider their infirmity and abstain from making them the butt of
your witty rhetoric. Even if you cannot and dare not declare for us,
yet at least you might leave us alone and mind your own business. If
they suffer from your bites, *you* certainly will confess that human
weakness has cause to fear the name and fame of Erasmus and that
it is a very much graver matter to be snapped at by you than to be
ground to pieces by all the papists together. I say this, excellent Erasmus, as an evidence of my *candid moderation*, wishing that the Lord
might give you a spirit worthy of your reputation, but if he delays
doing so I beg that meanwhile if you can do nothing else you will remain a spectator of the conflict and not join our enemies, and especially
that you publish no book against me, as I shall write none against you.
Remember that the men who are called Lutherans are human beings
like ourselves, whom you ought to spare and forgive as Paul says:
"Bear ye one another's burdens." We have fought long enough, we
must take care not to eat each other up. This would be a terrible
catastrophe, as neither one of us really wishes harm to religion, and
without judging each other both may do good. Pardon my poor style
and farewell in the Lord. . . .

MARTIN LUTHER.

Erasmus' answer, dated May 8, asserts that he is not less
zealous for the cause of religion than others who arrogate to
themselves the name "evangelic," and that he has as yet written nothing against Luther, though had he done so he would
have won the applause of the great ones of the world.

Very soon after this he finished the Diatribe on the Free
Will. On account of its pure Latinity, its moderation, wit, and
brevity, this work is still very readable. It is also distinguished
by the absence of scurrility; indeed it hardly makes the impres-

sion of a polemic at all, but rather of a conversation on the intellectual movement of the times, addressed to a wide audience.

The author expresses his perfect readiness to appeal only to reason and to Scripture, as these are the only grounds recognized by Luther. He defines free will as the power to apply one's self to the things leading to salvation, and appeals to the universal opinion of mankind that each one has such a power. His strongest argument is that it would be unjust for God to damn a man for doing what he could not help. He devotes long sections to explanations of Scriptural passages, such as "God hardened Pharaoh's heart," which would seem to militate against free will, and he refutes point by point Luther's arguments in the Assertion of All the Articles Condemned by the Bull — a part of the work in which he borrows much without acknowledgment from Bishop Fisher. Finally he sums up: "Those please me who attribute something to free will but much to grace." Both must coöperate to save a man, one may assign as small a part as one likes to the former factor, only it must be *some* part.

The Diatribe was published in September, 1524, and promptly sent to the author's patrons and friends, most of whom it had the good fortune to please. Even Melanchthon liked the moderation of tone and the reasonableness of the argument. Luther himself confessed that of all his opponents Erasmus only had gone to the root of the matter and instead of threatening him with ban and stake had undertaken to refute him by reasons. He once said that of all the books written against him, the Diatribe was the only one he read through, but even this made him feel like throwing it under the bench and heartily disgusted him. He did not answer it for more than a year, a delay partly accounted for by his preoccupations with the "heavenly prophets," the Peasants' War, and his marriage, and partly by the unusual care with which he prepared his reply. His book on the Unfree Will (*De servo arbitrio*) at last appeared in December, 1525.

This bulky volume has been acclaimed by most Protestant biographers of Luther as his ablest polemic and a work of extraordinary power. It is needless to remark that much of this ability is wasted on a generation for which the question, then so passionately disputed, has sunk almost into oblivion. In point of earnestness he is a striking contrast to Erasmus. What for the latter is the subject of an interesting discussion is to him matter of life and death. It is in this sense that he attributes eloquence and mastery of speech to his opponent, but to himself substance and real understanding of the issue.

Luther takes his former stand for extreme predestinarianism. His determinism is not founded, as that of a modern philosopher might be, on any conception of the immutability of natural law, but is simply and solely the logical deduction from his doctrine of justification by faith alone, or, as it is technically called, of the monergism of grace. Man is a simple instrument in God's hands, and the Almighty arbitrarily saves whom he wills and damns whom he wills. The extreme form in which Luther put this doctrine, which is certainly revolting to our ideas, can only be realized by a few quotations of his own words : —

The human will is like a beast of burden. If God mounts it, it wishes and goes as God wills ; if Satan mounts it, it wishes and goes as Satan wills. Nor can it choose the rider it would prefer, nor betake itself to him, but it is the riders who contend for its possession. . . .

This is the acme of faith, to believe that God who saves so few and condemns so many is merciful ; that he is just who at his own pleasure has made us necessarily doomed to damnation, so that, as Erasmus says, he seems to delight in the tortures of the wretched, and to be more deserving of hatred than of love. If by any effort of reason I could conceive how God, who shows so much anger and iniquity, could be merciful and just, there would be no need of faith. . . .

God foreknows nothing subject to contingencies, but he foresees, foreordains, and accomplishes all things by an unchanging, eternal, and efficacious will. By this thunderbolt free will sinks shattered in the dust.

Besides defending his main thesis Luther here puts forward his doctrine of infallibility of the Scripture. He is enraged at the assertion of his opponent that there seem to be contradictions in the Bible. According to Luther every text must be taken literally, and yet all must be made to agree, for as the whole is plenarily inspired by divine wisdom there can be no diversity of doctrine. Moreover he apologizes for his whole theology, especially replying to the charge that tumult followed it by asserting that uproar always follows the preaching of God's Word.

He sent a copy of the work, with a letter asserting his conviction of its truth, to his opponent, but the messenger was delayed and Erasmus did not receive it until April. In the mean time a friend in Leipsic (Duke George?) had sent him a copy, which he received on February 10. He commenced his reply at once, spending only twelve days in answering it so as to have the reply ready to be sold at the Frankfort Fair. He was astonished by the violence of Luther's invective of which he complained to the Elector of Saxony. To Luther himself he wrote as follows:—

DESIDERIUS ERASMUS TO MARTIN LUTHER AT WITTENBERG

BASEL, April 11, 1526.

Your letter was delivered to me too late and had it come in time it would not have moved me. . . . The whole world knows your nature, according to which you have guided your pen against no one more bitterly and, what is more detestable, more maliciously than against me. . . . The same admirable ferocity which you formerly used against Fisher and against Cochlaeus, who provoked it by reviling you, you now use against my book in spite of its courtesy. How do your scurrilous charges that I am an atheist, an Epicurean, and a sceptic, help the argument? . . . It terribly pains me, as it must all good men, that your arrogant, insolent, rebellious nature has set the world in arms. . . . You treat the Evangelic cause so as to confound together all things sacred and profane, as if it were your chief aim to prevent the tempest from ever becoming calm, while it is my greatest desire that it should die down. . . .

The Hyperaspistes, Part I, is a work three times as large as the Diatribe, of which it is a defence, and is moreover a general attack on all points of Luther's doctrine. In it the question of free will recedes behind the other question of the excellence of the Lutheran movement. Erasmus cannot convince himself that the Reformer is really inspired with the spirit of the gospel, as he has not learned to avoid giving offence. He attacks Luther's person and the results of his doctrine, among which are included the Peasants' War. As the book is written in such haste, he promises a continuation of it later with fuller consideration of the main argument.

After his first heat had cooled down, Erasmus put off this promised work for eighteen months. That he wrote it at all was again the work of Henry VIII. This monarch's answer to Luther, published in the early part of 1527, contains some references to free will which made the Reformer suspect Erasmus' hand in its composition. This charge, coupled with the violence of the Wittenberg reformer, which alienated many persons besides Erasmus, induced him to reply. This he did in a book six times the size of the Diatribe, which appeared about September 1, 1527, and was called Hyperaspistes, Part II.

Now at last the fundamental difference between Erasmus and Luther is revealed, the opposite trend of the two natures. The humanist reacts against Luther's absolutism; he cannot abide hard-and-fast rules admitting no exception. Of himself he said, "I am prone to those things like nature; I abhor portents"; of his antagonist, "He never recoils from extremes." For the dogmatic reformer there is one absolute right and one absolute wrong; for the classic scholar men and things cannot be divided into such uncompromising categories; there are shades and degrees. Luther is a logician; from premises impeccable, because directly revealed in the Bible, he draws conclusions of mathematical precision; Erasmus is an evolutionist and a rationalist, to whom all truth does not come through the Bible, but much from reason. He believes, moreover, that men have a natural trend to the good. At the close of this comprehensive work he tries to hedge and make peace again. After all, the strife is mainly one of words, and man should remember that salvation is God's work, but damnation that of sin. Just as the Hyperaspistes, Part II, appeared, its author wrote Duke George that Luther's spirit is neither a wholly good nor an entirely bad one.

The work was received by the Evangelic party as might have been expected. Justus Jonas, a quondam Erasmian, now at Wittenberg, referred to his former beloved master as a toad. Melanchthon, indeed, who resembled Erasmus in many ways, was half-convinced that determinism would be bad for the morals of the common man, for who would try to be good if he was convinced it was no use? Luther himself punned on the double meaning of aspis, which in Greek means both shield and viper (Hyperaspistes, a soldier), calling the work "super-viperean." He never deigned to answer it for reasons explained to Montanus in a letter of May 28, 1529 : —

Erasmus writes nothing in which he does not show the impotence of his mind or rather the pain of the wounds he has received. I despise him, nor shall I honor the fellow by arguing with him any more. . . . In future I shall only refer to him as some alien, rather condemning than refuting his ideas. He is a light-minded man, mocking all religion as his dear Lucian does, and serious about nothing but calumny and slander.

But the last word was not yet said. In 1533 George Witzel, a liberal Catholic and an admirer of Erasmus, begged "that Solon" to draw up a plan for pacifying the Church. The old scholar, who, in the mean time, had been forced to withdraw from Basel, now too Protestant for him, to Freiburg, flattered by the request, published a reasonable and irenic pamphlet, On Mending the Peace of the Church, advising that each side tolerate the other in non-essential matters, that all controversial writings be forbidden, and that a general council take measures with the civil authorities for restoring unity and healing the schism.

The anger of the reformers was roused afresh by this apparently inoffensive essay towards compromise. Corvinus answered it in full, Luther writing a preface for his work, proving that there could be no peace between Christ and Belial. At the same time he expressed himself more fully in a long printed letter to Amsdorf, written about March 11, 1534, calling Erasmus by the somewhat contradictory names of heretic, atheist, blasphemer, and Arian, and, worst of all, one who makes jokes of serious things and serious business of jokes.

Erasmus answered with A Justification against the Intemperate Letter of Luther, denying all the accusations point by point. Two years later he died, in the opinion of his adversary "without light, without the cross, and without God."

The table-talk (1531–46) is full of the most rancorous expressions about the great scholar: —

In writing his Folly, Erasmus begot a daughter worthy of himself. He turns, twists, and bites like an awl, but yet shows himself a true fool.

On my death-bed I shall forbid my sons to read his Colloquies. . . . He is much worse than Lucian, mocking all things under the guise of holiness.

He goes so far as to compare our Lord to the god Priapus. . . .

In his New Testament he is ambiguous and cavilling . . . trying to perplex the reader and make him think the doctrine doubtful. He reviles all Christians, making no exception of Paul or any pious man.

The battle between Luther and Erasmus was a real tragedy. The humanist had set himself, as his life task, a peaceful reformation of the Church; abuses, he thought, would fade away before gentle sarcasm and the cultivation of good letters and the sacred texts. The boisterous attack of the Wittenberg monk, said he sadly, destroyed all hope of this. He lived to see his ideal of peace shattered in war, the followers trained to carry on his work reft from him by one side or the other, and his own name spat upon by almost all.

For Luther the loss was hardly less. He saw the man in whom he confidently expected the most valuable of all allies gradually draw back from his side and become not only a neutral but an enemy, to the great scandal of his own followers and to the hurt of the Evangelic Church. In his anger and disappointment he more and more expressed himself in unmeasured terms, and more and more forgot the good in Erasmus and the services he had done the world. But those who regret his one-sidedness and especially his violence should not blame him too hastily. Every great leader of a new and struggling movement must feel that he who is not with him is against him and that he who gathereth not scattereth. The citizen who refuses to take arms in wartime is a public enemy. His scruples may be honorable, but one can hardly blame the general for expelling him from the ranks. In the American civil war no character was so much detested as the " copper-head," the Northern man who refused to fight for the Union.

The Reformation is still a living issue. A reflecting mind must have an opinion on its merits. Some judge it as a great step forward, others as a blow to human progress. A few are still Erasmians, approving the principle of the Reformation, they think it might have been accomplished without rending the peace of the world. But the mass of mankind are not led in that way. To reform any institution it is not sufficient to secure the intellectual adherence of a few choice spirits, the whole soul of a people must be aroused. One may estimate the Reformation as one pleases, but to think of it without Luther is as unhistorical as to fancy that Christianity might have grown up without its great Founder, or that Islam could have been born in the deserts of Arabia without the Prophet.

CHAPTER XIX

GERMAN POLITICS. 1522-1529

WHEN Martin Luther returned from the Wartburg in March, 1522, he found the state of affairs very different, not only at Wittenberg, but in the whole of Germany, from that which he had left a year before. He was no longer a lone man fighting single-handed against the official representatives of the universal Church; he was now at the head of a movement which gradually swept into its vortex the greater part not only of his countrymen but of all civilized Europe north of the Alps and the Pyrenees. By far the greater part of this revolution lies entirely beyond the ken of a biographer of Luther. He cared little or nothing for politics in themselves, partly because of his direct reliance on God, partly because he felt himself ill qualified to advise on such matters. Nevertheless in some phases of public affairs he was forced by his position to interfere.

Leo X died in December, 1521. His successor, Adrian VI, a pious man and a sincere Catholic, fought both the corruption within the Church and the schism without. His particularly close relations with the Emperor, to whom he had once been tutor, foreboded danger to the new cause, though as a matter of fact his short pontificate enabled him to do little. To the Diet called at Nuremberg in 1522 he sent an injunction to stamp out heresy in the Empire. Before this body also came the complaints of Duke George of Albertine Saxony against the fanatical programme of the prophets at Wittenberg. In defence of his subject, Frederic the Wise, now as always his best supporter, submitted the letter drawn up by Luther immediately after his return.[1] This, together with the restoration of order at Wittenberg, impressed the members of the Diet so favorably that they declined to take any decisive action against the outlawed heretic.

[1] Cf. *supra*, p. 146.

Nevertheless his position and that of his protector was very delicate. The Imperial Edict of Worms was still in force. Frederic had on this account been much opposed to his coming out of hiding, fearing that the electorate would become embroiled with the central government. In the letter of March 5, 1522,[1] Luther had answered his lord's question as to how far he, Frederic, was bound to obey the higher power in case it demanded the execution of the edict, by saying that it would be sufficient to allow the imperial officers a free hand, but that resistance to them would be rebellion and therefore forbidden by God. This disinterested advice was partly determined by the riots at Wittenberg; while the Reformer was preaching earnestly against these disturbers of the peace, he could hardly request his sovereign to defend him against the Emperor by arms. The letter gives the key-note to Luther's attitude toward the government for the next ten years; he consistently maintained that opposition to it should be confined to neglecting to execute its decrees, but that all armed resistance must be discountenanced as tantamount to treason. These principles were thoroughly worked out in a thoughtful little pamphlet, published in March, 1523, entitled: Of Civil Authority and how far Obedience is due to it.

Formerly, he begins, I wrote a book to the German Nobility, to point out their office and Christian work. Every one sees how well they have done their duty. But now I must carefully advise them what to leave undone, hoping that these men, who have hitherto striven to be Christians before they were princes, will now let themselves be guided by me. God Almighty has made our princes foolish, so that they think that they can command their subjects whatever they please, and the subjects likewise think they are bound to obey every command. . . . Indeed the civil authorities presume to sit in God's seat, mastering consciences and faith, and they try to teach the Holy Ghost. . . . Now since the fools rage to extirpate Christ's faith, to deny his Word, and to blaspheme his Majesty, I neither will nor can any longer acquiesce in their doings.

Nevertheless, he continues, we must not err on account of the spiritual tyranny of the lords. The powers that be are

[1] *Supra*, p. 144.

ordained of God and have been given a divine right from the beginning.

The world is divided into two parts, the Kingdom of God and that of the world; it is against the latter that the temporal power must bear the sword, but of the former that Christ spoke when he bade us turn the other cheek. In a somewhat labored argument Luther even proves that bearing the sword is an office of love, because it enables one to protect his neighbor from wrong.

In the second part of his treatise, the author considers the limitations of the secular power. The civil magistrate is not entitled to punish heretics or to force the faith of any one. Lords are no judges of such matters, " for since the foundation of the world a wise prince has been a rare bird and a just one much rarer. They are generally the biggest fools and worst knaves on earth, wherefore one must always expect the worst of them and not much good, especially in divine matters which concern the soul. They are only God's gaolers and hangmen." This harsh judgment of hereditary magistrates is the more surprising in a work dedicated to Duke John, the Elector's brother. In no case, the writer emphatically sums up, may the temporal power decide spiritual things nor even guard against plain false doctrine.

In conclusion he points out the duties of a Christian prince, of which the first and foremost is to attend to the weal of his subjects.

In summing up Luther's " political theory," Professor Dunning says that two doctrines can be deduced from his various writings on the subject: " first, the absolute distinction in kind between spiritual and secular interests and authority, and second, the Christian duty of passive submission to the established social and political order."

Both these doctrines were later modified by the course of events. When the political situation seemed to make it necessary for the Protestants to fight for their faith, the Reformer under a rather casuistical plea gave his consent to this course, which, however, was happily avoided. In a meeting of the jurists and theologians to discuss this point at Torgau in 1531, Luther let himself be convinced that resistance would in some cases be legal, justifying himself in a letter (dated February 15, 1531) to Lazarus Spengler who accused him of "recanting his former opinion that resistance to the Emperor was wrong."

> I am not conscious of any inconsistency (he writes) . . . The jurists first alleged the maxim that force might be repelled with force, which did not satisfy me; then they pointed out that it was a positive imperial law that "in cases of notorious injustice the government might be resisted by force," to which I merely replied that I did not know whether this was the law or not, but that if the Emperor *had* thus limited himself we might let him remain so . . . and, as the law commands, resist him by force.

The proposition that one might resist the Emperor only when and because he himself commanded it, is not really quite so absurd as it seems when thus baldly stated. The sixteenth century had no word for the idea "constitution," so familiar to us. Had Luther written four hundred years later, he would have said that the imperial laws might be resisted when they were unconstitutional, for it must be remembered that the Holy Roman Empire had a constitution, mostly unwritten, like that of England, but consisting partly of ancient charters like the Golden Bull.

On his first doctrine, that in no case the civil power has the right to interfere in matters of faith, the Reformer was also forced to weaken. The fanatical innovations of Münzer and the prophets, with their sequel in the Peasants' War, taught him the danger of allowing men to teach what they pleased under the guise of religion. Moreover, when, in 1525, an avowed Lutheran ascended the electoral throne, willing to support the till then struggling religion with powerful laws, the Reformer's ideas of the proper sphere of government considerably widened, so that he became almost, though not quite, an Erastian. Not that he ever allowed the right of the magistrate to compel faith, but he insisted on the duty of the government to enforce uniformity in religious externals. Thus, on November 11, 1525, he wrote Spalatin: "Our government does not force belief in the Evangelic faith, but only suppresses external abominations [such as masses and all forms of public worship save the Lutheran]. . . . For even our opponents confess that the government should put down crimes like blasphemy."

In the same tenor he wrote Joseph Levin Metsch, August 26, 1529 : —

No one is to be compelled to profess the faith, but no one must be allowed to injure it. Let our opponents give their objections and hear our answers. If they are thus converted, well and good ; if not let them hold their tongues and believe what they please. . . . In order to avoid trouble we should not, if possible, suffer contrary teachings in the same state. Even unbelievers should be forced to obey the Ten Commandments, attend church, and outwardly conform.

It is easily seen that all real freedom of conscience vanishes when the distinction between the suppression of heresy and the enforcement of conformity by the civil power is drawn so fine. If Luther's tolerance was far short of modern standards, in one respect he was greatly superior to his contemporaries, all of whom, Catholic princes, Henry VIII, Zwingli and Calvin, put dissenters to death. The man of Wittenberg, in this as in other things, following Augustine, who punished heretics with banishment, consistently refused to do this, for reasons presented in a letter to Wenzel Link, written July 14, 1528 : —

You ask whether the government may put false prophets to death. I hesitate to give capital punishment even when it is evidently deserved, so much am I terrified to think what happened when the papists and the Jews punished with death, . . . for in the course of time it has always come to pass that none but the most holy and innocent prophets were slain. . . . Wherefore it is sufficient to banish false teachers.

Returning from this digression on Luther's political theories to the course of history in the years following the Diet of Worms, we find that the Reformer's confidence, fostered by his continued immunity from persecution, that all would work together for good without the interference of man was not shared by his sovereign. On October 12, 1523, the professor wrote Spalatin : —

Now, almost two years since my return from the Wartburg you see that, contrary to the expectation of all, the Elector is not only safe but feels the rage of the other princes much less than he did a year ago. . . . If I knew any way of keeping him safe without discrediting the gospel, I would act accordingly even at the expense of my life. . . . I wish he possessed more equanimity, and power to dissimulate for a while. His way of acting does not please me, for it savors of I know not what unbelief and courtly infirmity of soul, preferring temporal to spiritual things.

This criticism of the Elector's policy was hardly justified by events. While he was procrastinating and gaining time the Evangelic faith won many powerful converts throughout the Empire. The cause was threatened for a moment by the rebellion and fall of the party of the knights under Sickingen, which claimed alliance with Wittenberg. True to his principles of obedience, the Reformer gave no countenance to the movement, designated by Melanchthon as brigandage, and when it was crushed in May, 1523, largely by the energy of the Evangelic Philip of Hesse, the recoil was not felt by the growing Church. Among the many gains made during these years the most important was that of Prussia, till 1523 a fief of the religious order of Teutonic Knights, whose grand master, Albert of Brandenburg, adopting the new faith, turned it into a temporal realm.

On September 14 of this same eventful year Adrian VI died. In his place was elected a Medici, Clement VII, whose main object was to restore the elegant humanism and corrupt privileges of the Curia enjoyed by the courtiers of his kinsman, Leo X. He wished, however, to stamp out the dangerous schism, and therefore sent to the Diet, summoned at Nuremberg January, 1524, Campeggio, an able legate, with strong representations urging the execution of the Edict of Worms. This appeal met with no success; the nuncio was obliged to speak very moderately to get a hearing at all, while thousands of persons, among them many members of the Diet, and even a sister of the Emperor, flouted the Pope and Campeggio by taking communion in both kinds from the hand of the Lutheran pastor, Osiander. All that could be wrung from the Estates was a resolution to enforce the edict as far as they were able, a nullifying qualification. In return they demanded an immediate calling of a free council of the Church to meet at Spires to compose the religious differences.

The year 1525 was the hardest through which the young movement had to go. The Peasants' War alienated many of

the nobles from the fermenting doctrine, and the Reformer's harshness to the poor rebels shook his popularity with
the people. In the very midst of the tumult, on May 5, the
Elector Frederic died. He was buried in his favorite church
at Wittenberg by the famous subject with whom he had never
spoken and whom he rarely saw. On May 23, Luther writes
to Rühel : —

My gracious lord departed this life in the enjoyment of his full
reason, taking the sacrament in both kinds and without supreme
unction. We buried him without masses or vigils, but yet in a fine
noble manner. Several stones were found in his lungs and three (wonderful to relate) in his gall, in fact he died of the stone. . . . The
signs of his death were a rainbow which Melanchthon and I saw one
night last winter over Lochau, and a child born here at Wittenberg
without a head, and another with feet turned around.

Though Frederic's talents were not of the dazzling order, he
had certainly shown consummate ability in protecting the Wittenberg monk during the crucial early years. Though he was too
prudent to flaunt his advanced views in the face of the world,
there can be no doubt that at heart he was a convinced disciple of the new teaching. His subject recognized and often
spoke highly of his first patron : —

When the genius of a financier, a statesman, and a hero concur in
the same prince, it is a gift of God. Such an one was Frederic.

He was, indeed, very wise. He took care of the administration himself and did not leave everything to a pack of fools, for he said:
" While I am alive I will be ruler."

He was succeeded by his brother John the Steadfast, a less
able but more open devotee of the Evangelic faith. With his
accession the Lutheran Church became the dominant one.
Spalatin, on the death of his master, retired from the chap-
laincy of the court and was appointed to the pastorate of the
first church at the capital, Altenburg. He remained the confidant and adviser of the new elector, and did invaluable service
to the cause by representing the Reformer's ideas at court.
There still existed a strong Catholic opposition, composed
mostly of nobles who feared the new doctrines, that they re-

garded as subversive. Indeed Luther feared to come to his friend Spalatin's wedding at Altenburg on account "of the ignoble crowd of nobles raging against me." He even said that he felt safer under the old elector who did not openly profess the gospel than under the new one who did.

The first Diet after John's accession, that of Augsburg, 1525, proved small and abortive, but that which met at Spires in June, 1526, was described by Spalatin as the boldest and freest ever held. Many innovations were suggested by the liberal majority, which Ferdinand, the Emperor's brother and lieutenant, vainly tried to obstruct. The Estates passed a decree (known as the Recess of Spires), providing that in matters of faith each state should act as it could answer to God and the Emperor. This was in effect a declaration of entire religious liberty, not indeed for each individual, but for each state of the Empire.

The division of Saxony between the Ernestine and Albertine branches of the house of Wettin has already been described. As the strongest support for the Lutherans came from the former, so the most determined opposition to them came from the latter during the lifetime of Duke George the Bearded. This prince had heard the Leipsic debate in 1519, and had been shocked by the Wittenberger's open avowal of a position regarded as heretical; for the next twenty years, until his death in 1539, he was the ablest and most active of the Reformer's opponents. Though both a moral and a sincere man, not bigoted according to the standards of the age, Luther regarded him, on account of his refusal to accept the "gospel," as the very instrument of Satan. The prince greatly provoked him in 1522 by sending a complaint to the Imperial Council, and by excluding the German New Testament from his lands. In March of this year the Reformer wrote a good friend, Hartmuth von Kronberg, alluding to "the straw and paper tyranny" of certain persons otherwise designated as "bladders." Hartmuth promptly published the letter, filling in the blank with the name of the duke. To a polite inquiry from George about the authorship of the obnoxious pamphlet, the writer thought fit to return the following insulting response: —

TO DUKE GEORGE OF SAXONY AT DRESDEN

WITTENBERG, January 3, 1523.

Instead of greeting I wish you would stop raging and roaring against God and against his Christ. Ungracious Prince and Lord! I received your Disgrace's letter with the pamphlet or letter I wrote Hartmuth von Kronberg, and have had read to me with especial care the part of which your Disgrace complains as injurious to your soul, honor, and reputation. The epistle has been printed at Wittenberg and elsewhere. As your Disgrace desires to know what position I take in it, I briefly answer that as far as your Disgrace is concerned, it is the same to me whether my position is standing, lying down, sitting or running. For when I act or speak against your Disgrace, be it secretly or openly, I intend it as right, and (God willing) will have it taken so. God will find the needful power. For if your Disgrace were in earnest, and did not so ignobly lie about my coming too near your soul, honor, and reputation, you would not so shamefully hurt and persecute Christian truth. This is not the first time that I am belied and evilly entreated by your Disgrace, so that I have more cause than you to complain of injuries to soul, honor, and reputation. But I pass over all that, for Christ commands me to do good even to my enemies, which I have hitherto done with my poor prayers to God for your Disgrace. I offer to serve your Disgrace in anything I can, save in what is wrong. If you despise my offer I can do no more, and shall not tremble for a mere bladder, God willing. May he lighten your Disgrace's eyes and heart and please to make me a gracious, kind prince of you. Amen.

MARTIN LUTHER,
by the grace of God Evangelist at Wittenberg.

Duke George, naturally still more antagonized by such a letter, endeavored by making strong diplomatic representations to his cousins to force the author to apologize. For a long time Luther steadily refused to do this, but about three years later he thought that the time was propitious for a reconciliation, and accordingly wrote his old enemy with that view. What decided him to do so is not clear; perhaps a sense of his weakened position at this time made him more conciliatory: —

TO DUKE GEORGE OF SAXONY AT DRESDEN

(WITTENBERG,) December 21, 1525.

. . . As I observe that your Grace does not turn from your dis-favor, I am minded once more to approach your Grace, perhaps for the last time, with this humble, affectionate letter. It looks to me as if God would soon take one of us away, and so makes it desirable that Duke George and Luther should speedily become friends. . . .

I fall at your Grace's feet and beg you in utter humility to leave off persecuting my doctrine. Not that much harm can come to me through your Grace's persecution, for I have little to lose but my poor body. . . . Truly I have a greater enemy than you, namely, the devil and his angels. . . . Persecution has greatly helped me and I thank my enemies for it. If your Grace's misfortunes were pleasant to me, which they are not, I would irritate you still more and provoke you to persecute me more. . . . Of my doctrine I can only say that it speaks for itself and does not need my exhortation to recommend it. . . . Let not your Grace despise my humble person, for God once spoke through an ass. . . .

Except by preaching my doctrine I beg to know how I have inad-vertently hurt your Grace. I forgive from my heart what your Grace has done to hurt me, and I will pray the Lord to forgive you what you have done against his Word. . . . Let me inform your Grace that I have always hitherto prayed *for* your Grace, and now write this letter in hopes of avoiding the necessity of praying *against* your Grace, for although we are a poor little flock, yet should we pray against you . . . we know that nothing good would happen to you. . . . Your Grace might then learn that it is a different thing to fight against Luther from fighting against Münzer. . . .

Your Grace's humble, devoted servant,

MARTIN LUTHER.

This missive reached its destination on Christmas and was answered on December 28 "for a New Year's gift." The Duke recalls the Kronberg episode, with the letter of 1523, and re-bukes the Reformer for "reviling us with slippery words, the like of which you will not find in the Bible, by which example you justify yourself." Moreover, "We heard you debate, and when accused by Eck of being a patron of the Hussites, blus-teringly deny the charge, although you asserted that certain articles of Huss, for which he was condemned, were right Christian. Then, acting as a friend, we had a private interview with you." In conclusion : " My dear Luther, keep the gospel you have drawn from under the bushel, we will stand by the gospel of Christ as the Church holds it, so help us God ! "

The hostility of Duke George to the new faith was more than balanced by the adherence of his son-in-law. After the death of Frederic of Saxony, the ablest champion of Lutheranism was Philip, Landgrave of Hesse. His enterprise and ambition made him a great contrast to the cautious, diplomatic elector. Early left fatherless, he had been declared of age by his guardian, the Emperor Maximilian, at thirteen. Four years later he had met Luther at the Diet of Worms, and, attracted by the monk's courage, had wished him godspeed. In spite of the alliance with Duke George, whose daughter Christina he married in 1523, he heartily embraced the new faith and entered into the league of Torgau, with Electoral Saxony and other states, for its support. The suppression of the successive revolts of the knights and of the peasants having been largely due to his ability, he had conceived high ambitions for extending his religion and for his personal aggrandizement.

In 1528 a plot almost precipitated a general war, to which, perhaps, he would not have been averse as a means to these ends. Such a conflict he may have regarded as inevitable ; at any rate he became convinced that there was an understanding between the supporters of the old faith to suppress the new heresy and expropriate himself and the Elector of Saxony. His suspicions were confirmed by an ex-counsellor of Duke George, Dr. Otto von Pack, who brought the Landgrave a document purporting to be a treaty between Ferdinand and a number of Catholic princes to extirpate Luther and his followers, and if necessary eject Philip and John the Steadfast from their respective domains. Though a forgery, this document concurred so aptly with the Landgrave's suspicions that, never doubting it, he at once communicated its contents to the equally unsuspecting Elector and Luther. Hesse armed forthwith and began a campaign against one of the bishops named in the treaty, and forced him to pay an indemnity. Philip urged John to do the same, but at Luther's advice the Elector first consulted the Imperial Executive Council and questioned Duke George. Explanations were simultaneously offered from all sides that nothing was known of the treaty. Philip, who has sometimes been charged with being the instigator of the whole affair, gave up his suspicions with the utmost reluctance. Neither was the Reformer ever convinced by the official dementis, but believed to his dying day that, treaty or no treaty, the conspiracy had actually existed. Of it he wrote : —

TO WENZEL LINK AT NUREMBERG

(WITTENBERG,) June 14, 1528.

Grace and peace. You know more news than I can tell you. You see what a commotion this confederacy of wicked princes has caused. They deny it, to be sure, but I consider Duke George's extremely cool denial as equivalent to a confession. Let them protest as they please, I know what I know; that confederacy is no mere chimæra, though it is a most monstrous monster. . . . May God confound that worst of fools [Duke George] who, like Moab, boasts more than he can do and waxes proud beyond his power. We shall pray against those homicides; hitherto we have spared them, but if they try anything again we shall pray God and exhort our princes to make them perish without quarter, inasmuch as those insatiable blood-suckers will not rest until they make Germany reek with gore. . . .

This letter was indiscreetly shown by Link to friends, one of whom sent a copy of it to Duke George. The insulted prince wrote imperiously to Luther, asking him if he had sent the obnoxious missive to Link. The Reformer replied on October 31, saying that he would answer neither yes nor no, and begging that in future he be left untroubled by such communications. The Duke complained to the Elector, and answered in a printed letter of November. In reply to this, Luther published, in December, an article On Secret and Stolen Letters, vehemently accusing his adversary of theft of the mails, and bidding him find out from the man who sent him the letter what he wanted to know about it. George answered again, in January, 1529, but the altercation was carried on no further until a new cause kindled the old hatred.

Though the Recess of Spires certainly did not intend to legalize the Reformation, nevertheless it was a considerable gain to the Evangelic party, giving them the possibility of a wide interpretation, at their own risk, of the course of action for which they would be answerable to God and the Emperor. Charles had strictly forbidden the Estates to meddle with the religious question, and after passing the Recess they had sent him a humble petition for more liberty. Had he been able to enforce the Edict of Worms and stamp out the heresy at once, he would certainly have done so, but he was for many years too much entangled with foreign wars to venture strong measures against powerful subjects. When, by the victory of Pavia, February 24, 1525, he had defeated the rival Valois, and by the sack of Rome, May, 1527, he had temporarily mastered the Pope, he still had an arduous task before him in the conflict with the Turks. At Mohacs, in August, 1526, Sultan Suliman had routed the Hungarian army, and slain its king. The imminent danger of an invasion of Germany was not averted until the Turks were repulsed at Vienna, in October, 1529. For a moment it looked as if the mutual animosities of the Christians would be buried in their fear and detestation of the common foe. Luther was strongly in favor of such a course and took pains to clear himself of the imputation that he shared the views of those Anabaptists who, like the later Quakers, taught that all war was wrong. This he did, first in a tract entitled Whether Soldiers can be in a State of Grace (1526), in which he says : —

What people now write and say about war being such a curse is true. But we should remember how much greater a curse may sometimes be avoided by war.

Men should not, indeed, he continues, fight in a cause they know to be wrong, but when in doubt they are bound to follow their sovereign, on whom God places all the responsibility. This pamphlet he followed up by another On the Turkish War, which he dedicated to Philip of Hesse, in a letter dated October 9, 1528. In it he says : —

Certain persons have been begging me for the past five years to stir up our people against the Turk, and now as he is actually approaching they have compelled me to fulfil this duty. I regret to learn that some mistaken preachers in Germany instruct the people not to fight against the Turk; some are so silly as to say it does not become a Christian to bear arms, and some say that the Germans are such a wild and wicked folk, half devil and half man, that they need the Turk to rule them. All the blame for such wicked nonsense is put upon Luther and upon my Evangelic doctrine, just as I had to bear the blame of the Peasants' War, and of all the rest of the evil in the world, although my accusers know that their charges are false. . . .

I dedicate this book to your Grace as a powerful, famous prince, both to make it more widely read and to give it greater influence with other princes if it comes to a campaign against the infidel. . . .

Philip was not, however, convinced by the arguments of the Reformer. He was one of the first to suggest that pressure be brought to bear on the Emperor by refusal of supplies for this war. If anything could justify such an attitude it was the hard position in which the Evangelic leaders found themselves at the Diet of Spires in 1529. The Catholic majority here passed a decree, called a Recess, most unfavorable to the reformers. All Catholic States were commanded to execute the persecuting Edict of Worms, although toleration for adherents of the old faith was demanded from Lutheran States. The governments of both religions were to refuse toleration to any new doctrine, a provision aimed both at Zwingli and the Anabaptists; finally no prince should take another's subjects under his protection. The Recess as a whole was intended to prevent further growth of the Lutheran Church and all toleration of other reformed sects. It called forth from the minority of the Estates the celebrated Protest from which the name Protestant is derived. In this proclamation the Lutheran princes and cities declared that they could not in conscience abide by the provisions of the Recess and appealed to the Emperor to annul them.

As Charles was far from inclined to accede to their wishes, the question soon came up in a practical form whether it were lawful to resist him by force. To decide this point a congress of the protesting princes was held at Nuremberg in January, 1530. Luther's opinion had been previously asked and given to the effect that armed resistance of the Emperor by individual states was tantamount to rebellion. Philip of Hesse was too ambitious to be content with this answer: he voted not only to resist the Emperor but to call in the national enemy France; failing this he proposed as next best to refuse Charles military aid against the Turks. He tried to get Luther's support in this measure, but with little success. The reply he received shows how little political were the Reformer's thoughts; nay, what a dislike, almost contempt, he entertained for temporal means of religious propaganda: —

TO PHILIP, LANDGRAVE OF HESSE

(WITTENBERG,) December 16, 1529.

Grace and peace in Christ. Serene, highborn Prince, gracious Lord. The messenger has just brought your Grace's letter, informing me what unrighteous plots are brewed by the priests and the Emperor. I trust in God, who boasts in the Psalter that he makes nought the plans of godless princes and peoples, that he will hear us now and make these plans, too, come to nought. My hope is confident, because those priests boast loudly and rely on the Emperor and on human help and do not call on God nor ask after him. May God guard us from relying on our wisdom and strength and make us desire his help and wait on it; then it will certainly come. Your Grace asks me to advise my sovereign not to give the Emperor help against the Turks until a general peace is made. I do not know, and have never cared to inquire what was done at Spires and at Schmalkalden, and so at this time I am unable to answer to you; but if my advice is asked, I will, with God's aid, give it to the best of my ability, and pray God that in this matter of binding consciences his will and not that of the princes may be done. Amen. I commend your Grace to Christ. Amen.

MARTIN LUTHER.

CHAPTER XX

CHURCH BUILDING

PERSECUTION of the Lutherans was first felt in the Netherlands. It was bitter to the founder of the new Church to hear that two of his followers arrested for heresy had recanted. On June 27, 1522, he wrote Staupitz that one of them, James Probst, deserved to lose his life on account of his damnable recantation. But the inquisitors soon found men of sterner stuff, and on July 1, 1523, they burned two young men at Brussels for their faith. When the Wittenberg reformer heard of their fate tears started to his eyes and he murmured that he had not been found worthy to suffer for Christ. This mood yielded to one of spiritual joy which found rich expression in a hymn describing the heroic death of the martyrs and in a letter to their countrymen: —

TO THE CHRISTIANS OF HOLLAND, BRABANT, AND FLANDERS

(WITTENBERG, July ? 1523.)

Praise and thanks be to the Father of all mercy, who at this time lets us see his wonderful light, hitherto hidden on account of our sins while we were compelled to submit to the terrible power of Antichrist. But now the time has come when the voice of the turtle is heard in the land, and flowers appear on the earth. Of what joy, dear friends, have you been participants, you who have been the first to witness unto us. For it has been given unto you before all the world not only to hear the gospel and to know Christ but to be the first to suffer, for Christ's sake, shame and injury, wrong and distress, imprisonment and death. Now you have become full of fruit and so strong that you have watered the cause with your blood. For among you those two precious jewels of Christ, Henry and John, have held their lives of no account for Christ's Word. Oh how miserably were those two souls condemned, but how gloriously with eternal joy will they meet Christ and justly condemn those by whom they were unjustly condemned! . . . How welcome was that fire which helped them from this sinful life to eternity, from this ignominy to everlasting dominion! . . . And although our adversaries will cry out that those saints were Hussites, Wiclifites, and Lutherans, we should not wonder but rather let this strengthen us the more, for Christ, too, had a cross and slanderers. Our judge is not far off, who will give another judgment; of that we are certain. . . .

While animating his cohorts to the fray, the captain was straining every nerve to supply an organization and discipline adequate to their needs. On returning from the Wartburg he had found things in great confusion and his first task was to restore order. The old form of service with slight alterations was reëstablished in the parish church. Communion was administered in one or in both kinds according to the preference of the recipient; and the only change in the mass was the omission of the words purporting to change the elements into Christ's body and blood, an alteration made easy, as the Reformer remarked, by the fact that the parishioners did not know Latin and hence could not perceive it. A like moderation was used in respect to images; believers were discouraged from praying to the saints, but the heads of neither the images nor their venerators were broken as under the Carlstadt régime.

But with time a new and improved service was introduced. An important change, made as early as 1524, was the use of the vernacular instead of the learned language in the house of God. In 1526, under the name of German Mass, Luther published an Evangelic plan for public worship, consisting of the Lord's Prayer, the Creed, the singing of hymns, the reading of the Bible, and a sermon. In the preface he carefully guards against the danger of having this service turned into a universal law; he is moved to write it by the general demand for such a work, but he leaves it free to any one to alter or improve as he will.

The material for this service was largely furnished by Luther. In translating the Bible — of which more will be said in a separate chapter — the foundation for the exposition of the Scripture in the vernacular was laid. More extraordinary is the fact that seeing the need of good German hymns the Reformer should have written them himself. It is one of the most surprising phenomena in literary history that a man of forty should suddenly develop considerable poetic talent in response to a definite practical requirement. Yet such is the case. In the last days of 1523 he began to collect hymns, to write them himself, and to urge his friends to do the like. The next year the fruit of his efforts appeared in a book of Spiritual Songs for which the tunes were supplied or adapted from older ones, by a local composer, John Walther. This contained twenty-four hymns, of which eighteen are by Luther. After this remarkable outburst the songs came more slowly but never ceased. A second hymn-book, printed probably in February, 1528, contained four new ones by Luther including *Ein Feste Burg*, composed during the dark days of illness and trial in the preceding year. From time to time new hymns by the same author are known to have been introduced into the Wittenberg service, and in 1543 another book was printed with several recently composed. In all there are extant forty-two hymns from the Reformer's pen, and fifteen other bits of versification, including an epitaph for his daughter, some verses on his housekeeping, and several lampoons.

It must be owned that much of this verse is almost without poetic inspiration. The Ten Commandments and the Creed are hardly happy subjects for this treatment, especially when the writer's object is to make his verse as literal, that is, as near prose, as possible. Most of the hymns are based on Psalms or other portions of Scripture; others are paraphrases of old Latin hymns. Little of the Gothic grandeur of these latter is preserved in the German version, the language of which is highly popular. In the instructions sent to Spalatin for hymn-writing, early in 1524, the author reveals his own principles. " Please omit all new-fangled court expressions," he says, "for to win popularity a song must be in the most simple and common language, although the words should be good and apt, and the meaning plain and as nearly like the original as possible. The translation may be free; only keep to the sense, changing the words where convenient. I have not as much talent in this direction as I wish I had, but I will do my best."

In applying these principles Luther took for his model the ballad poetry so popular in his own day, and many of his songs vividly recall these verses. The sing-song meter, the common-

place expressions, the rough rhymes often succeed in vulgariz-
ing religion rather than in making it poetical. But this is not
the case in all instances. Poetry is the language of strong feeling, and when moved to the depths of his deep nature Luther
produced an immortal lyric. Several of his efforts are good;
one is really great; the battle hymn of the Evangelic Church,
the Marseillaise, as Heine called it, of the Reformation : —

> AIn feste burg ist unser Gott,
> ain gutte wör un waffen,
> Er hilfft uns frey aus aller not,
> Die uns yetzt hat betroffen.
>> Der alt böse feynd,
>> mitt ernst ers yetzt meint,
>> gross macht un vil list
>> sein grausam rüstung ist,
>>> auff erd ist nicht seins gleichen.[1]

Not without a struggle was the improved form of public
worship introduced. The chief opposition came from the vested
interests of priests holding endowed masses. There were a large
number of these in the Castle Church at Wittenberg and also
in one of the churches at Altenburg, the capital of Ernestine
Saxony. From 1523–26 the Reformer's letters are full of fierce
denunciation of these " priests of Baal," whom, however, he was
unable to oust on account of Frederic's settled policy of laissez-
faire in religious matters. In a published letter to Bartholomew
von Starenberg, of September 1, 1523, after consoling him for the
loss of his wife he earnestly warns him against having masses
or vigils said for her soul, " for they are unchristian things
greatly angering God. Any one can see that there is no serious
faith in them but only useless mumbling. We must pray differently to be heard by God, for such services are a mockery of
him . . . instituted by priests for the sake of lucre."

---

[1] God is to us a fortress strong,
A weapon never failing,
He helps us freely in the throng
Of mortal ills prevailing.
> Our ancient foe accurst
> Now means to do his worst,
> Great craft and power are his
> And armed with them he is
>> On earth without an equal.

The victory for the reformed faith was not entirely won until the accession of John the Steadfast, in May, 1525, brought Ernestine Saxony under an avowed convert. From this time forth the Evangelic Church was the dominant religious body within that territory; to insure its supremacy laws were passed abolishing the objectionable rites and enforcing uniformity in the churches. Some form of church government had to be established, and this came in the institution of a system of visitation, first suggested by John Frederic in 1524, but not undertaken until 1527. Able and educated men, among them Luther and Melanchthon, were sent around to the various parishes to see that the incumbents were competent, to arrange for the finances, and to institute the reformed services. The result of the first tour of inspection was disheartening; many of the priests were still attached to the old Church; most of them were very ignorant, one or two not even knowing the Ten Commandments or the Lord's Prayer, and some were immoral. The people, too, were sunk in abject superstition and ignorance. To give method to the plan of visitation an Instruction was drawn up in 1528 by Melanchthon and Luther. The supervisors were to instruct the priests in doctrine, with especial emphasis upon repentance; the Ten Commandments were to be diligently preached; of free will the people were to be told that a man had the power of choice to do good or evil, but that this power availed nothing to salvation. The sacraments and services of the Church were explained. Above all the preachers were to exhort parents to send their children to school, and a proper curriculum was suggested. The first class was to learn to read from primers with the alphabet, the creed and certain prayers in them; next they should be taught to write, and Latin from the grammar of Donatus and the Disticha Moralia of Dionysius Cato, and the elements of music. The second class was to continue music and to read Æsop's Fables in Latin, and selections from Erasmus' Colloquies. The method was to be that recommended by Milton a century later; the teacher was to read, translate, and explain a certain portion of the text one day for the class to recite the next. Some poetry was to be learned by heart. Proper instruction in religion was to be given. The older children were to follow up this programme with Virgil, Ovid, Cicero, music, and more religion.

On education Luther relied the most. What is the use of forcing through reforms which the people are too ignorant to appreciate or even to want? It was with the object of training men and women in his ideas that early in 1529 he published two of his most influential works, the Long and Short Catechisms. The former came out in January under the title German Catechism, and was intended to supplement the German Mass. A few weeks later appeared the Enchiridion, or Short Catechism, which was merely an abbreviation and simplification of the previous work.

Luther's purpose was so practical, and his sources so obvious, that it is almost needless to seek for precedents for his catechisms. Nevertheless it is interesting to know that he had examples in the instruction given to catechumens in the mediæval Church. Characteristics of his work are: 1. There is no system of dogma set forth in technical terms, and no argumentation whatever. 2. There is no polemic against Rome or against the sacramentarians, a contrast to the contemporary and subsequent catechisms of other churches and leaders. 3. Theology is rescued from its old, stiff forms and made really simple and easy of comprehension.

In the preface to the smaller work the author begins : " The lamentable, miserable need which I saw when I visited the parishes has induced me to compose this summary of Christian doctrine in short, easy form." Good Heavens! how little the people, and even the pastors know! The object of the work is partly to introduce a uniform teaching of the Creed, Paternoster, and sacraments so as not to confuse the common man, but it must not be regarded as an irrevocable law. The people are free to choose another form if they prefer, only they must keep to it once chosen. The longer book begins with an earnest exhortation to a thorough study of its contents. Let not any one think that a single reading is sufficient, but let him con it by heart and read it every day. "For I do the same," says the author ; " like a child I study it every day, and each morning that I have time I say the Decalogue, the Creed, the Lord's Prayer, and some Psalms." The priests are exhorted (in the Short Catechism) to explain the contents to the people, see that they learn it and insist that they attend communion at least four times a year.

The Ten Commandments, the Creed, and the Lord's Prayer are set forth and explained clause by clause. In expounding the third commandment (as he numbers it), "Remember the Sabbath day to keep it holy," the Reformer says that this ceremonial law was only given to the Jews and that Christians are free from it; nevertheless it is useful to rest on one day in the week for natural reasons and for the cultivation of the spiritual life. The sacraments of baptism and the Lord's Supper are explained. In a later edition of the Short Catechism, of 1531, a similar explanation of penance was inserted, with a form of private confession. The use of this, however, is left to individual judgment; if a man does not know that he has committed any of the sins mentioned, which is stated to be hardly possible, he may receive absolution after the general confession in church.

Forms of family prayer and religious instruction are given, with blessing and grace for meal-times. Certain sayings from Scripture on the respective duties of pastors, husbands, wives, parents, children, masters, servants, and widows are set forth.

To the Small Catechism was added a marriage service, a baptismal service and form of private confession with instructions to the priest as to how to treat the penitent. Luther regarded marriage more as a civil contract than as a religious matter, and expressly states that each country may follow its own customs in the matter. According to his service a portion of the ceremony took place in the evening, the couple were then led to the bride bed, and the blessing on their union took place the following morning. In this Luther but followed the custom of his day. The baptismal service is strikingly different from that in use in most churches now. The evil spirit was first exorcised from the child, who was then asked a number of questions on its religious attitude, answered by the sponsors, of whom there were a considerable number.

The Catechism, many editions of which were printed and

rapidly used up, exerted an enormous influence, and is still the spiritual pabulum of the majority of Germans as well as of Lutherans in other lands. Its author had a justifiable pride in his work. He once declared that he would be willing for all his books to perish save the Catechism and the Unfree Will. During the Diet of Augsburg, in the summer of 1530, he wrote the Elector that thanks to this simple instruction the youth of Saxony now understood the Bible better than monks and nuns had done under the old régime. He sums up the position to which he assigned it in the words: " It is a right Bible for the laity."

The Evangelic faith spread from Saxony to neighboring lands, the first of which was Hesse. Philip, the young landgrave, set about the conversion of his subjects with characteristic promptness, drawing up an ordinance in 1526 commanding the adoption of the Saxon service and system and church visitation. This he submitted to the Wittenberg professor. The answer is highly characteristic of the Reformer. He had introduced his system as gradually as possible in his own country, and distrusted the rapid methods of Philip. The letter which he wrote in answer to the Landgrave's request for an opinion, is worthy, in its statesmanship, of Burke.

TO PHILIP, LANDGRAVE OF HESSE

WITTENBERG, January 7, 1527.

Grace and peace in Christ. Serene, highborn Prince, gracious Lord. To the request which your Grace makes for an opinion of your Ordinance, I answer unwillingly, inasmuch as many blame us, as if we of Wittenberg would force every one to do as we do, although we know that God wills otherwise and that others can do well without our aid. But to oblige your Grace, and since the Ordinance might raise an outcry if published without my consent, I humbly and faithfully advise you not to allow it to be printed at this time, for I have never had, and have not now, sufficient courage to pass so many radical laws at once. In my opinion we should act as did Moses, who only wrote down his laws after they had been put in practice among the people. Your Grace should provide the schools with good teachers and the parishes with good pastors, and begin by oral command and private instruction and let the innovations be gradual and proceed farther when things get started and are going of themselves. Then the Ordinance could be published and all priests commanded to obey it; I know well and have learned that laws passed prematurely are seldom well obeyed, as the people are not used to them nor ready for them, as those legislators who sit apart devising laws may think. Making laws and enforcing them are vastly different things. By this Ordinance you would change much arbitrarily. But when some of the reforms have been already put into practice it will be easy to pass the law. Legislation is a great, noble, comprehensive thing, and cannot be successful without the spirit of God, for which we must humbly pray. Moderation is necessary; after customs are rooted, laws will follow of themselves. This necessity has been experienced by the greatest law-givers; Moses, Christ, the Romans, and the Pope. . . .

Your Grace's devoted,

MARTIN LUTHER.

CHAPTER XXI

ULRICH ZWINGLI

THE tendency of Protestantism to split up into manifold sects has often been noticed and explained. When once individual judgment is set up against authority, all the revolting leader's followers will claim the same privilege against him. Even before the revolting Church had made its position secure against Rome, it divided into many sects. Most of these were small, and, though holding the most diverse and even opposite opinions, were classed together under the name of Anabaptist; but besides the Lutheran community there was one other of great importance. Its leader was Ulrich Zwingli; the doctrinal difference of the two Churches was on the eucharist.

The theory of the Roman Catholic Church, at least for several centuries, had been that the bread and wine in the Lord's Supper were actually turned into the body and blood of Jesus, though without a corresponding change in the accidents of taste, appearance, and so forth; this is transubstantiation. Luther's theory, known as consubstantiation, is nearly allied to it, namely, that though there was no actual change, yet the body of the Saviour was present with the natural bread and wine as fire is in red-hot iron, or a sword in a sheath, and that it was so truly present that it was "bitten by the teeth" of the communicant. The belief adopted by Zwingli and most of the other Reformed Churches was that the rite was merely commemorative and that the body and blood of Christ were partaken of in a purely figurative and spiritual sense.

This doctrine came to Luther's attention soon after his return from the Wartburg (if not before) in the writings of a certain Honius, in those of the Bohemian Brethren, and in the pamphlets of Carlstadt, who taught it, along with his other advanced tenets, while Luther was away. The Reformer speaks of it in his letter to the Christians of Strassburg, of December 14, 1524, as follows : —

ULRICH ZWINGLI

After a painting by Hans Asper; now at Zurich

I freely confess that if Carlstadt or any other could have convinced me five years ago that there was nothing in the sacrament but mere bread and wine, he would have done me a great service. I was sorely tempted on this point and wrestled with myself and tried to believe that it was so, for I saw that I could thereby give the hardest rap to the papacy. I read treatises by two men who wrote more ably in defence of the theory than has Dr. Carlstadt and who did not so torture the Word to their own imaginations. But I am bound; I cannot believe as they do; the text is too powerful for me and will not let itself be wrenched from the plain sense by argument.

And if any one could prove to-day that the sacrament were mere bread and wine, he would not much anger me if he was only reasonable. (Alas I am too much inclined that way myself when I feel the old Adam!) But Dr. Carlstadt's ranting only confirms me in the opposite opinion.

Luther's work Against the Heavenly Prophets of Images and the Sacrament has been noticed in a previous chapter. The second half of it, appearing January, 1525, was entirely on the subject of the sacrament. This work was not particularly successful; in fact it seemed rather to alienate some men who were hesitating between the two dogmas.

The controversy might have fallen into oblivion, especially after the disgrace of Carlstadt and Münzer in the Peasants' Revolt, had it not been taken up by one of the ablest men of the generation, Ulrich Zwingli.

Born at Wildhaus, Switzerland, January 1, 1484, he had received a humanistic education and entered the Church in 1506. After varied experiences as an army chaplain and parish priest, he was called to Zurich in December, 1519, and here, quite independently of the Wittenberg movement, he began a similar reformation. He at once protested against the sale of indulgences and with success; he then proceeded to other reforms, especially on lines suggested by the writings of Erasmus, whose ardent admirer he was. He soon rose to the leading position in the city, and, carrying his reform further than had Luther, was able, in April, 1525, to abolish the mass and substitute for it a simple communion service.

The wide difference between the personal experiences and

careers of the two reformers is chiefly accountable for the divergence of their opinions. The German had gone through a rebirth of spiritual anguish which made the forgiveness of sin the central point of his theology as of his life ; the Swiss had never felt this need so strongly; the central idea of *his* theology was that of Christian fellowship fostered by the analogy of the republican freedom of the canton. Again, Luther was at bottom a monk, reasoning with the depth, and also with something of the limitations, of scholastic philosophy ; Zwingli was a humanist, anxious only to get at the exact meaning of the Greek Testament.

It is possible that the two men might have agreed on this point, at least better than they did, had it not been for the unfortunate manner in which Zwingli first crossed Luther's horizon, as a supporter of Carlstadt and " the ranters." When the division of the two became recognized, it was deepened by the proud consciousness, on the part of each leader, of the independence of his own movement. How bitterly Luther felt against men whom he regarded as rebels and traitors may be seen in a letter : —

TO NICHOLAS HAUSMANN AT ZWICKAU

(WITTENBERG,) January 20, 1526.

Grace and peace in the Lord. I wrote Duke George [1] with good hope, but am deceived. I have lost my humility and shall not write him another word. Indeed I am not moved by his lies and his curses. Why should I not bear with him who am compelled to bear with these sons of my body, my Absaloms, who withstand me so furiously ? They are scourges of the sacrament compared with whose madness the papists are mild. I never understood before how evil a spirit is Satan, nor did I comprehend Paul's words about spiritual wickedness. But Christ lives. Now Theobald Billican, pastor at Nordlingen, writes against Zwingli, Carlstadt, and Œcolampadius. God raises up the faithful remnant against the new heretics ; we greatly hope that Christ will bless the undertaking. I would write against them if I had time, but first I wish to see what Billican does.

I am glad that my book on the Unfree Will pleased you, but I expect the same or worse from Erasmus as from Duke George.

[1] December, 1525, cf. p. 223.

That reptile will feel himself taken by the throat and will not be moved by my moderation. God grant that I be mistaken, but I know the man's nature; he is an instrument of Satan unless God change him. I have no other news. Farewell and pray for me.

MARTIN LUTHER.

In a similar strain the Reformer says in his Answer to the King of England's Libel (1527): "Hitherto I have suffered in all ways. But not until now did my Absalom, my dear son, hunt and shame his father David. My Judas [Zwingli] had not yet shamed the disciples and betrayed his master; but now he has done his worst on me."

The new "Judas" had simply published, in February, 1526, a pamphlet entitled True and False Religion, and followed it up soon after with A Clear Explanation of Christ's Supper. Along with cogent argument in support of his position that the elements were mere bread and wine, the author alleges that the truth of his opinion has been revealed to him in a dream. This method of proof unfortunately impressed Luther still more deeply with the idea that Zwingli's "spirit" was akin to that of Münzer and the prophets who had cultivated dreams with such disastrous results. His works had considerable success, however; so many of the South German pastors came over to the Swiss opinion that the leader was able to prophesy that within three years all Christendom would be converted.

Luther replied in a comprehensive treatise, entitled That these Words of Christ, "This is my Body," still stand against the Ranting Spirits (March, 1527). The greater part of this book is a proof from Scripture that the words quoted in the title are to be taken literally. The theory of the opposite party, that Christ's body cannot be in the bread because it is in heaven, is rebutted by showing, from mediæval philosophy, that it may be extended through space, and is, in fact, omnipresent. Again, a careful exegesis of John vi, 63, "The flesh profiteth nothing," is devoted to proving that Christ's flesh is not meant, as supposed by the Swiss. Further proofs are adduced from other passages of Scripture and from the fathers. The last part of the book is devoted to a practical exposition of the use, necessity, and significance of the sacrament, which last, in

Luther's opinion, would be entirely destroyed if the consecrating words were not taken literally.

While Luther was writing this, Zwingli had composed two treatises, A Friendly Exegesis of Christ's Words, and A Friendly Appeasement and Rebuttal, the former in Latin, the latter in the vernacular (Früntliche verglimpfung und ˏableynung), both of which he sent to his opponent with a letter of April 1. His tone was pastoral, not to say pedagogical; he seemed to instruct Luther in calm superiority ; though perhaps he intended to be conciliatory he was in fact extremely irritating to the older man, to whom he said : "You have produced nothing on this subject worthy either of yourself or of the Christian religion, and yet your ferocity daily increases." Luther wrote on May 4 to Wenzel Link : "Zwingli has sent me his foolish book and a letter written in his own hand worthy of his haughty spirit. So gentle was he, raging, foaming, and threatening, that he seems to me incurable and condemned by manifest truth. — And my comprehensive book has profited many."

In the mean time the Swiss received the last-named work of the Wittenberg professor. They were greatly exasperated by its violent tone; Zwingli writing Vadian on May 4 "that its whole contents were nothing but lies, slander, sycophancy, and suspicion."

A reply, composed by Zwingli and Œcolampadius, was published in June under the title That these Words of Christ, "This is my Body," still have the same old Sense. It was dedicated to John, Elector of Saxony.

Luther was too ill to read it at once. His answer, a huge Confession on Christ's Supper, appeared in February, 1528. He is glad, he declares, that his words have so greatly angered Satan, by which sign he knows that they have done much good. He goes over the old arguments with more thoroughness than before, refuting first Zwingli's philosophy and then his exegesis of Scripture, showing that he contradicts the Bible, the fathers, and himself.

The book only increased the rage without shaking the convictions of the sacramentarians. Capito wrote that Luther had

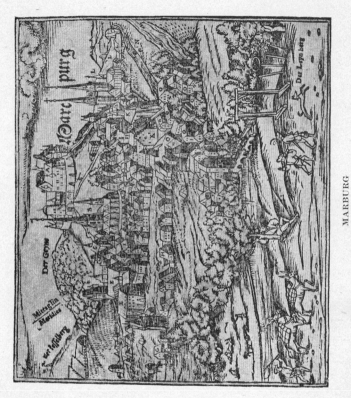

MARBURG

From a print of 1544

hurt himself by it; Zwingli judged that it was "a denial of
what Luther had said before, and a fog through which Christ's
mystery could not be discerned." He, and Œcolampadius, published in one book Two Answers to Martin Luther's Book. It
was dedicated, in a letter dated July 1, 1528, to the Elector
John and the Landgrave Philip of Hesse, whom Zwingli refused to salute with the customary titles "highborn" and
" serene," "because," as he explained to them, "you are only
highborn in comparison to the world and the flesh, but before
God you are mean ; and serene [German Durchlaut, literally
transparent] is a word which is only applicable to glass windows."

That one, at least, of the princes thus addressed did not take
the letter ill, is shown by the attempt of Philip of Hesse to reconcile the opposing sections of the Reformed Church. His main
motive was political, for he saw that in union was strength and
he wished to make an alliance between the German Protestant
states and the Swiss cantons. He was, however, something of a
theologian himself ; he had a clearer comprehension of Zwingli's
opinion than had Luther and was, perhaps, inclined to adopt it
himself. Hoping to bring about an understanding that would
enable both parties to present a united front to the common
enemy, he invited the reformers and other distinguished theologians to a conference at his capital, Marburg. After some
negotiation the consent of all concerned was secured and during
the last days of September, 1529, the famous divines gathered
in the pretty Hessian town on the banks of the Lahn. All were
received right royally by the host, of whom Luther many years
afterwards related the following characteristic bit : —

At Marburg Philip went around like a stable-boy, concealing his
deep thoughts with small talk as great men do. He said to Melanchthon : "Shall I suffer the Archbishop of Mayence to take away my
clergy by force ? " To which the latter replied : " Yes, if they are
under the jurisdiction of that see." Then the Landgrave said : " I have
asked your advice on this, but I won't take it."

The public discussion was preceded by private conference
of the leaders. At these, or perhaps at the main discussion,

Luther was annoyed by the display of humanistic learning made by his opponent. Long afterwards he spoke of him in these terms : —

People always want to seem more learned than they are. When we were at Marburg, Zwingli wanted to speak Greek. Once, when he was absent, I said : " Why is n't he ashamed to speak Greek in the presence of so many learned classicists — Œcolampadius, Melanchthon, Osiander, and Brent ? *They* know Greek." These words were carried to him, wherefore the next day he excused himself in the presence of the Landgrave by saying : " Illustrious Lord, I speak Greek because I have read the New Testament for thirteen years." No indeed ! It is more than reading the New Testament, it is vainglory that blinds people. When Zwingli spoke German he wanted every one to adopt the Swiss dialect. Oh, how I hate people who use so many languages as did Zwingli : at Marburg he spoke Greek and Hebrew from the pulpit.

The great colloquy took place on October 2, in the large, darkly wainscotted hall of a noble castle, the battlements of which, crowning the steep hill in the centre of the town, seem rather to protect than to overawe the smiling region round-about. Here, before an audience of some fifty or sixty notables, Luther debated, for some hours, that autumn day, with Zwingli and Œcolampadius. The speaking was temperate, the arguments in the main the old familiar ones. Though it can hardly be denied that the German showed himself the better debater, the result was indecisive, all persons retaining their former opinions.

Although nothing, or next to nothing had been accomplished, the Landgrave was anxious to have some tangible result to show for all his trouble. He therefore induced his guests to draw up a statement of their common beliefs, known as the Marburg Articles. Fourteen of these articles were on points agreed to by both sides ; the fifteenth defined the eucharist and stated that the subscribers were unable to agree " on the bodily presence of the body and blood " in the elements, with a prayer for enlightenment. The principal divines present signed this confession, but when Philip requested them to give each other the right hand of fellowship, Luther refused with the remark, es-

Martinus Luther

Justus Jonas

Philippus Melanchthon

Andreas Osiander

Stephanus Agricola
Joannes Brentius

Ioannes Oecolampadius

Huldrychus Zwinglius

Martinus Bucerus

Caspar Hedio

FACSIMILE SIGNATURES OF THE MARBURG ARTICLES
Now in the archives at Marburg

pecially unfortunate on account of its previous connotations, that the Swiss had a different spirit from his own. His idea of what had been accomplished is given in the two letters next translated, the former being especially interesting as his first known letter to Katie. It shows that he confided his deepest interests to her, though it appears that part of the letter, written in Latin never used elsewhere by Martin in addressing his wife, was intended rather for Bugenhagen than for her.

TO CATHARINE LUTHER AT WITTENBERG

(MARBURG,) October 4, 1529.

Grace and peace in Christ. Dear Lord Katie, know that our friendly conference at Marburg is now at an end and that we are in perfect union in all points except that our opponents insist that there is simply bread and wine in the Lord's Supper, and that Christ is only in it in a spiritual sense. To-day the Landgrave did his best to make us united, hoping that even though we disagreed yet we should hold each other as brothers and members of Christ. He worked hard for it, but we would not call them brothers or members of Christ, although we wish them well and desire to remain at peace. I think to-morrow or day after we shall depart to go and see the Elector at Schleitz in Vogtland, whither he has summoned us.

Tell Bugenhagen that Zwingli's best argument was that a body could not exist without occupying space and therefore Christ's body was not in the bread, and that Œcolampadius' best argument was that the sacrament is only the sign of Christ's body. I think God blinded them that they could not get beyond these points. I have much to do and the messenger is in a hurry. Say good-night to all and pray for me. We are all sound and well and live like princes. Kiss little Lena and Hans for me.

> Your humble servant,
> MARTIN LUTHER.

TO NICHOLAS GERBEL AT STRASSBURG

MARBURG, October 4, 1529.

Grace and peace in Christ. You will know, my dear Gerbel, how far we attained harmony at Marburg, partly by the verbal report of your representatives, partly by the Articles they are taking with them. We defended ourselves strongly and they conceded much, but as they were firm in this one article of the sacrament of the altar we dismissed them in peace, fearing that further argument would draw blood. We ought to have charity and peace even with our foes, and so we plainly told them, that unless they grow wiser on this point they may indeed have our charity, but cannot by us be considered as brothers and members of Christ. You will judge how much fruit has come of this conference; it seems to me that no small scandal has been removed, since there will be no further occasion for disputation, which is more than we had hoped for. Would that the little difference still remaining might be taken away by Christ. Farewell, brother, and pray for me.

Yours,

MARTIN LUTHER.

CHAPTER XXII

FESTE COBURG AND THE DIET OF AUGSBURG. 1530

THAT the Edict of Worms remained a dead letter was due to the excessive decentralization of the Empire. Since Charles had left Germany after the memorable visit of 1520–21, three important diets, one held at Nuremberg (1524) and two at Spires (1526 and 1529) had dealt with the religious question without being able to enforce any consistent policy. The Emperor himself had been too busy in his other dominions and with his French and Turkish wars even to attempt to suppress the German heresy. Toward the end of 1529, however, the success of his arms in other quarters enabled him to turn his attention northward. Fully bent on settling the religious dispute for his subjects, he summoned a diet to meet at Augsburg in 1530, announcing his intention of being present at it himself.

Early in April of this year Luther, Melanchthon, and other theologians set out from Wittenberg with the intention of appearing at the Diet. At Coburg, the most southern town of Ernestine Saxony, they met the Elector, and waited for an imperial safe-conduct before proceeding further. About the middle of the month an urgent summons from Charles V to the Elector John arrived, together with safe-conducts for himself and others of his party, but none for Luther, who was still, be it remembered, under the ban of both the Church and the Empire. In these circumstances it was impossible for the outlaw to attend the meetings of the Estates, and accordingly when John set out with the other theologians on April 22, he was consigned to the castle near the town where he spent nearly six months.

Feste Coburg, as the fortress is called, crowns a small eminence, the only one in the region, and, like a little city built on a hill, dominates the whole surrounding country. Within its ample walls, picturesque towers, and rambling battlements, a garrison might well be maintained. Without the austere grandeur of the Wartburg, with less of the romantic attraction of Marburg, Feste Coburg surpasses both these castles in size and situation.

With Luther were his amanuensis Veit Dietrich, his nephew Cyriac Kaufmann, and some thirty retainers of the Elector. From his retreat the Reformer kept up a lively correspondence with his friends at Augsburg as well as with those left at Wittenberg; there are extant almost as many letters written from the castle as days he spent there. Among these epistles are many of the finest he ever penned; in some the depths of his religious faith are sounded, in others the chinks and crannies of his deep love are searched. Whatever he wrote is full of humor, of fancy, of an idyllic love of nature and a childlike trust in God.

On the very day on which he moved into his new quarters the Reformer tells of them thus: —

TO PHILIP MELANCHTHON (AT NUREMBERG?)

THE REALM OF THE BIRDS AT THREE P.M. (April 23, 1530).

Grace and peace in the Lord Jesus. I have come to my Sinai, dearest Philip, but I shall soon make it a Zion and build three tabernacles, one for the Psalter, one for the Prophets, and one for Æsop — I speak after the manner of men. It is indeed a very pleasant place and convenient for study, save that your absence saddens it.

I am beginning to be stirred up against the Turk and Mohammed, even passionately when I see the intolerable fury of Satan waxing proud against body and soul. I shall therefore pray and weep nor cease until I know that my clamor has been heard in heaven. *You* are more affected by the home-bred monsters of the Empire. We are those to whom these last woes were predestined, to feel and suffer the furious impetus of the final assault. But the attack itself is a witness and prophecy of its own end and of our redemption.

I pray Christ to give you sleep and to free your heart from the cares which are the fiery arrows of Satan. Amen. I write this at leisure, not yet having received my books and papers. Neither have I yet seen either of the castle wardens. I lack nothing; this huge building crowning the hill is all mine; the keys of all the rooms are given to me. Thirty men are said to take their meals here, among them twelve night guards and two scouts who keep watch from the towers.

FESTE COBURG

Why should I write all this? Because I have nothing else to do. By evening I hope the post will arrive and then I shall hear some news. The grace of God be with you. Amen. Give my remembrances to Dr. Caspar Lindemann and Spalatin. I shall ask Jonas to greet Agricola and Adler for me.

MARTIN LUTHER.

To Wittenberg Luther also wrote of his new life. His large household had not been entirely depleted. The guests who remained wrote him a common letter giving the domestic news, and he promptly answered them in this delightful epistle : —

TO HIS TABLE COMPANIONS

AT THE DIET OF THE GRAIN TURKS, April 28, 1530.

Grace and peace in Christ. Dear gentlemen and friends, I have received the letter which you all sent me and so have learned how everything is. And that you may also learn how things are with us, I would have you know that we, namely, Veit Dietrich, Cyriac Kaufmann, and I, did not press on to the Diet of Augsburg, but stopped to attend another diet here. There is a coppice directly under our windows, like a little forest, where the daws and crows are holding a diet; they fly to and fro at such a rate and make such a racket day and night that they all seem drunk, soused and silly. I wonder how their breath holds out to bicker so. Pray tell me have you sent any delegates to these noble estates? For I think they must have assembled from all the world. I have not yet seen their emperor, but nobles and soldier lads fly and gad about, inexpensively clothed in one color; all alike black, all alike gray-eyed, all alike with the same song, sung in different tones of big and little, old and young. They care not for a large palace to meet in, for their hall is roofed with the vault of the sky, its floor is the carpet of green grass, and its walls are as far as the ends of the world. They do not ask for horses and trappings, having winged chariots to escape snares and keep out of the way of man's wrath. They are great and puissant lords, but I have not yet learned what they have decided upon. As far as I can gather from an interpreter, however, they are for a vigorous campaign against wheat, barley, oats, and all kinds of corn and grain, a war in which many a knight will do great deeds. So we sit here in the diet and spend time agreeably seeing and hearing how the estates of the realm make merry and sing. It is pleasant to see how soldierly they discourse and wipe their bills and arm them-

selves for victory against the grain. I wish them good luck — to be all
spitted on a skewer together. I believe they are in no wise different
from the sophists and papists who go for me with their sermons and
books all at once; I see by the example of the harsh-voiced daws
what a profitable people they are, devouring everything on earth and
chattering loud and long in return.

To-day we heard the first nightingale, who could hardly believe that
it was April. The weather has been splendid, with no rain except a
little yesterday. Perhaps you are not so fortunate in this respect. God
bless you all. Keep house well.

MARTIN LUTHER.

With his dear wife, too, he kept up regular correspondence.
Just after his father's death she sent him a picture of their year-
old baby Magdalene, a pair of needed spectacles, and a box of
home comforts, for which he thanks her: —

TO CATHARINE LUTHER AT WITTENBERG

(FESTE COBURG,) June 5, 1530.

Grace and peace in Christ. Dear Katie, I believe I have received
all your letters. This is my fourth to you since John left me for Wittenberg. I have Lena's picture and the box you sent. At first I did
not know the little hussy, she seemed so dark. I think it would be a
first rate thing if you weaned her; do it little by little as Argula von
Grumbach who has been here tells me she did with her son George.
John Reinecke of Mansfeld has also been to see me and so has George
Römer; in fact I shall soon have to go elsewhere if the pilgrimage
hither continues.

Tell Christian Döring that I have never in my life had worse spectacles than those that came with his letter; I could not see a line
through them. I did not receive the note sent in care of Conrad Vater,
as I am not at Coburg, but I shall try to get it. You can send your
letters care of the superintendent, who will forward them to me.

Our friends at Nuremberg and Augsburg are beginning to doubt
whether anything will happen at the Diet, for the Emperor still tarries
at Innsbruck. The prelates have some infernal plot, God grant the
devil foul them. Amen. Let Bugenhagen read the copy of my letter to
Link. I must hurry, as the messenger will not wait. Greet, kiss, hug,
and be kind to each according to his degree.

MARTIN LUTHER.

Katie was not entirely dependent for information on the letters of her husband. One to her from Veit Dietrich is too characteristic of that interesting person and too good of its kind to omit. The writer, now twenty-three years old, had come to Wittenberg to study medicine, but abandoned that vocation for theology when he came under the influence of Luther. He became the professor's amanuensis in 1527 and was taken into his house in 1529. His unbounded idolatry of the great man led him to treasure all he wrote and all he said; much of the table-talk he noted down, as well as the letter given below, is worthy of Boswell.

VEIT DIETRICH TO MISTRESS CATHARINE LUTHER AT WITTENBERG

FESTE COBURG, June 19, 1530.

Grace and peace in God. Kind, gracious, dear lady! Know that your husband and we are hale and hearty by God's grace. May God also bless you and the children. You did a mighty good stroke of work in sending the doctor the picture, for it makes him entirely forget his cares. He has hung it on the wall opposite the table in the Elector's apartment where we eat. When he first saw it he did not recognize it for a long time. "Dear me," said he, "Lena is so dark!" But now it pleases him well, and the more he looks at it the better he sees it is Lena. She looks extraordinarily like Hans in the mouth, eyes, and nose, in fact in the whole face, and she will grow more like him. I just had to write you this!

Dear lady, pray don't worry about the doctor; he is, thank God, hale and hearty, and, although his father's death was very bitter to him, he ceased mourning for it after two days. When he read Reinecke's letter he said to me, "My father is dead." And then he took his Psalter and went to his room and wept so much that for two days he could n't work. Since then he has not given way to grief any more. Saturday, June 3, the town clerk was our guest for the evening, and the doctor told us, among other things, how he had dreamed the night before that he lost a tooth so large that it astonished him beyond measure, and the next day came the news of his father's death! I thought you ought to know this, so pray take it with my service. May God bless Hans and Lena and the whole household. My friend George will give you three gulden, which please accept until I can get more.

VEIT DIETRICH of Nuremberg.

What a picture of the man these chatty letters give! As at the Wartburg he dressed in laymen's clothes and grew a thick beard. He had grown stouter and aged a little since then, more with toil and illness than with his forty-seven years. Sometimes he rambled about the wide-flung battlements, gazing with a smile at the busy birds in the tree-tops, or lost in thought and wonder at the mysteries of nature, the clouds, the rainbow, and the stars.

Most of the time he spent in his little wooden room with the narrow window, poring over the Hebrew prophets and the Psalter, or adapting an old German translation of Æsop to the needs of his own day, or writing letters. His first task was the composition of A Warning to the Prelates at Augsburg which was printed in May and sent to the Diet in June. He solemnly begs the clergy there assembled not to make the session vain and not to induce " the noble blood Charles " to damn him and his doctrine. He insists that he is not responsible for the tumults which have shaken Germany ; rather he alone withstood the turbulent spirits "so that I might truly say that I was your protector." He reminds them of his moderation at Worms and recounts the history of his attacks on indulgences, confession, penance, private masses, and monastic vows. If they ask what good has come of the new teaching, he replies rather what good has remained with his opponents? Have they not perverted all God's laws? Have they not abused the ban, the sacrament, which ought to be administered in both kinds, and vows of celibacy which ought to be left free? But they talk only of these and similar things indifferent, whereas they should first concern themselves with the primary things, the law, the gospel, sin, grace, the gifts of the spirit, right repentance, Christian freedom, faith, free will, and love, and next to these practical reforms such as the erection of schools, hospitals, and the regulation of poor-relief.

Just after he had finished this, he had one of his old nervous break-downs, partly due to overwork, partly to the unaccustomed richness of the fare. Thus he writes : —

TO PHILIP MELANCHTHON AT AUGSBURG

Feste Coburg, May 12, 1530.

Grace and peace in the Lord. Dear Philip, I began to answer your letter from Nuremberg on May 8, but business interfered to prevent me finishing my reply. I have completed my Warning to the Prelates and sent it off to the Wittenberg press. I have also translated the two chapters of Ezekiel about Gog and have written a preface to them, so that they can be printed at the same time. Then I took the Prophets in hand and attacked the labor with such ardor that I hope to finish it before Pentecost and after that turn to Æsop and other things. But the old outer man cannot keep up with the ardor of the new inner man ; my head has begun to suffer from ringing or rather thundering, and this has forced me to stop work. Yesterday and the day before when I tried to work, I narrowly escaped fainting, and this is the third day on which I am unable even to look at a letter of the alphabet. I get worse as the years go by. My head (caput) is now a mere heading (capitulum) or chapter, soon it will be a paragraph, and then a bare sentence. I can do nothing but idle . . . so now you know why I am slow in answering your letter. On the day that it came Satan was busy occupying my attention with an embassy. I was alone, Dietrich and Cyriac were away, and Satan conquered me so far that he forced me to leave my room and seek the society of men. I hardly expected to see the day when that spirit would have so much power and simply divine majesty.

Such is our domestic news ; other news comes from abroad, such as that you mention about the strife between Eck and Billican. What is happening at the Diet? What do those blockish asses think of the cause of the Church and how are they disposed? But let them be.

Camerarius has sent me some dainties[1] consisting of fine grapes[1] and sack[1] and has written me two Greek letters. When I feel better I shall write him in Turkish, that he too may have to read what he does not understand. Why should he write me in Greek?

I must stop now lest my head, still sensitive, go bad again. I pray ; do you pray also. I would most willingly write, as you suggest, to the Landgrave of Hesse and to the Elector and to all of you, but I must take my own time. The Lord be with you. Give heed to my example and be sure not to lose your head as I have done. I command you and all my friends to keep regular habits for the sake of your health. Do not kill yourself and then pretend you did it in God's service.

[1] These three words are in the rare Greek used by Camerarius.

For God is just as well served, if not better, by resting, wherefore he commanded the Sabbath to be rigidly kept. Do not despise this warning, for it is the word of God.

MARTIN LUTHER.

When the Elector heard of Luther's sufferings he sent him a kind message not to worry about his enforced idleness, and at the same time expressing some anxiety on his own part at the dark outlook of the Protestants in the present crisis. The answer encourages him in turn: —

TO JOHN, ELECTOR OF SAXONY, AT AUGSBURG

(FESTE COBURG,) May 20, 1530.

Grace and peace in Christ our Lord and Saviour. Amen. Most Serene, Highborn Prince, most Gracious Lord! I have delayed answering your Grace's first letter from Augsburg, kindly written to tell me the news and express your hope that time was not hanging heavy on my hands. Truly your Grace need not worry about me in the kindness of your heart, although I am anxious about you and pray God for you. The time does not seem long to me; I live like a lord and the weeks scarcely seem three days to me. It is your Grace who is really in the tedious place. . . .

Consider that God shows himself merciful to you in making the Word fruitful in your Grace's land. Verily Electoral Saxony has the greatest number and best ministers and preachers of all the world, men who teach pure, true, and peaceable doctrine. Now the tender youth of both sexes are growing up so well instructed in the Catechism and in the Bible that it does my heart good to see how the boys and girls can pray and believe and speak more of God and Christ than formerly any religious foundation, cloister, or school could or yet can. Such young people in your Grace's land are a fair paradise, the like of which is not to be found in all the rest of the world. It is planted by God in your Grace's land as a true sign of favor to you, just as if he should say: "Well, dear Prince John, I commend to you my most precious treasure, my pleasant paradise; you shall be father in it, for I put it under your protection and rule and give you the honor of being my gardener and care-taker." . . . It is just as if God himself were your daily guest and ward, as he makes his gospel and his children your guests and wards. On the other hand, consider what terrible harm the other princes have done, and yet do to their youth, making the paradise of God a sinful, worthless, foul slough of Satan, destroying all and inviting the genuine old devil to be their guest. . . .

May your Grace be pleased with my letter; God knows I speak the truth and do not flatter, for it is a sorrow to me that Satan can still trouble and disturb your heart. I know him somewhat myself, for he is accustomed to play with me. He is a gloomy, sour spirit who cannot suffer a heart to be glad or have peace, and especially the heart of your Grace, for he knows how much depends on you, not only for us but for the world, and I can truly say for heaven itself. . . . Wherefore we are bound loyally to pray for and encourage your Grace, for if you are happy we live, if you are in trouble we sicken. . . .

Your Grace's subject,
MARTIN LUTHER.

The Diet, though summoned to meet on April 8, did not really open until June 20, a few days after the arrival of the Emperor. Charles was now at the height of his power. The earnest boy who had heard the heretic at Worms nine years before had become a grave man of thirty. Though without brilliant talents he had by persistence and application made himself the most powerful monarch in Europe. He had repulsed the Turk, he had sacked Rome, he had beaten France. The fruits of the last victory, that of Pavia, in February, 1525, had been torn from him, for the concessions made by Francis and ratified by an oath and a pledge of his knightly honor, were forgotten as soon as the Pope, as the Lord's Vicar, absolved the French King from his oath and made with him the "holy" league of Cognac. By 1530 Charles had made peace again with these two powers, a state of things from which some augured ill for the Protestant cause. Luther, however, suspected, and rightly, that the present peace was not much more stable than the former one, as the following very witty letter to a magistrate in Wittenberg shows: —

TO CASPAR VON TEUTLEBEN AT WITTENBERG

THE WILDERNESS, (FESTE COBURG,) June 19, 1530.

Grace and peace in Christ. Honorable, learned doctor and dear friend! I am heartily glad to hear that you and your dear Sophie are well. I have no news for you from Augsburg, as our tongue-tied friends there write me nothing, which pains me not a little. I know your brother-in-law Nicolas von Amsdorf would be immoderately angry with them if he knew how reticent they were, especially at this time. He shall yet be their judge.

I have learned from hearsay that Venice has sent the Emperor a present of many hundred thousand gulden and that Florence offers him five barrels of gold, but that the Emperor won't take anything for the sake of the Pope, who has promised to stand by him with body and estate, just as Francis once did with his *"par ma foi"* and the Pope with his *"in nomine Domini,"* and that there is a precious holy league — all that we don't believe. But I have heard from Dr. Martin Luther himself that he will forfeit an eye and an ear if Venice, the Pope, and Francis turn true Emperor's men; they are three persons of one nature, namely, of an inconceivable wrath and hatred against the Emperor with all hypocrisy, lies, and fraud, and will remain so until they either go to the wall — may God help them to it — or bring pious, noble young Charles to need. For my Lord *Par-ma-foi* cannot forget the disgrace at Pavia; my Lord *In-nomine-Domini* is first, a low Italian — which is too much — secondly, a Florentine — which is worse — and third, the son of a harlot — which is the devil himself, and moreover he is ill at ease over the sack of Rome. Likewise the Venetians are nothing but Venetians, which is enough said, and they excuse their wickedness by pretending to take vengeance for Maximilian — all these things we firmly believe. But God will help pious Charles, who is like a sheep among wolves. Amen. Remember me to your dear Sophie. God bless you. Amen.

MARTIN LUTHER.

The silence of which Luther complains was at last broken by Melanchthon, who wrote on June 13 begging him to write at once to Philip of Hesse. This prince seemed likely to desert the Lutheran for the Zwinglian party, and was accordingly warned of the danger of doing so in the desired letter by the head of the former faction. This epistle is mainly a long argument against the theological errors of the sacramentarians, closing with the words, often turned against their writer by the Romanists : —

O God! it is no joke nor jest to teach new doctrine! Darkness, arbitrary opinion, and uncertain arguments must not move us to it, but only clear, powerful texts, such as the Zwinglians have not yet found.

Truly I have suffered great pain and danger for the sake of my doctrine and hope it will not all be in vain. I do not oppose them from hate or pride, for God knows I would long ago have adopted their doctrine if they could only prove it. But I cannot satisfy my conscience with their reasons.

When at last the Diet began to sit, on June 20, it decided to take up the religious question first. Melanchthon, as the active leader of the Protestants, had drawn up an official statement of their doctrine to be presented to the Estates, the so-called Augsburg Confession. This document had been submitted to Luther and approved by him, but after this Melanchthon had somewhat altered it, hoping to make its wording more acceptable to the Catholics and to show that the Protestants were the real defenders of the old faith against novel abuses. For example, the article on the sacrament was put into language which good Catholics could have subscribed to, had they not known that declarations on transubstantiation and on the mass as an offering had been intentionally omitted. Again, private masses were gently deprecated instead of being described as a horror in the style of the previous confession. In spite of these concessions Melanchthon was fearful that they might not satisfy his opponents, and when he wrote to Luther again on June 20, he made gloomy prognostications as to the outlook for the cause, and complained bitterly of the cares which were devouring him.

TO PHILIP MELANCHTHON AT AUGSBURG

The Wilderness (Feste Coburg), June 27, 1530.

Grace and peace in Christ — in Christ, I say, not in the world. Amen. I shall write again, dear Philip, about the apology you make for your silence. This courier has come unexpectedly and suddenly from Wittenberg and is going to leave at once for Nuremberg, so I must wait to write more fully for another post.

Those great cares by which you say you are consumed I vehemently hate; they rule your heart not on account of the greatness of the cause but by reason of the greatness of your unbelief. John Huss and many others have waged harder battles than we do. If our cause is great, its author and champion are great also, for it is not ours. Why are you therefore always tormenting yourself? If our cause is false, let us recant; if it is true, why should we make him a liar who commands us to be of untroubled heart? Cast your burden on the Lord, he says. The Lord is nigh unto all them that call upon him with a broken heart. Does he speak in vain or to beasts? I, too, am quite often smitten, but not all the time. It is not your theology which makes you anxious, but your philosophy, the same which has been gnawing at your friend Camerarius. What good can you do by your vain anxiety? What can the devil do more than slay us? What after that? I beg you, so pugnacious in all else, fight against yourself, your own worst enemy, who furnish Satan with arms against yourself. Christ died once for sinners, and will not die again for truth and justice, but will live and reign. If he be true, what fear is there for the truth? Will he be prostrated by God's wrath? rather let us prostrate ourselves before it. He who is our father will also be the father of our children. I pray for you earnestly and am deeply pained that you keep sucking up cares like a leech and thus rendering my prayers vain. Christ knows whether it is stupidity or bravery, but I am not much disturbed, rather of better courage than I had hoped. God who is able to raise the dead is also able to uphold a falling cause, or to raise a fallen one and make it strong. If we are not worthy instruments to accomplish his purpose, he will find others. If we are not strengthened by his promises, to whom else in all the world can they pertain? But saying more would be pouring water into the sea.

I forwarded your letters to Wittenberg, both that written before and that written after the arrival of the Emperor. For at home they are also troubled at your silence, as you will learn from Bugenhagen's letter, though the fault of their not hearing from you is not, as Jonas says, the messenger's, but yours, and yours alone. May Christ comfort, strengthen, and teach you by his spirit. Amen. If I hear that things are going badly or that the cause is in danger, I shall hardly be able to restrain myself from flying to Augsburg, to see what the Bible calls the terrible teeth of Satan roundabout. I shall write again soon; in the mean time give my greetings to all my friends.

MARTIN LUTHER.

The Confession was read before the Diet, though only in a secret session. Luther regarded this as a great triumph for the cause, for which he alone had stood nine years before, as he writes to a friend and ardent supporter:—

TO CONRAD CORDATUS AT ZWICKAU

THE WILDERNESS, July 6, 1530.

. . . Jonas writes me that he was present during the session when the Confession was read before the Diet and supported in a two-hour oration by Dr. Beier, and that he will tell me later what he gathered from the faces of the audience. . . . Our enemies certainly did their best to prevent the Emperor allowing it to be read, and they did succeed in preventing its being read in the public hall before all the people. But the Emperor heard it before the princes and estates of the Empire. I am overjoyed to be living at this hour, when Christ is openly confessed by so many in a great public assembly and with so good a confession. . . . Do not cease to pray for the good young Emperor, worthy of the love of God and of men and for the not less excellent elector who bears the cross and for Melanchthon who tortures himself with care. . . .

The reading of the Confession was only the beginning of negotiation, which, dragging along week after week, sorely tried the patience and firmness of the Protestant minority. In these dark days, when the sun was hidden and the way seemed lost, Luther, though absent, the heart and soul of his party, encouraged and revived their fainting spirits. One of the most wonderful letters he ever wrote is the following to the chancellor, or, as we might say, prime minister of Electoral Saxony.

TO DR. GREGORY BRÜCK AT AUGSBURG

THE WILDERNESS, August 5, 1530.

. . . I have recently seen two miracles. The first was, that as I looked out of my window, I saw the stars and the sky and the whole vault of heaven, with no pillars to support it ; and yet the sky did not fall and the vault remained fast. But there are some who want to see the pillars and would like to clasp and feel them. And when they are unable to do so they fidget and tremble as if the sky would certainly fall in, simply because they cannot feel and see the pillars under it. If they could only do this, they would be satisfied that the sky would remain fast.

Again I saw great, thick clouds roll above us, so heavy that they looked like great seas, and I saw no ground on which they could rest nor any barrels to hold them and yet they fell not on us, but threatened us and floated on. When they had passed by, the rainbow shone forth, the rainbow which was the floor that held them up. It is such a weak thin little floor and roof that it was almost lost in the clouds and looked more like a ray coming through a stained glass window than like a strong floor, so that it was as marvellous as the weight of the clouds. For it actually happened that this seemingly frail shadow held up the weight of water and protected us. But some people look at the thickness of the clouds and the thinness of the ray and they fear and worry. They would like to feel how strong the rainbow is, and when they cannot do so they think the clouds will bring on another deluge.

I permit myself such pleasantries with your Honor, although I write with earnest purpose. . . . I hope we can keep the peace politically, but God's thoughts are above our thoughts. . . . If he should hear our prayers now and grant us peace, perhaps it would turn out worse than we hoped, and God would get less glory than the Emperor. . . . I do not mean to despise the Emperor, and only hope and pray that he may do nothing against God and the imperial constitution. If, however, he does this, we as faithful subjects are bound to believe that it is not the Emperor himself who is so doing, but tyrannical advisers usurping his authority, and we should make a distinction between the acts of our sovereign and those of his wicked counsellors. . . .

While Luther was writing these lines bad news was on the way. A Refutation of the Confession, prepared by his old enemy Eck and others, was read before the Diet on August 3. Charles refused to allow the Protestants a copy of this, which they desired in order to frame a reply. Thereupon Philip of Hesse, thinking all was over, suddenly and secretly left Augsburg, August 6. Just a week before he had, in spite of Luther's warning to beware of the sacramentarians, entered into an alliance with Zurich and Constance. The Wittenberg professor did not hear of this for some time, and when he did judged the ambitious chief severely for a step likely to bring on a war between Lutherans and Swiss.

But negotiations were still continued by the Protestants who stood fast and by a Catholic peace party headed by Albert of Mayence. Crafty Eck had appointed a committee of six consisting of himself, four other Catholics, and Melanchthon. The one reformer in this body had not the stamina to withstand a hostile majority and made such concessions on all points save marriage of the clergy, the dispensation of the sacrament in both kinds and the abolition of private masses, that an agreement was almost reached. It must be remembered, however, that when articles of faith were expressed in purposely ambiguous terms acceptable to both parties, the interpretation of these words was diametrically opposite. In return for the Protestant agreement to call the mass an offering, if the word were qualified with the term commemorative, the Catholics conceded that communion might be administered in both kinds if it were taught that this was a matter of convenience and not of principle. One of the most dangerous points yielded by Melanchthon was that the bishops should be restored to their ancient jurisdictions, a measure justified by him as a blow to turbulent sectaries.

Negotiations continued, to the increasing prejudice of the Protestants, throughout most of August and September. Melanchthon, whose humanistic training gave him a broader outlook than that of many of his contemporaries, animated by a sincere love of peace, yielded on matters which to him were indifferent, but to his co-religionists vital. Justus Jonas, also a humanist by education, sided with him, but most of the other Protestant leaders raised an outcry that he was a greater enemy to the faith than any Catholic and appealed over his head to Luther. The numerous letters written by him to his friends at Augsburg, though they sometimes show perplexity as to what was actually being done, are consistently and energetically opposed to all compromise. To Melanchthon he wrote, August 26, that he was even sorry that Eck had told such a lie as to say that he believed in justification by faith; communion in both kinds must be insisted on as necessary in all cases, and there was great danger of civil war in restoring the bishops to their old power. "In short, all treaty about harmonizing our doctrines displeases me, for I know it is impossible unless the Pope will simply abolish the papacy." On September 20 he wrote : "If we yield a single one of their conditions, be it that on the Canon or on private masses, we deny our whole doctrine and confirm theirs. . . . I would not yield an inch to those proud men, seeing how they play upon our weakness. . . . I am almost bursting with anger and indignation. Pray break off all transactions at once and return hither. They have our Confession and they have the Gospel; if they wish let them hear those witnesses, if not let them depart to their own place. If war follows it will follow; we have prayed and done enough."

Luther has often been blamed for his uncompromising spirit and for his narrowness on this occasion. An age which has ceased to regard many points then hotly disputed as vital or even as interesting can hardly appreciate the opinion of a man who made so much of them. Nevertheless, while Melanchthon's conciliatory breadth is far more congenial to our modern spirit, I believe that in this case Luther was right. The problem before a statesman is not what is the best possible policy in perfect conditions, but what is the best practical course to pursue under given limitations. The question for the Protestants of 1530 was not what line might be safely followed in an enlightened, tolerant age, but what measures were necessary, in the face of an exigent and perilous situation. It was a plain fact that however much they might juggle with words their differences were far too fundamental to be composed by any treaty. Luther saw this, Melanchthon did not.

The Catholics also saw it. Notwithstanding the immense concessions wrung from their opponents, they voted, on September 22, that the Confession had been refuted and rejected, and that consequently the Protestants were bound to recant. The Diet, in this Recess, gave the heretics until April 15, while the Emperor was to use his influence with the Pope to call a general council for the decision of still doubtful points; after that respite they were to be coerced.

Luther was deeply disappointed at this result. "I think the Recess is worldly wisdom," he wrote on October 1, "but let us believe that Christ is yet strong enough to rule all fools and babblers who condemn him." A day or two later the whole Saxon delegation returned to Coburg, which the Reformer left on the fourth, arriving home on the thirteenth.

CHAPTER XXIII

THE GERMAN BIBLE

LUTHER'S greatest monument is the German Bible. The old error of supposing that his was the first German version and that before his time the book had been much neglected has been often exposed; yet it remains true that his translation, by its superior scholarship and wonderful style, marks an era in both religion and literature.

Begun at the Wartburg in the latter part of 1521, the work was prosecuted with such energy that the New Testament was completed by the time that Luther returned to Wittenberg in March, 1522. It was published the following September in a handsome quarto with woodcuts from Cranach's workshop, — some of them after Dürer's famous Apocalypse series, — a description of the Holy Land by Melanchthon, marginal explanatory notes and introductions to the whole and to the separate books by Luther.

Work on the Old Testament was begun at once with the help of Melanchthon, Aurogallus, and Rörer. The first part appeared in the summer of 1523 and the second in December of that year. Of the work taken up next, Luther writes, on February 23, 1524, to Spalatin: —

We have so much trouble translating Job, on account of the grandeur of his sublime style, that he seems to be much more impatient of our efforts to turn him into German than he was of the consolations of his friends. Either he always wishes to sit upon his dunghill, or else he is jealous of the translator who would share with him the credit of writing his book.

The third part of the Old Testament, however, containing this difficult book, appeared in September or October, 1524. There still remained the Prophets, and labor on them had to be postponed for some years by the controversies with Erasmus,

the Heavenly Prophets, and Zwingli. When they were taken
up again, in 1528, the Reformer wrote Wenzel Link, on June
14: —

I am now at work translating the Prophets. Good Heavens! how
hard it is to make the Hebrew writers speak German! They withstand our efforts, not wishing to give up their native tongue for a barbarous idiom, just as the nightingale would not change her sweet
song to imitate the cuckoo whose monotonous note she abhors.

In the same year Isaiah was finished, after which some portions of the Apocrypha were taken up. At Feste Coburg the
Prophets were almost completed, though it was not until March
16, 1532, that the last portion of the Old Testament came out.
This was shortly followed by the Apocrypha. In 1539 a careful revision was undertaken by a " Sanhedrim " as Mathesius
calls it, consisting of Melanchthon the Grecian, Cruciger with
the Chaldean paraphrase, Bugenhagen skilful in the Latin version, Jonas the rhetorician, Aurogallus professor of Hebrew,
Rörer the proof-reader, and Luther the president and inspiring
spirit of the whole. He took a legitimate pride in his own work,
of which he said: —

I do not wish to praise myself, but the work speaks for itself. The
German Bible is so good and precious that it surpasses all the Greek
and Latin versions, and more is found in it than in all the commentaries, for we clear the sticks and stones out of the way that others may
read without hindrance.

In point of scholarship Luther's version was far superior to
all that had preceded it. They had been made from the Latin
Vulgate, adding to the errors of their original others of their
own. The basis of Luther's translation was the original tongues:
the Hebrew Massoretic text of the Old Testament published by
Gerson Ben Mosheh at Brescia in 1494 and the Greek New
Testament of Erasmus in the edition of 1519. Modern critics
have been able to improve on the work of Erasmus, nevertheless
his text was better than anything which had preceded it and was
in some points, as for example in omitting 1 John v, 7, superior
to that from which our King James version was made.

Other helps were of course much scantier than they are to-day. For example a diligent search failed to secure a map of the Holy Land. Luther undoubtedly used the Latin and even the older German versions as aids, though in no sense did he copy them. The work was indeed done with astounding rapidity, but the manuscripts show how carefully he polished and revised, and the success of the work testifies to its excellence.

Luther's principles, indeed, were not strictly scientific, but rather apologetic. The protocols laid down for the revision of 1539 indicate this, and so does the following saying of 1540 : —

Dr. Forster and Ziegler conferred with us about our version and gave us much help. I gave them three rules : 1. The Bible speaks and teaches of God's works, of this there is no doubt. But these works are divided into three classes : the home, the State, and the Church. If a saying does not fit the Church, let us place it in whichever of the other classes it best suits. 2. When there is doubt about the words or construction, we must choose the sense — saving the grammar — which agrees with the New Testament. 3. If a sentence is repugnant to the whole of Scripture, we must simply throw it away, for the rabbis have corrupted the whole text with their notes, trying to make it appear that the Messiah will come to give us meat and drink and afterward will die. That is a horror and we must simply throw it away. I took many a questionable sentence to Forster ; if he said, " But the rabbis understand it so and so," I replied, " But could you not write the vowel points differently and construe so as to agree with the New Testament?" In case his reply was affirmative I would say that it should then be so construed. That sometimes surprised them, and they said that they would not have thought of that sense their whole life long.

Such a saying gives a rather unfavorable idea of the probable accuracy of the version ; nevertheless as a matter of fact Luther's scholarship was far sounder than that of his predecessors. But it was less remarkable for this excellence than for the superiority of its style. The English Bible has also become a classic, but hardly attains the exalted position of the German in this respect. Luther's influence, exerted chiefly through this work, has been so enormous on the literature of his people that it is sometimes said that he created the modern written language. Other scholars are inclined to see in him rather the culmination of a literary activity which began some centuries before.

It is certain that there existed before him a common German
apart from the numerous local dialects, spoken at the court
first of the Luxemburg and then of the Hapsburg emperors.[1]
Luther himself recognized this: —

I talk a common, standard German rather than a particular dialect,
and thus I can be understood in both Upper and Lower Germany.
I speak according to the usage of the Saxon chancery, the form used
by the German princes in addressing one another. Maximilian and
Frederic the Wise brought the whole Empire to a sort of common
speech by combining all the dialects in one.

Whatever may be thought of Luther's speech, whether he
merely gave currency to "the ugly dialect of the Luxemburg
emperors," or created a strong and flexible literary language,
it is certain that his writings were for a long time the standard
of good form and that they gave an immense impetus to German thought.

His own principles, which conduced to great freedom of treatment, are well set forth by himself: —

It is not possible to reproduce a foreign idiom in one's native
tongue. The proper method of translation is to seek a vocabulary
neither too free nor too literal, but to select the most fitting terms
according to the usage of the language adopted.

To translate properly is to render the spirit of a foreign language
into our own idiom. I do this with such care in translating Moses that
the Jews accuse me of rendering only the sense and not the precise
words. For example when the Hebrew says, "the mouth of the sword"
I translate "the edge of the sword," though in this case it might be
objected that the word "mouth" is a figurative allusion to preachers
who destroy by word of mouth.

I try to speak as men do in the market-place. Didactic, philosophic,
and sententious books are, therefore, hard to translate, but narrative
easy. In rendering Moses I make him so German that no one would
know that he was a Jew.

No Englishing of Luther's German can give any conception

[1] It is interesting to compare the formation of the common dialect in Germany
and Italy. As Luther claims to speak the tongue of the cultivated introduced by
the Emperor Maximilian (as he thinks), so Dante (De vulgari eloquio) states that
he wrote not the *Tuscan* dialect but a common Italian, originating, as he believed,
at the court of Frederic II.

of the peculiar flavor of his version, which, to be appreciated, must be read in the original. One or two examples, however, may serve to point out the extreme freedom of the rendering. The word "church" (Kirche) is never used, but for it "congregation" (Gemeinde), as more consistent with the original idea. Again "Repent ye" (Matt. iii, 2; iv, 17; Mark i, 15) is not "tut Busse" as in the older versions, but "bessert euch," "improve yourselves." In Romans iii, 28, "Therefore we conclude that a man is justified by faith without works of the law," Luther added "alone" after "faith," to bring out what he believed to be the meaning of the apostle. He was violently attacked for this alteration by his enemies, and defended himself in an angry Letter on Translation in 1530.

It is my testament and my translation [he bursts out] and if I have made any mistakes (though I never falsified intentionally) I will not let the papists judge me. . . . As to Romans iii, 28, if the word "alone" is not found in the Latin or Greek texts, yet the passage has that meaning and must be rendered so in order to make it clear and strong in German.

Luther's attitude to the Bible contains one striking contradiction. He insisted that it should be taken as a whole and literally as God's inerrant Word; and at the same time he was himself the freest of "higher critics." In his works against the Heavenly Prophets (1524) and against Erasmus (1525) he introduces long arguments to show that the Bible is consistent and binding in the literal interpretation of each text. In a work of 1530 he says: "Let no one think he can master the articles of faith by reason. . . . What Christ says must be so whether I or any other man can understand it." In his book Against the Papacy at Rome (1545) he says: "This writer would have done better to leave his reason at home or to ground it on texts of Scripture, rather than ridiculously and crazily to found faith and the divine law on mere reason." These and many another saying lend substance to the charge, often brought against Luther, of having merely substituted an infallible book for an infallible Church, or as a recent writer has expressed it, "of having set up Bibliolatry in place of ecclesiolatry."

But Luther was not the man to be bound by his own rule; few of his followers have ever interpreted, commented on, and criticised the Bible with the freedom habitual to him. The books he judged according as they appealed to his own subjective nature, or according to his spiritual needs. He often exercised his reason in determining the respective worth of the several books of the Bible, and in a way which has been confirmed to a surprising degree by subsequent researches. He denied the Mosaic authorship of part of the Pentateuch; he declared Job to be an allegory; Jonah was so childish that he was almost inclined to laugh at it; the books of Kings were "a thousand paces ahead of Chronicles and more to be believed." "Ecclesiastes has neither boots nor spurs, but rides in socks, as I did when I was in the cloister."

The Psalter was prized highly: "It should be dear to us," he said in his preface to it, "if only because it so clearly promises Christ's death and resurrection and prefigures his kingdom with the estate and nature of all Christendom, so that it may well be called a small Bible wherein all that stands in Scripture is most fairly and briefly comprehended."

But we must not make Luther more in advance of his time than he really was. He naïvely accepted all the miracles of the Bible, as illustrated by the following: —

I would give the world to have the stories of the antediluvian patriarchs also, that we might see how they lived, preached, and suffered. . . . I have taught and suffered, too, but only fifteen, twenty, or thirty years; they lived seven or eight hundred and how they must have suffered!

Like freedom was used in judging the books of the New Testament. In the preface of 1545 he says: "St. John's Gospel and his first epistle, St. Paul's epistles, and especially Romans, Galatians, and Ephesians, and St. Peter's first epistle are the books which teach all that is necessary for salvation, even if you read no other books. In comparison with them, James is a right straw epistle, for it has no evangelic manner about it."

In the introduction to Romans (1522), he says: "This epis-

tle is the kernel of the New Testament and the clearest of all
gospels, worthy and worth that a Christian man should not
only know the words by heart, but should converse with them
continually as the daily bread of the soul. It can never be too
much read nor considered, but the more it is used the more
precious it becomes." Then, by way of explaining the apostolic
use of such words as law, sin, grace, faith, justification, flesh,
and spirit, he gives an excellent summary of his own doctrine.

Revelation he holds neither apostolic nor prophetic, for
Christ is neither taught nor recognized in it.

Again, when he was asked what were the best books of the
Bible, he said the Psalms, St. John's and St. Paul's epistles for
those who had to fight heretics, but for the common man and
young people the first three gospels.

The often quoted condemnation of James as an epistle of
straw is far better known than the more drastic things he said
about it to his table companions : —

Many sweat to reconcile St. Paul and St. James, as does Melanchthon in his Apology, but in vain. "Faith justifies" and "faith does
not justify" contradict each other flatly. If any one can harmonize
them I will give him my doctor's hood and let him call me a fool.

Let us banish this epistle from the university, for it is worthless. It
has no syllable about Christ, not even naming him except once at
the beginning. I think it was written by some Jew who had heard
of the Christians but not joined them. James had learned that the
Christians insisted strongly on faith in Christ and so he said to himself : "Well, you must take issue with them and speak only of works,"
and so he does. He says not a word of the passion and resurrection
of Christ, the text of all the other apostles. Moreover, he has no order
nor method. He speaks now of clothes, now of wrath, jumping from
one topic to another. He has this simile : "For as the body without
the spirit is dead, so faith without works is dead also." Mary, mother
of God! He compares faith to the body when it should rather be
compared to the soul! The ancients saw all this and did not consider
the epistle canonical.

Luther's marginal notes in one of his own Bibles are equally
trenchant. To James i, 6 (But let him ask in faith, nothing
wavering), he remarks : "That is the only good place in the

whole epistle"; to i, 21 (Receive with meekness the engrafted word), "Other engrafted it, not this James"; to ii, 12 ff., "What a chaos!" and to ii, 24 (Ye see then that by works a man is justified, and not by faith only), "That is false."

CHAPTER XXIV

THE Recess of Augsburg was published in an imperial edict
of November 19, 1530, declaring that the Emperor and Estates
had resolved to remain in the ancient communion, that the
Protestants must therefore renounce their errors before the
fifteenth of the following April, that the Emperor would use
his influence with the Pope for the calling of the general council to which the final settlement of the religious difficulties was
referred, and that in the mean time the bishops should be restored to their former jurisdictions and no further innovations
allowed. Shortly after promulgating the edict, Charles summoned the imperial electors to meet at Cologne for the purpose
of making his brother Ferdinand King of the Romans — the
title regularly assumed by the Emperor's destined successor.
By this means he hoped to constitute a strong, permanent
authority in Germany from which he himself was generally
obliged to be absent.

To meet the exigencies of the situation thus presented, the
Protestant princes and delegates from the cities assembled at
Schmalkalden, a little town just outside the borders of Electoral Saxony. Here, in December, 1530, they formed for mutual
help and protection an alliance, soon to become, under the
name of the League of Schmalkalden, one of the great powers
of Europe. They then debated what means should be used to
withstand the Emperor — legal or military. Some pressure
might be brought to bear upon the central government by con-
stitutional means; an obvious opportunity to do so occurred in
the election of Ferdinand.

Writing to Luther for advice as to the proper course to pursue, his sovereign received the following answer: —

TO JOHN THE STEADFAST, ELECTOR OF SAXONY, AT SCHMALKALDEN

(WITTENBERG,) December 12, 1530.

Grace and peace in Christ. Most serene, highborn Prince, most gracious Lord! My dear friend, Chancellor Brück, has spoken privately to me, by your Grace's command, asking my opinion in the present contingency, namely, the election of the King of the Romans, at which the Emperor has asked your presence in your official capacity. Although in my lowly station I cannot advise nor even know much about such important affairs — for I have not the advantage of seeing all things, as does your Grace, from the inside, but only from the outside and from afar — yet will I humbly give your Grace my thoughts.

I hope your Grace will not abandon your intention of taking part in the election, for if you do, the enemy will find cause to take away your vote. But if your Grace assists at this election, you will be thereby confirmed in your vote and your fief, and their crafty stratagem to ruin your Grace will be frustrated. . . .

Let your Grace be assured that it is no sin to vote for a political enemy of the Evangelic faith, for your Grace alone could not hinder his election which would take place anyway, so that you will be obliged, under any circumstances, to obey an Emperor who rejects the Gospel. Moreover, it might happen that if your Grace were absent, your vote would be given to Duke George of Albertine Saxony or to some one else. . . .

Your Grace must know that the Landgrave of Hesse has spontaneously caused himself to be inscribed a citizen of Zurich,[1] which causes me little pleasure; for unless God help and protect us war must come from that alliance. Your Grace knows that in such a war the Swiss will protect the sacramentarian heresy, if not force it upon us, which God forbid. For they have not yet recanted; they fight not because it is necessary but to uphold their error. O God! in these worldly matters I am too childish simple! I pray and will pray God to guard and guide your Grace as heretofore; or, if worst comes to worst, that he will give us his grace and a blessed end. Amen. Your Grace will take my simple talk in good part. I speak as I understand. . . .

Your Grace's subject,

MARTIN LUTHER.

[1] For the alliance of Hesse, Zurich, and Constance, formed July 30, 1530, see above, p. 260.

The "simple talk" failed to convince John, who sent his son, John Frederic, to protest against the election. As Luther predicted, the action of Saxony did not prevent the choice of Ferdinand by the six other princes (January 5, 1531), and it was also made the excuse for a proposal to deprive the absent member of his vote.

While advising against extra-legal means of resisting the Catholics, Luther continued the warfare with his pen. The Recess of Augsburg, together with the Refutation of the Protestant Confession, was printed early in 1531. The Wittenberg professor answered at once in two pamphlets: A Commentary on the Putative Imperial Edict, and A Warning to his dear Germans. In the former he protests that he would not have what he now says understood of the pious Emperor or against any authority, but only against the wicked advisers who usurped their lord's power. He refutes their refutation point by point, and designates their claim to have conquered him by Scripture as a plain lie. In the second pamphlet he recalls his Warning to the Clergy at Augsburg, in which he had so heartily begged for peace but they had despised his prayer. Now they accuse him of sedition and rebellion. He defends the Protestants from this charge, by making a distinction between those who resist authority simply to become masters themselves and those who merely defend their rights. The former is wrong, the latter justifiable.

These pamphlets were at once denounced by the Catholics as seditious and libellous. Duke George especially sent a remonstrance to his cousin John of Ernestine Saxony, who in turn requested his subject to refrain from violence in future.

Luther replied with the following indignant protest: —

TO JOHN THE STEADFAST, ELECTOR OF SAXONY

(WITTENBERG,) April 16, 1531.

Grace and peace in Christ. Most serene, highborn Prince, most gracious Lord! The esteemed and learned Dr. Gregory Brück has sent me your Grace's letter forbidding me to publish sharp or violent books, of which I have recently written two with the purpose of preventing injustice. . . .

First, I can show that in these two sharp books I have said nothing turbulent nor incited any man to sedition; this I will maintain against every one, God willing.

Secondly, it is clear that in these books I have highly praised and celebrated the Emperor; in short I have proposed nothing except that Christians should judge conscientiously and discover the bad practices and abuses perpetrated in the Emperor's name, so that pious hearts may remain untroubled and unseduced.

Thirdly, I think that your Grace should remember how your party worked against the edict at Augsburg, thereby acting in a Christian, upright way, letting every one know that you protested against it.

But yet they incontinently condemned our Confession, without letting us have their Refutation to answer it, and they did not hear our prayers for peace, but passed a menacing, atrocious, bloodthirsty, false edict, thereby, if truth be spoken, drawing the sword against your Grace and our party, and setting the whole Empire at odds — for one cannot mince words in such matters. Moreover your Grace and our party have kept silence for more than six months, showing abundant and perilous patience without accomplishing anything thereby, for it has only made our antagonists more proud, confident, and arbitrary; wherefore I was obliged to speak for fear they would not be checked until they had ruined us. If your Grace and the other leaders of our party wish to suffer in eternal silence, nevertheless I have not the patience, especially as the cause is originally and chiefly mine. If I should finally acquiesce in this public condemnation of my teaching, it would be tantamount to abandoning or denying it; sooner than do this I would incur the wrath of all the world and of all devils, not to mention his Imperial Majesty's advisers.

Certain persons have represented to your Grace that my books are sharp and vehement. This, indeed, is true, for I can write nothing on this subject soft and mild. I am only sorry that what I write on this subject is not still more cutting and violent, for compared to the sharpness of their actions my speech is not sharp at all. It is no mild, gentle act to publish such an edict against your Grace and your friends, not allowing you to speak in your own defence, but drawing the sword of wrath and trying to fill Germany with blood and with widows and orphans.

When did the Catholics ever punish the scurrilous writings published against us? . . . Your Grace may see that these people think it right and fine for a hundred thousand authors to write against us, every sheet of whose voluminous works is full of poison and gall. . . . But if I,

poor man, alone cry out against these monsters, then no one has written
sharply but only Luther! . . . In short, whatever I do or say is wrong,
even if I should raise the dead; whatever they do is right, even if they
should drench Germany with innocent blood! Yet one must fight these
people with cotton wool, bow to them and say: " Gracious sirs, how
pious and fair you are! " . . .

Your Grace's obedient subject,
MARTIN LUTHER.

The day set for the final recantation of the Protestants
— April 15, 1531 — passed without any attempt being made to
coerce them. On the contrary negotiations still continued and
a new diet was summoned to meet at Ratisbon in January,
1532. Luther had little hopes of any agreement; as he wrote
Amsdorf on August 26, 1531: —

Whether there will be a diet or not I cannot say. I know, however,
that whether there is one or not, agreement is impossible; for who can
reconcile Christ and Belial, or how can the Pope concede that faith
alone justifies and that the works of popery are damnable, or how can
he withdraw and let Luther reign?

The Estates met as appointed, but it was not here that negotiations were carried on but at Nuremberg. The Catholics were
represented by the Electors of Mayence and of the Palatinate,
to whom Ferdinand delegated plenary powers, and the Protestants by the Elector of Saxony. As a result of the conference
a treaty, known as the Religious Peace of Nuremberg, binding
each party to respect the faith of the other until an œcumenic
council should be called to decide all religious questions, was
signed by the delegates on July 23 and received the sanction of
the Emperor and Estates on August 2. The result was diplomatic victory for the Lutherans, giving them time in which to
grow and for an indefinite period a recognized legal status in the
Empire.

The Elector John did not long live to enjoy the fruits of this
triumph. He died on August 16 and was buried in the Castle
Church at Wittenberg two days later. In officiating at the funeral the Reformer wept unaffectedly for his departed sovereign.
On the day of the interment he spoke as follows at dinner: —

The bells sound differently when we know they ring for a dead friend. . . . In John we saw the greatest clemency, in Frederic the greatest wisdom; had the two princes been united it would have been a miracle. . . . How great a prince has now died, and how lonely, for no son, cousin, nor friend was with him. The physicians say that a convulsion killed him.

Four days after this, Luther said to the new elector, John Frederic, as they were dining together at Wittenberg : —

The death of a prince is a much more pitiful thing than that of a peasant. A prince must be left by all his friends and nobles and at last strive alone with the devil, for no one will remind him that he has lived like a prince.

John Frederic the Magnanimous was twenty-nine when he succeeded his father. Like Philip of Hesse he belonged to a generation more susceptible to the influence of the new teaching. Brought up by Spalatin in a strongly Lutheran atmosphere, he was a yet more ardent disciple of the Reformer than his father had been. The Wittenberg professor at first had some doubts of the youth : —

With the Elector Frederic, wisdom died, with the Elector John, piety. Now the nobles will reign and piety will vanish. They know that my young lord has a mind of his own and that he does not care for learning, and that pleases them much. The nobles preach opinion to him. Let them look to it that they do not put the land through a sweat bath and then lay the people on the pavement to cool off. If the Elector only had his uncle's wisdom and his father's piety I would like also his insistence on having his own way and wish him success with it.

In this case, however, familiarity bred respect, for Luther came to have an increasingly high opinion of his prince. About 1540 he said : —

We certainly have a prince adorned with many gifts. He has a reverend tongue and listens to no base or blasphemous word. He loves the Bible, schools and churches; he upholds a heavy weight and alone keeps the faith. He would gladly attend to everything, but he cannot. His only vice is that he drinks too much with his friends and perhaps he also builds too much. But he works like a donkey. If we did not pray earnestly for him we should not do right.

After the peace of Nuremberg languid negotiations looking to a more definite settlement still continued. The main question was the calling of a council. Pope Clement, who desired nothing less than such an assembly, procrastinated. In June, 1533, ambassadors from him and the Emperor came to treat with John Frederic on the subject. The Elector took them to Wittenberg to consult Luther. A letter from the latter to an old friend partly explains why the conference was futile:—

TO NICHOLAS HAUSMANN AT DESSAU

(WITTENBERG,) June 16, 1533.

Grace and peace in Christ. Dear Nicholas, I have not leisure to write at length on account of the presence of the Most Illustrious Elector, before whom I daily preach, and with whom I have to confer on the answer to be given to the papal and imperial ambassadors. The Pope has sent them to propose to us certain articles about calling a council, in which he intends that all shall be done according to his pleasure; that is, that we should be condemned and burned; but he conceals his purpose with slippery words worthy of himself. We shall return an answer worthy both of himself and of ourselves. They are rascals to the core and will remain so. The ambassadors are treated most honorably, not on account of the Pope but on account of the Emperor, whose name we reverence while despising that of the Pope. The ambassadors have spoken to neither me nor to Melanchthon nor to any of our theologians. Why indeed should the servants of our despoilers and murderers hear us? More at another time. At present farewell in the Lord and pray for me.

DR. MARTIN LUTHER.

What could not be obtained by peaceful means was sometimes wrested by force. Of the numerous gains made by the Protestants in the early thirties, the most important was the conquest of Württemberg by Philip of Hesse in May, 1534. The tyrannical Duke Ulrich had been expropriated some fifteen years previous by the Swabian League and the territory given by the new emperor to his brother Ferdinand. After many unsuccessful attempts to reconquer his dominions, Ulrich at last found an opportunity, by embracing the Protestant religion, to secure the military support of their ablest statesman. The campaign was, however, undertaken contrary to the advice of the reformers, true to their pacific principles. Their meeting with Philip at Weimar, in January, 1533, as well as the result of the campaign, is described by Luther in a saying recorded some seven years later : —

Philip of Hesse undertakes much and accomplishes much. Great was his audacity to oppose the bishops,[1] but greater to restore the Duke of Württemberg and expel Ferdinand. Melanchthon and I dissuaded him from doing this with all our powers at Weimar, thinking that he would bring shame on the Evangelic cause and disturb the peace. He got all hot and red, though he is usually pale. . . . So he kept on and did what he said he would and fired three hundred and fifty shots into the city and castle [2] and waited for an answer at Cadan. Duke George said to Ferdinand : "If you could only raise an army in two or three days, I would not advise peace, but as you can't you must come to terms."

[1] Of Bamberg and Würzburg at the time of the Pack affair, 1528. Cf. *supra*, p. 224.

[2] Asperg, June 1 and 2, 1534.

CHAPTER XXV

THE CHURCH MILITANT

THE philosopher, says a great historian, may indulge in the pleasing task of portraying Religion as she descended white-robed from Heaven; it is the melancholy duty of the historian to show how she has been maltreated by men, and her immaculate garments torn and spotted by human passion. The early annals of the Protestant, as of the Apostolic Church, are full of difficulty and dissension. After the peace of Nuremberg had given the Protestants a firm position against the Roman Catholics, the main energies of the reformers were applied to fighting each other and dealing with the numerous contrarieties which arose in their own folds.

A main problem with all associations as with all individuals is the financial one. This chronic difficulty is thus spoken of in a letter from Luther to John Sutel of Göttingen, March 1, 1531: —

I see your friends are worried for fear they will have to pay their ministers a little more. . . . Formerly the people gave thousands of guldens to every impostor that came along, whereas now they won't give any man a hundred. Let them go to. It is better for them to serve the Pope and be subject to the devil than to lord it over Christ and trample on his Word. Many such cases come up elsewhere, but the Lord knows his own. They imagine that we must flatter them and could not do without them. This is not to seek the gospel earnestly.

About the time that Luther was writing this discouraged note a perfect tempest was brewing at Zwickau — a tempest in a teapot, to be sure, but one which occupies more space in the Reformer's correspondence and table-talk, than do the Diet of Worms and the Peasants' Revolt put together. The cause of the disturbance was the expulsion of a clergyman, Lawrence Soranus, early in 1531, by the town council. The accused secured the interest of the government and of Luther, who wrote the following vigorous letter to one of the principal citizens: —

TO STEPHEN ROTH AT ZWICKAU

(WITTENBERG), March 4, 1531.

Grace and peace in the Lord. Among many sorrows undergone in the ministry of God's Word, I feel keenly, my dear Stephen, that you and your fellow citizens show such overbearing contempt for God and his ministers. You have cast out Lawrence Soranus with ignominy, branded with a public punishment, though not convicted of crime nor even heard in his own defence, and every one cries out that you, Roth, were the author and perpetrator of this crime. Excuse yourself as much as you like, you will never clear yourself of this arbitrary, or rather presumptuous act, done without the knowledge and consent of your excellent pastor Hausmann, who had every right to know and participate in the proceedings. Do you really think, my dear young fellows, that you can domineer in the Church, appropriate and steal revenues which you have not given, and can distribute them to whom you wish as if you were lords over the Church? I am minded to write a book to humble you and those beasts of Zwickau and to make a public example of your iniquity, as the Lord lives. This is the thanks that you give us, friends, for our sweat and agony in the service of God's Word. I wish you and yours excluded from the communion of my Lord Jesus Christ so that you and all may see how safe you are in your pride. May the Lord Jesus confound the undertakings of you all. Amen.   MARTIN LUTHER.

Roth and the town council replied, standing by their former action, and expressing surprise at Luther's hasty judgment. The other local preachers, Hausmann and Cordatus, encouraged by support from headquarters, took the part of Soranus, and the quarrel soon made their position as untenable as his. Cordatus, a man of passionate temper, was the first to be obliged to go. He would have preferred to stay even at some personal risk, but his chief, more gentle in deed than in word, advised him "to leave that Babylon and give place to wrath." Cordatus accordingly came to Wittenberg, where he was for ten months the guest of the Black Cloister, during which time he made a collection of his host's table-talk, naturally recording the many violent denunciations of "that cursed, recalcitrant city."

In hopes of composing the quarrel a meeting was arranged between Luther, Jonas, Hausmann, and Cordatus, and some representatives of Zwickau, headed by the burgomaster Mühlpfort, to whom in happier times the Reformer had dedicated his work on the Liberty of a Christian Man. As the altercation waxed hot, Mühlpfort said, "Doctor, you will never bring us under another Pope: we have learned too much for that"; to which Luther replied, "Is it not a curse on me that I have made others so learned and yet know nothing myself?"

The attempt came to nothing, and Hausmann was eventually forced to follow Cordatus. On November 22 his leader invited him thus: —

I write again to beg you for Christ's sake to come to me as soon as possible. There is a little new room waiting for you. Think not that you will be a burden to me, but rather a support and a solace.

Hausmann accepted the invitation. In the autumn of 1532 he found employment as court preacher to the princes of Anhalt at Dessau, and in 1538 accepted a call to his native town Freiberg. His death on October 17 of that year was a great blow to Luther, who burst into tears upon hearing of it.

Before the storm at Zwickau had been laid, another dissension arose at Nuremberg. Osiander, a reformed priest who had taken a prominent part in the Diet held here in 1523, endeavored, about ten years later, to abolish the practice of private confession. The stricter party, headed by Link, opposed this step, referred the question to Wittenberg, and received an answer, dated April 18, 1533, from Luther and Melanchthon, to the effect that public and private confession might well be continued at the same time. Osiander refused to bow to the decision, and for a long time harbored resentment against the other clergymen. Luther treated the matter in a large and conciliatory spirit, writing Link on October 8: —

I pray you for Christ's sake not to close the eyes of mercy, but consider how far the man is captured and sick with his own opinion, and therefore try not to confound or condemn him publicly, lest from this spark a conflagration should arise. Endeavor rather to free and

heal him by the exercise of moderation, patience, and prudence, studying only how to profit his soul.

The threatened breach happily yielded to this gentle treatment, and Luther was able to write Osiander an affectionate
letter styling him the true partner of his faith.[1]

Far different was the result of another schism, which tore
the very heart of the Evangelic Church before it was quelled.
The leader of the Antinomian heresy — so the new sect was
denominated — was John Agricola, a native of Eisleben, about
ten years younger than his great compatriot. His ambition was
not satisfied with the humble position of village schoolmaster,
and he several times brought himself into prominence, notably
by an attack on Melanchthon during the church visitation of
1527. His abilities and his personal friendship for Luther
moved the latter to nominate him for a position in the university. During the Reformer's absence at Schmalkalden in the
early part of 1537, Agricola and his family were guests at the
Black Cloister, while he assisted in supplying the vacancy caused
by his host's absence, taking some of the professorial and pastoral duties.

It was now first noticed that his theology was not free from
the taint of false doctrine; he was accused of teaching justification by faith to the disparagement of morality, asserting, it was
charged, that as long as a believer was in a state of grace it
made little difference what he did or what sins he might commit. On his return Luther felt obliged to preach against this
doctrine, and the Elector prohibited Agricola from the pulpit.
In December the Reformer issued a series of propositions, containing the gist of the Antinomian doctrine, intending to debate them with its leader. The man against whom they were
directed declined the challenge, and, in January, 1538, gave
such quieting assurances that he was again allowed to preach.
Hardly had he been forgiven, however, before he gave new
offence. He issued a stronger statement of his previous position, defending it by quotations from the Reformer's own works.
Luther was irritated both by the contents and the manner of
the apology; he saw that Agricola's doctrine was dangerous to

[1] June 3, 1545. Burkhardt: *Luther's Briefwechsel.*

morality and proposed to suppress it whether supported by former expressions of his own or not. He accordingly issued a pamphlet against the Antinomians early in 1539, to which Agricola promptly responded with a list of rather enigmatical theses, thus explained by one of the reporters of the table-talk : —

January 31, 1539, Dr. Martin Luther read Agricola's propositions for debate. They were all about Jonathan and Saul. . . . At last he understood the deceit of Agricola, who played with allegories and double meanings, and yet exposed himself in all his thoughts. . . . His meaning was that Jonathan was himself, who ate honey, that is, preached the gospel, but that Saul was Luther, who forbade the use of this honey in the Church. When the doctor had at last fathomed this meaning he exclaimed : " O Agricola, are you such a man ? May God forgive you for being so bitter and thinking that I am your enemy. God is witness that I loved you and yet do. Why don't you come out openly and not fight so treacherously ? "

During the long controversy the poison had spread to other parts. When Melanchthon went to the Congress of Frankfort in February, 1539, he wrote accounts of other Antinomians who had made themselves known. At the same time Luther heard that the heresy was being taught at Saalfeld and other places, as he wrote his friend on March 2. On the same day, probably, he said: —

Satan, like a furious harlot, rages in the Antinomians, as Melanch-thon writes from Frankfort. The devil will do much harm through them and cause infinite and vexatious evils. If they carry their law-less principles into the State as well as the Church, the magistrate will say : I am a Christian, therefore the law does not pertain to me. Even a Christian hangman would repudiate the law. If they teach only free grace, infinite licence will follow and all discipline will be at an end.

The strain between the two protagonists at Wittenberg continued without coming to an open breach. Indeed, sundry attempts were made to bring about a reconciliation, and on one occasion, apparently in January or February, 1540,[1] Luther

_____

[1] The date is doubtful. The story was noted by one of the guests, Spangen-berg of Nordhausen, in his Bible, and taken from him by Aurifaber into his col-

invited his opponent with other theologians to a banquet at his house.

When they had eaten and made merry Dr. Martin Luther took a glass which had three rings around it marking divisions. Pledging his guests in this he said to Agricola : " Friend Agricola, note this glass ; the first division is the Ten Commandments, the second the Creed, the third the Lord's Prayer ; the glass itself which contains them is the Catechism." Then he drank all the wine in the glass, and filling it again gave it to Agricola. But he could only drink the upper division, nay, he was obliged to set the glass down and could not bear even to look at it again. Then said Luther : " I knew well that Agricola could drink the Ten Commandments, but that he would leave the Creed, the Lord's Prayer, and the Catechism alone."

In March Agricola laid a complaint against Luther before the Elector, saying that he had been trampled on for three years by his enemy and had never taught the doctrine of which he was accused. Before the committee of theologians appointed to investigate the merits of the case had come to a conclusion, Agricola had the opportunity to leave Wittenberg to accept a position in Brandenburg. He eagerly embraced this offer, in June, 1540. Even here, however, he found that the friendship of the Wittenbergers was desirable.

Luther, however, steadily refused to forgive him unless he recanted in the following formula : " I was a fool and wronged the Wittenberg divines ; they teach aright and I wronged them much. I repent from my heart and beg for God's sake that they will forgive me." The breach was therefore never healed. The Antinomian played in the religious history of the time a chequered part which gave some color to Luther's designation of him as a chameleon.

The most important follower of the Antinomian was James Schenk of Freiberg. Notwithstanding some complaints against him he was called to be court preacher to the Elector in July, 1538. While on a visit to Lochau, September 10 and 11, Luther heard Schenk preach and afterwards invited him to a

lection of table-talk (Förstemann-Bindseil, ii, 144) where the date 1540 is given. Many of the dates in Aurifaber are incorrect, but if this is right it seems likely that the banquet took place before Agricola's complaint to the Elector in March.

meal for the purpose of coming to an understanding. Schenk, when accused of teaching false doctrine, said: " I must speak as I do for the sake of Christ's blood and precious passion; the great pain of my conscience forces me to it. . . . I have a God as well as you." After some vain expostulation Luther replied: " If you are so badly torn the devil must mend you. Poor Freiberg will never get over it, but God will destroy him who has violated the temple. The proverb says ' Bad mind, bad heart.' A desperate bad fellow." To this Schenk only retorted: " If I make the court as pious as you have made the world, it will be all up."

He soon lost his position with the orthodox sovereign, and, failing to find another, wandered around for some years in deep poverty, until, about 1545, he died, apparently either of starvation or by his own hand. On Luther, who in his later years occasionally spoke of " Grickel and Jäckel " (Agricola and James Schenk) as lost men, the unhappy altercation left an abiding and melancholy impression.

Other fierce, if petty, quarrels broke out in Luther's immediate circle. By a bit of dramatic irony the centre of these storms was the peace-loving Melanchthon. This highly gifted teacher and writer by his very wish to please all men laid himself open to the charge of holding the faith and the interests of his Church too lightly. While Luther was absent at the Wartburg, the fatal weakness of Philip's character had been revealed in his dealings with the Zwickau prophets. A few years later he had been attacked by Agricola for his supposed backsliding to Catholicism. In 1530 at Augsburg he had drawn down upon himself the cutting animadversions of more resolute if less talented Protestants by his concessions to the enemy. In 1536 again Cordatus scented heresy in Melanchthon's teaching. The quarrel was suspended during the absence and illness of Luther at Schmalkalden, but later was renewed with greater violence, Cordatus calling his younger but more noted antagonist " a crab crawling on the cross." James Schenk, too, of Antinomian notoriety, in his orthodox days attacked Melanchthon with almost equal fierceness.

At times it seemed as if the relations of the two leading

reformers of Wittenberg would become strained. Luther took
very ill the approaches made by Melanchthon to his opponents,
whether papist or sacramentarian. He was angry when, in
return for a good sum of money, his friend dedicated a book
to Albert of Mayence ; he disliked the action of his colleague
and of Bucer when, in the reformation at Cologne, they
seemed to slur over the doctrine of the sacrament for the sake
of unity.

On the other side, too, the younger man often felt the influence of his older friend dictatorial and overbearing. Once or
twice it seemed that he tried to free himself from it, but always
anxiously avoided an open quarrel. His wife, moreover, was
jealous of Katie, for according to the rule of academic etiquette,
the doctor's wife preceded the master's.

But fortunately the mutual strain never came to an open
breach. The pair had too much respect and affection to allow
that. Luther was greatly impressed by his friend's intellectual
excellence and splendid services to the common cause. Not
only in his writings but by his active participation in politics,
Melanchthon did a great deal for the Protestant cause. After
the Diet of Augsburg he was the most active, though not the
most powerful, theologian of the reformed faith. He was almost
always present at the diets and conferences from which Luther
was kept by his health, and it was Melanchthon rather than
his friend who was invited by the kings of France and England
to visit their capitals. Katie may have felt some jealousy now
and then, but her magnanimous husband was never tired of
celebrating his friend. Among many testimonies of his affection and respect, the following are important.

August 1, 1537, Luther wrote on his table : —

> Deeds and words, Melanchthon,
> Words without deeds, Erasmus,
> Deeds without words, Luther,
> Neither words nor deeds, Carlstadt.

While he was writing, Melanchthon and Basil Monner entered
by chance. Melanchthon said that Luther had spoken truly of
Erasmus and Carlstadt, but that he had spoken too highly
of him and that Luther also had words.

VIVENTIS·POTVIT·DVRERIVS·ORA·PHILIPPI
MENTEM·NON·POTVIT·PINGERE·DOCTA
MANVS

MELANCHTHON

After an etching by Albrecht Dürer

No one has done so much as Melanchthon in logic in a thousand years. I knew the rules before, but Philip has taught me the thing itself.

The little man is pious; when he does wrong it is not with malice prepense. In his way he has accomplished much, but he has often been unfortunate in the dedications of his books.[1] To judge by results I should say that my way was the better, to speak out and hit like a boy. Blunt wedges rive hard knots.[2]

[1] Melanchthon had dedicated works to Albert of Mayence and Henry VIII.

[2] *Malo nodo malus cuneus*, a proverb several times quoted by Luther. My rendering is borrowed from *Troilus and Cressida*.

CHAPTER XXVI

THE WITTENBERG AGREEMENT. 1536

A PREVIOUS chapter [1] has traced the history of the schism of the two great reformed Churches as far as the unsuccessful attempt to reconcile them at the Marburg colloquy of October, 1529. To the Diet of Augsburg in the following year Zwingli sent a confession of faith in which he designated the Lutherans as men who longed after the flesh pots of the old Egypt. Still another confession, more irenic in tone, was brought by the German Zwinglians. Their representative, Martin Bucer of Strassburg, since 1518 a friend and admirer of the Wittenberg reformer, visited Feste Coburg in hopes of bringing about a union. He succeeded in convincing Luther of the good intentions of the South German cities, and, wishing to push his advantage, sent to him, not long after the close of the Diet, a very conciliatory creed, for which he received the following acknowledgment : —

TO MARTIN BUCER AT STRASSBURG

WITTENBERG, January 22, 1531.

Grace and peace in Christ. I have received the confession sent by you, dear Bucer; I approve it and thank God that we are united in confessing, as you write, that the body and blood of the Lord is truly in the supper, and is dispensed by the consecrating words as food for the soul. I am surprised that you say that Zwingli and Œcolampadius believe this too, but I speak not to them but to you. [Here follows an exposition of the minute differences in the belief of Luther and of Bucer.]

I cannot, therefore, admit a full, solid peace with you without violating my conscience, for did I make peace on these terms I should only sow the seeds of far greater theological disagreement and more atrocious discord between us in future. . . . Let us rather bear a little

[1] Chapter XXI

discord with an imperfect peace, than, by trying to cure this, create a more tragic schism and tumult. Please believe what I told you at Coburg, that I would like to heal this breach between us at the cost of my life three times over, for I see how needful is your fellowship to us and what damage our disunion has done the gospel. I am certain that, were we but united, all the gates of hell and all the papacy and all the Turks and all the world and all the flesh and whatever evil there is could not hurt us. Please impute it not to obstinacy but to conscience that I decline the union you propose. After our conference at Coburg I had high hopes, but as yet they have not proved well founded. May the Lord Jesus illumine us and make us more perfectly at one. . . .

How insistent Luther was that all with whom he claimed Christian fellowship should believe exactly as he did, and how sensitive he was lest it be thought that he had changed an iota of his opinion, is set forth in a letter to John Frosch, a minister of Augsburg, dated March 28, 1531: —

I have heard of the boasting of your Zwinglians that peace is made between us and that we have gone over entirely to your opinion. But, my dear Frosch, you must know that we have yielded nothing. Martin Bucer, indeed, seems to be thoroughly convinced that we believe and teach the same doctrine, and of him personally I therefore entertain some hopes. Of the others I know nothing certain, but if they desire peace I should wish to indulge them little by little, tolerating their opinion for a time while holding fast to our own as heretofore. This much charity demands.

Luther not only condemned the Swiss theology, but he entertained a deep, and as it proved, a well-founded distrust of the political aspirations of their leader. From the alliance of Hesse, Zurich, and Constance [1] he predicted disaster.

His gloomy prognostications were strikingly confirmed by the battle of Cappel, October 11, 1531, in which the Protestant cantons were defeated by the Catholic; Zwingli lost his life and the Swiss allies of Hesse were rendered powerless. As in the destruction of Münzer and the prophets six years before, the radical wing of the Protestant party was cut off and the leadership left to the conservative Lutheran branch. The Re-

---

[1] See letter to Elector John, December 12, 1530, p. 272.

former regarded both events as providential judgments on error. Far from being moved by the heroic death of his rival, he was, if possible, more confirmed than ever in his unfavorable estimate of his opinions and character. When he first heard of Cappel, he exclaimed: —

God knows the counsels of the heart, and it is therefore a good thing that Zwingli, Carlstadt, and Pellican lie prostrate, for otherwise we could not have withstood them and Strassburg and Hesse altogether. What a triumph for us it is that they have thus stultified themselves!

Again, when he learned of the death of Œcolampadius, which followed a few weeks later, he said: —

Erasmus, Œcolampadius, Zwingli, and Carlstadt all relied on their own wisdom and were therefore confounded. But I know that God knows more than I do and I thank him for it. . . . Who would have believed ten years ago that we should have been so successful?

Regarding the heresy of Zwingli as so poisonous, Luther naturally continued to combat it vigorously. Not long after his rival's death he wrote a letter to one of the earliest converts to his faith, expressing his views with a freedom deeply resented by the Swiss. The unkindest cut was the juxtaposition of the name they revered with those of the ranters, for Luther obstinately persisted in confounding them: —

TO DUKE ALBERT OF PRUSSIA

(WITTENBERG, February or beginning of March, 1532.)

Grace and peace in Christ our Lord and Saviour. Serene, highborn Prince. I have received your Grace's letter on the sacrament and the sixth chapter of John. [Here follows a long exposition of this and other pertinent texts.]

Such counsel of the Holy Ghost we must not despise, nor turn ourselves to others' boasting, but avoid them. He who has counselled us will turn their boasting to shame, as he has already begun to do. For we saw what he did to Münzer and his company, making them a horrible example to all ranters. For they boasted of the spirit and despised the sacrament, but they found out thoroughly what kind of a spirit it was. In like manner God has chased Carlstadt to and fro ever since he began his game and has left him no country for his body and no rest for his heart, but has made him a true Cain, branded and cursed with fear and trembling. And recently God has notably punished the poor people of Switzerland, Zwingli and his followers, for they were hardened and perverted, condemned of themselves, as St. Paul says. They will all experience the same.

Although neither Münzerites nor Zwinglians will admit that they are punished by God, but give out that they are martyrs, nevertheless we, who know that they have gravely erred in the sacrament and other articles, recognize God's punishment and beware of it ourselves. Not that we rejoice in their misfortune, which is and always has been a sorrow to our hearts, but we cannot let the witness of God pass unnoticed. We hope from the bottom of our hearts that they are saved, as it is not impossible for God to convert a man in a moment at his death; but to call them martyrs implies that they died for a certain divine faith, which they did not. We do not send criminals whom we execute to hell, but we do not for that reason make martyrs of them.

It astonishes me that the surviving Münzerites and Zwinglians do not become converted by the rod of God; they not only remain hardened in their former error, but give out that they are martyrs. . . .

It is true that the victory of the Catholic Swiss over Zwingli is not at all happy, nor does it win the victors great glory, inasmuch as they let the Zwinglian faith (as they call it) stand undisturbed by their treaty, and do not condemn this error, but let it pass, as they say, along with the rest of their old, indubitable faith; this, perhaps, will only confirm the sacramentarians. We must believe that this is a chastisement of God, of which they cannot boast, for by it he has closed their mouths against their enemies and all godless papists, and has given the latter cause to boast, which I fear will finally bring down a judgment of God on both parties. . . .

Wherefore I warn your Grace, and beg that you will avoid such people and not suffer them in your land. Your Grace must think that if you tolerate such ranters in your dominions when you can prevent it, you will terribly burden your conscience, so that perhaps you can never quiet it again; you would be troubled not only for the sake of your soul, which would be damned thereby, but for the sake of the whole Christian Church, for if you allow any to teach against the long and unanimously held doctrine of the Church when you can prevent it, it may well be called an unbearable burden to conscience. I should rather have not only all ranters, but all powerful, wise emperors,

kings, and princes testify against me than let one jot of the holy
Christian Church hear or see anything against me. For we must not
trifle with the articles of faith so long and unanimously held by
Christendom, as we can with papal or imperial law or the human
traditions of the fathers and the councils.

This is my brief, humble, and Christian answer to your Grace. May
Christ our Saviour richly enlighten and strengthen you to believe and
act according to his holy Word. Amen.

Your Grace's devoted
MARTIN LUTHER.

Some months after writing the above missive Luther expressed himself as to the probability of his enemies' salvation
as follows : —

It is much better and easier to pronounce Zwingli and Œcolampadius damned than saved, even if they did die for their faith. It is
profitable to do this to deter others, both those now living and posterity,
from their errors, for to call them saints and martyrs hurts many and
confirms the sectaries in their opinions.

Zwingli took the sword and received his reward, for Christ says:
Whoso draweth the sword shall perish by the sword. If God has
saved his soul he has done it extra regulam.

The blow to Protestantism in Switzerland made it all the
more advisable that German Lutherans and Zwinglians should
unite, and the danger of sacramentarian leadership being averted
removed the obstacle to doing so on the part of Wittenberg.
Philip of Hesse was again the mediator. Judging that better
results would follow from a conference at which Luther was
not present, he invited Melanchthon to meet Bucer at Cassel in
December 1534, to discuss terms of agreement. Fearing that his
friend would yield too much, Luther sent with him a written
statement of his opinion in the strongest form, namely, that the
body of the Lord was bitten by the teeth of the communicant.
The meeting was, however, successful ; Bucer admitted the absent reformer's contentions in such a way as to convince the latter
that the Church of Upper Germany, at least, was on the right
road. Thus he wrote to Philip of Hesse, January 30, 1535 : —

I have now arrived at the point, thank God, where I can confidently
hope that the ministers of Upper Germany heartily and earnestly be-

lieve what they say. But inasmuch as neither side has completely as-certained the opinion of the other, it seems to me that we have done enough for the present until God helps us to a real, thorough union. A long standing and deep difference cannot come to an end suddenly.

Nevertheless he wrote to Gerbel [1] November 27, 1535 : —

What more joyful could happen to me, now that I have discharged the duties of life, used up with labor and sorrow and overtaken with old age, than that before my death I should see an unexpected peace? . . . I say this that you may not doubt that I am heartily desirous of an agreement whatever may seem to interfere with one. If you will mediate I am willing to do and suffer all. I wish to be found a faith-ful servant of Christ in the Church even if I am not a very wise one.

With such a spirit of eagerness on one side and of willing-ness on the other, it was natural that a still closer approach to unity should be made. Free correspondence between the leaders of both parties impressed on them the belief that all that was needed for perfect mutual understanding was a personal inter-view. The Upper Germans appealed to Luther to fix the time and place for such an assembly and he in turn consulted the Elector in a letter of January 25, 1536 : —

The ministers of Strassburg and Augsburg are anxious for a meet-ing, for having thoroughly canvassed the subject, we are convinced that nothing remains but to draw up an agreement. There is no need, as they themselves acknowledge, of a great concourse, among whom some might be restless and recalcitrant and thus spoil our peaceful in-tentions. I therefore humbly beg your Grace to state what city would be best.

The Elector at first assigned Eisenach as the place of meeting, but this was later changed, on account of Luther's health, to Wittenberg. A small number of the leading clergy of Upper Germany arrived on May 21, and the next day the conference began at the Black Cloister. After a week's deliberation Luther was finally convinced that the men present believed and taught the orthodox doctrine of the sacrament, namely, that the body and blood are really present in the elements of the eucharist. When he announced that he regarded them all as brothers

[1] Enders, xi, 126. On dating, see note, *ibid.* 128.

tears sprang to the eyes of many. The conference was closed Saturday, May 27. The day following, one of the visiting divines, Alber, preached in the morning, Bucer at noon, and Luther in the afternoon. The same evening Bucer and others were guests at the Black Cloister; of their conversation on that occasion the following interesting fragment has been recorded: [1]—

Luther — I liked your sermon right well, friend Bucer, and yet I think mine was better.

Bucer — I gladly admit your superiority, doctor.

Luther — I don't mean to boast; I know my weakness and that I am not so acute and learned as you in my sermons. But when I enter the pulpit, I consider my audience, mostly poor laymen and Wends,[2] and preach to them. Like a mother I try to give my children milk, and not some fine syrup from the apothecary. You preach over their heads, floating around in the clouds and in the " shpirit." [3]

In the mean time Melanchthon had drawn up a formula embodying the results of the conference, the Wittenberg Concord, as it was called, which was signed by all present, save one, on Monday, May 29. The same day the guests departed. With them Luther sent several letters on the agreement, one of which may be transcribed: —

TO THE TOWN COUNCIL OF AUGSBURG

WITTENBERG, May 29, 1536.

Grace and peace in Christ. Honorable, wise, and dear friends! I have heard both of your preachers, together with others, and have done all in my power for them, as they themselves will tell you. At last, thank God, we are at one on all things, so far as human power can tell; wherefore I kindly and humbly beg you, as much as you can, to make our union strong and permanent. I have earnestly prayed and admonished your ministers to do the same, that we may not only teach the same doctrine with our mouths but also trust one another from the bottom of our hearts, eradicating all offence as true love is bound to do. If our agreement please you and your ministers, kindly inform us, as

---

[1] *Die handschriftliche Geschichte Ratzebergers*, edited by Neudecker, 1850, pp. 87 f.

[2] The Wends were the remnants of the Slavonic population which had inhabited Germany before the arrival of the Teutons.

[3] Luther ridicules his guest's pronunciation of " *Geist* " (spirit) as " *Gaischt*."

we shall tell you and others how we are pleased with the union. Then we will have it publicly printed, to the praise of God and the hurt of the devil and his members. Amen. The Father of all comfort and peace strengthen and guide your hearts with us in the right knowledge of his dear Son our Lord Jesus Christ, in whom all the riches of wisdom and knowledge are hidden. Amen.

Your devoted

M. L.

Although the Wittenberg Agreement had reunited the Lutherans with the German followers of Zwingli the breach with the Swiss still remained. Bucer, cheered by the success of his last venture, hoped to heal this schism also, and, finding the Swiss divines ready to meet him halfway, approached Luther. His letter reached the Reformer while he was lying at Schmalkalden very ill, and was therefore not answered until December 6, 1537. This noncommittal reply left matters as they had been.

In 1538 the Swiss again addressed themselves to Wittenberg. On April 15 one of their ministers, Simon Sulzer, visited Saxony and was received with friendliness at the Black Cloister. A little later Zwingli's successor at Zurich, Henry Bullinger, wrote Luther with the same end in view. The Reformer replied on May 14: —

Of Zwingli I will say freely that when I saw and heard him at Marburg I judged him an excellent man, as I did Œcolampadius. Their fate deeply shocked me, being, as I am forced to believe, a retribution on their obstinately held errors.

After this no further efforts at unification were made.

CHAPTER XXVII

RELATIONS WITH FRANCE, ENGLAND, MAYENCE AND ALBERTINE SAXONY

By 1535 the League of Schmalkalden had become one of the great powers of Europe. The Emperor was forced to treat with this combination of his subjects as with a foreign state, and the puissant monarchs of France and England sought alliance with it to bridle the overbearing dominion of the Hapsburgs. Francis, in courting the fellowship of the German Protestants, was moved by purely political motives, for there was never any serious question of his conversion. So earnest was he, however, in soliciting the heretics' support, that he not only sent a special embassy to Ernestine Saxony, but invited Melanchthon to visit his capital. Little as Luther trusted him he thought the invitation should be accepted for reasons explained in a letter.

TO JOHN FREDERIC, ELECTOR OF SAXONY

(TORGAU ?) August 17, 1535.

Grace and peace and my poor paternoster. Most serene, highborn Prince, most gracious Lord! I beg your Grace humbly and earnestly in God's name to let Philip Melanchthon go to France. I am moved to make this petition by the piteous letter of pious, honorable men [in France] who have barely escaped being burned. Melanchthon's reception by the king would bring such slaughter to an end. But if we fail these people the bloodhounds will have a pretext to do their worst with stake and axe, so that I think Melanchthon can hardly with a good conscience leave the men in such need and rob them of their desired comfort. Besides which the king might take offence against us all if we refused, for he himself graciously wrote the invitation and sent an embassy. Your Grace can leave the issue to God's mercy while Philip is absent three months. Who knows what God, whose thoughts are higher than our thoughts, will do? . . .

DR. MARTIN LUTHER.

This letter was without effect, for John Frederic feared the acceptance of the invitation would provoke the Emperor, and moreover he thought that Melanchthon, whose yielding nature was only too well known, might be brought to make concessions prejudicial to sound doctrine.

England, too, was now seeking the aid of the Schmalkaldic princes. As soon as Henry heard of the act of Francis, he dispatched Barnes in post haste with a similar invitation to Melanchthon to visit London. Luther also advised that this be accepted, but it was again denied.[1]

Two Catholic princes nearer home divided Luther's attention with the rulers of France and England. Ever since 1517 he had been in communication with Albert of Mayence. At the Diet of Worms, as Capito wrote to the Reformer, this ecclesiastic had advised moderation in dealing with the heretic. His letter of December 21, 1521, had been the beginning of a rapprochement, for Albert toyed with the idea of changing his religion and turning his archbishopric into a temporal fief.

At Augsburg the Hohenzoller had again used his influence for peace. Shortly after this he drew down Luther's displeasure by certain acts hostile to the Evangelic faith, and in 1535 a furious quarrel was caused by a tyrannical act of the Macchiavellian prince in the execution of one John Schenitz.

This artisan had risen from a humble position to be a minion of the powerful Elector of Mayence, at whose request he was even ennobled by the Emperor in 1532. Two years later his power suddenly collapsed. He was accused, perhaps with justice, of fraud; envious courtiers poisoned the mind of their lord; an intrigue of Schenitz with one of Albert's mistresses aroused the prelate's jealousy, and finally a scapegoat was needed to satisfy the loud complaints of Albert's subjects against the extravagance of his administration. So in September, 1534, he was arrested, and notwithstanding bribes offered by his brother Antony and an appeal to the Emperor, he was hanged at Giebichenstein in June, 1535. Antony, with Lewis Rabe, another courtier, fled to Wittenberg, where they

[1] Cf. chapter XVII on Luther and Henry VIII, p. 197.

gave the Reformer their own account of the trial. When Albert complained that he misrepresented the facts he received the following stern letter from Luther: —

TO ALBERT,' ARCHBISHOP OF MAYENCE

WITTENBERG, July 31, 1535.

I wish you repentance and forgiveness of sins, most noble Prince, gracious Lord! I am moved to indite this letter to your Holiness, not in the hope that it will do you any good, but only to satisfy my conscience before God and the world and not to connive at your crimes by keeping silence. Lewis Rabe has read me a letter in which your Holiness threatens to call him to account for mentioning John Schenitz whom you condemned. As he is my guest and your Holiness doubtless knows that you are doing him wrong and do not speak the truth, I am forced to think that you are privily seeking a quarrel with me, or are vexed at the honest words of honest men. I can testify conscientiously that Rabe sits like a maiden at the table and often speaks more good of his infernal cardinal than I can well believe. He does not gad about the town but sits still in his room. The whole city was full of Schenitz' fate at least two days before either Rabe or I heard of it, and we could hardly believe this noble deed of your Holiness, that Schenitz, so highly favored a minion, should suddenly be hanged by his dearest lord. Neither Rabe nor I invented the story; the cardinal's name was spit upon and damned without our motion.

If it is your intention to pick a quarrel with me it is my devout prayer that your Holiness should not strike at my guests and friends. . . . I hope your Holiness will not hang me as quickly as you did Schenitz. I propose to have my thoughts and opinions and also my conversations with my friends free and unforbidden by your Holiness, just as I must allow you a similar privilege. If I am a little incredulous about what might be said against Schenitz and for your Holiness — though I have not heard anything like that hitherto — it is a sin which may be forgiven me without one of your Holiness's indulgences. If your Holiness would hang all who speak evil and shame of you in this and in other matters, you would not find rope enough in all Germany. No matter how busily the infernal cardinal plied the hangman's trade, some would escape. . . . If your Holiness is anxious to know what people are saying about you throughout Germany, I can very well publish it, and relate everything which stands to the credit of such a horrible holy man, clear from the beginning about indulgences fifteen years ago. Your Holiness is not well advised to stir up so foul a matter nor to raise that bitter enemy Rumor against you. . . .

In writing this letter to your Holiness for the last time, I must take comfort that you cannot hang all your enemies, though it were indeed an easy matter to hang all who wish you well. Leave off your attacks on God and his Church and let a few live until the infernal torturer gets hold of you. Amen.

DR. MARTIN LUTHER, Preacher at Wittenberg.

Albert endeavored to appease Luther by turning to their common friends John Rühel and Prince George of Anhalt as mediators, but he only succeeded in making him angrier than before. About the end of January, 1536, the Reformer wrote him another letter in the tone of that last given, threatening a book against him charging him with a number of crimes and vices as well as with the murder of Schenitz. The archbishop applied to his powerful relative the Elector of Brandenburg, who, with himself, made diplomatic representations at the court of Saxony too strong to be ignored. The chancellor of John Frederic, Gregory Brück, writing to Luther on the subject, received an answer, dated December 10, 1536, containing the following paragraph : —

You have informed me that my gracious lord, moved thereto by letters from the Elector of Brandenburg and his family, has instructed you to ask me about my proposed pamphlet against the cardinal of Mayence. I give you to know that I intend to write it, but wish the Elector of Brandenburg and his relatives nothing but good. I told them at Torgau and elsewhere that I should prefer to see them take their noble cousin the cardinal in hand themselves and make him cease from evil, for truly I am of the opinion that he has mocked our dear Lord Jesus Christ and plagued poor folk enough. If they did so it would do more good than for them to complain against my writings. My pamphlet will contain little that is new ; I simply mean to uncork that prelate's nose, for it is stopped up so tight that he cannot smell how he stinks unless he is forced to.

Business and ill health delayed the publication until Luther had cooled off sufficiently to allow himself to be persuaded not to write the obnoxious pamphlet at all. He often thought over the cardinal's sins, however; on July 1, 1538, for example, he sighed and said : " Dear Lord Jesus Christ, give me life and strength and I will shave that parson's head, for he is a wicked and crafty mocker of all men."

Another magnate with whom Luther's relations were chronically bad was Duke George of Albertine Saxony. Ever since the Leipsic debate the Reformer had hated him as the most consistent enemy of the gospel. The quarrel which had flamed up in 1529 as a sequel to the Pack affair [1] broke out again in 1531, when the Duke answered Luther's Warning to his dear Germans, and when one of his clergy replied to the Gloss on the Putative Imperial Edict.[2] The Reformer received his opponent's work before it had been published and replied in a characteristically severe pamphlet Against the Assassin of Dresden. This booklet was ready for the Leipsic fair of the spring of 1531, for notwithstanding the supervision of the Duke many of Luther's works found their way to his capital. It may have been as a reply to this that in 1532 he passed a law that his subjects should take the sacrament once a year at least according to the rites of the Catholic Church, making exile the punishment of those who refused — exactly the measure of persecution adopted against the papists in Ernestine Saxony. Luther was furious when he heard of this law against his co-religionists : —

They say a mad dog lives only nine days, but Duke George has been mad nine years. He will be a lunatic soon. He has just exiled some of his subjects on account of the sacrament.

To the Protestants of Albertine Saxony, who wrote Luther asking what was their duty at this conjuncture, he answered : —

TO THE EVANGELIC CHRISTIANS AT LEIPSIC

WITTENBERG, April 11, 1533.

Grace and peace in Christ, who suffers and is put to death among you, but who will certainly rise and reign.

I have heard, dear friends, that some of you wish to know whether they may take the sacrament under one kind with good conscience, saying that if they only do that the government will be satisfied. Although I know none of you nor how your hearts and minds are fixed, yet this is my counsel : Whoso is convinced that God's Word commands

---

[1] Cf. Chapter XIX.   [2] Chapter XXIV.

the sacrament to be dispensed in both kinds should not do anything contrary to his conscience, for that would be tantamount to acting against God himself. And as Duke George has undertaken to search out the secrets of conscience, he will deserve to be deceived, as an apostle of the devil, which could easily be done, as he has no right to make such an inquiry, but sins against God and the Holy Ghost. And yet, as we must not do wrong because others do — though they be murderers and brigands — but must only decide what is right for us to do, in the circumstances it would be better to say to the murderer and brigand openly : "I will not do what you command; take my body and estate, and thereby injure him by whom you will be called to strict account, for Peter says, ' Jesus Christ is ready to judge the quick and the dead.' Wherefore, dear brigand, go on as you like ; what you will I will not, but what I will, God wills also, as you shall soon find out." We must smite the devil in the face with the cross and not whistle to him nor flatter him, so that he will know with whom he has to do. May Christ our Lord strengthen you and be with you. Amen.

Dr. MARTIN LUTHER, with his own hand.

It is hardly surprising that the prince designated as the "devil's apostle" should complain that Luther was stirring up revolt among his subjects. Peace was made by a meeting of diplomats of each branch of the house of Wettin, only to be broken the next year when Duke George's son complained that Luther was praying against his father. To the Elector's inquiries Luther guardedly answered that he did not know whether he had done so or not, but at his sovereign's request he consented to abstain from public prayers of such a kind in future. A truce was thus observed during the five remaining years of George's life. The quarrel is not wholly to Luther's credit. The Duke was in many ways an estimable character, sincerely convinced of his faith, and yet never, like so many other princes, staining his hands in the blood of the Protestants.

The Reformer's opinion of his demerits was only confirmed by his peculiarly tragic end. One by one all of his sons died, last of all Frederic, an idiot who succumbed to powerful remedies administered to make him capable of having children. The forlorn old duke made a will leaving his domains to his brother Henry, known to be a Lutheran, only on condition that he embraced the Catholic faith; otherwise he devised his lands to King Ferdinand. On his death, April, 1539, Henry the Pious succeeded, and, disregarding the will, at once introduced the Reformation with the general consent of his subjects, most of whom had already become secretly converted. Luther and Melanchthon accepted his invitation to visit Leipsic during the festival attending the public adoption of the Protestant faith. The journey was a triumph contrasting strongly with the visit of twenty years before, when, frowned upon by the government and hooted by the populace, the Wittenbergers had come to debate with Eck.

Luther was hardly convinced of the sincerity of the conversion. When his friend Link was called to fill a position in the capital of Albertine Saxony, the Reformer wrote him, October 26, 1539: —

I would by no means advise you to change your present position for one at Leipsic. There they were debating who or what will support the ministers of the Word. If the people are well disposed, nevertheless the nobles regard Wittenberg with their old hatred. Duke George is not dead there as yet, and it is uncertain whether he will die or rather come back again soon. Indeed I hate that sink of usury and other wrongs, that Sodom which must be saved for the sake of Lot only. The remnant of the city is provided for by a happy introduction of the Evangelic Church.

CHAPTER XXVIII

THE LEAGUE OF SCHMALKALDEN. 1535-1539

A NEW phase in the history of the Reformation was ushered in by the death, in October, 1534, of Clement VII, and the election of Paul III, a man of very different type, whose main interest was not to enjoy the temporal benefits of the papacy, but to forward the cause of the Church and especially to stamp out the growing heresy. He hoped to accomplish this by means of an œcumenic council, for to such a body the Protestants themselves had often appealed for a final settlement of orthodox faith. To arrange for the summoning of such an assembly he sent to Germany as nuncio Vergerio, Bishop of Capo d'Istria. On the way from Berlin to Dresden this prelate took the longer road by Wittenberg, excusing himself in a letter to a friend for visiting this sink of heresy, by saying that he was forced to do it to avoid the plague endemic in the smaller villages. At Wittenberg, where he arrived November 6, 1535, he was received with ceremony by the bailiff, John von Metsch, and lodged in the electoral castle. On the very night that he came he invited Luther, Bugenhagen, and their English friend Barnes, now here on official business, to " dinner after the bath," according to the then polite usage. This was declined, but the following day the Germans — not Barnes — accepted a second invitation to the ten o'clock lunch which was then the principal repast. Luther's preparations for this meeting, which, by the way, was on Sunday, are recorded by one of the reporters of the table-talk : —

Luther sent for the barber early to shave him. When he asked why he was thus summoned, Luther replied : " I am told that an agent of the Holy Father the Pope has come and that I am to speak with him. If, therefore, I have a young appearance the legate will think : ' The devil ! If Luther who is not yet old has been able to give so much trouble, what will he do when he gets on in life ? ' "[1]

[1] The doctor's desire to appear young was realized ; the nuncio wrote that

When shaved, the doctor put on his best clothes and a gold chain around his neck. " Professor," said the barber, "you will offend them. " Luther replied : " I do it for that very purpose ; they have offended us enough and one must deal thus with foxes and serpents." The barber: " Go in peace ; the Lord grant that you may convert them." Luther : " I shall not do that, but it is possible that they may be reproved by me before they are dismissed."

Luther and Bugenhagen then drove to the castle, where they were met by the bailiff, John von Metsch. Here, in a dining-room, was enacted the following little drama : [1] —

Enter John von Metsch with Luther and Bugenhagen.

Metsch — My Lord, let me present Dr. Luther and our pastor Bugenhagen — the best company we have for you in Wittenberg. (Turning to Luther) This is my lord the legate of his Holiness Paul III.

Luther (taking off his cap) [2] — How do you do ? So you come from Paul III, do you ? I remember hearing when I was in Rome many years ago (smiling sarcastically), celebrating masses by the bushel, that he who is now Pope was better than the average run of priests.

Vergerio — Let us sit down to table, gentlemen. (They do so ; Metsch, who waits on the table himself, pours wine.)

Luther (taking a sip of wine) — I daresay that before you came to Germany you heard that I was drunk most of the time ?

Vergerio — I did hear some things, professor. — I regret that the Englishman was unable to accept my invitation to dinner. Who is he, anyway ?

Luther — Oh, he is King Henry's private secretary sent as special ambassador to us. He mentioned that his monarch had just put to death a couple of bishops ; [3] I told him I wished it had been a hundred.

Vergerio — How can you praise sufficiently what he has done to these two holy men ?

although fifty he looked only forty. The Italian gentleman, however, ridiculed the ex-monk's dress and poor way of living.

[1] For the sources of this see the bibliography at the end of the book. I have followed them as accurately as possible, simply turning some indirect into direct discourse and supplying a few absolutely necessary junctura.

[2] This courtesy was so much less than the legate expected that he found it an insult.

[3] Luther means Fisher, Bishop of Rochester, and Sir Thomas More, who was not a bishop.

Luther — It would be hard to do so. (Vergerio gnaws his lips and makes a furious gesture.) England is certainly coming over to our side and would support the German Protestants against the Catholics.

Vergerio — Don't be deceived by his arguments and his bribes. We should do far better to make common cause against this monster than to eat each other up. (Pause.) Speaking of bishops how do you get along here without any to ordain your priests?

Luther (pointing to Bugenhagen) — There sits the bishop appointed for that purpose.

Bugenhagen (solemnly nodding) — Aye, we ordain them according to the method taught by the Apostle Paul.

Vergerio (sarcastically) — Indeed!

Luther (warmly) — You see, my lord, we are *compelled* to; and men publicly approved are thus ordained.

Vergerio — What do you mean by "compelled"?

Luther (hotly) — Your Roman bishops are too *holy* for us; they despise us and won't do it, so we have to provide for our own souls, and we appoint one of ourselves to take the place of the bishop.

Vergerio — I suppose these priests think it better to marry than to burn?

Luther — Aye, they are husbands of one wife. I have an honorable nun myself; we have three boys and two girls. The eldest boy is nine.[1] I expect he will be a great Evangelic theologian some day to take my place.

Vergerio — Do you teach him to fast and pray?

Luther (fiercely) — Not when the Pope orders him to.

Vergerio — Do you mean to say that you refuse to fast just because our Holy Father the Pope commands it?

Luther — Precisely; if it were the Emperor, now, we would; we respect *him*.

Vergerio — What you say is really incomprehensible. Don't you know that the Emperor himself is a mere creature of the Pope? The Supreme Pontiff crowns him and our Holy Mother Church created the Empire. But to come to the point. If the Pope, whom you insult, were to summon a general council of the Church, would you come to it?

Luther — I think a general, free, Christian council would be an extremely useful and necessary thing; not for us, indeed, for we know the truth, but for foreign nations. But you only pretend to call a council, not acting sincerely nor really wishing for one. But supposing

[1] Vergerio says Luther said "twelve"; this is a mistake.

you did call a council, you would only discuss useless things, cowls, priests' tonsures, food and drink, and such external things as, we know, justify no man before God. But of faith, true penitence, justification and other necessary things, and how those who believe in spirit and in truth may live at one — of these things you will not so much as make mention. Wherefore we do not need a council, but you, miserable men, do need one, for your faith is vain and uncertain.

Vergerio — Luther, what do you mean? Beware lest you take too much on yourself; you are a man and can err. Do you think you are wiser, more learned, more holy than so many councils, holy fathers, and learned men throughout the whole world who confess Christ and profess his religion? It is only your arrogance that rebels.

Luther (fiercely) — My arrogance! I tell you, man, my wrath is God's wrath!

Vergerio — But would you come?

Luther — Yes, and lose my head. I will appear, God willing, if you burn me for my faith.

Vergerio — Tell me in what place or city you think the council should be called.

Luther — Mantua, Padua, Florence — it's all one to me.

Vergerio — Would you come to Bologna?

Luther — To whom does Bologna belong?

Vergerio — To the Pope.

Luther — Good God! Has the Pope seized that city, too? Well, I will come to you there.

Vergerio — Neither would the Pope refuse to come to you at Wittenberg.

Luther — Let him come, we will receive him cordially.

Vergerio — If he came armed or in peace?

Luther — As he pleases. Only let him come, we will expect and await him. (They rise from table, and go outside where Vergerio's retinue are awaiting him. Vergerio mounts his horse.)

Vergerio — Be sure and be ready for the council.

Luther — Yes, my lord, with my life.

Of the nuncio's visit Luther wrote on November 10 to Jonas: —

The Pope's legate appeared unexpectedly in this city. He is now with the Margrave of Brandenburg; one would think he rather flew than rode. Would that you had been here to see him! He invited Bugenhagen and me to lunch when we had declined his invitation "to dinner after the bath" the night before. I went and ate with him in the castle, but what I said is not lawful for a man to write. I played Luther in the *disagreeablest* words, of which I shall tell you when I see you. I also had to play the part of Barnes, who was invited but did not go as he will inform you.

On June 2, 1536, the Pope actually summoned the long talked of council to meet at Mantua on May 23, 1537. When the news reached Wittenberg in December, 1536, Luther said:

If the Pope cites me I will not go. I spit on his citation because he is my adversary. But if the council summons me I will obey, and I would like to be welcome and kindly received. But the bull Cœna Domini [1] has most horribly damned me and excommunicated all my friends. Even you, dear Katie, if you were with me, would be tortured although you adored the whole papacy. The Lord keep me in his Word! I have bitter enemies and Vergerio said the Roman See had no worse enemy than me.

Various methods were suggested by which the Protestants might meet the invitation of the Pope to take part in the council. John Frederic proposed that they should call a counter-council, an act from which Luther dissuaded him, as savoring of wilful schism. To decide on a consistent course of action the Protestant princes and theologians met in a congress at Schmalkalden in February, 1537. In preparation for this Luther drew up a confession of faith, known as the Schmalkaldic Articles. In emphasizing the differences of the Protestants and Catholics the Articles formed a strong contrast with the intentionally conciliatory Augsburg Confession. The chief points of variance were stated to be the following: 1. That men are saved by faith, not by works. 2. That the mass, considered as a good work, is a horror and ought to be abolished. 3. That all foundations for the endowment of perpetual masses be abolished. 4. That the Pope is not the head of the universal Church but only Bishop of Rome. Melanchthon modified this statement by adding that if the Pope left the Protestants to rule themselves, they would not interfere with his *de facto* supremacy in other parts. Sundry other demands, of subordinate importance, were added.

[1] 1521.

Luther intended to present his articles to the congress in
person, but after he arrived a severe attack of the stone prevented him from taking part in the sittings of the princes.
Melanchthon was left at the helm, and he induced the Elector to
substitute for the articles the Augsburg Confession, supple-
mented by a statement written by himself on the extent of the
papal power. These documents were accordingly accepted by
the allies, who decided not to attend the council and sent back
the Pope's invitation unopened. This was a significant step.
Hitherto the Protestants had claimed to be a party within the
old Church, and had repeatedly requested a council to decide on
the orthodoxy of their claims. Now, however, they boldly proclaimed that their communion was distinct from that of Rome.

All other interests, however, were for the moment overshadowed by Luther's illness; the chief fears of the allies were
for his life. It often happened to him that a change of scene
and diet proved unwholesome, never more so than now. His
old malady the stone became very acute. His sufferings began
almost as soon as he arrived; after February 11 he was obliged
to keep to his room in the inn. He kept up his good spirits,
however, as is shown by his letter to a friend at home.

TO JUSTUS JONAS AT WITTENBERG

CHALCIS [1] (SCHMALKALDEN), February 14, 1537.

Grace and peace in Christ. I wrote you yesterday, dear Jonas, that
is, on St. Valentine's eve; now I write you on the saint's day, as he
keeps me here against my will. Last night Valentine [2] began to make
me convalescent from the stone; not indeed that Valentine who is the
idol of epileptics, but the true and only valiant Valentine who saves
those that trust in him. I hope that I shall at length be well by his
grace. This is the eighth day since I stick or rather hang here, sick
and tired of the place and of the inn and desirous of returning. For I
am useless here. The princes and estates act differently from what I
advised regardless of me.

Dr. Pauli and Dr. Sindringer have become the bitterest enemies of
the Pope. How they tear him to pieces with his own decrees! I will

---

[1] Pun on "*calculus*," the stone.

[2] Pun on the name of the saint as the patron of health, *valens*.

tell you of it when I see you. Dr. Held, the Emperor's ambassador, arrived yesterday and perhaps spoke before the congress to-day.

I am a beggar here, eating the bread of the Landgrave of Hesse and the Duke of Württemburg (for they have the best loaves and fishes) and drinking the wine of Nuremberg; our own Elector sends me meat and fish. You told me heavy bread caused the stone and now I learn it by experience, for that is the kind of bread we get here. I have the very best trout, but they are cooked in the same way and with the same water as the other fish. Oh, it is a merry dish! I am accustomed to ask for them uncooked from "the cooks of the earth," [1] and give them to the Nuremberg chef to be prepared. Our Elector cares for me in all things and orders everything to be supplied to me as carefully as possible, but his orders are interfered with by his toadies, moadies, noadies, and loadies. I have nothing else to write. Farewell in the Lord and pray for me.

Yours,

MARTIN LUTHER.

After the temporary respite just spoken of, the disease resumed its course. The patient suffered intense pain, as well as great discomfort in other ways. The doctors used all the remedies in their power, some of which perhaps did more harm than good, but at last despaired of his life. During these days his old amanuensis Veit Dietrich, now a Nuremberg clergyman attending the congress, was constantly with him and according to his old practice again took down his master's sayings. A few of these [2] illustrating the bravery of the sick man may be of interest: —

Saturday, February 24, when Melanchthon burst into tears on seeing Luther, the latter said: "John Löser is accustomed to say that it is no credit to drink good beer, but that the real test is drinking bad beer; I have need of the philosophy now. Have we received good at the hands of the Lord and shall we not also receive evil? As the Lord willed so it has happened; blessed be the name of the Lord. In times past I have often played a dangerous game with the Pope and with the devil, but the Lord marvellously saved and strengthened me; why

---

[1] "Cooks of the earth" is an allusion to a joke made by Luther's little son. Asked by his father who was the dirtiest (*immundus*) cook, he replied "a cook of the earth (*in mundo*)."

[2] Taken from Köstlin-Kawerau: *Martin Luther*, ii, 388, where they are quoted from Dietrich's unpublished notes.

should I not now bear with equanimity what the Lord inflicts? My death is as nothing compared with that of the Son of God; many great and holy men have died before me, whose companions I am not worthy to be, but if I wish to be with them I must also die. Therefore I pray God with good courage, for our Lord is the Lord of life and has us in his hand.

"How quickly I am changed by disease — *Quantum mutatus ab illo!* But lately I wandered through the woods in good health. O God, we are nothing! I should like to pray our Lord God — even to complain a little — that I might die in my Saxony; if that cannot be I am ready to die when and where he calls me, and I shall die the enemy of all the enemies of my Lord Jesus Christ. If I die under the ban of the Pope, the Pope will die under the ban of my Lord Christ."

The next day, after a violent attack of vomiting, he said: "Dear Father, take my soul in thy hand. . . . Let me die. If this pain lasts longer, I shall go mad and fail to recognize thy goodness. If it were not for my faith in Christ I would kill myself. The devil hates me and has his claws in me, but do thou, God, avenge me on mine adversary; let me die and pay thou the devil as he deserves."

Long afterwards he said : —

Oh, how I wanted my wife and children at Schmalkalden! I thought I would never see them more. How sorrowful that separation made me! I believe that the natural love of husband for wife and parents for children is greatest in dying people. But now that I am well again by God's grace, I love my wife and children all the more. No one is so spiritual as not to feel natural inclination and love, for the union of man and wife is a great thing.

Luther was anxious to leave Schmalkalden so as not to die in the vicinity of "that monster" the Pope's legate, and also to spend his last hours in Saxony. Melanchthon would have held him back on account of the new moon, but Luther was free from this form of superstition and insisted on setting out. He did so, in company with Bugenhagen, Sturtz, Myconius, and Schlaginhaufen, on February 26. The jolting of the carriage on the rough road was such torture to him that he cried out: "Would that some Turk would fall upon me and kill me!" At Tambach, only two miles away, he was forced to halt. The same night he was unexpectedly, as he believed miraculously, relieved. He lost no time in dictating the following letters: —

TO PHILIP MELANCHTHON AT SCHMALKALDEN

TAMBACH, February 27, 1537.

Dearest Philip: Blessed be God the Father of our Lord Jesus Christ, the Father of mercies and of all consolation, who this night at two o'clock took pity on me and relieved my sufferings. . . . At last I was able to pass water. . . .

I am writing at once. Please tell the news to my dear and gracious lords and all others, for I know how gladly they helped me. Let it go with me as God wills; I am ready to live or die, now that I have escaped from the pit into our own Saxony, and have here obtained grace. I have written this in haste. Schlaginhaufen will tell you the rest. He cannot be kept back but will fly to you. Thank God for what has happened and continue to pray that he may perfect his work. This is an example of how we should pray and trust in help from heaven. May God preserve you all and beat down Satan and all his monstrous Roman allies under your feet. Amen. Written at two thirty in the night from Tambach, the place of my blessing, which is my Phanuel in which God appeared to me.

Yours,
MARTIN LUTHER.

The next morning as Schlaginhaufen galloped into Schmalkalden with this letter, he saw the Pope's legate looking out of the window and shouted to him: "Luther lives." In the mean time word had been dispatched

TO CATHARINE LUTHER AT WITTENBERG

TAMBACH, February 27, 1537.

Grace and peace in Christ. Dear Katie, if you need horses on the farm you must hire them a while longer, for the Elector is going to keep your horses and send them home with Melanchthon.

Yesterday I left Schmalkalden in the Elector's private carriage. The reason I left was that for three days I have been very unwell, unable to pass water the whole time. I could not rest nor sleep at night nor keep anything on my stomach. In short I was dead and commended you and the children to God and to my gracious Elector, thinking that I would never see you more. My heart was moved for you, for I thought I was surely in the grave. But men have prayed hard to God and perhaps some have wept before him, so that he has healed me this night. Wherefore thank God and ask the children and Aunt Lena to do the same, for you almost lost me. The good Elector did everything in his power for me but in vain. Moreover your medicine [1] did not help me. But God wrought a miracle on me this night, and will continue to do so at the prayers of pious people.

I am writing to you because I heard that the Elector ordered his bailiff to send you to me so that if I should die on the road you might speak with me again. There is no need of this now, as God has helped me so much that I expect to come soon and happily. To-day we are going to Gotha. I have written you four letters since I left home and am surprised that nothing has come from you.

MARTIN LUTHER.

The crisis was past, but a period of lassitude and weakness followed. This was so great that when Luther reached Gotha he believed he was going to die after all. The following day he accordingly dictated a farewell document usually known as his first will, though it is not at all what we understand by a testamentary disposition of property, but rather a few valedictory precepts and messages : —

LUTHER'S (FIRST) WILL

(GOTHA, February 28, 1537.)

God be praised. I know I did right to attack the papacy, which injures the cause of God, Christ, and the gospel.

Ask my dear Melanchthon, Jonas, and Cruciger to forgive me what wrong I have done them.

Console my Katie that she may bear this, and let her consider that she has been happy with me twelve years. She has served me not only as a wife but as a servant. May God reward her ! Care for her and the children as you can.

Greet the deacons of my church for me. The pious citizens of Wittenberg have often served me.

Say to my Prince the Elector and my Lord the Landgrave not to be disturbed by the charges of our enemies who allege that they will steal the church property, for they will not seize it as some others have done. I see that they rather use the church property to support religious undertakings. If there is any surplus, why should it not go to them ? It certainly belongs to the princes rather than to papal

---

[1] A mixture of garlic and horses' dung.

wretches. Bid them act boldly in the Evangelic cause, and do what the Holy Spirit may suggest; I do not prescribe the way. May God the merciful strengthen them to remain in the sound doctrine, and let them give thanks that they are freed from Antichrist. I have earnestly commended them to God in prayer, and hope that he will preserve them and that they may not relapse into papal impiety. Even if they are not pure in all things but sinners in some, let them nevertheless confide in God, notwithstanding the calumnies and accusations of our adversaries. For their sins are as nothing compared to the impiety, blasphemy, hatred, and murders of our antichristian enemies. From these sins God has freed our princes. Therefore let them be strong and proceed in the Lord's name.

Now I am prepared to die if the Lord will. But I should like to live until Pentecost, that I may more solemnly and publicly accuse the Roman Beast and his reign. I will do this if I live; I shall not need spurs. Others will come after me who will deal more rudely with that beast, although I, too, if I live, will deal more roughly in future.

Now I commend my soul into the hands of my Lord Jesus Christ, whom I have preached and confessed on earth.

The weakness was not fatal after all, and in five or six days Luther was able to move on by slow stages. Jonas met him on the road with one of Luther's nieces as nurse, and Katie came as far as Altenburg to see her husband. Here she was entertained by George Spalatin. Luther was soon able to move on again and reached home on March 14; a week later he was able to write this note: —

TO GEORGE SPALATIN AT ALTENBURG

(WITTENBERG,) March 21, 1537.

Grace and peace in Christ. I am able to write again, dear Spalatin, after my long vacation from literary labors. By God's grace I am convalescing slowly, and am learning to eat and drink again, although my knees and bones sink in and are not able to bear my body steadily. More of my strength is exhausted than I would have believed possible, but I will rest and take care of myself until God makes me strong again. My Katie greets you and says that she regrets that she brought your daughters no present, but that she is going to have some books bound and send them as a souvenir of her visit. In the mean time she asks to be kindly remembered to you. She often speaks at length of your urbane benevolence and benevolent urbanity. Farewell in Christ and pray for me.

Yours,

MARTIN LUTHER.

In anticipation of the calling of a council, Luther published, in March, 1539, an important book On Councils and the Church, at which he had worked during the winter of 1536-37 until interrupted by the events just recorded. The first two sections, which the author himself termed " weak and verbose," set forth the history of the early councils of the Church for the purpose of demolishing their authority, and especially of proving that such bodies have no claim to inerrancy or obedience at present. The third section is on the Church, of which the writer exclaims : "Praise God, every child of seven years old knows what it is." Nowadays we speak of many churches, to Luther there was only one, " the true," set over against " the false church " of the papacy. The true Church he defines as the holy community of Christians, and one may recognize it by a number of outward signs, of which the following are the most important : The Church exists wherever : (1) God's Word is preached, (2) baptism is administered, (3) the Lord's Supper is eaten, (4) the power of the keys (forgiveness and punishment) is exercised, (5) there is a regular priesthood, (6) public prayer, praise, and thanks are offered up, (7) there is the cross and persecution. In closing, the Reformer gives a short exposition of his ideas of the divine economy, according to which the family, the State, and the Church are the three providential ordinances for the governance and well-being of mankind.

It being now clear that the Protestants would not submit to a council, to which they had earlier appealed, the Emperor continued to treat with them about other means of settling the religious question. For this purpose a conference was arranged at Frankfort in the spring of 1539, the Lutheran Church being represented by Melanchthon. The Emperor agreed to suspend all proceedings against the Protestants for fifteen months, and the settlement of the religious question was relegated to a German national synod, called to meet at Spires in June, 1540.

No mention of a general council was made. That called for 1537 had been postponed, and did not in fact meet until 1545. The treaty of Frankfort, signed April 19, 1539, marks the most important advance made by the Lutherans since the peace of Nuremberg, seven years before.

CHAPTER XXIX

CHARACTER AND HABITS

THERE is no good portrait of Luther after his forty-third year, but from the numerous inferior pictures painted by Lucas Cranach's sons and apprentices and from a number of descriptions it is possible to get a fairly good idea of his personal appearance. The accounts are somewhat contradictory in details, as, for example, his eyes are variously reported to have been black, brown, and dark with yellow rings around the pupils. Almost all, however, were impressed by the restless fire that flashed from them, and by the lion-like mien of the man. In later life his form became portly, but in spite of illness he retained a look of uncommon youth and vigor. His hair turned gray but did not become sparse. In his last years traces of suffering and irritability appeared, though when he was forty-two even an enemy found his expression pleasant and serene.[1]

In dress Luther's tastes were of the simplest. His ordinary habit was the layman's jerkin and hose, which were sometimes poor and patched. He occasionally mended his clothes himself; in the first half of 1539 Lauterbach heard Katie complain that her husband had cut a piece out of his son's trousers to supply his own. He defended himself thus : —

The hole was so large that I had to have a large patch for it. Trousers seldom fit me well, so I have to make them last long. If the Electors Frederic and John had not better tailors than I have they would mend their own breeches. The Italian tailors are the best. They divide the labor, some making coats, some cloaks, and some trousers. But in Germany they do it hit or miss, making all trousers according to one pattern. We praise the good old times but we live in the present. Think what an eye-sore it is to see a man with trousers like a pigeon and a coat so short that one can see his back between it and

[1] Cf. *supra*, visit of Vergerio, Chapter XXVIII.

the trousers. There is a proverb that "short-coated Saxons jump like magpies."

On festive occasions and when preaching, Luther wore a gown and on gala days a gold chain around his neck, an attempt at adornment which a polished and hostile Italian gentleman who saw him in 1535 found rather ridiculous.[1] At all times a silver ring graced one finger. Luther's standards of cleanliness were relatively high. He had a bath-room with tubs in his house; after using it one day he remarked, at dinner : —

Why is the water so dirty after bathing? Ah! I forgot that the body is dirt, as the Bible says, "Thou art dust and ashes." Why art thou proud, O man?

The day began early, the time of rising varying according to the season. The morning was devoted to lecturing and preaching, though Luther frequently felt headache and dizziness which prevented him from doing much work. The principal meal of the day came at ten o'clock, after which the long afternoon was spent in writing and other business. After supper at five o'clock the evening was spent in conversation, reading, or work until nine, the regular bedtime. Of his evening devotions he once said : —

I have to hurry all day to get time to pray. It must suffice me if I can say the Ten Commandments, the Lord's Prayer, and one or two petitions besides, thinking of which I fall asleep.

Luther's enemies called him a glutton and a wine-bibber. But in the monastery he had fasted until he became emaciated, and in later life his ill health often made it difficult for him to eat. In general he tried to eat, thinking it good for his health and spirits, as when he said : —

This morning the devil had a dispute with me about Zwingli and I found a full head better able to withstand the fiend than one weakened with fasting.

And again :—

We ought to do our part and take care of our bodies ; when we are tempted, abstinence is a hundred times worse than eating and drink-

[1] Vergerio. Cf. *supra*, Chapter XXVIII.

ing. Had I followed my appetite I should have taken nothing for three days, but I do eat though without pleasure. The world sees it and calls it drunkenness, but God will judge it rightly. . . . Sleep is also a good thing; when I lie awake the devil comes at once to dispute with me until I say: " Devil, go hang,[1] God is not angry with me as you say."

Of good drink Luther was undoubtedly fond, but his practice in this respect must be judged by the standard of his age. No one advocated total abstinence, and the greatest licence was allowed not only to moderate indulgence but to intemperance. Charles V is reported to have taken habitually three quarts of wine at dinner — some authorities say more — and he was never charged with excess in this respect, as was the Elector John Frederic. Luther had special reasons for his potations. It is now believed that alcohol is little better than poison to one suffering as he did from diseases of the nerves or of the kidneys, but four centuries ago drink was actually prescribed for these ailments, and moreover he took a " strong little potation " at bedtime to make himself sleep. Other motives are more questionable, as, for example, when he tells Weller that he often drinks freely to " spite the devil." [2]

Nevertheless, Luther certainly stopped short of intemperance. No one who did the enormous amount of work that he did could have been an habitual drunkard. In a sermon to the courtiers he tells them that, though constant intemperance is not to be borne, an occasional carouse may be overlooked. Did he allow himself these occasional carouses? The argument from silence is in this case decisive in the negative; knowing almost every act of his private life for fifteen years, we never once hear of such an outburst. At times, however, his conviviality bordered on the extreme, and that he was always appreciative of the merits of good liquor may be gathered from the fact that when he is away from home he almost always writes of the cheer he is having. For example, while visiting the Princes of Anhalt, he sent the following epistle : —

[1] Luther's stronger expression will not bear literal translation.
[2] Letter to Jerome Weller, July, 1530.

TO CATHARINE LUTHER AT WITTENBERG

(DESSAU,) July 29, 1534.

Grace and peace in Christ. Dear Master Katie, I have nothing to write, as Melanchthon and others are going to Wittenberg and will tell you all the news. I must stay here for the sake of good Prince Joachim. Imagine if you can why I should stay so long or why you ever let me go. I think Francis Burkhardt [1] would be willing to see me depart, as I would him. Yesterday I shipped some bad beer for which I had to sing out.[2] There is nothing fit to drink here, for which I am sorry as I like it, and think what good wine and beer I have at home, and also a fair lady (or should I say lord?) It would be a good thing for you to send me the whole wine-cellar and a bottle of your own beer as often as you can. If you don't I shall not come back for the new beer. God bless you and the children and household. Amen.

Your lover,

MARTIN LUTHER.

The most damaging evidence, however, has been found in an autograph of the Vatican Archives, first published in 1880. The content of the epistle is somewhat unguarded, and the signature, which is very hard to decipher, was read " Dr. plenus "[3] and interpreted " Dr. Full," a welcome proof to the Catholic publisher of the author's intoxication at the time he wrote. I believe, however, that this is not the true reading, and accordingly give another, with a translation of the most important part of the jocose missive: —

TO CASPAR MÜLLER, CHANCELLOR OF MANSFELD, AT EISLEBEN

(WITTENBERG,) March 1, 1536.

. . . Pray tell his Grace of Mansfeld from me to be merry, as in the story of the two students and the cook. People begin to say, or murmur, that a great deal depends on cheerfulness, and I half believe them. I have n't written to his Grace myself for fear that the Buck

---

[1] The Saxon agent, later vice-chancellor.

[2] The English slang expression, " to sing out," is given in Grimm's *Deutsches Wörterbuch*, x, 1, 1069, as a translation for the German colloquialism here used.

[3] So also in *Enders*, x, 137. Other readings are " Dr. Hans," " Dr. plures," and " Dr. parvus." After a careful comparison with photographs of the original, I have adopted the reading of Prof. H. Böhmer (*Luther im Lichte der neueren Forschung*, 2d ed. 1910, p. 116).

of Lübeck [1] would make a fool of me. Yet as I now and then cast an inquisitive eye on his Grace, please tell him my opinion. What harm does a little jollity do? The beer is good, the maid fair, the boys young. The students are so merry that I am sorry that my health prevents me being oftener with them. Understand me like the poor, simple sheep you are said to be. I would willingly be good but I fear that I can never be as simple as you are. God bless you and greet all good friends. Amen.

Dr. Martin.

Dr. Luther.

Dr. Johannes.

P. S. — My Lord Katie sends her greetings and so does your godson Hans.

The three signatures are for the three persons who send greetings to Müller, Dr. Martin, "my Lord Katie" as Dr. Luther, and nine-year old Hans (Dr. Johannes).

Occasionally good stories [2] are told as to the quantity Luther drank, but that he became intoxicated is never recorded. Of the charges brought by his enemies, he once said: "If God can forgive me for having crucified him with masses twenty years long, he can also bear with me for occasionally taking a good drink to honor him. God allows it, the world may take it as it pleases."

Luther has been charged by his enemies, from his own day to the present, with being a profligate as well as a drunkard — the two usually going together. This accusation may be summarily denied. In the age of Henry VIII, Francis I, and Philip of Hesse, the example of the monk of Wittenberg was a striking contrast to the prevalent immorality. So light indeed was the condemnation visited upon sexual offences in that licentious age that one of the Reformer's guests once asked him if simple fornication was a sin at all. He replied by quoting 1 Corinthians, vi, 9. At another time he wrote a most uncompromising opinion of houses of ill-fame; the conversion of Freiberg had been accompanied by the abolition of these dens, but it was later proposed to reinstate them on the customary plea that regulated vice was the lesser of two evils. When Weller, now the pastor

---

[1] Was the Buck of Lübeck, a person, a spirit, or a tavern?

[2] As at the banquet given to Agricola. Cf. Chapter xxv, p. 284.

of that town, wrote to his chief to ascertain the stand he should take in the matter, he received the following injunctions : —

TO JEROME WELLER AT FREIBERG

(WITTENBERG,) September 8, 1540.

Grace and peace. Dear Jerome, have nothing to do with those who wish to reintroduce houses of ill-fame. It would have been better never to have expelled the devil than to have done so only to bring him back again stronger than ever. Let those who favor this course deny the name of Christ and become as heathen ignorant of God. We who are Christians cannot do so. We have the plain text: " Whoremongers and adulterers God will judge," much more, therefore, will he judge those who protect and encourage vice. How can the priests preach against impurity if the magistrates encourage it ? They allege the precedent of Nuremberg, but forget that she is the only town that has thus sinned. If the young men cannot contain, let them marry — indeed, what is the use of marriage if we permit vice unpunished ? We have learned by experience that regulated vice does not prevent adultery and worse sins, but rather encourages them and condones them. . . . Let the magistrate punish one as well as the other, and if there is then secret vice, at least he is not to blame for it. We can neither do nor permit nor tolerate anything against God's command. We must do right if the world comes to an end. Farewell in haste.

DR. MARTIN LUTHER.

If Luther's life was pure, his words certainly were not so at all times. It strikes the modern reader with no less than astonishment, almost with horror, to find the great moralist's private talk with his guests and children, his lectures to the students, even his sermons, thickly interlarded with words, expressions, and stories, such as to-day are confined to the frequenters of the lowest bar-rooms. The only justification for this is to be found in the universal practice of the day. Not only was the popular literature of the time unspeakably filthy, but the conversation of the best society had a liberty exceeding that of the men and women of Shakespeare's plays. Shocking stories are told of the conversation of England's virgin queen, and Margaret of Navarre, one of the most devout and refined women of the sixteenth century, wrote a series of stories that no decent woman can now read with pleasure. In that day it was thought strange that any one should be forbidden to speak of things of which every one knows.

With all possible excuses allowed in extenuation of the Wittenberg professor's talk, it is to be regretted that he did not rise above the level of his age. If his student Mathesius found nothing shameful in his words his friend Melanchthon did. No amount of precedent can excuse the disgusting things he sometimes said about his private relations with Katie.[1] At times it seemed as if he allowed himself liberty in this regard as in drinking, "to spite the devil"—a strange expression which he undoubtedly meant literally. At other times his good humor ran away with him. In one letter he seems to condone loose talk under certain circumstances:—

TO PRINCE JOACHIM OF ANHALT

WITTENBERG, May 23, 1534.

Grace and peace in Christ. Serene Prince, gracious Lord! Hausmann has told me that your Grace has been a little unwell, but are now, thank God, again in good condition.

It often occurs to me that, as your Grace leads a quiet life, melancholy and sad thoughts may be the cause of such indisposition; wherefore I advise your Grace, as a young man, to be merry, to ride, hunt, and keep good company, who can cheer your Grace in a godly and honorable way. For loneliness and sadness are simple poison and death, especially to a young man. God has often commanded us to be joyful before him, and will suffer no sad offering, as Moses often wrote, and as it is often written in Ecclesiastes: "Rejoice, young man, in thy youth, and let thy heart be of good cheer." No one knows how it hurts a young man to avoid happiness and cultivate solitude and melancholy. Your Grace has Hausmann and several others with whom to be merry. Joy and good humor, in honor and seemliness, is the best medicine for a young man, yea for all men. I, who have hitherto spent my life in mourning and sadness, now seek and accept joy wherever I can find it. We now know, thank God, that we can be happy with a good conscience, and can use God's gifts with thankfulness, inasmuch as he has made them for us and is pleased to have us enjoy them.

---

[1] These are quite unquotable, but are sufficiently numerous to be easily found in the originals, e. g., Bindseil: *Lutheri Colloquia*, ii, 299.

If I have not hit the cause of your Grace's indisposition and have thereby done you a wrong, your Grace will kindly forgive my mistake. For truly I thought your Grace might be so foolish as to think it a sin to be happy, as I have often done and still do at times. It is true that joy in sin is the devil, but joy with good, pious people, in the fear of God, and with moderation pleases him, even if an indecent [1] word or two now and then slips in. Your Grace should be happy in all things, inwardly in Christ and outwardly in God's gifts; for he gives them to us that we may have pleasure in them and thank him for them. Sorrow and melancholy bring on old age and other evils before their time. Christ cares for us and will not leave us. I commend your Grace to him eternally. Amen.

DR. MARTIN LUTHER.

This letter is characteristic of Luther's naturally joyous temper. He was, as Mathesius called him, " a joyous, frolicsome companion." His good humor bursts forth on all occasions when not crushed out by ill health or overwork. Another letter bubbling over with it is to the same good friend : —

TO PRINCE JOACHIM OF ANHALT AT DESSAU

(WITTENBERG,) June 12, 1534.

Grace and peace in Christ. Gracious Prince and Lord ! John Beichling has brought me very good news, namely, that your Grace is very merry. For truly I prayed without ceasing (as did my gracious lord,[2] the cathedral provost), " O God, make my prince sound and happy," and I expected he would. And as soon as I have fed the printer a little bit [3] so that I can have rest, I will come to you with Pomeranian

---

[1] *Wort oder Zötlein zu viel.* Luther's defenders try hard to prove that " *Zote* " here means nothing more than " idle talk " or " anecdote," and they are supported by the excellent German dictionary of Daniel Sanders (Grimm's monumental lexicon being complete only to the letter S), iii, 1779. Sanders assigns the meaning of " indecency " to every other use of this word, modern and by Luther and his contemporaries, *except* this place. This is of course arguing in a circle from a preconceived notion. The innocent meaning here given, besides being otherwise unsupported, would have no sense, for why should Luther especially excuse what is entirely innocent, or how can a " simple anecdote " be " too much " ?

[2] Joachim's brother, Prince George of Anhalt.

[3] With the German Bible now coming out as a whole for the first time. The intended visit took place in July. Cf. the letter to Katie of July 29, 1534, translated just above, p. 319.

Bugenhagen and his little pomeranians and marmots, so that my gracious lady your wife may see how like the old dog the puppies are and how merry. God bless you. Amen. Your Grace must really look out for that marvellous chess-player, Francis Burkhardt,[1] for he is quite sure that he can play the game like a professional. I would give a button to see him play as well as he thinks he can. He can manage the knights, take a castle or two, and fool the peasant-pawns, but the queen beats him on account of his weakness for the fair sex, which he cannot deny.

Your Grace's obedient servant,

MARTIN LUTHER.

Luther's constant advice to his friends to cultivate the virtue of cheerfulness was made the more emphatic by the fact that he himself was often subject to melancholy and depression. His letters and table-talk are full of counsel to young friends on the subject, the best perhaps being in an epistle written to Jerome Weller at Wittenberg while the Reformer was at Feste Coburg in the summer of 1530. He says : —

Whenever this temptation comes to you beware not to dispute with the devil nor allow yourself to dwell on these lethal thoughts, for so doing is nothing less than giving place to the devil and so falling. Try as hard as you can to despise these thoughts sent by Satan. In this sort of temptation and battle contempt is the easiest road to victory ; laugh your enemy to scorn and ask to whom you are talking. By all means flee solitude, for he lies in wait most for those alone. This devil is conquered by despising and mocking him, not by resisting and arguing. Therefore, Jerome, joke and play games with my wife and others, in which way you will drive out your diabolic thoughts and take courage. . . .

Be strong and cheerful and cast out those monstrous thoughts. Whenever the devil harasses you thus, seek the company of men or drink more, or joke and talk nonsense, or do some other merry thing. Sometimes we must drink more, sport, recreate ourselves, aye, and even sin a little to spite the devil, so that we leave him no place for troubling our consciences with trifles. We are conquered if we try too conscientiously not to sin at all. So when the devil says to you : " Do not drink," answer him : " I will drink, and right freely, just because

---

[1] Later vice-chancellor of Electoral Saxony. Luther played a good game of chess, himself.

you tell me not to." One must always do what Satan forbids. What other cause do you think that I have for drinking so much strong drink, talking so freely and making merry so often, except that I wish to mock and harass the devil who is wont to mock and harass me. Would that I could contrive some great sin to spite the devil, that he might understand that I would not even then acknowledge it and that I was conscious of no sin whatever. We, whom the devil thus seeks to annoy, should remove the whole decalogue from our hearts and minds.

No picture of Luther would be complete without making his humor conspicuous.[1] He was as fond of a joke or a good story as was Abraham Lincoln; his letters and table-talk are as full of puns as are Shakespeare's plays. Like all puns they can only be appreciated in the original. But of his stories, many of them indeed old in his time, some specimens must be given, in order, as the old English translation of the table talk-puts it, "to re-fresh and recreate the company":—

Whatever one does in the world is wrong. It is with me as in the fable of the old man, his son, and the ass;[2] whatever I do is wrong. One physician advises me to bathe my feet at bedtime, another before dinner, a third in the morning, and a fourth at noon; whatever I do displeases some. So it is in other things; if I speak I am turbu-lent, if I keep silence I spit on the cross. Then Master Wiseacre comes along and hits the poor beast on the rump.

Rustics are not equal to public affairs and spectacles, as is proved by the passion play. When a cobbler began to say his lines he could only stammer out, "I am .. I am ..." at which the manager re-torted, "What are you then?" He replied, "I am a cobbler," and the manager rejoined, "What are you doing here, then? Go home and mend shoes."[3]

I am the father of a great people, like Abraham, for I am respon-sible for all the children of the monks and nuns who have renounced their monastic vows.

[1] Cf. E. Rolffs: *Luther's Humor ein Stück seiner Religion.* In *Preussische Jahr-bücher*, 1904, clv, 468–488.

[2] Luther may have read this fable in Æsop. It is also found in Poggio: *Sales et Facetiae*, 1470, and from him in La Fontaine, who entitles it, "*Le meunier, son fils et l'âne.*"

[3] The two chief cycles of miracle plays at this time given in Germany were the nativity cycle and the resurrection cycle. They were evidently sometimes given in the style of Pyramus and Thisbe, played by Bottom the Weaver and company.

Women wear veils because of the angels; I wear trousers because of the girls.

Peasants are proudest of wealth and yet uncouth, as can be seen by the story of one who could not keep a fly from lighting on his spoon and so finally ate it with his food. Another rustic in Mansfeld had trouble in keeping a robin from perching on his bowl and so at last ate *it* alive, and when he heard it still chirping in his stomach, said, "So you keep on peeping, do you?" and poured down a schooner of beer to drown it.

A man was burned at Prague for teaching his dog to jump through a ring when he said, "Luther." O Lord, how wondrous are thy ways!

When I am dead I shall be a ghost to plague bishops and priests and godless monks, so that they will have more trouble with one dead Luther than with a thousand living.

A liar must be careful. I sinned against this rule when I was a student and said that permission had not been granted to take baths on Sunday. An excellent story illustrating the same point is told about a man who said he had seen some bees as big as sheep. When asked how they could get through the little holes into their hives, he replied, "Oh, I let them think of that for themselves."

Cannon are the very invention of Satan himself, for here one cannot fight with sword or fist and all bravery perishes. Death comes before one sees it. If Adam had seen such instruments as his children were to make he would have died of sorrow.

Some of the stories will surprise those who conceive of a reformer as a grave and proper curate; such is the comparison of three preachers with the persons of the Trinity : —

Bugenhagen is Minos, Rörer Aeacus, and Crödel Rhadamanthus. They are one substance in three persons, Bugenhagen the Father, Rörer the Son, and Crödel the Holy Ghost. They simply won't let me alone, I have to do the *Kyrie Eleison* for Crödel because he gave me three or four kegs of beer; Rörer orders me about the gospels and collects; and if Bugenhagen hears of some things I do, I shall have to leave.

Another joke on Bugenhagen, who, notwithstanding his dignified position in both the upper and lower worlds, seems to have been unable to deliver a palatable sermon, was made about the same time as the last : —

When a woman put badly cooked food before her husband, he said, "Oh, I expected that Bugenhagen would preach to-day."

Some of Luther's remarks have a humor to us not intended by him. Such is his naïve opinion of the French mode of address : —

The question was mooted whether it were a sin to curse a Frenchman, for they themselves have the custom of greeting their best friends with a curse, as, "Pest and pox take you, my dear sir." Is it then a sin when the mind is free from hatred? Luther said : "Our words should be Yea and Nay, and the name of the Lord is not to be taken in vain, but it may well be that their curses are more innocent than many a good-morning with us."

Luther's constant good spirits and joyousness are remarkable when it is considered that he was a prey to several torturing diseases. Indigestion with painful complications had set in at the Wartburg, and occasionally returned. In 1523 he first experienced that nervous disease which throughout his life made him suffer from dizziness, ringing in the ears, and sleeplessness. Stone, at that time a very common disease of kidneys and bladder, began in 1526 and became continually worse until the almost fatal attack in 1537. Gout, rheumatism, sciatica, ulcers, abscesses in the ears, toothache, and palpitation of the heart gradually added their pains to make his life a constant agony. He obtained little relief from physicians. He believed alcohol, a certain irritant, to be good for the stone and for insomnia. Other medicines prescribed undoubtedly made him rather worse than better; such were the disgusting remedies he took at Schmalkalden.[1] His troubles become increasingly prominent in his letters and table-talk. He always used what means were available for recovery, though, indeed, the medical science of that day was barbarous. Once he said : —

Our burgomaster asked me whether it was against God's will to use medicine, for Carlstadt publicly preached that the sick should not use drugs, but should only pray to God that his will be done. In reply I asked the burgomaster if he ate when he was hungry, and when he answered in the affirmative, I said, "You may then use medicine

[1] Cf. letter to Katie, February 27, 1537, p. 312, note.

which is God's creature as much as food, drink, and other bodily necessities."

It is no wonder that irritability and world-weariness grew upon the afflicted man. To his friend Müller, Luther writes, for example, in a very melancholy way : —

TO CASPAR MÜLLER AT MANSFELD

(WITTENBERG,) January 19, 1536.

Grace and peace. My dear Chancellor, I have long been desirous of writing you but have been laid up with a cold and cough. But my chief illness is that the sun has shone on me too long, a disease, you know, common and fatal to many. It makes some blind, others gray, sallow and wrinkled. Perhaps the trouble with your toe is that you stubbed it on a piece of mud hardened by the sun, albeit it is not the fault of the dear sun that it hardens mud and softens wax, for everything must act according to its nature and find its own place at last.

Of all things I should have liked to take Kegel as a boarder, but as our student eating-club is just back from Jena [1] the table is full and I cannot turn away old friends. But when a place is vacant, as may happen at Easter, I will take him if my Lord Katie is gracious to me.

Of the English embassy,[2] as you at Mansfeld are so curious, I know nothing especial. Queen Catharine has just died, and they say her daughter is mortally ill. She lost her cause with all the world except with us poor beggars the Wittenberg theologians. We would have kept her in her royal honor as was right. But this is the end and final decision. The Pope acted in this matter like the Pope, promulgating contradictory bulls and playing such a double game that it served him right to be turned out of England, even if the Evangelic teaching did not profit thereby. He cheated the king so that I could almost excuse his Majesty, though I do not approve all his acts. Friend, let us pray that the Pope get a stroke of epilepsy. The Pope's nuncio was here, as you know, but I have not time to relate the answer he took back to Schmalkalden. My cough prevents me hunting for it; if I stop coughing I will look for it. I think my cough would leave off if you would pray for me. . . .

My Lord Katie greets you and asks, although I am already too much

[1] The university, and with it Luther's student boarders, had removed to Jena during the visitation of the plague.

[2] On this and on the visit of the Pope's nuncio, Vergerio, cf. chapters XVII and XXVIII.

in the sun, that you won't outshine yourself without shining on me. Your godson, master Martin,[1] greets you; he is getting big but not bad, God keep him! God bless you. Don't mind my ways, for you know that I am so hard and cross, gross, gray, and green, so overladen, overcrowded and overstocked with business that once in a while, for the sake of my poor carcass, I have to break out to a friend. A man is no more than a man save that God can make what he will of one if we only let him. Greet all good gentlemen and friends.

DR. MARTIN LUTHER.

Much the same tone prevails in a letter written two years later to Justus Jonas. This true friend had been a student at Erfurt when Luther passed through on his way to Worms. He left all to follow his hero, first to the memorable diet and then back to Wittenberg, where his abilities soon won him a position in the university and that of canon and provost of the Castle Church. Till 1541, when he left to preach the gospel at Halle, he was often a guest at Luther's table. His wife Catharine was a great friend of Frau Luther.[2] Jonas was a fine stylist and a polished preacher. While he was absent on a visit Luther wrote him this letter, in which sadness is mingled with that love of nature so often expressed elsewhere: —

TO JUSTUS JONAS AT BRUNSWICK

(WITTENBERG,) April 8, 1538.

Grace and peace in Christ. Dear Jonas, I do not wish to contend with you in writing letters, and not without reason, first, because you surpass me in genius and eloquence even by your hereditary gifts, and then because you have much more material to write about, living, as you do, among heroes and great deeds. I beg leave to think that the armies of Trojans and Greeks would have grown cold before Troy had not Homer blown so small a matter big with his immense gift of language.

We confess Christ in quietness and confidence, but sometimes without much strength. We are oppressed by business, especially Melanchthon and I, on account of your absence, and I am sick of it, for I am an old veteran who has served his time and would prefer to spend my

---

[1] Luther's four-year-old son. Cf. chapter XXXII.

[2] Cf. letter to her, March 26, 1542, and to Jonas, December 25, 1542, and May 4, 1543.

days in the garden enjoying the senile pleasures of watching God's wonders in the blooming of the trees, flowers, and grass, and in the mating of the birds. I should have merited this pleasure and leisure had I not deserved to be deprived of it on account of my past sins. . . .

Yours,

MARTIN LUTHER.

CHAPTER XXX

AT WORK

AFTER the return from Feste Coburg, Luther continued to occupy the Wittenberg pulpit. His pastoral duties were especially heavy during the frequent absence of Bugenhagen, the parish priest. On December 1, 1530, he wrote Link: —

I have not time to write to all, as I am not only Luther but Bugenhagen and notary-public and Moses and Jethro and what not? all in all, Jack of all trades and master of none.

As time went on his style became freer. He preached *ex tempore*, no longer writing out his sermons, many of which were taken down by Rörer. He often alluded in his sermons to questions of the day. One thing he especially cultivated was simplicity, for, as he said: —

A preacher should bare his breast and give the simple folk milk, for every day a new need of first principles arises. He should be diligent with the catechism and serve out only milk leaving the strong wine of high thoughts for private discussion with the wise. In my sermons I do not think of Bugenhagen, Jonas, and Melanchthon, for they know as much as I do, so I preach not to them but to my little Hans and Lena and Elsa.[1] It would be a foolish gardener who would attend to one flower to the neglect of the great majority.

Luther's professorial work was also continued till his death. An estimate of his contributions to Biblical exegesis has been given in previous chapters. Some conception of his methods in the classroom may be formed from this saying: —

Some masters rate the proud youngsters to make them feel what they are, but I always praise the arguments of the boys, no matter how crude they are, for Melanchthon's strict manner of overturning the poor fellows so quickly displeases me. Every one must rise by degrees, for no one can attain to excellence suddenly.

[1] Luther's niece, Elsa Kaufmann.

Luther also exercised a certain supervision over the morals of his pupils, warning them against impurity, and endeavoring to see justice done when they got into scrapes. An amusing letter, written during a summer when a light epidemic of the plague swept over Wittenberg, may be translated as showing how like were the students of the sixteenth to those of the twentieth century : —

TO JOHN FREDERIC, ELECTOR OF SAXONY

WITTENBERG, July 9, 1535.

Grace and peace in Christ and my poor paternoster. Most serene, highborn Prince, most gracious Lord! Your Grace's chancellor, Dr. Brück, has communicated to me the kind invitation to visit you while the plague is here. I humbly thank your Grace for your care, and will show myself ready to comply if there is real need. But your bailiff, John von Metsch, is a reliable weather-cock; he has the nose of a vulture for the plague, and would smell it five yards under ground. As long as he stays I cannot believe that there is any plague here. A house or two may be infected, but the air is not tainted. There has been neither death nor new case since Tuesday, but as the dog-days are near the boys are frightened, so I have given them a vacation to quiet them until we see what is going to happen. I observe that the said youths rather like the outcry about the plague; some of them get ulcers from their school-satchels, others colic from the books, others scurvy from the pens, and others gout from the paper. The ink of the rest has dried up, or else they have devoured long letters from their mothers and so got homesickness and nostalgia; indeed there are more ailments of this kind than I can well recount. If parents and guardians don't speedily cure these maladies it is to be feared that an epidemic of them will wipe out all our future preachers and teachers, so that nothing will be left but swine and dogs, which perchance would please the papists. May Christ our Lord give your Highness his grace and mercy (and to all Christian rulers) to guard against such a plague as this, to the praise and honor of God and to the vexation of Satan, that enemy of all decency and learning. Amen. God bless you. Amen.

Your Grace's obedient

MARTIN LUTHER.

The most abiding portion of the Reformer's work is of course contained in his writings. These are voluminous; an incomplete

edition fills more than one hundred volumes. During his lifetime he was often urged to publish a complete edition of them,
but he disliked the idea, writing Capito that he felt a Saturn-
ian hunger to devour his offspring rather than a wish to give
them a new lease of life. To the citizens of Wittenberg and
Augsburg who made the same request he replied that he would
prefer that all his writings perish, so that only the Bible might
be read. He was finally induced, however, to supervise such an
edition undertaken by Rörer and Cruciger, of which, however,
only two volumes appeared before his death.

A number of Luther's letters were also published during his
lifetime, but not in large collections, as were those of Erasmus.
Those that saw the light were rather single epistles like pamphlets or newspaper articles of the present day. Nevertheless,
Luther's secretaries preserved a large number of letters, and
in 1540 some one told him they would be published. He replied : —

Don't believe it! No one will do it, though, to be sure, nothing has
given me more thought and trouble. I must often consider my answer
so as to say neither too much nor too little. . . . My letters are not
Ciceronian and oratorical like those of Grickel, but at least I have
substance if not elegant Latin.

Luther was, perhaps, too conscious of his own imperfect
Latinity. In 1516, writing to Mutian he apologizes that "this
barbarian Martin, accustomed only to cry out among geese,"
should venture to address so learned a man, and he rarely fails
to make similar excuses whenever he writes to a noted humanist. At these times he took especial pains with his diction, and
was capable of a certain refinement. He always wrote, indeed,
with correctness, and though he lacks the labored and often
pedantic Ciceronian style, so carefully cultivated by the scholars of the Renaissance, he more than makes up for this de-
ficiency by the freshness and force of his Latin, which he treats
as if it were a living language.

In German, as has been pointed out, Luther was one of the
first authors. His greatest fault, perhaps, is verbosity. His
works contain endless repetition. He was conscious of this
defect himself, and regretted that he was unable "to be as

concise and perspicuous as Melanchthon and Amsdorf." " I am garrulous and rhetorical," he said at another time, and once confessed, "Formerly I almost talked the world to death. Then I could say more about a feather than now about a farm, and yet I do not like verbosity."

Another quality, nearly allied to this, very obvious in all Luther's writings, and felt by him as a lack, is the absence of system. The Reformer was no organizer ; he had not the gift of ordered presentation. This quality, which he admired so much in Melanchthon and would have admired still more in Calvin, has sometimes been said to be usually lacking in Germans. These deep thinkers, patient searchers after truth, and great poets have not the ability, so characteristic of the French, of presenting their thought in a clear, systematic form. Even the greatest German masterpiece, Faust, with all its sublime poetry and profound thought and feeling, has, according to classic standards, little unity and at times imperfect coherence. To say that Luther and his countrymen are somewhat less gifted in this regard is not saying anything against them. The deepest thinking is not always the most systematized. It has often been charged against Shakespeare that he had no philosophy, and Plato has been accused of being inconsistent.

Among the four hundred and twenty works from Luther's pen, none, therefore, is to be found which gives in succinct form the essentials of his philosophy. All his commentaries are concerned with the text alone ; all his tracts are written to meet the exigencies of some particular situation. Moreover he habitually wrote at great speed, often finishing a work while the first part was in press. Of his rapidity in composition he once observed : —

I bring forth as soon as I conceive. First, I consider all my arguments and words diligently from every point of view, so that I have a perfect idea of my book before I begin to write. . . . But my enemies the papists and others burst forth and bawl whatever comes into their heads first.

Whatever his faults, however, Luther remains one of the greatest of writers. His fury and his mirth are alike Titanic ;

his polemics are informed with matchless vigor, and his musings over the cradle of his baby are in the grand style. It is well known that Goethe and Lessing and many another great German author drank deep of the great river of his inspiration. To foreign writers, too, he has been a mighty influence. Thomas Carlyle, in his suggestive, impressionistic way, thus hits off his qualities : [1] —

But in no books have I found a more robust, I will say noble, faculty of a man than in these of Luther. A rugged honest homeliness, simplicity ; a rugged sterling sense and strength. He flashes out illumination from him ; his smiting idiomatic phrases seem to cleave into the very secret of the matter. Good humor, too, nay tender affection, nobleness, and depth : this man could have been a poet too !

And Michelet, the greater historian of France, thus vividly brings him before our eyes : [2] —

See how Luther appears, sublime and ridiculous (bouffon) musician of this divine Yule-tide ; mirthful, angry, and terrible ; an Aristophanic David, something between Moses and Rabelais. Nay, more than all that, the People, or, as he magnificently named the people : " My Lord Everybody " (Herr Omnes). This lord is in Luther.

No English writer of his time can be compared with him. Only Burke has equalled him in passion, sometimes degenerating into scurrility. His prose is perhaps nearer that of Milton than of any other of our authors. Milton, to be sure, lacks Luther's humor ; but they possess in common the long complex sentences ; the vocabulary of each has the same taste of originality and radicality ; in both there is the same scholarly background ; the same vehemence, occasionally the same foulmouthed invective in the interest of piety. In another point, not without its influence on style, the pair resembled each other, namely, in their fondness for music and relative indifference to other arts.[3]

[1] *Hero and Hero-Worship.* **The Hero as Priest.**

[2] *Histoire de France,* x, 108.

[3] Cf. Chapter xxxi, p. 348. Milton had some familiarity with Luther's Latin works, though he confesses that he had not " examined through them " all. Cf. *supra,* p. 87.

CHAPTER XXXI

RELIGION AND CULTURE

THE deepest part of Luther's life was his religion. Any picture which failed to give a strong idea of this would be like Hamlet with the prince left out. To him the relation of the individual to God was not only the most serious fact in life, but also the most practical, the atmosphere in which he lived and moved and had his being. His formal writings are mainly concerned with religion, his letters are saturated with it, and his table-talk reveals the constancy with which his thoughts were occupied with this subject. To his contemporaries these sayings were mainly interesting as authoritative expositions of dogma, to posterity they are hardly less valuable as keys to the heart of a great prophet. The dogmatic system of the Evangelic Church may be best studied in the treatises of its leader and in those of his disciple Melanchthon, but the ethical part, taking the word in its broadest sense as that which concerns the man's ἦθος, comes out most strongly in his incidental remarks. Luther is greater than his work. His dogmatic system has lost part of its hold upon mankind, and seems likely to lose still more, but his influence on the ideals and culture of many an age to come will remain.

To Luther himself, however, religion and doctrine were nearly allied. The centre of his theology was the idea of justification by faith in Christ, and the most important part of the Saviour's work was the atonement; indeed he warns his followers against regarding Jesus merely as an example for imitation.[1]

His faith and childlike trust are strongly painted in the following fragments of his conversations : —

We must rejoice in the Lord, but such joy will often lead us astray, too. David had to endure many a temptation, to murder, adultery,

[1] In the letter to the Christians of Strassburg, December 14, 1524, p. 155.

and rapine until he turned to the fear of God and remained therein. Therefore he says in the Second Psalm, "Serve the Lord with fear and rejoice with trembling." They go together — joy and fear. My little son Hans can do it before me, but I cannot do it before God. If I sit and write and Hans sings a song over there and plays too noisily, I speak to him about it and he sings more quietly with care and reverence. So God will have us always joyful, but with fear and honor to him.

The principal study of theology is to learn of Christ and know him well. As we trust a good friend, knowing that he will show us all good will, so we should trust the Lord to be gracious and merciful to us. Therefore St. Peter says: "Grow in the knowledge of Christ," that is, believe that he is the best, most merciful and kindest Lord, on whom alone we should depend and to whom we should cleave. Christ also teaches that we know him only in the Holy Scripture, for he says: "Search the Scriptures, for they are they which testify of me." But the devil hinders and greatly darkens this high knowledge in us and brings it to pass that we trust a good, human friend more than the Lord Christ.

I have studied diligently, but as yet I do not understand one word of the Bible. I have not yet passed the primary class, but I am always turning over in my mind what I know, and asking for comprehension of the decalogue and the creed. It irks me not a little that I, a doctor, with all my learning should willy nilly stay in the class with my little Hans and Magdalene and go to school with them. Who has ever understood all the meaning of the words: "Our Father which art in heaven"? By faith in these words we know that the God who made heaven and earth is our father, and that we are his children and none can hurt us. The Angel Gabriel is my servant, Raphael is my groom, and all other angels are ministering spirits to my various needs. Then, perhaps, my good Father turns to and has me cast into prison or beheaded or drowned, to try whether I have really learned these words, or even the one "Father." For the faith in our hearts wavers and our weakness suggests a doubt, "How do I know whether this is true?" The hardest word in all Scripture to understand is "thy" in the First Commandment.

No one is able to calculate the wealth God spends feeding the birds, even the useless ones. I fancy it costs God more than the revenue of the King of France for one year to feed two sparrows. And what about the other birds, larger and more rapacious?

One night two little birds flew into the room, but were frightened by us and would not let us approach. The doctor said to me : " Schlag-inhaufen, these birds lack faith. They do not know how glad I am to have them here nor that I would let no harm be done them. Thus do we act toward God, who loves us and has given his Son for us."

Dr. Luther was playing with his dog and said : " The dog is the most faithful of animals and would be much esteemed were it not so common. Our Lord God has made his greatest gifts the commonest. Eyes are the greatest of all gifts to living creatures. Little birds have eyes like stars, so that they can see a fly across the room. But we fools don't think of these gifts now, though we shall in the next life."

From the first years in the monastery Luther's later life in-herited a tinge of melancholy. Though he rarely again felt the terrible despair of those days, he often had periods of depres-sion. He was therefore very kind in understanding and helping younger friends who felt the same trials. At times he said he found relief from such thoughts in a good drink, or in other pleasures of the senses. To Schlaginhaufen he gave the fol-lowing more spiritual advice : —

The greatest temptation is this, when Satan says, " God hates sin-ners and therefore hates you." Some feel this temptation one way, some another. The devil always makes me think of my misdeeds, as for example that in my youth I celebrated the sacrifice of the mass. Thus he attacks some on their past life. But in his syllogism the major premise is to be denied, for it is false that God hates sinners. If the devil brings up the example of Sodom and such places, we must reply by citing the fact that Christ was sent in the flesh. If God hated sinners he would certainly not have sent his Son. He hates only those who do not wish to be justified, that is, those who think they are not sinners. Temptations of this sort are most valuable to us ; they are not, I believe, our ruin but our education, and every Christian should think that he cannot know Christ but by tempta-tion.

About ten years ago I first felt this despair and fear of divine wrath.[1] Afterwards I obtained rest when I married and had good

---

[1] Luther speaks December 14, 1531. For the moment he is speaking of the doubts he entertained when he first broke with the Church of Rome, a subject to which he returns later. He next digresses to the old monastery days when he felt doubts about his own salvation.

days, but later it returned. When I complained to Staupitz he said he had never felt such trials, " but as far as I can see," said he, " they are more necessary to us than food and drink." Who feel such temptations should accustom themselves to bearing them, for so doing is real Christianity. If Satan had not tried me thus I could not hate him so much, nor do him so much harm, so that my trials seem to me gifts of God, for I should have fallen into the abyss of hell through pride had it not been for them. God has taught me that they are his free gifts, for when it comes to a battle, I cannot single-handed conquer one venial sin.

The papists and Anabaptists teach that if you would know Christ you must be alone and not associate with men, like a hermit. This is devilish advice. . . . Good-bye to those who say : —

" Keep to yourself apart.

" Then you are pure in heart."

The world does not know the hidden treasures of God. It cannot be persuaded that the maid working obediently and the servant faithfully performing his duty, or the woman rearing her children are as good as the praying monk who strikes his breast and wrestles with his spirit.

One part of Luther's religion, borrowed from the popular superstition of the age, was his belief in a personal devil. The anecdote of his throwing his inkstand at the fiend, is, to be sure, apocryphal, but it admirably expresses both the vividness with which the Reformer objectified his spiritual foe and the energy of the means taken against him. He attributed all his sufferings, as well as all the misfortunes to the Church or people, to the direct interposition of Satan, and his fury resembled a personal hatred more than a philosophic detestation of an abstract principle. He was ready to do anything " to spite the devil," with whom he talked nightly in the rudest as well as in the coarsest manner. To understand the intensity of this conception, so foreign to our sophisticated century, we must remember that Luther imbibed the superstition from his earliest childhood. Throughout life he continued to attribute even meteorological phenomena, if at all startling, to supernatural agency. A thunderstorm frightened him into his vow to be a monk; of one on December 16, 1536, he said : —

It is simply Satanic. I believe the devils were going to hold a debate and some angel interposed this crash of thunder and tore up their propositions.

Among a great number of stories told by the Reformer about Satan, one is especially interesting for its mention of Faust. It will be remembered that the historical personage who bore this name was a contemporary of Luther's, and may have been known to him, as he lived at Wittenberg for a time during the third decade of the sixteenth century. The first literary treatment of the Faust story, that published by Spies at Frankfort in 1587, brings its hero into close relations with the Wittenberg theology. He is made a student at the university and his fall from grace is an apostasy from the Evangelic faith. Many things in the work, such as Faust's impression of Rome and his ideas of the devil, are suggested by passages from Luther's table-talk. Through this channel the Reformer is brought into direct connection with Marlowe's Dr. Faustus and with the greatest masterpiece of German literature.

They spoke much of Faust, who called the devil his friend and talked with him. Luther said: " If I had only reached my hand out to Satan he would have destroyed me. But I feared him not and stretched forth my hands to God my protector. I believe many use incantations against me. At Nordhausen there was a devil named Wildfire,[1] who so dazed a peasant that the man wandered about several hours with his horse and wagon and at last found himself in a puddle. In like manner a devil assumed the garb of a monk, and meeting a peasant on the road asked him how much he would charge to let him eat all the hay he wanted. The peasant asked a farthing, whereupon the monk ate more than half the load of hay, so that the rustic had to drive him away by force. Again as a pardoner the fiend pulled off a Jew's leg. You see what power Satan has in deluding our external senses: what can he not do with our souls ? "

Luther sometimes gives advice as to the best way of counteracting the incantations of witches and the malice of devils. One way to harass those who turned butter and milk sour was to

---

[1] *Wildfeuer:* the sense leads us to translate " will o' the wisp," but such a meaning is apparently unsupported, the German word for will o' the wisp being *Irrlicht.*

put the articles on ice ; another way, used by Bugenhagen, was "to plague them with filth" in a manner which Luther describes freely but which will hardly bear repetition after him.[1] Sometimes Luther's advice was more drastic, as when he advised that a boy whom he believed to be a changeling be strangled and that a witch at Altenburg be tortured.[2]

Occasionally, the Reformer took a rational view, as when he disavowed a belief in astrology, which was Melanchthon's pet superstition. Again he often advised those who applied to him for advice on how to treat diabolic possession, to be sure that they were not deceived. "For," he once admitted, "I have found many impostors in my own experience, not to mention those I have read about, and have been afterwards much annoyed to think of my gullibility."

One idea which Luther possessed, in common with many Christians from the times of the apostles to our own, was that of the near approaching end of the world.

If conduct is three fourths of life, culture is one fourth, and in estimating a man this must be taken into account, both for its own sake and because even his conduct will be influenced by his knowledge of and attitude towards books, art, and the world of beautiful ideas.

Luther was one of the best read men of his time. Like all natures with an abnormally developed religious faculty, he found his spiritual ancestry rather in Judea than in Greece, even preferring tho literature of the Hebrews, an opinion in support of which the great English poet-scholar Milton has elaborately argued in Paradise Regained. "Compared to the wisdom of the Hebrews," said the German professor, "that of the Greeks is simply animal, for there can be no true wisdom without knowledge of the true God." From the first years in the cloister to the day of his death, Luther's chief spiritual nourishment was the Bible.

This does not mean that he was a man of one book, for of

---

[1] Lauterbach's *Tagebuch*, p. 121. Disgusting methods of putting the devil to flight appear to have been very common. St. Francis recommended Bugenhagen's way to his follower Rufinus, and Cellini speaks of similar doing in his *Memoirs*.

[2] Or put to death? "Da solde man mit solche ad supplicia eilen." Lauterbach's *Tagebuch*, p. 117.

classic, mediæval, and contemporary writers he read a great deal. Greek he never knew well enough to enjoy the classical authors of that tongue, in which respect he was exactly on a par with the most famous humanists of the Italian Renaissance.[1] True, " he bought a Homer to become a Greek," and a few quotations show that he really studied it, but occasional references to other authors, such as Demosthenes and Aristophanes, seem to have behind them little more than literary commonplace.

With the Latin authors it is different. Luther read them quite widely and critically. In college he learned to know Virgil, Ovid, and Baptista Mantuan, a late humanist whose eclogues enjoyed a great reputation. Later he studied Terence, in whose stories he took great delight, though he entertained the theory, not original with himself, that the plays were really written by Scipio or Laelius. Cicero he often praised, as, for example : —

Cicero is the best philosopher, for he felt that the soul is immortal. He wrote best on natural, moral, and rational philosophy. He is a valuable man, reading with judgment and able to express himself well. He wrote in earnest and did not fool like the Greeks Plato and Aristotle. I hope God will forgive such men as Cicero their sins. Even if he should not be redeemed, he will enjoy a situation in hell several degrees higher than that destined for our cardinal of Mayence.

In the Latin Christian writers Luther's reading was very extensive though not exhaustive. His favorite was Augustine ; of some others, especially Jerome, he had a poor opinion. His knowledge of the later schoolmen was ready to his tongue, as his debates at Marburg and Leipsic proved. It would be tedious to give a list of the now obsolete authors whom the German professor mastered; suffice it to say that almost the only one of the first importance with whom he was unacquainted was Thomas Aquinas, who, with the realists, was then regarded as the champion of a vanquished theology.

[1] The proof of this statement, which at first may sound paradoxical, is found in an article by Dr. L. R. Loomis in the *American Historical Review*, xiii, 246 (1908). It is well known how much Petrarch revered a Greek manuscript, and how little of it he could construe.

Luther studied Church history with considerable thoroughness and much independence of judgment. He was familiar with Eusebius and Cassiodorus as well as with the legends of the saints, almost all of which he regarded with a justifiable suspicion. Sometimes he was biased by preconceived ideas, as when he convinced himself that the rise of the papal power was to be dated only four centuries before himself, with the introduction of the Canon Law. With this great code he was thoroughly familiar.

Among the more recent theologians Luther's special proclivity to Tauler and the mystics, Staupitz and Gerson, has been mentioned. One of his favorite writers was John Huss, whom he learned to know early in 1520. In 1536 he edited a collection of his great predecessor's letters. Wicliffe is often mentioned by Luther, but it is probable that he knew him only through the reports of others.

Of all writers the one whom Luther most relished, at least until the Diet of Worms, was Desiderius Erasmus. We get a fresh impression of that great scholar's enormous power and influence by reading in Luther's correspondence of the eagerness with which his works were looked for and with which they were perused. For one reference to any other author in the Reformer's letters before 1521 there are at least ten to Erasmus, and this does not count the numerous citations from his Adages, a book of familiar quotations by which the aspiring stylist might add graces to his composition without the trouble of reading through the vast body of the classics. Luther's indebtedness to Erasmus' edition of the New Testament, both for his translation and for his lectures, has been noted. Among the other theological works of the Dutch scholar, the Saxon speaks of the Apologia ad Fabrem, the Ecclesiastæ, the Querela pacis, the Ratio theologiæ, the Enchiridon militis Christiani, and the Catechismus. The Colloquies and the Praise of Folly are frequently alluded to, though generally in a hostile tone. Of Erasmus' controversial works the Spongia against Hutten, and of course the Diatribe on Free Will, were known to Luther. To the older scholar he was indebted for an edition of Jerome's Epistles and a translation of Lucian's Dialogues.

The satire, Julius exclusus, made such an impression upon the
Reformer that he thought of translating it, but gave it up
as too difficult. Erasmus' epistles were bought and devoured as
soon as published : the Auctarium of 1518, the Farrago nova
of 1519, and the Epistolæ ad diversos of 1521.

Other contemporaries were perused only less eagerly. More's
Utopia and Epigrams were ordered at the Frankfort fair of
1518. Lefèvre d'Étaples was well known and so were the
Epistolæ Obscurorum Virorum, of which, however, Luther,
like Erasmus, highly disapproved. The writings of Valla and
Hutten each had their place in the Reformer's library.

Later in life, Luther developed a great fondness for the
contemporary German fables, plays, ballads, and satires. The
characteristics of this literature were intense nationalism, a
powerful appeal to the common man and strong religious feeling, with all of which the Wittenberg professor deeply sympa-
thized. The age loved sententious precept and satire. Indeed
the most famous works of the time were satires. Erasmus'
Praise of Folly, Brant's Ship of Fools, and the Letters of
Obscure Men attest the taste of Luther's contemporaries, a
predilection which he also shared. This taste was not refined ; the apotheosis of St. Grobianus, a character invented by
Brant and often spoken of by Luther, is typical of the least
pleasant side of the exuberant vitality manifest everywhere.
Again, the age was one delighting in fables and short moral
stories, as in Reinecke Fuchs and Æsop and the adventures
of Till Eulenspiegel. Luther also appreciated and represented
the intense nationalism of his countrymen — a quality prominent in the fiery dialogues of Hutten as well as in the works of
minor men. Luther's fondness for this literature with which he
has so many points in common, finds appropriate expression in
a letter — half Latin, half German — to one who dwelt in the
old poetic city of Nuremberg : —

TO WENZEL LINK AT NUREMBERG

(WITTENBERG,) March 2, 1535.

Grace and peace in Christ. As it is now several centuries, dear
Wenzel, since I have spoken or written Latin, I fear that I have for-

gotten it, at least our good old kind ; however, I believe that you are in like danger, and I hope that this my faith will justify me to you, without works, good or bad, for you are a propitious god to such sinners as I, for you need the same indulgence yourself. Amen.

I have nothing to write, except that I would not let these fair Evangelists, Lady Tetzel and her daughters, go from here to Nuremberg without taking you a letter. I would have sent you mountains of gold besides, but our Elbe has overflowed this year and washed away all the golden sands, leaving us only stones, of which two lodged in Jonas's body to reward him for his enmity to our sceptics. I have joked enough, ill and well, weak and strong, a sinner and righteous, dead and alive in Christ. Do you, who live by rivers of gold and silver, send me some poetic dreams or poetic songs of the kind I love. You don't understand ? Well then, I will speak German, gracious Lord Wenzel. If it is not too hard, nor too much, nor too long, nor too wide, nor too high, nor too deep, nor too anything, please have some boy collect all the German pictures, rimes, songs, books, lays of the Meistersinger, which have this year been painted, composed, made, and printed by your German poets, publishers, and printers. I have a reason for wanting them.

We can make Latin books for ourselves, but we wish to learn how to make German ones, as we have hitherto made none that please anybody. Farewell in Christ and pray for me. The Lord be with you and all your household. Greet all our friends.

Yours,
Martin Luther, as much doctor as you are.

Of the kind of literature of which he has spoken to Link the fables so characteristic of the period especially appealed to Luther. At Feste Coburg he had already busied himself with Æsop's fables,[1] for which he wrote an introduction. Another author whom he was constantly quoting was Dionysius Cato, who flourished about the time of Constantine, and wrote a set of short moral verses much used in schools.

He loudly praised Æsop's fables, and said they were worthy of being translated and put in their proper topical order, for the book was not composed by one man at one time, but by many men in different ages. . . . Serious anecdotes, sententious and redolent of age, useful to the state, should be gathered into the first book, lighter ones

---

[1] Cf. letter to Melanchthon, April 23, 1530, pp. 248, 252.

into the second, and the rest into the third. " It is a providential dispensation that the writings of Cato and Æsop remain in the schools; each is a weighty author. Cato has the most useful words and precepts, Æsop the pleasantest conversation and fables. If these moral books are used in education the youth profit much. In short, after the Bible, these two books please me better than those of all other philosophers and jurists, just as Donatus seems to me the best grammar."

In contemporary productions Luther took a warm interest. One of his humanistic friends was Eoban Hess, who had welcomed him so warmly on his journey to Worms. Hess had been called to teach the humanities at the first Protestant university, that of Marburg, founded by Philip of Hesse. Here he published a translation of the Psalms in Latin verse, for which Luther warmly thanked him in a letter of August 1, 1537 : —

I confess, he wrote, that I am one of those who are more moved and delighted by poems than by the polished orations of even Cicero and Demosthenes. This is true even of profane poems, how much more of the Psalms.

Though perhaps the chief means of culture, books are far from being the only ones. Luther was a thorough master of one of the fine arts — music. The old legend that he composed the tunes to his hymns has been exposed, but he both played the lute and sang. He had an exalted opinion of the function of music in divine service ; indeed it would be difficult to speak more strongly than does he in this letter : —

TO LEWIS SENFEL AT MUNICH

COBURG, October 4, 1530.

Grace and peace in Christ. Although my name is so hated that I must fear, my dear Lewis, that this letter will not be safely received and read by you, yet my love of music has overcome my fear, and in musical talent I see that God has richly endowed you. It is this that makes me hope my letter will bring no danger to you, for who even in Turkey would be offended at me for loving art and honoring an artist? Moreover I greatly honor and esteem your two Dukes of Bavaria, although they are not very favorable to me, because I see they love and foster music. I doubt not that there are many seeds of virtue in a mind touched by music, and I consider those not affected by it as stocks and stones. We know that music is hateful and intolerable to devils. I really believe, nor am I ashamed to assert, that next to theology there is no art equal to music, for it is the only one, except theology, which can give a quiet and happy mind, a manifest proof that the devil, the author of racking care and perturbation, flees from the sound of music as he does from the exhortation of religion. This is the reason why the prophets practised no other art, neither geometry nor arithmetic nor astronomy, as if they believed music and divinity nearly allied; as indeed they declare in their psalms and canticles. Praising music is like trying to paint a great subject on a small canvas, which turns out merely a daub. But my love for it abounds; it has often refreshed me and freed me from great troubles.

I pray you and beseech you if you have a copy of the canticle, I will lay me down in Peace, to transcribe and send it to me. The tune delighted me even as a youth and does so more now that I know the words. I have never seen it arranged for several voices. I would not add to your labor, but if you have it so arranged I would be pleased. I hope my life is nearly at an end, for the world hates me and I am sick of it. I wish the good and faithful Shepherd would take my soul. So I keep humming this canticle, and wishing I had it properly arranged. In case you do not know it I send along the air, which you can arrange after my death if you like. The Lord Jesus be with you always. Amen. Pardon my bold and tedious letter. Give my greetings to your whole choir.

Again he said: —

"Singing is a fine noble exercise. It has nothing to do with the world or business troubles. He who sings drives out care, and that is an excellent thing."

At the house of Wolfgang Reissenbusch they sang at table. Luther said: "Music is a noble gift of God, next to theology. I would not change my little knowledge of music for a great deal. Youths should be trained in this art, for it makes fine, clever people."

The meals at the Black Cloister were enlivened by singing, of which a lively picture is given in a letter to Jerome Weller's brother, who had sent the Reformer one of his own compositions: —

TO MATTHEW WELLER AT FREIBERG

(WITTENBERG,) January 18, 1535.

Grace and peace in Christ. I am rather late with my thanks, dear friend, for your kindness in sending me the song and the Pomeranian apples. But Jerome is my witness how often I have intended to write, but have had no messenger. Please take my intentions kindly, for of a truth I believe you are my hearty friend as I am yours, as I shall prove when I have a chance.

We sing your song as well as we can at table and afterwards. If we make a few mistakes it is not your fault, but that of our skill, which is small enough even after we have sung the song over twice or thrice. Virgil says we are not all equal to all things. No matter how well our composers do, we are too much for them and sing their songs badly. If indeed all the governments of the world were to punish us and if God and reason were to write the tunes, nevertheless we would make such mince-meat [1] of them as might be sold at the butcher's and make people wish us and our tongues hung as high as church bells. You composers mustn't mind if we do make howlers of your songs, for we insist on trying them whether we fail or not. My dear Katie says she hopes you won't take offence at my jokes and she sends you her kind regards. God bless you.

MARTIN LUTHER.

Of Luther's appreciation of the other fine arts, it is more difficult to speak. If it can be argued that because he rarely speaks of painting, sculpture, and architecture, he did not care for them, the same must be said of Milton, who, having visited Italy in a later age, and with far greater opportunities of seeing her masterpieces, is silent about them in his works, though he takes every occasion to praise music both in prose and verse.[2] When Luther visited Italy in 1510, many of the great works both of classical antiquity and of the Renaissance which have

---

[1] Luther puns on the double meaning of Sau, which means both pig and mistake.

[2] I make this statement on my general familiarity with Milton's works, without having examined them expressly to ascertain how often he speaks of painting and sculpture. Such references are certainly absent in places where one might expect them, as, for example, in the description of the glories of Athens in *Paradise Regained*, though here Milton would have had the example of Virgil's tribute to Greek art; nor, again, does the essay on education, while especially recommending music, mention the other fine arts.

been the delight and study of all subsequent times, were already on exhibition. At Rome, at Florence, at Milan, and at many other cities, the pilgrim might have learned to know not only the great sculptors and painters of Greece and Italy, but those of other lands. And yet what a meagre opportunity was one month in a whole lifetime to become acquainted with a world of art! Luther's attitude towards the masterpieces that he saw is well illustrated by one of his few references to them, namely, that it was a shame that the money paid for indulgences should go to pay for such things as the Apollo Belvedere. When souls were perishing what was it to him that the popes were enriching the life of this world by their enlightened patronage of the arts? Even thus Luther was too much alive to all the best in life, too cultured, in fact, not to notice the immortal works of great artists which he saw in Italy and possibly also in some German cities. Though the men who reported the table-talk were not particularly interested in this phase of their master's personality, they have fortunately preserved one saying which indicates that he was not blind to the merit of what he saw : —

The Italian painters are so able and so full of genius that they can, in a masterly way, follow and exactly imitate nature in all their paintings ; not only do they get the proper color and form in all the members, but they even make them appear as if they lived and moved. Flanders follows Italy and imitates her in some measure, for the men of the Low Countries, especially the Flemish, are cunning and artful ; they quickly and easily learn a foreign language, for they have ready tongues. If one sends a Fleming through France or Italy, he soon knows the speech.

Of the German painters on the other hand he has nothing to say. Dürer once sent him some of his engravings, of which the Reformer expresses no opinion. Cranach's art is only mentioned to blame a certain picture for its indecency. In general, it is fair to say that if Luther was little appreciative of the arts appealing to the eye, the fault was rather in his limited opportunities than in his nature.

In many other matters, trifling in themselves, a man's culture, temper, and view of life may be tested. In all these the Wittenberg professor showed that he was no narrow fanatic. He approved of all innocent forms of amusement. He played a good game of chess, and speaks of cards as a harmless diversion for children. Again, he is delighted when some young people make up a party for "fools' bells" (a game I am not able to describe), and he warmly recommended outdoor sports to the young nobles as a substitute for drinking. Of another form of recreation which has fallen under the ban of some of his followers, he says: —

Dances are instituted that courtesy may be learned in company and friendship and acquaintance be contracted between young men and girls. Here their intercourse may be watched and occasion of honorable meeting given, so that having tried a girl we can afterwards let her go about more safely and easily. The Pope formerly condemned dances because he was an enemy of marriage. But let all things be done decently! Let honorable men and matrons be invited to see that everything is proper. I myself would attend them sometimes, but the youth would whirl less giddily if I did.

Luther approved not only of dances but of the theatre, which was, indeed, in that day, a vehicle of religious instruction. When George Held of Forscheim asked him, in 1543, whether such plays[1] were to be encouraged, intimating that they were disapproved by certain ministers, Luther answered with a strong affirmative.

[1] The plays complained against, by the clergy of Magdeburg, were those of Joachim Greff. Cf. W. Scherer, Deutsche Studien, Sitzungsberichte der phil. hist. Klasse der k. k. Akademie zu Wien. vol. xc (1878), pp. 193 ff. Luther's letter, De Wette, v, 552. Cf. Burkhardt, *Luther's Briefwechsel*, p. 424.

CHAPTER XXXII

THE LUTHER FAMILY

MARTIN and Katie had six children, of whom four, three sons and one daughter, survived their parents. The eldest, John (Hans), was born on June 7, 1526. On December 10 of the following year a little daughter named Elizabeth came, but left her parents in less than a year. On August 5, 1528, Luther wrote to Hausmann : —

Little Hans thanks you for the rattle of which he is inordinately proud. . . . My little daughter Elizabeth is dead. She has left me wonderfully sick at heart and almost womanish, I am so moved by pity for her. I could never have believed how a father's heart could soften for his child.

The birth of another daughter, on May 4, 1529, brought comfort to the bereaved parent. She was baptized Magdalene, after Katie's aunt, who had come from the Nimbschen cloister to live with her niece.

When Hans was four years old, his father, then at Feste Coburg, wrote him a letter which has been a children's classic from that day to this : —

TO HANS LUTHER AT WITTENBERG

(FESTE COBURG, June 19 ? 1530.)

Grace and peace in Christ, dear little son. I am glad to hear that you are studying and saying your prayers. Continue to do so, my son, and when I come home I will bring you a pretty present.

I know a lovely, pleasant garden where many children are ; they wear golden jackets and gather nice apples under the trees and pears and cherries and purple plums and yellow plums, and sing and run and jump and are happy and have pretty little ponies with golden reins and silver saddles. I asked the man who owned the garden whose children they were. He said : "They are the children who say their prayers and study and are good." Then said I : "Dear man, I also have a son whose name is Hans Luther ; may he come into the garden and eat the sweet apples and pears and ride a fine pony and play with these children?" Then the man said: "If he says his prayers and is good, he can come into the garden and Phil and Justy [1] too, and when they all come they shall have whistles and drums and fifes and dance and shoot little cross-bows." Then he showed me a fine large lawn in the garden for dancing, where hang real golden whistles and fine silver cross-bows. But it was yet early and the children had not finished eating and I could not wait to see them dance, so I said to the man: "My dear sir, I must go away and write at once to my dear little Hans about all this, so that he will say his prayers and study and be good, so that he may come into the garden, and he has an Auntie Lena whom he must bring with him." Then the man said: "All right, go and tell him about it." So, dear little Hans, study and say your prayers and tell Phil and Justy to say their prayers and study too, so you may all come into the garden together. God bless you. Give Auntie Lena my love and a kiss from me.

Your loving father,

MARTIN LUTHER.

Another son was born on November 9, 1531, and named after his father, whose birthday was so near his own. Luther, who was uncommonly fond of children, said of him, rather sublimely: —

"The youngest children are always the most loved by the parents. My little Martin is my dearest treasure. Hans and Lena can now speak and do not need so much care, therefore it is that parents always love the little infants who need their love the most. What a heart-stab it must have been to Abraham when he was commanded to kill his only son. Truly I would dispute with God if he bade me do such a thing." Then Katie said: "I cannot believe that God would really want any one to kill his own child."

Luther: "God must be kinder to us and speak more gently to us than Katie does to her baby. Katie or I would not gouge an eye out or knock the head off our own child, and neither will God with his children. He gave his only son to make us trust him."

At other times the moralizing was less lofty if equally human. One day when the baby, as is the manner of them, dirtied the parental lap on which he was sitting, the father grimly bade

---

[1] Philip Melanchthon and Justus Jonas, juniores, both born 1525.

his guests remark that it was symbolic of the way most people treated their Father in heaven. Again he said : —

What cause have you given me to love you so? How have you deserved to be my heir? By making yourself a general nuisance. And why are n't you thankful instead of filling the house with your howls?

On January 28, 1533, a third son was born. When the sponsors gathered the next day, the proud parent said to them : —

A new Pope has just been born; you will help the poor fellow to his rights. . . . I have called him Paul, for St. Paul has given me many good sayings and arguments, wherefore I wish to honor him.

The last child, named Margaret after her father's lately deceased mother, first saw the light on December 17, 1534.

The Reformer took a lively interest in the education of his children. Hans began to study under the tutorship of a student, Jerome Weller, before he was four years old. At seven he apparently knew some Latin, by no means a dead language but one frequently used in conversation by the members of the learned classes. At the same time he was enrolled in the university, but this was a mere honor usually accorded to sons of professors. At nine he was sent away to school, though where is not known. One of his father's letters, of January 27, 1537, warns him of the curse which God will send upon him if he does not do right. Hans was not a very bright boy, and in August, 1542, his father sent him to one of the best schools of the day, that conducted by Mark Crodel at Torgau.

About three weeks after he had first entered the school, he was called home by the serious illness of his sister Magdalene. The little girl, then in her fourteenth year, died on September 20. Luther's life was so little private that the whole death-scene has been preserved from the pen of one of the household who happened to be present. Few tragedies are more touching than this simple narrative, showing how the great, strong man was utterly broken by the affliction: —

As his daughter lay very ill, Dr. Luther said: "I love her very much, but dear God, if it be thy will to take her, I submit to thee." Then he said to her as she lay in bed: "Magdalene, my dear little daughter, would you like to stay here with your father, or would you willingly go to your Father yonder?" She answered: "Darling father, as God wills." Then said he: "Dearest child, the spirit is willing but the flesh is weak." Then he turned away and said: "I love her very much; if my flesh is so strong, what can my spirit do? God has given no bishop so great a gift in a thousand years as he has given me in her. I am angry with myself that I cannot rejoice in heart and be thankful as I ought."

Now as Magdalene lay in the agony of death, her father fell down before the bed on his knees and wept bitterly and prayed that God might free her. Then she departed and fell asleep in her father's arms. . . .

As they laid her in the coffin he said: "Darling Lena, you will rise and shine like a star, yea, like the sun. . . . I am happy in spirit, but the flesh is sorrowful and will not be content, the parting grieves me beyond measure. . . . I have sent a saint to heaven."

Three days later he wrote to Justus Jonas:—

I believe that you have already heard that my dearest daughter Magdalene has been reborn to the eternal kingdom of Christ; and although my wife and I ought only to give thanks and rejoice at such a happy pilgrimage and blessed end, whereby she has escaped the power of the flesh, the world, the Turk, and the devil, yet so strong is natural affection that we must sob and groan in heart under the oppression of killing grief. . . . Would that I and all mine might have such a death, or rather such a life. She was, as you know, of a sweet, gentle and loving nature.

The other children survived their father. Hans entered the university in 1543. Here he continued to study after his father's death, taking up the law, although the Schmalkaldic war, 1546–1547, interrupted his work. In 1552 the Elector John Frederic gave him a position in the government, which he continued to serve till his death in 1575. In 1553 he married Elizabeth, daughter of Caspar Cruciger. He had but one daughter, who died childless.

Martin studied theology, but never held a position, being sickly and perhaps weak-minded. He married, but died childless in 1565.

Paul became a successful physician. After taking his degree

at Wittenberg, in 1557, he taught some time at Jena, and was later called to be court physician first to Elector Joachim II of Brandenburg and then to Elector August of Albertine Saxony. He married in 1553 and had several children, of whom some have descendants now living.

Margaret Luther was but eleven at her father's death. Nine years later she married a student at Wittenberg, the rich and noble George von Kunheim. She left three children, of whom one, her daughter Margaret, has posterity at the present day.

Besides his own children, Luther brought up no less than eleven of his orphaned nephews and nieces. With his brother and sisters he had had little to do since his fourteenth year, though occasionally one of them is mentioned in a letter or in the table-talk. Their relations were strained by the division of old Hans Luther's estate, but this was amicably adjusted on July 10, 1534, when the heirs assembled at Wittenberg, and Martin drew up an instrument dividing the estate, reckoned at 1250 gulden, in five equal parts, one to each child or his heirs. The house, which may still be seen at Mansfeld, went to James Luther, who paid the other heirs for their share.

Luther did not always have an easy time with his young relatives. Two of them, George Kaufmann and Hans Polner, were given to drink. To the latter he said in 1540 : —

On account of you I hear an evil report among strangers. My enemies examine all that I do ; if I break wind they smell it at Rome. If in drink you should do some harm, do you not know how you would brand me and this house and the town and the Evangelic faith ? Other men when drunk are happy and mild, as my father was ; they sing and joke, but you fall into a fury. Such men ought to flee drink like a poison, for it is a deadly poison to such natures. Men of better humor may indulge more freely in liquor.

Polner may have reformed ; at any rate he became a clergyman, and Katie liked him better than the parish minister.

Like other German professors, Luther took a certain number of students as boarders, though they usually paid for their entertainment by service, both literary and menial, rather than by money. The Black Cloister was filled not only with them and with the poor relatives, but with needy priests, and frequently with distinguished visitors. In 1542 George Held described the house as "inhabited by a miscellaneous and promiscuous crowd of youths, students, girls, widows, old maids and children, and very unrestful."

Among these guests a round dozen took notes of their host's conversations — and thus arose the famous table-talk. The first to conceive this idea was Conrad Cordatus, a grizzled Austrian convert, who, notwithstanding some qualms of conscience and a rebuke from Melanchthon, began in the summer of 1531 to make entries of his chief's best sayings at table. Veit Dietrich, the amanuensis of the Reformer, hastened to follow his example. A third reporter was Antony Lauterbach, the most diligent of all, whose notes, taken on two visits, the first from September, 1531, to February, 1533, the second from October, 1536, to July, 1539, fill several small volumes. Lewis Rabe, the councillor of Albert of Mayence, who fled to Wittenberg after the execution of Schenitz, also took some notes during a former visit of 1532.

Another reporter was John Schlaginhaufen, a student who matriculated in 1529. His table-talk, from November, 1531, to September, 1532, shows that he was an inmate of the Black Cloister during that time. His assiduity in taking notes is illustrated by an amusing incident told by himself: —

After the doctor had gone to his room for the night, a messenger came with a note from the widow of a pastor of Belgern with a request for a husband. Luther said to the messenger : "She is of age and must look out for herself ; I cannot help her." When the messenger had gone, he laughed and said to me: "For Heaven's sake, Schlaginhaufen, write that down too. Is n't it a nuisance ? They must think I am a matrimonial agent. Fie on you, old world ! Friend, write it down and mark it."

A sixth note-taker was little Hans's tutor, Jerome Weller. He was the guest of the Reformer for many years, and so was his brother Peter, who owned a dog of which the doctor once said : —

If I were as devoted to prayer as Peter's dog is to food I could get anything from God. For the beast thinks of nothing the livelong day but licking the platter.

It was a great occasion when Jerome crowned his years of study by taking the doctorate in the fall of 1535. Luther gave a banquet to celebrate, sending far and wide for provisions. Of this feast Luther wrote to Justus Jonas on September 4, 1535 : —

Now our head cook, Lady Katie, begs you to take this thaler and buy us all sorts of birds and fowls of the air, and whatever else is subject to man's dominion and lawful to eat in the aerial kingdom of feathers — but not crows. As to sparrows, God loves them so that we would like to eat them all up. If you spend more than this thaler — I 'll give it to you. Moreover if you can buy or catch — which would cost you nothing — any hares, or such tidbits, send 'em on, for we are minded to satisfy your stomachs for once, especially if it can be done with malt liquor, as they call it. My Lord Katie has brewed seven kegs in which she put thirty-two bushels of malt, hoping to gratify my palate. She trusts that the beer will be good, but you and the rest will find that out by testing it. . . . We shall certainly live merrily if you come to us with all those winged creatures whom we shall force to give up their free kingdom of the air and go into a prison pot under the watch and ward of a practised cook. My Lord Katie greets you with respectful friendship, but the worse for you, for vice versa, if my wife salutes you, I salute yours, tit for tat. . . .

The game arrived and the feast went off well. The next year Weller married and set up housekeeping for himself. He wanted Luther to give him a wedding banquet, too, but the Reformer demurred, remembering the crowd and the bad markets of the year before.

As the older reporters of the table-talk left the hospitable house their places were taken by others not less zealous. At the head of the younger circle, both in point of time and of importance, was John Mathesius, a man who attained some little fame in his day. His notes fall within 1540. With him were George Plato, Caspar Heydenreich, Jerome Besold, and lastly John Aurifaber, whose intimacy with Luther began in the last years of the latter's life. Aurifaber was the first editor of the Reformer's letters and table-talk.

Such was the company of disciples who during the last fifteen years of their master's life frequented his hospitable home. It is easy to imagine what the evening meal must have been like in the darkly wainscotted dining-room. If it is winter, a large German tile stove diffuses a pleasant warmth. At the head of the long table the large form and strong face of the host is conspicuous. Near him may be seen the gray hair and irascible countenance of Cordatus; the Englishman opposite is Dr. Robert Barnes, struggling with the difficulties of the Teutonic tongue, though, indeed, he hardly needs it here, as most of the conversation among the men is carried on in Latin. Further along the table are gentle Hausmann, Lauterbach, tall and blond, and mournful Schlaginhaufen, intent upon his sins. Dietrich's boyish face is filled with adoration divided between his master and his master's niece; hard by are the Weller brothers with their dog, or perhaps Mathesius, with other students and guests. At the far end of the table sits a capable, plain, motherly woman surrounded by a host of children. As the students bend over their note-books, hurrying to let no gem of wisdom escape them, she laughs and says: " Doctor, don't teach them for nothing; they all get a lot that way, but Lauterbach gets the most and the best," to which her husband replies, " I have taught and preached gratis for thirty years, why should I begin to sell anything in my decrepit old age ? "

These men, indeed, recorded everything they heard, good, bad, and indifferent. No experience too sacred for their curiosity, no word too trivial for their indiscriminate veneration. Luther at the death-bed of his daughter, and Luther in all the freedom of after-dinner expansiveness, telling the idlest and coarsest of stories, are revealed with equal frankness.

The conversations deal with every subject which could possibly have come within the range of Luther's experience. He discusses his whole system of doctrine and philosophy; he speaks of books, ancient and modern, of history, of his contemporaries, of politics, and of nature. He makes jokes and tells many a tale of the world, the devil, and the flesh. Compared with his human breadth and refreshing unreserve, how dry and

jejune is the table-talk of Melanchthon[1] or of Coleridge.[2] Only
in Boswell's life of Johnson have we the same vitality, frankness, and living interest.

The conversations are no less interesting and hardly less
valuable for being very inaccurate as historical sources. Luther's information about contemporary events is imperfect and
his judgment nearly always partisan. Even his own reminiscences, owing to the fallibility of human memory, are often
demonstrably inaccurate. But if the sayings cannot be used as
a register of facts and dates, or as a chronicle, they have an
enormous value for the picture they give of the opinions, the
reading, the daily life and personal attitude of the Reformer.
However much the table-talk may distort history, it surely never
belies psychology.

It is for this reason that it has enjoyed such enormous popularity. The reprints in German are legion, and translations
have been made into several other languages. The first English
version was made in 1652 by Henry Bell, a second by Hazlitt,
son of the well-known essayist, in 1848, and both have been
often reprinted. Carlyle thinks the table-talk " the most interesting now of all the books proceeding from Luther, with many
beautiful unconscious displays of the man, and what a nature he
had." Coleridge devoted much time and thought to them, —
perhaps a little too much for some tastes, for he read into them
his own metaphysics and read out of them their own charm.
Michelet, who stopped his own great work on the history of
France to write a biography of Luther, has them in mind when
he says, in his wonderful way : —

And among these joys Luther had those of the heart, of the man,
the innocent happiness of the family and home. What family more
holy, what home more pure ? . . . Holy hospitable table, where I myself, for a long time a guest, have found so many divine fruits on
which my heart yet lives. . . . Yes, the happy years I spent reading

[1] Partly preserved in Lösche, *Analecta Lutherana et Melanthonia* (Gotha, 1892).
Its interest is indicated by the history of a dinner at Melanchthon's table, during
which most of the time was occupied in hearing the children read Greek and
Latin authors and recite parts of Scripture and of the Catechism.

[2] Coleridge's table-talk is not really table-talk at all, but sundry aphoristic
observations written down by himself at his study-desk.

Luther have left me a strength, a vigor (sève), which I hope God will preserve to me until death.

Luther's relations with his servants were usually pleasant. Katie was a little parsimonious in her dealings with them, and Martin often had to plead hard with her to give a departing domestic a tip, as in the case of John Rischmann, a faithful youth. The names of several of the servants are known to us and thus enjoy the immortality so cheerfully promised by Napoleon to his secretary. The oldest and most devoted was Wolfgang Sieberger, who started as a student of theology, but was unable to keep up with the classes, and even before the Reformer's marriage became the janitor of the Black Cloister, a position which he kept throughout his master's life. Luther bought him a little plot of ground next the monastery, which had belonged to the ex-prior Brisger. Here Wolf tried the profession of fowler, but his unsuccessful efforts only provoked the mirth of the Reformer, who to tease him wrote the following letter purporting to come from the birds. With the charming humor of the composition is mingled that love of nature and wild things which always found expression when not crowded out by more urgent matters : —

TO WOLFGANG SIEBERGER AT WITTENBERG

(Wittenberg, Autumn, 1534.)

Complaint of the Birds to Luther against Wolfgang.

We, thrushes, blackbirds, finches, linnets, goldfinches, and all other pious, honorable birds, who migrate this autumn over Wittenberg, give your kindness to know, that we are credibly informed that one Wolfgang Sieberger, your servant, has conceived a great wicked plot against us, and has bought some old, rotten nets very dear, to make a fowling-net out of anger and hatred to us. He undertakes to rob us of the freedom God has given us to fly through the air, and he puts our lives in danger, a thing we have not deserved of him. All this, as you yourself can imagine, is a great trouble and danger to us poor birds, who have neither houses nor barns nor anything else, and so we humbly and kindly pray you to restrain your servant, or, if that cannot be, at least to cause him to strew corn on the fowling-net in the evening and not to get up in the morning before eight, so that we can continue our journey over Wittenberg. If he will not do this, but keeps on wickedly seeking our lives, we will pray God to plague him, and instead of us to send frogs, locusts, and snails into the fowling-net by day and at night to give him mice, fleas, lice, and bugs, so that he will forget us and leave us free. Why does he not use his wrath and industry against sparrows, swallows, magpies, crows, ravens, mice, and rats? They do you much harm, rob and steal corn, oats, and barley even out of the houses, whereas we only eat crumbs and a stray grain or two of wheat. We leave our case to right reason whether he has not done us wrong. We hope to God, that as many of our brothers and friends escaped from him, we too, who saw his dirty old nets yesterday, may also escape from them.

Written in our lofty home in the trees with our usual quill and seal.

Behold the fowls of the air: for they sow not, neither do they reap nor gather into barns; yet your heavenly Father feedeth them. Are ye not much better than they? Matthew vi, 26.

Luther was not always so fortunate in his servants as in the faithful Sieberger. His hospitality was so unbounded that no wonder it was sometimes abused. The worst experience he ever had, though not the only one, is fully related by himself, with a terrible passion of hatred only to be explained by the nervous irritability brought on by his torturing illnesses: —

TO JOHN GORITZ AT LEIPSIC

(WITTENBERG,) January 29, 1544.

Grace and peace. Dear Judge and good friend! I am informed that you have at Leipsic, as a guest, one who calls herself Rosina von Truchses, such a shameful liar as I have never seen the equal of. For she first came to me with that name, giving herself out to be a poor nun of noble family, but on inquiry I found she had deceived me. When I asked her about it and inquired who she really was, she confessed that she was the daughter of a citizen of Minderstadt, in Franconia, who had been killed in the Peasants' Revolt; she said she had been forced to wander around and was a poor child and begged me to forgive her for God's sake and to pity her. I told her henceforth not to tell such lies and not to take the name of Truchses. But while I took her obedience for granted and thought she did as I bade, she played the harlot behind my back and foully deceived every one with the name Truchses. I found this out after she had left, and can only think she was sent me by the papists as an archwhore, desperate character, and sack of lies, who did all sorts of harm to my cellar, kitchen, and rooms, and yet no one can be held accountable for it. Who knows what else she planned to do, for I took her into my own house with my own children. She had lovers and became pregnant and asked one of my maids to jump on her body and kill the unborn child. She escaped through the compassion of my Katie; otherwise she would have deceived no more men unless the Elbe ran dry. Wherefore pray keep an eye on this Truchses, and make it your duty to inquire where she is, that this cursed harlot, this lying, thievish wretch be not tolerated among you. Protect the Evangelic cause, oblige me, and beware of her devilish frauds, thefts, and impostures. I fear that if a strict inquiry should be made, she would be found to deserve death more than once, as so many witnesses have appeared against her since she left. I have written to show you what I know about this case, so that my conscience may not be burdened by having kept silence instead of having warned you against this damned, lying, thievish harlot. Now do what you like; I am excused. God bless you. Amen.

Before we leave the Black Cloister one humble inmate must not be forgotten, the little dog named Tölpel, or Clownie: —

One of Luther's children had a dog. The doctor said: "We see now the meaning of the text, 'Ye shall rule over the beasts of the field,' for the dog bears everything from the child."

Asked about the restoration of all things and whether there would be dogs and other animals in that kingdom, he said: "Certainly there will be, for Peter calls that day the time of the restitution of all things. Then, as is clearly said elsewhere, he will create a new heaven and a new earth. He will also create new Clownies with skin of gold and hair of pearls. There and then God will be all in all. No animal will eat any other. Snakes and toads and other beasts which are poisonous on account of original sin will then be not only innocuous but even pleasing and nice to play with. Why is it that we cannot believe that all things will happen as the Bible says, even in this article of the resurrection? Original sin is at fault."

CHAPTER XXXIII

DOMESTIC ECONOMY

WITTENBERG lies along the inner curve of the winding, eddying Elbe, in the midst of a sandy plain neither fertile nor beautiful. Frequent floods and poor drainage made the town unwholesome. Prior to the close of the fifteenth century it was a mere hamlet, with about three hundred and fifty low, ugly, wooden houses and few public buildings. As previously stated, Frederic the Wise, anxious to build up a capital equal to Leipsic, adorned the town with a new church and a university. The rise of the Evangelic teaching made Wittenberg one of the capitals of Europe, and its growth and improvement kept pace with its more exalted position.

One of the handsomest buildings was the Black Cloister, a large red-brick edifice situated at the extreme southeast of the town, near the Elster Gate and about ten minutes' walk from the river. It was on the main thoroughfare, named College Street, from which it was separated by a court, or lawn, on which has since been built the Augusteum, a theological seminary. This court was surrounded by a brick wall, and contained some trees, including a large pear tree. The house is a long quadrangle, with three stories and an attic; in the middle of the front is a tower with a spiral staircase which was the principal approach to the living-rooms situated one flight up. The ground floor contained the kitchen and some storerooms. Climbing the stairs one comes to a large ante-room, a living-room, a chamber now shown as Luther's bedroom, and a corner room, which at that time had a spiral staircase to the kitchen, all looking north over the court. On the south side, facing a small garden, also enclosed with a high wall, are three large rooms then used as lecture-halls — for Luther held his classes here instead of in the university buildings hard by. The rest of the house was used for the numerous guests and dependents of the hospitable professor.

Luther was greatly annoyed for many years by the fortifications built by the electors after 1526. The public works came so near his property that he was obliged to make alterations. In 1532 he complained of them, and nine years later[1] he wrote on this subject one of his rudest letters to the inspector of the fortifications, Frederic von der Grüne: —

I *command* you, for I will not *beg* one who is my enemy and God's and perhaps the secret enemy of the Elector also, that upon receipt of this warning to remove the said operations, for, mind you, I won't stand them. Likewise you must mend the door of the brewery. . . . I say nothing of those great lords the ditch-diggers, whom you have set over me to drive me from my windows and act as they please. . . . God bless you and convert you and make you different! If you don't turn about you will soon be in the abyss of hell. This I do not wish; if I did, I would tell you so frankly. . . . There have been much greater tyrants and devils than you and the bailiff, but they have all gone and had to leave the sun in the sky.

Besides the changes necessitated by the public works, Luther undertook extensive alterations to adapt the building to his convenience. He took down the tower-like passage between the main building and an outhouse, and removed his study, formerly situated here, to one of the south rooms overlooking the garden in the second story. In July, 1532, a cellar he was building fell in and would have crushed him had it not been for the interposition of an angel, as the student who records the incident says. Of his other alterations in the rooms, including the equipment of a bathroom, most of what is known comes from his household account. From this document we also learn that a building (the so-called new house) was erected directly back of the Black Cloister, though what it was used for is unknown to me.

While such extensive alterations were being made, the living-rooms gradually assumed a pretty and even rich appearance.

[1] If the date of a letter from him to Grüne, published in Burckhardt: *Luther's Briefwechsel*, p. 403, is right. The editor places it in this year because the Weimar archives show that Grüne was then at Wittenberg; Köstlin supposed the saying to come from the same time as a saying in the table-talk which can be dated 1532, a mistake allowed to stand in the last edition. Cf. Köstlin-Kawerau, i, 690, note to p. 491.

LUTHER'S HOUSE AT WITTENBERG, THE BLACK CLOISTER

The wainscotting, not so dark then as now, was handsome, and the solid furniture in perfect harmony with it.[1] Gold, silver and crystal goblets[2] presented by nobles and cities, adorned the rooms, and the walls were covered with pictures. Among these were probably Cranach's portraits of Martin and Katie painted at the time of their wedding, and possibly one or two others by this well-known artist. Others were by the inferior artists of his school, many of them representing allegorical subjects, as for example, one large painting illustrating the Ten Commandments, and another of the vineyard of the Lord, with Luther clearing away the thorns and Melanchthon following after to water the seed. On one picture of the Virgin, Luther sweetly commented: —

The child Jesus sleeps on Mary's arm; should he wake he would ask us what we had done and how we had lived.

His fondness for sententious precepts led him to decorate his walls with them — a taste not unknown at the present day. In July, 1543, he wrote with his own hand above the handsome tile stove in the living-room these very characteristic words :—

Whoso is faithful in little things will also be faithful in great things, and who is unfaithful in little things will be unrighteous in great things. The reason is : Dogs learn to eat by lapping.
Who is diligent in little will be diligent in much.
Who esteems not a penny will never have a gulden.
Who wastes an hour will waste a day.
Who despises the small will never get the large.
Who despises the gizzard will not get the hen. . . .
Who will not learn his letters will never learn anything.
Who cannot live on a hundred gulden cannot live on a thousand.

It is probable that flowers often added to the beauty of the living-rooms. Luther was very fond of them and had carried a bouquet in his hand at the Leipsic debate. One day in the spring of 1533 some violets were brought to him. His thoughts on

[1] The furniture now in the Luther house is said to be the original ; this is highly improbable, but at any rate it may be assumed to be like the original, as it is very old.

[2] Two of these in rock crystal chased with gold are to be seen in the Grüne Gewölbe at Dresden.

them, if not too deep for tears, are abundantly worth transcription : —

What do we give God for these little flowers? Reviling, evil, and shame. This first summer flower is as blue as the sky. Neither the Grand Turk nor the Emperor could pay for them in all the world.

There were at least two clocks, instruments which interested the Reformer almost as much as they did his contemporary, the Emperor. Indeed he observed : —

How wonderful is the invention of the clock! If it could only speak it would be simply human!

These things had to be ordered from other cities. Link sent Luther several manufactured articles from industrial Nuremberg, and with them a satire on the papacy by Hans Sachs, the celebrated dramatist. On May 19, 1527, Luther writes him : —

I have received the planes and the quadrant with the cylinder and the wooden clock, for which I thank you. You only forgot one thing, to tell me how much money I ought to send you, for I do not suppose what I sent you before was enough. I shall not order any more instruments at present, unless you have a new kind of lathe which will turn itself while Sieberger snores and neglects it. I am a past-master of clock-work myself, especially when I have to point out the lateness of the hour to my drunken Saxons, who look more at the tankards than at the clock, and do not mind in the least the course of the sun or of the clock or of its owner.

Previous to his marriage, Luther had a salary of one hundred gulden. He also had regular presents of clothes from the Elector, and of course his lodging in the monastery cost him nothing. After 1525 his salary was doubled, but as the endowment of the monastery was dissipated, he was obliged to buy his own provisions. That he found it difficult to do so may be inferred from a letter to Brisger, of February 1, 1527, mentioning that he has contracted a debt of one hundred gulden for which he has given cups as a pledge. Nevertheless on August 17, 1529, he wrote the Elector asking him not to send any more clothes : " For," said he, " I already have more from your Grace than I can reconcile with my conscience; it does not become me as a minister to have superfluity, nor do I wish it."

His salary was raised again in 1532 to three hundred gulden, and in 1536 the equivalent of another hundred was added by regular donations of wood, grain, and hay. Luther sometimes feared that these payments were tampered with by the nobles, and wrote an earnest protest to Spalatin, on July 13, 1542: —

Although I care but little for the meats and dainties of this life, as Paul advises, yet am I married, and therefore, as the same Paul says, a debtor to my family, for whoso neglects to care for those of his house is worse than an infidel. Wherefore I beg of you to see to it that I be not cheated of the Elector's gifts.

About 1541 Luther's income was further increased by a pension from the Elector, to him and his heirs, of fifty gulden per annum on a capital of one thousand gulden. In the last year of his life a pension on the same terms was granted him by the King of Denmark. Again he made a good deal from gifts, sometimes in money, oftener in plate and other valuables. He mentions a legacy of a hundred gulden left him about 1520, and Henry VIII gave him fifty gulden in 1535.

Luther might greatly have increased his income from two sources by which he preferred not to profit. Professors were expected to receive something from each student (the honorarium still collected in German universities) in addition to their salary. But like Socrates the Reformer wished to make his teaching free. Again, the printers offered him four hundred gulden per annum for his manuscripts, but desiring to have his works as cheap as possible, he refused to take it, though as a matter of fact the benefit accrued to the publishers rather than to the public.

Money, of course, is worth just what it will buy, and for that reason a comparison of its value in different ages is of all things the most difficult. If the comparison is confined to those articles which are common to the sixteenth and twentieth centuries it will be found that a gulden (intrinsically worth fifty cents or two shillings) would then buy twenty times as much of them as it will now. Luther's salary of two hundred dollars, for example, must be multiplied by twenty or more to get the equivalent of the stipend of the leading professors in the larger American universities. Cows were reckoned at an average of three gulden apiece. Real estate is somewhat hard to compare, as it differs in each individual case. The Black Cloister, with its adjoining land and outhouses, fetched 3700 gulden in 1564. Shoes sold at thirty-six cents a pair. Wheat varied from three groschen to one gulden a Scheffel, or in our money from seven tenths of a cent to fourteen cents a bushel. The higher price was during a famine, and was so abnormal that Luther protested against it in a letter to John Frederic, April 9, 1539. The lower limit, though only reached when living " was so cheap as never before," was probably nearer the average.

On the other hand, it may plausibly be argued that a gulden now is worth more than a gulden then. Such cheap luxuries as coffee, tea, chocolate, and tobacco were unobtainable by Luther. Books are rather cheaper now, and of course newspapers and photographs were then unknown. Travel was cheaper then, but it is infinitely safer, quicker, and more comfortable now. With all his passion for music the professor could never hear an opera. His secretaries could have no typewriters, his house no electricity or gas, and his wife no sewing-machine.

Luther's expenses were heavy, owing to the generosity with which he helped his friends and the almost reckless hospitality with which he entertained poor students, clergymen, and relatives. That in spite of these drains he should have managed to accumulate a considerable property must be largely attributed to the business ability of Katie. She brewed beer in the cloister, raised vegetables, kept swine, cattle, and fowls, and as time went on farmed a good deal of land. His savings were all invested in real estate, though there were other forms of placing money. He once declined a present of two shares in a mine offered him by the Elector, saying : —

Satan deludes many in mines, making them think they see great store of copper and silver where there is none. If he can bewitch men in full daylight above ground, he can do so much more in a subterranean mine. . . . I know I would have no luck in mining, because Satan would not favor me with the free gift of God, and I am satisfied as it is.

The Black Cloister was legally deeded to Luther on February 4, 1532. About the same time he bought a small garden adjacent, moved by the prayers and tears of Katie. Some time in the thirties he bought for nine hundred gulden the large house and property of Claus Bildenhauer, on the swine market, a little north of the Cloister, near the present post-office. The " lazy brook " which flowed through it is still to be seen. Katie made a fishpond of it, in which, as her husband said, she took more pleasure than many a noble in his large preserves. About 1534 Luther bought a very small garden for his servant Wolfgang Sieberger. In 1541 he purchased for four hundred and thirty gulden another cottage and land adjoining the Black Cloister which had once belonged to Brisger, who had previously sold it to Bruno. In 1544 he bought a hop-garden for three hundred and seventy-five gulden.

All these purchases had been in Wittenberg. About 1540 he bought from Katie's brother Hans von Bora, the little farm of Zulsdorf, some twenty miles south of Leipsic on the road to Altenburg. This was Katie's favorite property; she spent much time there cultivating the land, which was richer than that around Wittenberg. The price was 610 gulden, of which the Elector gave six hundred.

Besides the property that Katie bought, she also rented a large bit of meadow land, the Boos Farm, from the Elector. She had a good deal of trouble getting it, on account of the dislike of the Chancellor Brück for her husband, but her persistence was at length successful. One of the few letters in her hand now extant was written on April 28, 1539, to the receiver-general of taxes, John von Taubenheim, begging him to let her have the property for her growing herd of cows.

Luther naturally thought at times of what he should leave his wife and children. In 1540 he said : —

I approve Philip Melanchthon's prudence in making a will, but I do not know how to do it myself.

My books are at hand. I leave them to my children. Let them see to it that they be wiser than their father. Katie, I make you heir of my estate ; you have borne my children and given them suck ; you will not mismanage their property. I am averse to guardians, they rarely do well.

Early in 1542, however, Luther made a testamentary disposition of part of his property. His will is a remarkable document in two ways; first, because it does not mention all the property, but only that settled on Katie as a widow's portion. The Black Cloister, having been conferred on Luther and his wife jointly, needed not to be specified. But besides this there were other pieces of property, the most important of them being Bildenhauer's house, passed over in silence. Secondly, it is noteworthy that Luther's profound dislike of lawyers led him to act without the help of a notary. As this was requisite, according to the law of the time, his will was broken.

LUTHER'S (SECOND) WILL

WITTENBERG, January 6, 1542.

I, Martin Luther, recognize with my own hand, that I have given to my dear and faithful wife Katie, as her portion, or whatever it may be called, for her life, and to use at her pleasure and to her profit, and that I give her by this letter now and to-day, the following : —

The property of Zulsdorf, as I bought it with the improvements, and all things as I have had it hitherto.

Item, Bruno's house, which I bought in the name of my servant Wolfgang Sieberger for him to dwell in.

Item, cups, jewels, rings, chains and gift-coins, which should be worth about a thousand gulden.

I do this,

First, because she has always been dear, worthy, and fair, as my pious, true wedded wife, and has, by God's blessing, borne and brought up five children yet living (may God grant them long life).

Secondly, that she may meet the debt with which I am encumbered unless I do it during my lifetime, and pay it; as far as known it amounts to about four hundred and fifty gulden, but may well be more.

Thirdly and chiefly, because I want her not to look to the children but the children to her, to hold her in honor and submit to her as God has commanded. . . . Moreover I think a mother is the best guardian for her children, who will not use her property and portion to their injury and disadvantage, as they are her flesh and blood and she has carried them under her heart. . . .

Finally, I beg every one, that as in this bequest I do not use legal forms and words (for which I have good cause) they will recognize me to be what I am in truth, and am publicly known to be in heaven, on earth, and in hell, namely, one who has sufficient power and authority, and who may be trusted and believed more than a notary. . . .

M. L.

Witnessed by Melanchthon, Cruciger and Bugenhagen.

There is extant in Luther's hand a household account, completed about the time he made his will, as an inventory of his property, debts, income, and expenses. It contains many a curious item both about his domestic economy and about the conditions of family life in his day. Much of the information set forth in the present chapter is drawn from it. Were it not so long and so technical it would be well worth while translating in full, but those who are curious about these matters must refer to the original.[1]

Luther estimated his personal property at a thousand gulden. At about the time he made his will a tax for the Turkish war was levied. The real estate was assessed at nine thousand gulden. This was perhaps too high; the Black Cloister, for example, with its adjoining property, was valued at six thousand gulden, though when sold in 1564 to the university it fetched only thirty-seven hundred.

The letter in which Luther informs the wife of Justus Jonas, now in Halle, of the property on which he is taxed, is also interesting for the evidence it gives of the relative value of money and wheat : —

TO CATHARINE JONAS IN HALLE

(WITTENBERG,) March 26, 1542.

Grace and peace. Kind, dear Friend! I humbly beg you to admonish your husband not to write so many promissory letters, for I don't like them and will excuse his promises for the future. His letters only say: "I will write soon, I will write more, I will write something wonderful"; if he can write nothing but that, or what I know already, let him omit it.

Everything is going well here except that the treasury and taxation

---

[1] De Wette-Seidemann: *Luthers Briefe*, vi, 323 ff.

has run wild. Otherwise, living is so cheap as never before, a sack of corn for three groats. God bless you and yours. My Katie, now lord of Zulsdorf, greets you kindly. She lets herself be rated at nine thousand gulden, including the Black Cloister, although she will not have an annual income of one hundred gulden from the property after my death. But my gracious lord has kindly given more than I asked. God bless you. Amen.

DR. MARTIN LUTHER.

CHAPTER XXXIV

THE BIGAMY OF PHILIP OF HESSE. 1540

NOTWITHSTANDING the signal success of Luther's work, his last years were far from happy. He died an embittered, almost a disappointed man. The main cause of his increasing irritability and sadness is undoubtedly to be found in his torturing diseases, which, after their manner, became worse and worse. He was also grieved by the death of friends and of his daughter. Neither did public matters suit him. In the unstable political condition he foresaw, vaguely but uneasily, the storm about to burst, as it did just after his death, sweeping back, for a moment at least, the dykes and barriers of the Evangelic faith. Fierce quarrels within his Church, like that with the Antinomians, and that between Cordatus and Melanchthon, at times almost made him doubt. Finally, in 1540, a terrible scandal crippled the infant Church and made it a reproach to its enemies.

This was the bigamy of Philip the Magnanimous, Landgrave of Hesse, for many years the foremost political champion of Protestantism. Before he was quite nineteen he had married Christina, daughter of Duke George of Albertine Saxony, but, a debauchee, like most of the princes and many of the prelates of the age, he lived in flagrant immorality, confessing that he had broken his marriage-vow within three weeks after the wedding. Though his conversion to the Evangelic faith did not alter his mode of living, his religion was sufficiently real to make his sins a burden to conscience. Desiring to reconcile his pleasures with his duty, he was attracted by the preaching of the Zwickau prophets and other fanatics, who taught that polygamy was lawful, and in 1526 wrote Luther for advice. Receiving the answer that a Christian might have but one wife, he continued living as before, but refrained from going to the sacrament save once when he was ill.

In 1539 he contracted that terrible disease (the syphilis) then first epidemic in Europe. While convalescing at the house of his sister, he was attracted by seventeen-year-old Margaret von der Saal, and determined, Luther or no Luther, to make her his wife. According to the custom of the age, he treated with her mother, who insisted that the marriage, if not publicly recognized, as she preferred, be at least sanctioned by some of the leading lights in the Church. Philip easily obtained satisfactory advice from the obsequious divines of his own court, and, with more difficulty, the assent of Martin Bucer, with whom he had, for many years, been in correspondence. This not being sufficient to satisfy Frau von der Saal, he induced Bucer to go to Wittenberg to obtain the assent of Luther and Melanchthon, and also to secure a guarantee of support from the Elector John Frederic in case of need, for the Emperor had made bigamy a capital crime, and political complications might well follow. So determined, however, was the Landgrave to take Margaret at any cost that before he heard from Saxony he secured the written consent of his first wife — December 17 — and made preparations for the wedding.

Bucer arrived in Wittenberg early on December 9 with a missive from the Landgrave, who urged that his wife was disagreeable to him (though she had borne him many children), that his temperament was uncontrollable, and failing lawful satisfaction, he must continue to live in sin. He said he wished but one wife more; if the theologians would grant this trifle, he would not trouble them again. He cited precedents from early Christian history, as well as Luther's own advice to Henry VIII, that it would be better for him to take a second wife than to divorce a first. Finally, he intimated that if the Protestants did not give him what he wanted, he would turn to the Emperor and Pope.

The reformers allowed themselves to be convinced, and that very soon. The day after Bucer's arrival Melanchthon drew up a dispensation which was signed by himself and Luther (later by several other divines). This extraordinary document begins by thanking God for having relieved Philip of his recent illness; it then states the general law that in the beginning God

PHILIP OF HESSE

After the portrait by M. Müller, at Cassel. The signature reads: Philips der Grossmutige

ordained monogamy and that Christ confirmed this rule, but that there may be some exceptions. The theologians decline Philip's invitation to publish something on the subject, for fear that they will be reproached with making polygamy a general rule, like the Anabaptists, and they exhort him to continence and patience, but finally state that if he finds this impossible, they will allow him privately to take another wife, considering that bigamy is better than adultery.

Though unable to get the support of the Elector, Bucer returned with this dispensation to Hesse, and the Landgrave, with it, and especially by the promise of a public wedding, finally secured the consent of Frau von der Saal. The marriage took place on March 4, 1540, in the presence of Melanchthon, Bucer, and other " honorable men."

The honeymoon was a happy time for Philip, who again felt able to take the sacrament. On April 5 he wrote Luther, whom he addressed as "brother-in-law" on account of the distant relationship between Margaret and Katie, thanking him for the dispensation, offering continued support to the Evangelic cause, and promising to keep the marriage secret and not act in any matter without asking his advice. Luther returned the following answer: [1] —

TO PHILIP, LANDGRAVE OF HESSE, AT SCHMALKALDEN

(WITTENBERG,) April 10, 1540.

Grace and peace. Most serene, noble Prince, gracious Lord! I have received your Grace's letter and note that you are pleased with our counsel, which we would willingly have kept secret. Melanchthon has written me nothing about your Grace, but will certainly do so, or tell me about it orally. But we want to keep the business a secret for the sake of the example, which every one would follow, even at last the coarse peasants. There are also other reasons as great or even greater why you should keep it to yourself and not avow it which would make us a lot of trouble. Wherefore your Grace will please be secret and improve your life as you promised. Our dear Lord be with your Grace. Amen.

Your Grace's obedient servant,

MARTIN LUTHER.

[1] Lenz: *Briefwechsel des Landgraf Philipps mit Bucer* (1880), i, 362.

That Philip's act soon after this became generally known was largely his own fault. Notwithstanding his promise to keep the matter secret, he had celebrated an almost public wedding at the instance of Frau von der Saal, and after that he took less pains than his letters would lead one to suppose to conceal the "said person," as he called Margaret. A rumor of the bigamy reached Antony Lauterbach in May, and when he wrote Luther to inquire the truth of the matter he received the following answer : —

TO ANTONY LAUTERBACH AT PIRNA

(Wittenberg,) June 2, 1540.

Grace and peace. In answer to your question about the Landgrave's second marriage, dear Antony, I can say nothing. I have only heard that the girl Von der Saal has given birth to a boy,[1] but I know not whether it was true. If it is true and he recognizes that he is the father and supports the mother and child, it seems that he will do right. Perhaps this is the cause of the rumor. I only know that no public proofs of the marriage have been shown me. There are heirs from the legitimate wife who will not permit — nor will the princes — that the children of another wife should become co-heirs, especially if the second wife be of inferior rank. Therefore let those rail who wish to do so until time show what the monster really is. One must not pronounce rashly on insufficient evidence about the doings of princes. I will instruct your assistant about the other things.

MARTIN LUTHER.

The public proofs of the marriage came shortly after this in a peculiarly forcible way. The Duchess of Rochlitz, Philip's sister, was beside herself when she heard of her brother's act, and wrote an account of it to both the Saxon courts, to Henry the Pious, Christina's uncle, and to John Frederic, whom she accused of abetting the Landgrave. The Elector forwarded the correspondence to Luther with a request for an explanation. The long answer of the Reformer is one of the most interesting letters he ever wrote. It shows that he had nothing to take back. It also shows that he was extremely angry with Philip for two

---

[1] The rumor was false ; Margaret's first child was born March 12, 1541. She had a number of children.

reasons; first, because the marriage had been so open, and secondly, because Philip had concealed from him that at the time he asked permission to marry Margaret he was living with a mistress, "her of Eschwege," and was therefore no longer free to choose.

TO JOHN FREDERIC, ELECTOR OF SAXONY [1]

(WITTENBERG, June 10, 1540.)

Most serene, highborn Elector, most gracious Lord! I am sorry to learn that your Grace is importuned by the court of Dresden about the Landgrave's business. Your Grace asks what answer to give the men of Meissen.[2] As the affair was one of the confessional, both Melanchthon and I were unwilling to communicate it even to your Grace, for it is right to keep confessional matters secret, both the sin confessed and the counsel given, and had the Landgrave not revealed the matter and the confessional counsel, there would never need have been all this nauseating unpleasantness.

I still say that if the matter was brought before me to-day, I should not be able to give counsel different from what I did. Setting apart the fact that I know I am not as wise as they think they are, I need conceal nothing, especially as it has already been made known. The state of affairs is as follows: Martin Bucer brought a letter and pointed out that, on account of certain faults in the Landgrave's wife the Landgrave was not able to keep himself chaste and that he had hitherto lived in a way which was not good, but that he would like to be at one with the principal heads of the Evangelic Church, and he declared solemnly before God and his conscience that he could not in future avoid such vices unless he were permitted to take another wife. We were deeply horrified at this tale and at the offence which must follow, and we begged his Grace not to do as he proposed, but we were told again that he could not abandon his project, and if he could not obtain what he wanted from us, he would disregard us and turn to the Emperor and Pope. To prevent this we humbly begged that if his Grace would not, or, as he averred before God and his conscience, could not, do otherwise, yet that he could keep it a secret. Though necessity compelled him, yet he could not defend his act before the

[1] Letter published, Seidemann: *Lauterbach's Tagebuch auf das Jahr 1538*, p. 196 ff. On dating see Rockwell, p. 137, note 3.

[2] Meissen was the county in which the capital of Albertine Saxony, Dresden, was situated.

world and the imperial laws; this he promised to do and we accordingly agreed to help him before God and cover it up as much as possible with such examples as that of Abraham. This all happened as though in the confessional, and no one can accuse us of having acted as we did willingly or voluntarily or with pleasure or joy. It was hard enough for our hearts, but we could not prevent it; we thought to give his conscience such counsel as we could.

I have indeed learned several confessional secrets, both while I was still a papist and later, which, if they were revealed, I should have to deny or else publish the whole confession. Such things belong not to the secular courts nor are they to be published. God has here his own judgment and must counsel souls in matters where no worldly law nor wisdom can help. My preceptor in the cloister, a fine old man, had many such affairs, and once had to say of them, with a sigh: "Alas, alas, such things are so perplexed and desperate that no wisdom, law, nor reason can avail; one must commend them to divine goodness." So instructed, I have accordingly in this case also acted agreeably to divine goodness.

But had I known that the Landgrave had long satisfied his desires, and could well satisfy them with others, as I have now just learned that he did with her of Eschwege, truly no angel would have induced me to give such counsel: I gave it only in consideration of his unavoidable necessity and weakness, and to put his conscience out of peril, as Bucer represented the case to me. Much less would I ever have advised that there should be a public marriage, to which (though he told me nothing of this) a young princess and young countess should come, which is truly not to be borne and is insufferable to the whole Empire. But I understood and hoped, as long as he had to go the common way with sin and shame and weakness of the flesh, that he would take some honorable maiden or other in secret marriage, even if the relation did not have a legal look before the world. My concession was on account of the great need of his conscience — such as has happened to other great lords. In like manner I advised certain priests in the Catholic lands of Duke George and the bishops secretly to marry their cooks.

This was my confessional counsel about which I would much rather have kept silence, but it has been wrung from me and I could do nothing but speak. But the men of Dresden speak as though I had taught the same for thirteen years, and yet they give us to understand what a friendly heart they have to us, and what great desire for love and unity, just as if there were no scandal nor sin in their lives which are ten times worse before God than anything I ever advised. But the world must always smugly rail at the moat in its neighbor's eye and forget the beam in its own eye. If I must defend all I have said or done in former years, especially at the beginning, I must beg the Pope to do the same, for if they defend their former acts (let alone their present ones) they would belong to the devil more than to God.

I am not ashamed of my counsel, even if it should be published in all the world, but for the sake of the unpleasantness which would then follow, I should prefer, if possible, to have it kept secret.

MARTIN LUTHER, with his own hand.

A few days after writing this letter, Luther excused the bigamy to his table companions on much the same grounds : —

We have suffered greater scandals than this, but the papists excuse all their lusts of Sodom by this bigamy. What can we do? If they had only followed my advice![1] As it is done, we cannot abandon the Church. The scandal will be blamed on me. I believe that he will get some one to defend his deed publicly! They cannot make a rule out of it; it is no precedent. We are under our own jurisdiction and follow our own laws as Paul commands. They can't blame us. Well, such scandals drive philosophers from public affairs and monks from the Church. We must not and cannot yield, let our enemies be as impudent as they like!

After the conference at Schmalkalden, Melanchthon fell ill of a disease something like malaria, then called "tertian fever." He attributed it to the shame he felt over the Hessian scandal; undoubtedly the worry tended to make him worse. On June 18 Luther received letters from Chancellor Brück telling him of this, and of the conference at Hagenau, and also from the Elector, ordering him to come to Weimar to talk over the situation.

When a letter from Chancellor Brück was brought, Luther read it and said : "Melanchthon is almost worn away with grief and is falling into a tertian fever. But why does the good man torment himself so with this matter? He cannot remedy it by worrying about it. I wish I were with him, for I know his frailty and the pain the scandal causes him. I have grown callous; I am a peasant and a devilish hard Saxon; I believe I am called to Melanchthon." Some one said : "Doctor, perhaps the conference will be interrupted." The doctor :

[1] To keep the marriage secret.

"They must wait for us." Then he added with a serene countenance: "It is fine to have something to do. This gives us food for thought, otherwise we should only swill and gorge. How the papists will cry out! But let them cry to their own confusion. For our cause is good and our lives are blameless, because they are earnest. If Philip of Hesse has sinned, it is not only a sin but a scandal.[1] We often give the best and holiest answers, but they will not see our innocence because they do not want to. Let them go to the devil! . . . Our sins are venial, but those of the papists unforgivable, for they despise God and crucify Christ and deny their own blasphemies against better knowledge. What do they expect? They slay men; we labor to have them born and thus marry several wives." This he said with a merry face and not without a great laugh. . . . Rising from the table with a happy visage, he said: "I won't pay the devil and the papists the compliment of bothering myself about them."

If Luther cared little for the results of the bigamy, Philip soon found himself in a most unpleasant position. The court of Dresden arrested his new mother-in-law on June 2, and thus obtained most of the documents in the case. Such pressure was brought to bear upon the Landgrave that he felt the need of more advice, and accordingly invited Luther to Weimar, where the Reformer arrived on June 28. There he cheered up Melanchthon, whom he found in a desperate state. He himself attributed his friend's recovery to prayer, as he writes his wife on July 2. The letter is interesting as showing how little the scandal apparently weighed upon his mind. Among other things he wrote: —

Dear maiden Katie, gracious lady of Zulsdorf, and whatever else you may be. I humbly beg your ladyship to know that I am well, eat like a Bohemian and drink like a German, thank God. Amen. It is because Melanchthon was dead and has risen again like Lazarus from the grave. God the dear Lord hears our prayers; *that* we see and know, although we never believe it. May no one say Amen to our shameful unbelief! . . .

God willing, next Sunday we shall go from Weimar to Eisenach with Melanchthon.

The journey to Eisenach was for the purpose of conferring with representatives of Hesse about the best way of managing

[1] Fouché: "It is not only a crime but a blunder."

the unfortunate affair. Philip was for publicly avowing his marriage, wishing above all things that it be not held for an illicit amour; this Luther strongly deprecated. On the first day of the Conference, July 15, he stated that a public acknowledgment of the bigamy would create a great scandal, and continued : [1] —

Is it not a good plan to say that the bigamy had been discussed and should not Philip say that he had indeed debated the matter, but had not yet come to a decision? All else must be kept quiet. What is it, if for the good and sake of the Christian Church, one should tell a good, strong lie? . . . And before he, Luther, would reveal the confession which Bucer had made him in the Landgrave's name, or let people talk so about a pious prince whom he always wished to serve, he would rather say that Luther had gone mad, and take the blame on himself.

Luther further declined to take any responsibility if the matter was published; in that case he saw himself absolved, for he had never advised that bigamy be made a general practice, and, therefore, he threatened to withdraw and disavow his permission completely. This enraged Philip, who wrote the professor that it was the most horrible thing he had heard for a long time, that such a brave man should threaten to recall the dispensation he had given to relieve a needy conscience. He added: "I will not lie, because lying is wrong and no apostle nor Christian ever taught it; yea, Christ forbade it strictly and commanded people to stand by their yea and nay." Luther answered the letter as follows: —

TO PHILIP, LANDGRAVE OF HESSE

(EISENACH,) July 24, 1540.

Grace and peace in Christ. Serene, highborn Prince, gracious Lord! I have received your Grace's letter, which seems to me to have been written in a rather angry mood, although I am not aware that I have deserved your Grace's ire. For it seems to me that your Grace thinks we act in this matter to please ourselves and not, as is really the case, to serve your Grace and prevent future trouble for you. Wherefore I give your Grace to understand my real reason for

---

[1] First protocol to the Eisenach conference, Lenz, *op. cit.*, 373.

advising and warning against the publication of this confessional counsel. Let your Grace not doubt that if all the devils wanted to publish this counsel, I could, by God's grace, give them such an answer that they would not get any satisfaction out of me by doing so.

For in case you publish it, I have this advantage over your Grace and all devils, too, that you must bear me witness, first, that it was a secret confessional counsel, and second, that I have always truly begged that it be not published, and thirdly, that it will never be published by me. As long as I have these three advantages I defy the devil himself to move my pen. By God's grace I know well how to distinguish between things that should be allowed to consciences privately by way of dispensation and those which should be publicly preached. I would be sorry to see your Grace get into a war of words over this matter, for you have enough else to do. . . .

If your Grace should publish this marriage, you could not get the world to recognize its legality if a hundred Luthers and Melanchthons defended it. . . .

And as to what you say about not wishing your second wife to pass for a whore, I do not see why your Grace should mind that, for she has had to pass for one hitherto, at least before the world, though we three persons and God know that she is a wedded concubine. . . .

I write these things to your Grace to show you that it is not for my own sake that I wish this matter concealed ; for if it came to a war of pens, I well know how to draw myself out of it and leave your Grace sticking in it; which, however, I would not do if I could avoid it. Nor do I think to abandon your Grace during the present crisis as long as my life lasts. . . .

Your Grace should think what an offence it would be were it published, and . . . also whether you could answer for it to the Emperor, for the Bible says : " All men are liars," and, " Put not your trust in princes." . . .

Wherefore I advise you to give an ambiguous answer by which you could remain. I commend you to God and assure you that I advise you to do exactly what I should advise my own soul.

Your Grace's obedient,

DR. MARTIN LUTHER.

Luther returned to Wittenberg early in August and straightway wrote Justus Menius, his host in Eisenach, thanking him for the delightful entertainment his wife had given them, and adding: " We taught your son to steal nuts to amuse ourselves. It was great fun to watch him; he was a comedy in himself."

In spite of the attempt to hush the matter up, inquiries kept coming in. Luther still insisted that denial was the best answer: —

TO PHILIP, LANDGRAVE OF HESSE [1]

(WITTENBERG,) September 17, 1540.

Grace and peace. Most serene, highborn Prince, gracious Lord! It pleases me right well that your Grace has given such a reserved answer to the unnecessary and dangerous questions of the Margrave [2] and Meissen, [3] for, as they wish to be so holy and so friendly, they should be before others in hushing up this hue and cry, as, thank God, every one else does. The Margrave has also tried to pump me, but I will answer him, as I have done others, though perhaps even more strongly, and I shall do it with good conscience, as Christ does when he says in the gospel, "The Son knoweth not the day," [4] or like a pious father confessor, who must say publicly in court that he knows nothing of what he has learned in secret confession; for what one knows only in a private capacity one cannot know publicly. So that even if such a thing were said openly, one should not believe it. And since your Grace does not desire to defend your conduct as a public example, but only to use the grace for your conscientious need, it seems good that, should they trouble your Grace again, your Grace should be a little tart with them. . . . I would be unwilling for the court of Dresden to get a full acknowledgment from your Grace, by which perhaps they might make things more unpleasant than they have yet done. It is better to leave them in uncertainty and let them stumble around for proof which they can never get, for a mere copy of a letter would not be proof and your Grace is not bound to give them the originals nor even to acknowledge such originals. God grant that they make no trouble with their copies and do not substitute other letters they have never had nor seen! Why don't the coarse, inconsiderate people keep quiet when they know we want them to? God bless you. Amen. I have written in haste and keep no copy. If I dare

[1] Lenz, *op. cit.*, p. 389.

[2] The Margrave of Brandenburg.

[3] Duke Henry of Saxony, whose capital was in the county of Meissen.

[4] Mark xiii, 32. Luther believed, as he explained more fully elsewhere, that as Christ was omniscient he must have known the day of the last judgment, but that he thought it right to avoid inconvenient questions by denying his knowledge.

ask it, your Grace will return this letter, for I act in this matter as confidentially with your Grace as with my own heart.

Luther's letters tell the truth but not the whole truth. Regrettable as is his connection with the bigamy, an impartial student can hardly doubt that he acted conscientiously, not out of desire to flatter a great prince, but in order to avoid what he believed to be a greater moral evil. His statement in the Babylonian Captivity that he preferred bigamy to divorce, and his advice to Henry VIII in 1531, both exculpate him in this case. Moreover the careful study of Rockwell has shown that his opinion was shared by the great majority of his contemporaries, Catholic and Protestant alike. It is perhaps harder to justify his advice to get out of the difficulty by a lie. This, however, was certainly an inheritance from the scholastic doctrine of the sacredness of confession. A priest was bound by Church law to deny all that passed in the confessional. Moreover, many of the Church Fathers had allowed a lie to be on occasions the lesser of two evils. Nevertheless, though these considerations palliate Luther's guilt, the incident will always remain, in popular imagination as well as in historic judgment, the greatest blot on his career.

The last pretence of secrecy was given up when a Hessian clergyman under the pseudonym of Neobulus defended the bigamy of his sovereign in a pamphlet of 1541. When Luther heard of it his anger was aroused to an uncommon degree. Still maintaining that all he had allowed was exceptional and never intended to sanction bigamy as a common practice, he was able to say : —

If any one shall follow the advice of that wretch, and take more than one wife, the devil will prepare him a bath in the abyss of hell.

This is not the place to go into the political effects of Philip's act. In return for personal immunity he made concessions to the Emperor which greatly weakened the League of Schmalkalden. In the pact he signed was included his son-in-law, Duke Maurice of Saxony, who had succeeded his father, Henry the Pious, in August, 1541. The young prince had hardly ascended the throne before he almost came to blows with his cousin John

Frederic over the bishopric of Würzen in which both had
rights. Philip was anxious to make peace between his allies,
and asked Luther's coöperation in this. The letter in which the
Reformer answers is doubly interesting for its opinion of Maurice
and of Neobulus.

TO PHILIP, LANDGRAVE OF HESSE [1]

(WITTENBERG,) April 10, 1542.

Grace and peace in Christ our Lord. Serene, highborn Prince,
gracious Lord. I am very glad to hear that your Grace has hopes of
making peace in this deplorable and dangerous quarrel. May God
grant more and sufficient grace, as we earnestly and confidently pray.
I had not expected that Duke Maurice would act so unthankfully and
unkindly towards the Elector, for all the world knows he would never
have been born, much less would have been so mighty a prince, had
it not been for the late Elector Frederic. He is working for God's
wrath, which will come upon him sooner than he thinks unless he
solemnly repents of the crime he has done for the sake of a dunghill,
though the misunderstanding could have been set right with one word.
May God guard the people, that if a campaign is undertaken against
the Turk, Duke Maurice may not go with them, lest not only the
Turk but thunder and lightning smite them, on account of this im-
penitent, stiff-necked bloodhound, cousin-killer, fratricide, friend-
killer, patricide, and son-killer. I will speak against him to a Lord
who will be able to cope with him and who sits securely on the right
hand of God.

As to the other matter on which your Grace writes, you know how
loyal I have always been to your Grace, and have borne enough hardship in it to spare you. But this vile book of Neobulus has made it all
in vain by stirring up with his silly prattle such noisome filth, an act
not only unserviceable but also very harmful. It seems to me that
every one has blamed and mocked your Grace. Otherwise I should
not mind it. I pray for your Grace and must do so, as the times are
very bad, so that it is necessary to pray for rulers. They act evilly
and fall into trouble when they should administer justice. God bless
you. Amen.

Your Grace's obedient,

MARTIN LUTHER.

[1] M. Lenz: *Nachlese zum Briefwechsel des Landgrafen Philip mit Luther und
Melanchthon.* In *Zeitschrift f. Kirchengeschichte,* iv (Gotha, 1881), 136 ff. The copy
in De Wette-Seidemann, vi, 312, is faulty.

Luther feared the scandal that the division of the Protestants would cause, as he said to Melanchthon: —

They will say at Rome that we are coming to blows and that we will root out our own doctrine. We must listen to such words, but God will do what is right. Only pray diligently without doubting and God will bring it to pass. I prayed Duke George to death ; we will laugh Carlowitz and Pistorius to death. God grant that these authors of the treachery end as Judas and Ahithophel did. . . . Duke Maurice is a young man with little intelligence ; he trusts his counsellors, but he will learn by experience, for no one will trust him in future.

War was, however, averted by the efforts of Hesse. Luther's estimate of Maurice as a man of little intelligence is hardly justified by his later career. This prince was to rob his cousin of the electoral vote and of half his land.

CHAPTER XXXV

CATHOLIC AND PROTESTANT. 1539-1546

THE treaty of Frankfort, signed in April, 1539, stipulated for a truce of fifteen months between Catholic and Protestant;[1] before the expiration of which time it was hoped that a German national assembly would meet and settle the religious differences. Political exigencies forced the Emperor to deal cautiously with his heretical subjects, and so he arranged for a series of conferences, at Hagenau, at Worms, and finally and most important, at Ratisbon in 1541.

Charles V and Luther were for so long opponents that it is interesting to inquire what each thought of the other. The monarch had first seen the " presumptuous monk " at Worms, and then felt nothing but horror for his stout defiance of the universal Church. According to Charles's most recent biographer[2] the sincerest and most outspoken utterance of the usually reticent Hapsburg was his declaration, written by himself immediately after hearing Luther, that on supporting the cause of the Church against this heretic he " staked all his dominions, his friends, his body and blood, his life and his soul." A few years later, thinking the heretic might be useful in curbing the Pope, he had said, that " some day or other, perhaps, Luther may become a man of worth,"[3] but this cautious utterance never for an instant indicated that he entertained the slightest leaning to the new faith or the least liking for its leader.

The Wittenberg professor, on his side, was long inclined to

---

[1] The truce was to run in all circumstances for six months, till November 1, 1539; but in case the Emperor agreed to the provision that the league of Catholic States should receive no addition during fifteen months it was to be valid during that time, *i. e.*, until August 1, 1540. In case it expired the old basis of the peace of Nuremberg (1532) was to be restored.

[2] Edward Armstrong: *The Emperor Charles V* (London, 1902), i, 70 f.

[3] *Ibid.*, p. 162.

a much more favorable opinion. In the first stages he had hoped much " from the noble young blood Charles," to whom he had written an appeal.[1] Long after the Emperor showed his disposition by persecuting the Protestants, Luther maintained his opinion with an almost naïve obstinacy. At the Diet of Augsburg in 1530, he had persisted in ascribing the hostilities of the Catholics to the counsellors of Charles, who was himself "like a sheep among wolves." [2] This reverence can only be explained by the magic of the Imperial name. Long after the fall of the Latin world-state, Rome was a word to conjure with; throughout the Middle Ages men were awed by the fortune of the Eternal City. To a poetical and pious mind like Luther's the Cæsar of Virgil and of the New Testament was hedged with a more than royal divinity. At last, however, facts were too strong for him, and in 1540 he expressed the following unfavorable, though for him very mild, opinions : —

Our adversaries are now convinced, and have nothing more on which to oppose us. Wherefore the Emperor simply alleges his faith as a pretext to confiscate bishoprics to his own profit. (For I am something of a prophet and understand the wiles of the devil.) He sees that whenever a prince falls away from the popish religion he seizes the bishoprics in his territory, as the Duke of Brunswick did Hildesheim. Wherefore he acts like a dog named Wimmar at Linz, who used to carry meat home from the butcher's. One day, when attacked by other dogs which wanted the meat, he at first defended it, and then, when he could do so no longer, began to eat it himself.

The Emperor is a melancholy man and more of a voluptuary than a hero. He does not understand our position, although he sometimes hears our books read. If he were a Scipio or an Alexander or a Pyrrhus he would burst the pontifical net and bind the Germans to himself. He begins much but carries little through. He took Tunis, now he has lost it ; he captured the French king and let him go, and the same with Rome. He does not persevere. He is remiss in business. Noble souls are not so. What shall I say ? Germany lacks a head. Melanchthon has called it a blinded Polyphemus. We are a gigantic mass but lack direction.

The Emperor's brother and successor Ferdinand was also a

---

[1] Letter of August 31, 1520, p. 99.
[2] Letter to Teutleben, June 19, 1530, p. 255.

THE EMPEROR CHARLES V

After the painting by Titian, engraved by Rubens; in the Bibliothèque Nationale at Paris

staunch Catholic. His saying that he had had inclinations toward Lutheranism but had been deterred from it by the scandal of Philip of Hesse's bigamy, does not indicate that his leanings were very strong. For him Luther had no superstitious reverence; his opinion is more unqualified : —

Ferdinand is a monk ; he prays seven times a day and neglects the business of the state. Faber the Bishop of Vienna will have it so, for Ferdinand always listens to him. He neither understands our position nor reads our arguments, for the prelates take care not to allow that. They know that our theology is convincing. I believe if the King understood it, he would boldly drive the Pope from Germany. His errors and weaknesses are not such grave wrongs as are the open blasphemies of Albert of Mayence and of Duke George, who said, " Their cause is just but is not approved by the Church." For this the impious blasphemer died and went to hell, living a life of groaning under the shades.[1]

As he grew older the Reformer became more decided; in 1542 he said : —

Ferdinand is the plague of Germany. His father Maximilian [2] predicted it. He was an astrologer, and when he saw the horoscope of his son is reported to have said, " The best thing for you will be to drown in your baptism." A father's sayings are prophecies. Erasmus judged Ferdinand and Charles well, when he said : " These two cubs will make Germany smart some day."

Of the princes of the Empire he said, in 1532 : —

I hate to see our princes have such an appetite for bishoprics. . . . The nobles seek their own profit and devour monasteries which will soon turn their stomachs as grass does a dog's. They all try to get rich from the monastery's purse, but let them beware lest it be a beggar's purse they get.

These two parties — the Emperor and the princes — thus stood face to face in the beginning of 1540. As a general council, to which both sides had so long appealed, was no longer acceptable to the Protestants, the means chosen to reconcile them with the Catholics were the aforementioned religious

[1] Luther has in mind, "*Vitaque cum gemitu fugit indignata sub umbras.*" Virgil, *Æneid*, 11, 831.

[2] Maximilian was Ferdinand's grandfather; his father Philip was never Emperor.

conferences. The first of these, originally called at Spires, was prorogued to meet at Hagenau in June. In order to decide on the proper course of action, the Protestant leaders held another congress at Schmalkalden in March. Luther, remembering his former almost fatal visit to that city, was excused from coming, but in common with other theologians sent a memorial to the effect that in all things his Church should stand by the Augsburg Confession. Melanchthon attended the congress, on the way assisting at the Landgrave's second marriage. To him his chief wrote as follows : —

TO PHILIP MELANCHTHON AT SCHMALKALDEN

(WITTENBERG,) April 8, 1540.

You write, dear Philip, that the Emperor has promised a private audience ; I wonder what he wants. I believe he is uncertain as to the best course to pursue. He needs a secret heart, placed as he is among so many vipers, so that he cannot openly satisfy either them or us with certain promises. In his place it would puzzle me to know what to do, especially as I am not well versed in affairs. We must pray God for him. It is no small sign from God that he has withheld the Emperor's hands for so many years, while the cardinals and popes raged and stirred him up and pressed him forward and urged him on, but all in vain. Let us thank God for this. For whatever is or shall be, we shall effect all things by prayer, the only omnipotent empress of human affairs ; by her we shall overrule the decrees of fate, correct mistakes, take away what is too bad to mend, conquer all evils, preserve all that is good, as we have hitherto done, having proved the power of prayer of which the reprobate and baffled papists know nothing — for they neither will nor can be wise. The wrath of God has finally come upon them who have drenched their hands in the blood of Christ and Christians, who, indeed, are totally submerged in the blood of the saints. Although we, too, are miserable offenders, in the body of sin, yet are we pure from blood ; rather we hate the men of blood and the god of blood who possesses and animates them. I have only written this to answer your letter, that you may know I received it. Thus are we accustomed to talk in private when we touch upon such matters. I hope you will receive another letter before your return.

All is well with us, by God's grace, except that we desire your return as soon as possible, or rather at once. I am angry with Grickel,[1]

---

[1] Agricola; cf. *supra*, p. 285.

whom, with all his virtues, I hope to leave to you before I die. Farewell in the Lord. Salute all friends and tell them their households are well. Yesterday there was an eclipse of the sun which we saw sadly laboring from five till seven. O Lord, turn the evil upon our enemies and save us by thy name! Amen. My Katie is perfectly restored to health. She sends her greeting to you whom she esteems much and loves kindly.

The meeting at Hagenau, June, 1540, came to nothing, and another conference was called at Worms in the autumn of the same year. Discussion did not actually begin until January 14, 1541, Melanchthon and Eck having the leading parts. That Luther despaired of any result may be gathered from the next letter : —

TO FREDERIC MYCONIUS AT GOTHA

(WITTENBERG,) January 9, 1541.

Grace and peace. I have received your letter saying that you are sick unto death, that is, if you interpret it rightly and blessedly, unto life. It is a singular joy to me that you are so unterrified by death, that sleep into which all good men fall, nay, that you are rather desirous of being freed and living with Christ. We should have this desire not only on the bed of sickness but in the full vigor of life, at all times and in all places and circumstances, seeing that we are Christians who have risen, revived and ascended into heaven with Christ, where we shall judge angels, and the veil and the dark glass will be removed. Although I am uncommonly glad that you feel thus, yet I pray and beseech the Lord Jesus, our life and salvation, that he may not add this calamity to my sorrows, that I should live to see you or any of my friends break through the veil to the rest beyond, while I am left without among devils, to suffer after your death, seeing that I have already suffered so much that I am most worthy of going before you. I pray that the Lord will take me in your place, and let me lay aside this useless, worn-out, exhausted tabernacle. I am no longer of any value. Wherefore please pray the Lord with us to preserve you the longer to profit the Church and to despise Satan. You see, and God our life sees, how much need his Church has of men and of gifts.

At last we have received news from Worms, after having waited five weeks and almost given up hope; George Rörer will send you some of the letters. Our friends act strongly and wisely in all things; contrariwise our opponents act childishly, foolishly, and inanely, telling

gross and silly lies. You see that when the dawn appears Satan becomes impatient of the light and seeks darkness in a thousand ways
with subterfuge and indirection, but yet clumsily, for it is necessary
that he who wishes to defend and furbish up an open lie against the
manifest truth should fail in his impossible task. Why do we doubt?
Glory, power, victory, salvation, and honor are due to the Lamb who
was slain and rose again, and with him to us also, who believe that he
was slain and rose again. There is no doubt about this. I hope our
friends will soon return. Farewell, dear Frederic, and may the Lord
not let me hear that you have died, but may he make you survive me.
This I pray, this I wish, my will be done (Amen), for it is not for my
own pleasure but for God's glory that I wish it. Farewell again. I
pray for you from my soul. My Katie and all my friends send their
greetings, for they are deeply moved by your illness.

Yours,

MARTIN LUTHER.

Before anything definite was accomplished at Worms the
religious conference was adjourned to meet at Ratisbon where
the Emperor opened a diet on April 5. Here the most determined efforts were made to reunite the Catholics and Protestants. Bucer drew up a plan of comprehension, thus drawing
down on himself the severest judgment of Luther, who could
bear anything better than lukewarmness.

That little wretch has lost all credit with me. I shall never trust
him, for he has cheated me too often. He acted badly at the Diet of
Ratisbon, wishing to be mediator between me and the Pope, saying,
" It is a pity that so many souls should be lost for the sake of an article
or two." They look at it from the political standpoint, for political
matters are temporal and changeable.

Another mediator was the Landgrave of Hesse, on whom
Luther expresses a similarly severe judgment in the next letter
to Melanchthon, written to strengthen the friend suspected of
not being sufficiently firm himself : —

TO PHILIP MELANCHTHON AT RATISBON

(WITTENBERG,) April 4, 1541.

Grace and peace. Dear Philip, I write this second letter to you,
hoping that your letter to me is already on the road. I pray the Lord

to guide and preserve you from the wiles of Satan and especially from that Jason [1] and his ilk. Our good elector yesterday sent me through Chancellor Brück that man's advice about making peace with the Emperor and our opponents. I see they think this is a comedy of men instead of a tragedy of God and Satan, as it is. Where Satan's power waxes that of God grows rusty. But the tragedy will have its catastrophe, as such always have had from the beginning, and the omnipotent author of the drama will free us at last. I write with rage and indignation against those who trifle in such matters. But thus it must be, for throughout history the Church has suffered, like St. Paul, the dangers of false brethren that the seal of God may be certain in us. God knows who are his own. I would write more did I not know that you hate such men and measures as much as I. What do they mean by saying that we neglect the primary articles of faith to dispute about things indifferent? Is the Word of God and the sacrament, in perverting which they tempt, slight, and insult God, a thing indifferent? Peace will be easy " in things indifferent" if, by our impenitence, we relegate serious and important matters to this category. . . .

About the time he was writing this, Luther was publishing one of his fiercest books: Against Jack Sausage (*Hans Wurst*). The person to whom this sobriquet was applied was Duke Henry II of Brunswick. Succeeding to the government in 1514, he at once put his brother William in prison and kept him there ten years. A little later, with the connivance of the Emperor, he seized Hildesheim. With his neighbors he lived in constant strife. When the League of Schmalkalden held its congress at Brunswick in 1538, he refused passage through his territory to the Elector John Frederic and Philip of Hesse, and when the latter passed through notwithstanding, he shot at him with cannon. He was accused of hiring agents to set fire to buildings in Saxony and Hesse, by which three hundred men lost their lives. His private life was also scandalous. Outwardly professing the Catholic religion, he ventured to mock one of its most sacred rites by pretending to have his mistress, Eva von Trott, buried, though for years afterwards he kept her privately in one of his castles.

[1] Philip of Hesse; Jason took to wife the daughter of the King of Corinth, while Medea, his first wife, was alive.

The constant strain between him and his Evangelic neighbors broke out in a war of pens about 1540. The titles of the books, unthinkable nowadays between crowned heads, sufficiently show the character of this conflict. They are : *The true, wise, well founded, Christian and right Answer of the Serene Prince John Frederic, against the shameless, Calpurnian, mendacious Libel of that hard, godless, cursed, damnable Slanderer, that wicked Barrabas, Whore-master and Holophernes of Brunswick who calls himself Henry the Younger ;* and : *The considerable, well grounded, true, godly and Christian Reply of the Serene Prince Henry the Younger to the false, lying, shameless Libel vomited forth against the said Duke by that godless, infamous, hard, heretical, sacrilegious, cursed, wicked Antiochus, Novatian, Severian, and Pander who calls himself John Frederic of Saxony.*

Luther was drawn into the controversy by the taunt of Henry that "Frederic's dear Martin Luther calls him Jack Sausage." Taking this name to designate his enemy of Brunswick, the Reformer published his book against him about April 1. The nickname, first found in Sebastian Brant's Ship of Fools (1494), refers to the custom of the fools at carnival time of wearing a huge leather sausage. "This name," says Luther, "was not invented by me, but is used by other people against coarse clowns who try to be wise, but speak and act without rime or reason." The tone of the book is the usual violent invective; the substance is mainly concerned with Henry's charge that the Protestants are heretics and rebels. The author proves by a history of the schism, from the indulgence controversy on, that the Evangelic Church has been the true one and that the Romanists are the real heretics. He closes with a parody of a popular song, "Poor Judas," reviving the charge of arson against the Duke of Brunswick: "O wicked Heinz, what have you done to slay so many men by fire? For this you will suffer great pain in hell and be Lucifer's companion forever. *Kyrieleison!*"

The book had an enormous success, three editions being called for before the year was ended. John Frederic, a rather coarse man, was especially pleased with it, and sent a number of copies around to his friends. Like Warren Hastings, Luther was astonished at his own moderation. A contemporary letter alluding to it is also interesting as showing the sufferings which the Reformer underwent in his later years: —

TO PHILIP MELANCHTHON AT RATISBON

(Wittenberg,) April 12, 1541.

. . . I have re-read my book against that devil of Brunswick and wonder how I could have been so moderate. I attribute it to the sufferings of my head, which did not permit my mind to display a more upright and stronger vehemence. But, if the Lord will, it profits the Church that I write thus. My illness has turned the corner. I am troubled with that tumor in the head which you predicted. So much phlegm, rheum, and matter flows from my neck and nostrils that I wonder how my head, broken down with age and labor, could bring forth such monsters, and that I was not suddenly taken off with apoplexy, vertigo, epilepsy, or something like them. On Palm Sunday the tumor reached my ear and attacked not only my head but my soul, so that the intolerable anguish forced tears from my eyes (though I do not easily nor often weep), and I said to the Lord: "May these pains cease or may I die." I could not have borne that terrible fight with nature two full days, but on the second day the tumor broke. . . . Now the winds of all the seas and of all the forests blow through my head, so that I can hear nothing unless it is shouted at me. . . . At least I have the advantage of being able to read and write even if I cannot sleep as I used to. . . .

This letter reached Melanchthon still engaged in negotiations at Ratisbon. A committee of three Catholics and three Protestants, Eck, Pflug, and Gropper against Melanchthon, Bucer, and Pistorius, had reached a semblance of harmony on some of the chief points at issue. For example, justification by faith was conceded by the Catholics with the proviso that faith meant operative faith. Even on the articles where both sides agreed to the same formula, it must be remembered that their interpretation of the words was very different, and moreover there were some points, such as that on the primacy of the Pope, on which no harmony whatever could be found. The Emperor finally decided to publish the articles for which a common statement had been drawn up, reserving the others for the arbitrament of a future council and forbidding the publication of polemic books. He also promised that adherence to the Augsburg Confession should not be made the ground of action against any prince. On the whole, the result of the conference, which terminated in July, was favorable to the Protestants.

Their party continued to gain strength by the adhesion or conquest of new domains. One of these was Brunswick. Duke Henry, in spite of warnings both from the Schmalkaldic League and from Ferdinand, attacked the city of Goslar. The Protestant princes promptly came to the help of the town and expelled Henry not only from it but from his whole territory, which was at once converted to the Protestant faith (1542).

Another acquisition was the bishopric of Naumburg. When the bishop died in 1541, the chapter chose Julius Pflug, a good Catholic who had been prominent at Ratisbon, but his installation was prevented by John Frederic, who occupied the city with three hundred cavalry in January, 1542, and compelled the election of Nicholas von Amsdorf, Luther's old friend and colleague. The Reformer, pleased with the honor bestowed upon his faithful follower, went in person to consecrate him. This he did on January 20 and defended the act in a pamphlet entitled, How to Anoint a Right Christian Bishop. "We poor heretics," says he, "have committed a great sin against the hellish unchristian Church and against the most hellish father the Pope by anointing a bishop at Naumburg without ointment, butter, suet, bacon, grease, or smoke."

Still another gain for the Evangelic party was the conversion of Halle, a small thing in itself, but particularly dear to the Reformer as a personal triumph over his old enemy Archbishop Albert of Mayence, whose capital and favorite residence this town was. As the Reformation made way in Halle, Albert at first sold the town the right to hold Evangelic services in return for a sum of money, but by 1542 his capital became too hot to hold him and he was obliged to retire to Mayence, taking with him a large collection of relics. As a song of triumph over the discomfiture of his opponent, Luther wrote the lampoon next translated. The superstitious objects ridiculed, among them being a piece of the clay from which Adam was formed and a bit of Noah's ark, had figured in the previous indulgence trade at Halle which had brought down Luther's wrath in 1517 and 1521.[1] In making fun of such relics he was not original; they had been the butt of wits for centuries.[2]

NEWS FROM THE RHINE

(WITTENBERG, circa October, 1542.)

An order has gone out from all the pulpits under the jurisdiction of the Archbishop of Mayence on the Rhine, saying that the archbishop has, for good reasons and the prompting of the Holy Ghost, transferred all relics, bless'd and endowed with great Roman indulgences, graces, and privileges, which his Reverence formerly had at Halle in Saxony to St. Martin's Church in Mayence. There they shall be honored with great solemnity every year on the Sunday after Bartholomew's day, with public proclamation of the same and of great forgiveness of sins, so that the beloved men of the Rhineland may help clothe the poor, bare bones with new garments. For the coats they had at Halle have been torn, and had they staid longer there they would have been frozen.

There is a persistent rumor that the Elector of Mayence has added many new relics to the old ones, and secured a special indulgence for them from the Most Holy Father Pope Paul III. Among the new relics are : —

I. A fair piece of Moses' left horn.

II. Three flames from Moses' burning bush on Mount Sinai.

III. Two feathers and an egg of the Holy Ghost.

IV. A whole end of the banner with which Christ harried hell.

V. A large wisp of Beelzebub's beard which remained stuck to the same banner.

VI. Half a feather of St. Gabriel the archangel.

VII. A whole pound of the wind which blew for Elijah in the cave on Mount Horeb.

VIII. Two yards of the tones of the sackbuts on Mount Sinai.

IX. Thirty notes of the drum of Miriam, Moses' sister, heard on the Red Sea.

[1] Cf. letter to Albert of Mayence, December 1, 1521, p. 127.

[2] A similar, though in no particular identical list of relics in Boccaccio: *Decamerone. Giornata sesta, Novella decima.* Cf. also; the old English play, *The Four PP.* The strangest of all relics, the foreskin of Jesus, is shown at Rome, Antwerp, Charost (Berry) and Hildesheim and works miracles in every place. Cf. O. Clemen in *Archiv für Kulturgeschichte,* vii, 2.

X. A great big piece of the shout of the children of Israel with which they cast down the walls of Jericho.

XI. Five, fair, clear strings of the harp of David.

XII. Three locks of Absalóm's hair, by which he was caught on the oak. We must remember that this is shown not for holiness but for curiosity, as Judas' cord is shown at St. Peter's in Rome.

A special good friend has privately told me that the Elector of Mayence is going to bequeath by will a whole dram of his true, pious heart, and half an ounce of his veracious tongue. For these an indulgence will be secured from the Most Holy Father Pope, so that whoever honors these relics with a gold gulden shall have all his sins forgiven up to date, and moreover all the sins he can possibly commit during the next ten years shall not be allowed to prejudice his salvation. This is a great rich grace, never before heard of, which must be the source of joy to many.

The lampoon stung; Luther rejoiced in the writhing of his enemy, "the bride of Mayence," as he now called Albert, and wrote this letter to the pastor of Halle, intending it for public inspection : —

TO JUSTUS JONAS AT HALLE

(WITTENBERG,) November 6, 1542.

Grace and peace in the Lord. My dear doctor, you know that the lampoon on his Holiness the Cardinal is mine. The printer knows it, so does the university and the town, so that it is quite public and no secret at all. The bride of Mayence will also know it well, for I made the style easy to be recognized. Whoever reads it and has ever known my manner of writing and thinking must say, "That is Luther!" The bride herself will say: "That is the rascal Luther, whose heart, well known to me, is especially apparent." Had I wished to keep it secret I should have better disguised my style. The bride has no power to make me fear her arts, devilish as they are. And if it were a notorious libel, which it is not, yet would I have the right, authority, and power, against the cardinal, the Pope, the devil, and all their followers to have it not called a libel. Have the ass-ists — I mean jurists — not studied their law, that they are so ignorant of its purpose and subject? If I have to teach the guttersnipes I will do it gratis. How has fair Moritzburg [1] so suddenly become a stable for asses! If they wish to pipe, I wish to dance, and if life is spared me, I will yet tread

[1] Albert's castle, still to be seen at Halle.

a measure with the bride of Mayence, for I have a few more sweet kisses to press on her rosy red mouth. Help! jurist, or whatever you are that trouble God. Let her spleen boil and bubble, what matters it? I will roast her again, if I live, so that she will wish, for her honor, she had never noticed the lampoon. For I do not fancy keeping silence before that desperate enemy of God, that blasphemer of Mayence, whose devilish tyranny does ever worse and worse against the blood of Christ. Let them come and go as they please. I will teach them what right and might I have, even to publish a notorious libel (if that were possible!) without heeding their wrath and the disfavor of the jurists. For they will sit under God's judgment, not over it. I write this letter of my own accord, rather than suffer them to let me, an old man, alone. If they will not do so they must take the risk. I will let them find me if God will.

DR. MARTIN LUTHER.

The battle with Rome never ceased till the day of Luther's death. The occasion of his last and fiercest book against her was as follows: At the Diet of Spires, which closed June 10, 1544, the Emperor, anxious to secure the help of the Protestants in the war against France, promised that they should be recognized until a free German National Council was called to pass upon the religious question. When Pope Paul III heard of this he wrote the Emperor a sharp letter (August 24), forbidding him to meddle in the affairs of the Church, especially as an œcumenic council had already been called to meet at Trent. The Imperial Chancellor Gattinara sent this brief to Luther, who also had knowledge of another letter from Pope to Emperor, denouncing the summons of a German synod. John Frederic asked Luther to write an answer to these epistles, which he did in the early months of 1545, publishing in March of that year, Against the Papacy at Rome, founded by the Devil.

In the first part, considering the title of the Pope to be called head of the Church "over council, Emperor, angels, and all," he says: "The most hellish father, St. Paul III, as though he were a bishop of the Roman Church, has written two letters to our Lord Emperor, showing that he is very wroth, and snarls and rants as his predecessors have all done, and says no one has a right to call a council, even a national one." He then gives the history of the Council of Constance, which deposed three popes, and says : —

It would be a first-rate thing if the Holy Ghost, that poor heresiarch, should come to grace and be let into a holy, free, Christian council. If he were not stubborn he might humble himself before that holy virgin, St. Paula III, Lady Papess, fall on his knees, kiss her feet and recognize, repent, and recant his heresy. He would surely get a free indulgence both for himself and for his holy Church.

" Alas," sighs Luther, after continuing in this jocular vein for some time, "I am infinitely too small to mock the Pope, who has mocked the world for six hundred years."

In Part II the author considers the claim of the Pope that none can judge him. After painting his vices in lively colors, he goes on : —

So this Sodomite Pope, founder and master of all sins, threatens the Emperor Charles with excommunication and accuses him of sin, although he knows that his villainous tongue lies herein. These damnable rascals persuade the world that they are the heads of the Church, the mother of all churches, and masters of faith, although even stones and stocks would know that they were desperately lost children of the devil, as well as gross, stupid, ignorant asses in the Bible. One would like to curse them, so that thunder and lightning would smite them, hell fire burn them, the plague, syphilis, epilepsy, scurvy, leprosy, carbuncles, and all diseases attack them ; but they are simple slanderers, and God has anticipated us and cursed them with a greater plague, as he curses those who despise him, the plague mentioned in Romans i, 26, to wit, that they become so mad that they know not whether they are men or women. . . .

In the third and last part of this violent book Luther again takes up the question as to whether the Pope gave the Empire to the Germans. If the Pope had done so, he says, it would be much like his, Luther's, giving the kingdom of Bohemia to Saxony. He proves, however, by relating the history of Charlemagne, that in reality the Pope did no such thing.

A further effort was called forth by the action of the university of Louvain, in publishing, December, 1544, a condemnation of " the Lutheran, Zwinglian, and Anabaptist heresy." The Emperor gave his official approval to these articles in March,

1545. When he heard of this, Luther wrote the following letter to his sovereign, in which he speaks rather sceptically of the council which had at last really assembled at Trent: —

TO JOHN FREDERIC, ELECTOR OF SAXONY

(WITTENBERG,) May 7, 1545.

Grace and peace in the Lord and my poor paternoster. Most serene, highborn Prince, gracious Lord! I return the articles published by Louvain, as I received a printed copy of them a week ago. O unhappy Emperor, to be the father of such a great, shameful, horrible whore! Truly the Pope is silly and foolish from top to toe; the papists know not what they say nor do. No doubt if there is a council they will display wisdom superior or equal to that which they have just shown. But I think that they, and especially their Holy Ghost, Mayence, are wise enough to let the council remain like unripe barley in the sheaves, although they are not wise enough to let the Word alone. As to the other bit of news, about the council at Trent, I consider it a Romish and Mayence-ish chatter and babble, which he of Mayence would be very sorry to have come true. God won't have it and it won't have itself, either. Let things go of themselves and they will come out all right. May our dear God bless, rule over, and guard your Grace in his good and perfect will. Amen.

Your Grace's obedient subject,

DR. MARTIN LUTHER.

CHAPTER XXXVI

LUTHERAN AND SACRAMENTARIAN. 1539-1546

It sometimes seems that Luther hated the other branches of the Protestant Church more than he did even Rome, and his wrath against them, far from being healed with time, became more and more bitter until his death. In October, 1540, he speaks of his first opponents in the doctrine of the sacrament thus : —

Verily Œcolampadius' curse has come true, for he wrote, in his work against Pirkheimer : "If I act with evil intention, may Jesus Christ smite me!" Good God! how bold these men are! And others are not frightened by Zwingli's fate! Verily it is not good to joke with Christ!

John Calvin, Zwingli's great successor, was born too late (1509) to be well known to Luther. The Wittenberg professor read one of his books in 1539, liked it, and sent the author his greeting. On the other hand, when Calvin wrote him, in February, 1545, Luther never answered, and in the saying next translated he gives a very dubious opinion of the great divine of Geneva : —

(October or November, 1540.) When some one pointed out to Luther that Watt had written against Schwenkfeld, he said, "I have seen the book but not read it. These books written to refute others need refutation themselves. Thus Calvin hides his opinions on the sacrament. They are mad and cannot speak out, though the truth is simple. Don't read their books to me!"

(Spring, 1543.) Against the sacramentarians who complain that we sin against the law of charity he said : "They plague us with their charity in all their books, saying, 'You of Wittenberg have no charity.' If you say, 'What is charity?' they reply, 'To agree in doctrine. Let us not strive about religion.' Well, what of that? There are two laws, primary and secondary; charity belongs to the second class, although she precedes all works. It is written : 'Fear God and obey his Word.' They don't ask about that. 'Whoso has loved father or mother more than me,' says Christ, 'is not worthy of me.' You must have charity to parents and children; love, love, be kind to your father and mother! But, 'whoso hath loved them more than me.' Where 'me' begins charity stops. I am willing to be called obstinate, proud, headstrong, what they will, but not their fellow. God keep me from that!"

The old animosity broke out again in the summer of 1544 on the occasion of the conversion of Cologne from the Catholic to the Protestant faith. Melanchthon and Bucer went to that important city, and drew up for it a Plan of Reform, in which, to avoid altercation, they minimized the differences of the several bodies of reformers on the doctrine of the sacrament. This plan was sent to Nicholas von Amsdorf, now Bishop of Naumburg, who forwarded his criticism of it, together with the original document, to Luther. The latter expresses himself on both papers as follows: —

TO CHANCELLOR BRÜCK

(WITTENBERG, end of July or beginning of August, 1544.)

Honorable, learned Sir, dear Friend. The bishop's [1] articles please me right well. . . . But the Plan of Reform does not please me. It speaks at length about the use, fruit, and honor of the sacrament, but mumbles about the substance, so that one cannot gather what it believes. . . . In short, I am sick and disgusted with the book . . . which, besides other objections, is much, much too long, a great tedious talk, in which I see traces of that chatterbox, Bucer. I will say more at another time.

Your Honor's devoted,

MARTIN LUTHER.

The above letter did not make things any easier for Luther's friends, and when he announced definitely that he was going to write a book expressly against the sacramentarian heresy, Melanchthon feared the worst. The treatise, A Short Confession on the Holy Sacrament, came out toward the end of September. It contains these words: "As I am about to descend into the grave, I will take this testimony and boast before the

[1] Amsdorf.

judgment seat of my Lord, that I have always damned and shunned the ranters and enemies of the sacrament, Carlstadt, Zwingli, Œcolampadius, Stenkefeld,[1] and their disciples at Zurich and elsewhere, according to the command in Titus iii, 10." The book did not, however, attack Melanchthon, and caused no further schism in the Church; that it was taken ill by the Swiss had been expected. Luther speaks of their answer to the work in a letter to Amsdorf: —

TO NICHOLAS VON AMSDORF AT NAUMBURG

(WITTENBERG,) April 14, 1545.

Grace and peace in the Lord. I thank you, reverend father in Christ, for your strongly favorable opinion of my book against the papacy.[2] It does not please every one so much. Yet it so pleased the Elector that he sent around copies worth twenty gulden. You know it is not my habit to regard the dislike of the multitude, if what I write is only pious and useful and pleasing to a few good persons. Not that I think all who dislike this book are wicked, but they do not understand the substance, quantity, quality, and all the circumstances, kinds, manners, properties, differences, and attributes of the papal abomination, in short, all its monstrous horrors. For the eloquence and genius of none is able to reach them, even though they do not fear the wrath of kings.

The sacramentarians of Zurich have written in Latin and German against my Short Confession. As I have so often condemned them before, I have not decided whether to answer them. The men are fanatic, proud, and yet shirking; in the beginning of the reformation, when I alone sweated to bear the fury of the Pope, they kept resolute silence and watched my dangers and my success, but as soon as the papacy was somewhat broken they burst forth in triumphant boasting, saying that they owed nothing to others but all to themselves. Thus, thus does one labor and another enjoy the fruit of his labor. Now at last they turn and attack me by whom they were freed. They are a cowardly swarm of drones, skilful only to filch the honey others have made. Their judgment will come upon them. If I see best to answer them I shall do it briefly, merely reiterating my condemnatory

---

[1] That is, Schwenkfeld, on whom see just below. Luther's pun means "Stinkfield."

[2] *Against the Papacy at Rome,* the work condemned by Louvain.

opinion. But I am determined to finish the book against the papacy while I have strength.

The Emperor in Belgium, the French King in France, rage cruelly against the Evangelic cause, and Ferdinand is just as bad in Hungary and Austria. It is as when Caiphas advised to slay the Son of God that the place and the nation might not perish; they think they cannot conquer the Turk unless they drench their lands with the blood of the martyrs and brethren of Christ. The wrath of God has come upon them at last. May the Lord hasten the day of our redemption. Farewell in him, reverend father.

Yours,

MARTIN LUTHER.

In the next letter, written a month before his death, Luther expresses his final hatred of the sacramentarians: —

TO JAMES PROBST AT BREMEN

(WITTENBERG,) January 17, 1546.

Greeting and peace. Dear James, old, decrepit, sluggish, weary, worn out, and now one-eyed, I write to you. Now that I am dead — as I seem to myself — I expect the rest I have deserved to be given to me, but instead I am overwhelmed with writing, speaking, doing, transacting business, just as though I had never done, written, said, or accomplished anything. But Christ is all in all, able to do and doing, blessed world without end. Amen.

I greatly rejoice at what you tell me about the Swiss writing against me so vehemently, condemning me as an unhappy man of unhappy genius. This is what I sought, this is what I wished my book, so offensive to them, to do, namely, to make them publicly testify that they are my enemies; now I have attained this, and, as I have said, rejoice at it. The blessing of the Psalm is sufficient for me, the most unhappy of all men: "Blessed is the man that walketh not in the counsel of the sacramentarians, nor standeth in the way of the Zwinglians, nor sitteth in the seat of the men of Zurich." [1] You have my opinion. . . .

I have begun to write against Louvain, according as God gives me power; I am more angry at those brutes than is becoming to an old man and a theologian; but we ought to resist the monsters of Satan, even if we expended our last breath in doing so. Farewell. You

[1] Cf. Psalm i, 1.

know that you are most dear to me not only on account of our old
and intimate friendship, but on account of Christ, whom you teach
as I do. We are sinners, but he, who lives forever, is our righteousness. Amen. Greet your friends and ours in the name of us all.

Yours,

DR. MARTIN LUTHER.

Besides the Zwinglians there were the Anabaptists; a sect detested still more, if possible, than the others. It is fair, however,
to give Luther credit for standing out against the death penalty
for their belief, contrary to the practice not only of the Catholics
but of Zwingli and Calvin.

Some one asked if the Anabaptists were to be put to death. Luther
replied: "There are two kinds. Those who are openly seditious are
rightly punished by the Elector with death; the others who merely
have fanatic opinions ought in general to be banished."

One of the lesser religious leaders of the time, usually classed
as an Anabaptist, though he aspired to found a new sect of his
own, the "Middle Way," was a certain Silesian gentleman named
Casper von Schwenkfeld. He had been known to Luther for
a great many years and detested for his heresy concerning the
nature of Christ. Submitting his opinions to the theologians
who met in the Congress of Schmalkalden early in 1540,
Schwenkfeld was warned of his errors by them, whereupon he
had the poor judgment to appeal from them to Luther. The
opinion of the latter, together with his terribly rude answer, are
recorded by Besold, November 8, 1543: —

Schwenkfeld sent the doctor his book on the humanity of Christ,
entitled Dominion. Luther said: "He is a poor man, without genius
or talents, smitten like all the ranters. He knows not of what he
babbles, but his meaning and sense is: 'Creatures are not to be
adored, as it is written: "Thou shalt worship the Lord thy God and
him only shalt thou serve."' Then he argues: 'Christ is created,
therefore we should not pray to the man Christ.' He makes two
Christs. He says the created Christ, after his resurrection and glori-
fication, was transformed into a deity and is therefore to be adored,
and he foully cheats the people with the lordly name of Christ, saying
all the while that it is for Christ's glory! Children go to the heart
of the doctrine with: 'I believe in Jesus Christ our Lord, conceived

of the Holy Ghost, etc.,' but this fool will make two Christs, one who hung on the cross and the other who ascended into heaven, and says I must not pray to the Christ who hung on the cross and walked on earth. But he let himself be adored when one fell down before him, and he says : ' Whoso believeth in me, believeth in him who sent me.' This maniac has stolen some words out of my book." . . .

Katie said : " Dear husband, you are too rude." Luther answered : " They teach me to be rude." . . . To the messenger he answered : " My dear messenger ! Tell your master Schwenkfeld that I have received his letter and pamphlet. And would to God he would stop ! Formerly he kindled a fire in Silesia which is not yet quenched and which will burn him eternally. And he adds to that the heresy of Eutychianism on the creation of Christ, and makes the Church err, as God has not commanded him to do. The senseless fool, possessed of the devil, understands nothing and knows not whereof he babbles. But if he will not cease writing, at least let him leave me in peace, untroubled by the books of which the devil has purged him, and let him take this as my last judgment and answer : The Lord rebuke thee, Satan, and may the spirit which called you, and the race you run, and all your fellow sacramentarians and Eutychians, go with you and your blasphemies to perdition." . . .

War with Rome, war with Zurich, war with the innumerable lesser sects ! This is apt to be the thought with which one closes the history of Luther's public career. He was, indeed, a born fighter. His amazing strength and courage, animated by the strongest of all motives, devotion to conscience, and fortified by the intolerance of his age, found ample scope in the great load of wrong and superstition to be combated. However much some of the excesses of his passion may be regretted, it must be remembered that they are the defects of his qualities ; that, had he not been such a man, he would not have been the leader of the great Revolt.

And the wars, though the most conspicuous, are not the most enduring portion of Luther's work. If Napoleon wished to go down to history with his code in his hand, Luther gave posterity the German Bible and a great volume of poetry and prose which has permanently enriched the world. Luther was, indeed, — the point must be repeated, — the founder of a new culture. Like other such men, Voltaire for example, he has suffered by the very effectiveness of his own work. Much that he was the first to make valid has become commonplace now; in proportion as he raised the standard he is judged by the severer rule. In fable, Cadmus is less renowned for inventing the alphabet than for sowing the dragon's teeth. So it has been with Luther. The new culture, the fresh spirit, the glorious life he imparted to Europe has become as commonplace as the alphabet, whereas the fierce wars he waged are remembered to his discredit, and have made him, especially in recent years, the object of misunderstanding and dislike.

CHAPTER XXXVII

DEATH

INCREASING ill health made Luther's last years sad and bitter. Though he sometimes had cheerful days, they were sufficiently uncommon to be remarked, as for example : —

On Sunday, October 3 (1540), he was happy in mind and joked with his friends and with me (Mathesius), and disparaged his own learning. " I am a fool," said he ; " you are cunning and wiser than I in economy and politics. For I do not apply myself to such things, but only to the Church and to getting the best of the devil. I believe, however, if I did give myself to other business I could master it. But as I attend only to what is plain to view any one can overreach me, until, indeed, I see that he is a sharper, and then he can't cheat me. . . . Don't take it ill of me that I am happy and light-hearted, for I heard much bad news to-day, and since then have read a letter of the Archbishop of Mayence saying that he had released his subjects from prison. The devil makes it go hard with us, but we shall win, for God is with us."

Again in 1542 he said : —

Nothing is more hurtful than sadness. It eats the marrow of the bones, as it is written : " A broken spirit drieth up the bones." A young fellow should be merry. There I write for such an one, over the table : " sadness slayeth many."

Such a tone was, however, very exceptional. Luther often wished and sometimes thought he was going to die. Once in the winter of 1542 to 1543 he felt a pain in his head for several days together, and said, at dinner : —

" Katie, if I am not better to-morrow I will have our Hans brought from Torgau, for I would like him to be with me at my end." Katie : " Look ye, sir, you imagine it." Luther : " No, Katie, it is not imagination ; I shall not die suddenly, however, but be stricken down and become ill, though not for very long. I am tired of the world and it is tired of me, which I do not mind. It thinks if it were only rid of me, all would go well. But it is as I have often said. . . . We must part.

O God I thank thee that thou lettest me be of thy little flock, to suffer persecution for thy Word's sake, for I am not persecuted for impurity nor for usury, that I know well."

Like some other old men, Luther was inclined to look back on his youth as a better period for the world. With increasing frequency and bitterness he judged the immorality of his age. His enemies have often taken his words as proof that the new teaching had a disastrous moral effect. Periods of religious fermentation have often been accompanied by moral retrogression, a striking proof of it in the Reformation is the frequency with which polygamy was preached and practised by small sects. In general the change of standards, the revaluation of moral goods, may tend to upset not only bad but good customs, and in individual cases work with detrimental effect. On the other hand, evidence seems to show that in places the religious revival was accompanied by an ethical uplift, notably in the suppression of houses of ill-fame. The basis of Luther's criticisms must be chiefly looked for in subjective conditions; how gloomy his outlook at times was, is shown by the following records :[1] —

I (Mathesius) once stood with the doctor in the garden; he said that he was so oppressed and borne down by his own followers that he must get the Elector to build a preachers' tower in which such wild and troublesome people might be imprisoned, for many of them would no longer bear the gospel; all who had entered the cloister for the sake of their bellies and a good time burst out again for the sake of carnal freedom, and only a few of them, as far as he could see, had left their monasticism behind them in the cloister.

Again, a little later :[2] —

Now we have good books and bad scholars, formerly we had bad books and good scholars ; then there were golden preachers and wooden images, dark churches and bright hearts; now there are wooden preachers and golden images, bright churches and dark hearts.

The same tone is taken in the summer of 1542 : —

[1] Lösche : *Mathesius Ausgewählte Werke*, Luther Historien, p. 269. For dating see Kroker, *Luther's Tischreden*, no. 163.

[2] The text of this saying is from Melanchthon's lectures above referred to, *Corpus Reformatorum*, xx, col. 575. On dating, see Kroker, *op. cit.*, no. 194.

Paul Knoth once said to me that while a page at court he had asked an old priest how it was that there was so much arrogance among the nobles. The priest replied: "Don't ask such silly questions. There is no noble who wishes well to the peasant, the burgher, or even to the prince; they do not even wish each other well." It is true! There are three kinds of devils: house-devils, court-devils, and church-devils. The last are the worst; when they enter a priest the man does not wish another well, and each thinks he is more learned than another. Grickel [1] thinks he is more learned than I; Jeckel [2] thinks he is more learned than Melanchthon. Ah, well-a-day!

A letter to the devoted Lauterbach expresses, as strongly as it is well-nigh possible, the writer's despair at the moral condition of the people: —

TO ANTONY LAUTERBACH AT PIRNA

(WITTENBERG,) November 10, 1541.

Grace and peace. Although I have nothing to write, dear Antony, yet I prefer to write that I have nothing to write rather than leave your letter unanswered. May God strengthen Duke Maurice [3] in the true faith and in sound policy. Perhaps you have heard all the news of the Turk. I almost despair of Germany since she has received within her walls those true Turks or rather those true devils, avarice, usury, tyranny, discord, and that whole cesspool of perfidy, malice, and iniquity, in the nobles, the palaces, the courts of justice, the towns and the villages; worst of all is contempt of the Word and unexampled ingratitude. With these Turks ruling us savagely and cruelly, what success can we hope against the human Turks? May God have mercy upon us and make the light of his countenance to shine upon us. For while we pray against our enemies the Turks, it is to be feared that the Holy Ghost will understand us to pray against ourselves and yet for our good. For I see that it will come to pass that unless the tyranny of the Turk terrifies and humbles our nobles, we shall have to bear worse tyranny from them than from the Turks. Verily the nobles think to put chains on our princes and fetters on the burghers and peasants, and most of all on books and authors. Thus they avenge the papal slavery by subjecting the people to a new

[1] Agricola, see above, p. 285.
[2] James Schenk, see above, p. 285.
[3] The new Duke of Albertine Saxony; Luther was soon to form a very bad opinion of him. Cf. *supra*, p. 386.

slavery under the nobles. But enough. My Katie sends her greetings
to you and to your wife and daughter, as do we all, and we all pray
and beseech the Lord together to give us the pestilence instead of the
Turkish scourge, for without the special help of God our arms and
armies can do nothing.

Yours,

MARTIN LUTHER.

The complaints against the general immorality of the age
sometimes became specific, as in the beginning of 1544, when
certain students, including a son of Melanchthon and, probably,
Luther's own nephew, contracted secret engagements to marry.
One of these students, Caspar Beier, broke his engagement at
his father's wish, but was condemned by the court of Wittenberg for breach of promise. Luther took the matter up with
passion, seeing that the permission to make secret engagements
was likely to lead to immorality, or at least to cast a bad name
on the university. He accordingly wrote : —

TO JOHN FREDERIC, ELECTOR OF SAXONY

(WITTENBERG,) January 22, 1544.

Grace and peace and my poor paternoster. Most serene, highborn
Prince, most gracious Lord ! I humbly give your Grace to know that
the secret engagement is becoming prevalent again. We have a great
horde of young men from all countries and the race of girls is getting
bold, and run after the fellows into their rooms and chambers and
wherever they can, and offer them their free love ; and I hear that
many parents have ordered their sons home and others are ordering
them home now, saying that if they send their children to our university we hang wives around their necks and take their children from
them, for which cause the university is getting a bad name. But I
know what every one must know that your Grace has ordered that
secret engagements are worth nothing, but are null and void. But
while I remain quiet in this assurance, out goes a judgment from our
law-court assuming the validity of a secret engagement, so that I was
shocked and deeply moved and insisted on a stay in execution. The
next Sunday I preached a strong sermon, telling men to follow the
common road and manner which had been since the beginning of the
world, both in the Bible and among all heathen and even in the papacy
to the present day, namely, that parents should give their children to

each other with prudence and good will, without their own preliminary engagement. Such engagements never have been in the world, but are an invention of the abominable Pope, suggested to him by the devil to destroy and tear down the power of parents given and commended to them earnestly by God, and to incite disobedience to God's command, and to bring consciences into unnumbered entanglements, and moreover to rob parents of their children, and give them great woe and sorrow of heart instead of the honor owed them by the children according to God's commandment. This would have happened to Melanchthon and his wife had it not been for my sermon, which was almost too late. They would have been put to scorn by their son, who was so led astray by bad fellows that he betrothed himself secretly and solemnly, and I had great trouble to turn him, or rather frighten him from it. . . . Such a thing almost happened to me in my own house.

Therefore it is certain that secret vows are and can be nothing but the affair of the Pope and the invention of the devil against the will of parents, that is against the command given parents by God, and they are simply great misery and sorrow of heart (as must be the fruit of the devil's acts), from which come all entanglements and dangers to consciences. But men can well and happily marry in a right and godly way. As the shepherd of the souls of the flock in this church, to which God has commended me and for which he will hold me to account, I simply neither could nor would bear it and take it on my conscience. I brought it up before the eyes of all in the pulpit and said : " I, Martin Luther, minister of this church of Christ, take you, secret vow, and the paternal consent given to you, together with the Pope, whose business you are and the devil who invented you, and throw you into the abyss of hell in the name of the Father and of the Son and of the Holy Ghost. Amen." I said that children could not engage themselves, and if they did they were as good as not engaged, except that they had committed a great sin in becoming engaged. Likewise that no father could consent to such an engagement, and if he did his consent would be invalid, for we cannot consent to the business of the devil, but should know who is the master and inventor of such misery.

Wherefore it is my most humble prayer to your Grace to turn your attention to this matter anew for the sake of God and the salvation of souls, and maintain the command of God against the Pope and the devil as you have hitherto done with great earnestness and zeal. For if we have the command of our sovereign, we can more solemnly drive out and keep out this devil of the secret vow, that cursed, blasphemous, damned business of the Antichrist, and then we can keep our children for their poor parents and bring them up and care for them safely. But if we allow an engagement in the form suggested by the court of justice, namely, "I betroth you subject to the approval of my father," then we leave a hole for the devil, and instead of preventing secret engagements make them stronger than before. For how easily can a child talk over or stun a father into consent, or snatch a word out of his mouth by some hook or crook, although the father's heart is not inclined to his son? . . .

Your Grace's obedient subject,
MARTIN LUTHER.

The next letter to the Electress Sybilla of Saxony, during the absence of her husband at the Diet of Spires, sums up all the world-weariness and disgust with life which has come out indirectly in the last letter.

TO SYBILLA, ELECTRESS OF SAXONY

(WITTENBERG,) March 10, 1544.

Grace and peace in the Lord. Most serene, highborn Princess, most gracious Lady! I have received your Grace's letter, and humbly thank your Grace for asking so particularly and carefully after my health, and how it goes with wife and children, and for your good wishes. We are, thank God, well — better than we deserve of God. That my head is sometimes weak is no wonder, for it is old, and age is senile, frigid, impotent, sick, and weak. But the jug goes to the water until it is broken. I have lived long enough. May God grant me a blessed hour before this sluggish, useless body be taken to its like under the earth to become a prey to worms. I think, indeed, that I have seen the best days I ever shall see on earth. Things look as if they were going to the bad. May God help his own. Amen.

I can well believe what your Grace writes that it is tedious to you to have your husband, our gracious lord the Elector, absent. But since it is necessary, and his absence is for the advantage and good of Christendom and the German nation, we must bear it with patience according to the divine will. If the devil could keep peace we should have more peace, too, and less to do and especially less to suffer. But with it all we have the advantage of having the dear Word of God, which comforts and supports us in this life, and promises and brings us salvation in the world to come. Moreover we have prayer, which, as your Grace also writes, we know pleases God and will be heard in time. Two such inexpressible treasures neither the devil nor the Turk nor the Pope nor their followers can have, and are therefore much poorer and more wretched than any beggar on earth. . . . My Katie humbly offers her poor prayers for your Grace and humbly thanks you for thinking of us so kindly. God bless you. Amen.

Your Grace's obedient subject,

DR. MARTIN LUTHER.

Notwithstanding his bodily afflictions never once did Luther relax his enormous energy. The last year of his life saw the publication of eleven books or pamphlets, besides sermons and lectures at the university. For the same period there are extant more than seventy letters, only a part of his correspondence. Some idea of the variety of his occupations is given in an extract from a letter to Lauterbach, dated December 2, 1544 : —

You often urge me to write a book on Christian discipline, but you do not say where I, a weary, worn old man, can get the leisure and health to do it. I am pressed by writing letters without end; I have promised our young princes a sermon on drunkenness; I have promised certain other persons and myself a book on secret engagements; to others one against the sacramentarians; still others beg that I shall omit all to write a comprehensive and final commentary on the whole Bible. One thing hinders another so that I am able to accomplish nothing. Yet I believe that I ought to have rest, as an emeritus, to live and die in peace, and quietness, but I am forced to live in restless action. I shall do what I can and leave undone what I cannot do.

Some six months after writing this, during his last summer, Luther's disgust with life reached a crisis. He had another disagreeable experience with a servant, which reminded him of that detested impostor Rosina.[1] Throughout the town he saw signs of moral corruption, objecting especially to the immodest, low-necked dresses of the women. When he could bear it no longer he left home, intending never to return, taking with him his son Hans and his boarder Ferdinand von Maugis. The party

[1] Cf. letter to Göritz, January 29, 1544, p. 361.

travelled the well-known road to Leipsic, and thence to Zeitz, to share, at Amsdorf's wish, in settling a dispute between two clergymen of the diocese of Naumburg. At Zeitz they found Cruciger on the point of returning to Wittenberg. With him Luther sent this letter: —

TO CATHARINE LUTHER AT WITTENBERG

(ZEITZ,) July 28, 1545.

Dear Katie, Hans will tell you about our journey, unless, indeed, I decide to keep him with us, in which case Cruciger and Ferdinand will tell you about it. Ernest von Schönfeld entertained us well at Lobnitz, Henry Scherle still better at Leipsic. I should like to arrange not to have to go back to Wittenberg. My heart has grown cold so that I do not care to live there, but wish you would sell garden and the farm, house and buildings, except the big house, which I should like to give back to my gracious lord. Your best course would be to go to Zulsdorf; while I am alive you could improve the little estate with my salary, for I hope my gracious lord will let my salary go on, at least during this last year of my life. After my death the four elements will not suffer you to live at Wittenberg, therefore it will be better for you to do during my lifetime what you will have to do after my death. It looks as if Wittenberg and her government would catch — not St. Vitus' dance or St. John's dance, but the beggar's dance and Beëlzebub's dance; the women and girls have begun to go bare before and behind and there is no one to punish or correct them and God's Word is mocked. Away with this Sodom. Our other Rosina [1] and deceiver is Leak's [2] dung, and yet not in prison; do what you can to make the wretch stultify himself. I hear more of these scandals in the country than I did at Wittenberg, and am therefore tired of that city and do not wish to return, God helping me. Day after to-morrow I am going to Merseburg, for Prince George [3] has pressed me to do so. I will wander around here and eat the bread of charity before I will martyr and soil my poor old last days with the disordered life of Wittenberg, where I lose all my bitter, costly work. You may tell Melanchthon and Bugenhagen this, if you will, and ask the latter to

---

[1] One MS. reads Rosinus; at any rate the deceiver this time was a man, as the next clause shows.

[2] Leak seems to have been Agricola, who had been at Wittenberg recently. Particulars of this affair, and his part in it, if he had any, are unknown.

[3] Of Anhalt, Canon of Merseburg.

give Wittenberg my blessing, for I can no longer bear its wrath and displeasure. God bless you. Amen.

MARTIN LUTHER.

When this news reached Wittenberg, consternation followed. Melanchthon said that if Luther left he would leave, too. The university sent him and Bugenhagen, and the town her burgomaster, to persuade Luther to return; the Elector, too, when he heard of it, dispatched his physician to induce the old man to change his plan. They met him at Merseburg and found him so amenable to reason that by August 16 he was home again. Here he continued his usual activities, though feeling that his end was drawing near. On November 10 he celebrated his last birthday with his friends. On the 11th he gave his last lecture at the university, completing his course on the book of Genesis with the words: —

This is dear Genesis; God grant that others do better with it after me; I can do no more, I am weak. Pray God to grant me a good, blessed hour.

His labors were indeed near their end. Having accomplished a great work, he crowned it by dying like a brave man. When another call to danger came the worn old warrior went out to his last battle — his splendid courage undaunted to the end. It is characteristic of Luther that all his bravest and best acts were done in the simple course of every-day duty. He never seems to have had the thought of achieving fame, which inspired so many others — Loyola, for example, confesses to this motive. He simply saw the duty before him and did it. In the present case he well knew that he would get no advantage or reputation by leaving home.

Nevertheless, when a dispute broke out between the brother counts of Mansfeld, to whom, as a native of their dominions, Luther always felt especially loyal, and when they asked the mediation of the Reformer, without hesitation, with broken health, in the bitterest winter weather, he twice left home to give them his services. The first journey was to the town of Mansfeld, in December, 1545. Christmas was celebrated here, but Melanchthon's frail health forced the party to return home with the work half done. Later it was decided to continue the arbitration without Melanchthon's assistance, and the older man again left home for Mansfeld — this time for the town of Eisleben — attended by his three sons, and his *famulus* John Aurifaber. The party set out on January 23, reaching Halle two days later.

TO CATHARINE LUTHER AT WITTENBERG

HALLE, January 25, 1546.

Grace and peace in the Lord. Dear Katie, we arrived at Halle this morning at eight o'clock, but have not journeyed on to Eisleben because a great lady of the Anabaptist persuasion met us, covering the land with waves of water and blocks of ice and threatening to baptize us. We could not return on account of the Mulda, and so lie here between waters. Not that we venture to drink it, but we take good Torgau beer and Rhenish wine while the Saale is trying to make us angry. All the people, the postillions as well as we ourselves, are timid, and so we do not betake ourselves to the water and tempt God ; for the devil is furious against us and lives in the water, and is better guarded against before than repented of after, and it is unnecessary for us to add to the foolish joy of the Pope and his gang. I did not think the Saale could make such a broth, which has flooded the embankments. No more at present. Pray for us and be good. I think had you been here you would have advised me to do as I did, in which case I should have taken your advice for once. God bless you.

MARTIN LUTHER.

On the 28th the party crossed the Saale, and passed on to Eisleben with a cavalry guard of honor, through the little village of Rixdorf inhabited by the Jews. From Eisleben Luther wrote often to his wife, the most beautiful letters he ever penned, full of affection, trust, and gentle humor. In spite of his approaching end his good spirits seem to have come back to him.

TO CATHARINE LUTHER AT WITTENBERG

(EISLEBEN,) February 1, 1546.

I wish you grace and peace in Christ, and send you my poor, old, infirm love. Dear Katie, I was weak on the road to Eisleben, but that was my own fault. Had you been with me you would have said it was the fault of the Jews or of their God. For we had to pass through a village hard by Eisleben where many Jews live ; perhaps they blew on me too hard. (In the city of Eisleben there are at this hour fifty Jewish residents.) As I drove through the village such a cold wind blew from behind through my cap on my head that it was like to turn my brain to ice. This may have helped my vertigo, but now, thank God, I am so well that I am sore tempted by fair women and care not how gallant I am.

When the chief matters are settled, I must devote myself to driving out the Jews. Count Albert is hostile to them, and has given them their deserts, but no one else has. God willing, I will help Count Albert from the pulpit.

I drink Neunburger beer of just that flavor which you praised so much at Mansfeld. It pleases me well and acts as a laxative.

Your little sons went to Mansfeld day before yesterday, after they had humbly begged Jack-an-apes [1] to take them. I don't know what they are doing ; if it were cold they might freeze, but as it is warm they may do or suffer what they like. God bless you with all my household and remember me to my table companions.

Your old lover,

M. L.

On the same day Luther wrote Melanchthon more fully of his ill health and of the progress of negotiations. The two disputants were the brothers Count Albert and Count Gebhard. Among the several questions at issue, the hardest was that of the legal rights of each brother in Neustadt Eisleben, recently founded by Count Albert. Luther urged mutual concession and brotherly love ; he made much progress and, in his own opinion, would have made more had it not been for the lawyers.

---

[1] Hans von Jena ; at Jena under the clock on the tower of the Rathaus is a wooden head of a man, which, whenever the clock strikes, opens its mouth and snaps at an apple offered him by an angel, but which is always withdrawn before he gets it. This is Hans of Jena, though some think that the wooden head was made later than the Reformation. At any rate the expression was proverbial and is often used by Luther to signify a person who stands around gaping and minding other people's business. Cf. Enders, viii, 163. Whom he means here I cannot say ; the boys probably visited their uncle James.

TO PHILIP MELANCHTHON AT WITTENBERG

EISLEBEN, February 1, 1546.

Grace and peace in the Lord. I thank you, dear Philip, for praying for me and I ask you to keep on doing so. You know that I am an old man, and that some of the rough work even of my own calling should be spared me, whereas now I am involved in a quarrel alien to my interests, beyond my power to cope with and distasteful to my age. I should wish that you were with me did not the argument of your health rather force me to think that we did well to leave you at home. To-day, by God's blessing, we stuck that supernaturally prickly porcupine Neustadt, though not without a hard struggle. We hope it will please God to make the remaining battles easier. I have offended Dr. Kling [1] rather deeply, I think, because I am angry at the severity and sharpness of the law; but he first offended me by his enormous and ill-considered vice of proclaiming victory before the battle. A little learning makes lawyers mad. Almost all these men seem to be ignorant of the real use of the law, base and venal pettifoggers caring not at all for peace, the state of religion about which we care now as always.

A fainting fit overtook me on the journey and also that disease which you are wont to call palpitation of the heart. I went on foot, overtaxed my strength and perspired; later in driving my shirt became cold with sweat; this made my left arm stiff. My age is to blame for the heart trouble and the shortness of breath. Now I am quite well again, though I do not know for how long. When even youth is not safe, age can little be trusted.

God has hitherto granted that all the counts [2] of Mansfeld show wonderful good-will to each other. Pray that God may increase and continue this. Now that we have conquered Enceladus and Typhoeus we will proceed to-morrow to pursue the rest among whom we suspect the citizen. [3] God lives; may he conquer. Amen. Farewell in the Lord, dear Philip, and give my greetings to all — Pastor Bugenhagen, Cruciger, and the rest, whom we thank for their prayers, with no small faith that God will grant them.

DR. MARTIN LUTHER.

Of the progress of negotiations and of his health Luther gives constant news.

[1] Professor of law at Wittenberg and Mansfeld counsellor.

[2] It will be remembered that on the continent of Europe all the children of a count bear that title.

[3] Purherr. I am not sure of the meaning of the word, which I take to be Burger. The identity of the person is also unknown to me.

TO CATHARINE LUTHER AT WITTENBERG

(EISLEBEN,) February 10, 1546.

Grace and peace in Christ. Most holy lady doctoress! I thank you kindly for your great anxiety which keeps you awake. Since you began to worry we have almost had a fire at the inn, just in front of my door, and yesterday, due to your anxiety no doubt, a stone nearly fell on my head which would have squeezed it up as a trap does a mouse. For in my bedroom lime and cement had dribbled down on my head for two days, until I called attention to it, and then the people of the inn just touched a stone as big as a bolster and two spans wide, which thereupon fell out of the ceiling. For this I thank your anxiety, but the dear angels protected me. I fear that unless you stop worrying the earth will swallow me up or the elements will persecute me. Do you not know the catechism and the creed? Pray, and let God take thought as it is written: "Cast thy burden on the Lord and he shall sustain thee," both in Psalm 55 and other places.

I am, thank God, well and sound, except that the business in hand disgusts me, and Jonas takes upon himself to have a bad leg, where he hit himself on a trunk; people are so selfish that this envious man would not allow me to have the bad leg. God bless you. I would willingly be free of this place and return home if God will. Amen. Amen. Amen.

Your holiness's obedient servant,

MARTIN LUTHER.

TO CATHARINE LUTHER AT WITTENBERG

EISLEBEN, February 14, 1546.

Grace and peace in the Lord. Dear Katie, we hope to come home this week if God will. God has shown great grace to the lords, who have been reconciled in all but two or three points. It still remains to make the brothers Count Albert and Count Gebhard real brothers; this I shall undertake to-day and shall invite both to visit me, that they may see each other, for hitherto they have not spoken, but have embittered each other by writing. But the young lords and the young ladies, too, are happy and make parties for fools' bells and skating, and have masquerades and are all very jolly, even Count Gebhard's son. So we see that God hears prayer.

I send you the trout given me by the Countess Albert. She is heartily happy at this union.

Your little sons are still at Mansfeld. James Luther will take care of them. We eat and drink like lords here and they wait on us so well — too well, indeed, for they might make us forget you at Wittenberg. Moreover I am no more troubled with the stone. Jonas's leg has become right bad; it is looser on the shin-bone, but God will help it.

You may tell Melanchthon and Bugenhagen and Cruciger everything.

A report has reached here that Dr. Martin Luther has left for Leipsic or Magdeburg. Such tales are invented by those silly wiseacres, your countrymen. Some say the Emperor is thirty miles from here, at Soest in Westphalia; some that the French and the Landgrave of Hesse are raising troops. Let them say and sing; we will wait on God. God bless you.

Dr. Martin Luther.

This was the last letter Luther ever wrote. A treaty between the brothers he had reconciled was drawn up on February 16 and signed by him the day following. On the same day he felt faintness and pressure around the breast, but was somewhat relieved by the application of warm towels and doses of brandy before he went to bed. He felt ill in the night, rose and went into the next room — the house and apartments may still be seen at Eisleben; it was at that time an inn — where he lay down on the couch. This was about two o'clock on the morning of February 18. His friends were soon aroused, and with him, in this last hour, were Jonas, Aurifaber, and Cölius, the Mansfeld priest, his two sons Martin and Paul (where Hans was is not known), and one of the countesses of Mansfeld. Among his last words the following were remembered : —

Dr. Jonas and Cölius and you others, pray for the Lord God and his Evangelic Church because the Council of Trent and the wretched Pope are wroth with him.

O Lord God, I am sorrowful. O dear Jonas, I think I shall remain at Eisleben where I was born and baptized.

O my heavenly Father, one God and Father of our Lord Jesus Christ, thou God of all comfort, thou God of all comfort, I thank thee that thou hast given for me thy dear son Jesus Christ, in whom I believe, whom I have preached and confessed, loved and praised, whom the wicked Pope and all the godless shame, persecute, and blaspheme. I pray thee, dear Lord Jesus Christ, let me commend my soul to thee.

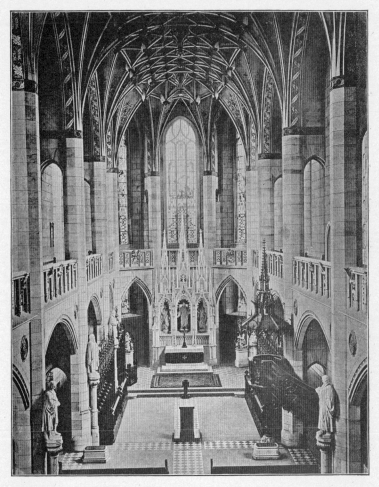

CASTLE CHURCH AT WITTENBERG, WHERE LUTHER IS BURIED

O heavenly Father, if I leave this body and depart I am certain that I will be with thee for ever and can never, never tear myself out of thy hands.

God so loved the world that he gave his only begotten son, that whosoever believeth in him should not perish but have everlasting life. (This he said thrice.)

Father, into thy hands I commend my spirit. Thou hast redeemed me, thou true God.

The immediate cause of Luther's death was apoplexy, which deprives the patient of power of speech instantly. The stroke, the proof of which was found by the apothecaries who examined the body the next day, must have come during a fainting spell. As Luther was losing consciousness, Jonas and Cölius had to speak loud to make him hear: "Reverend father, will you stand steadfast by Christ and the doctrine you have preached?" The dying man answered "Yes," the last word he spoke distinctly, though the friends around him thought they made out one more murmur: "Who hath my word shall never see death."

The body was taken back to Wittenberg, and buried, on February 22, in the church where he had long ago nailed his theses on indulgences — those words that shook the world.

EPILOGUE

THE LAST YEARS AND DEATH OF LUTHER'S WIFE

WHEN Luther's death became known a loud cry of sorrow went up from all who had known him. Great men are usually deeply loved, and the many letters still extant, mourning the death of a "father," prove that he was no exception to the rule. A biography may well pass over them all, even that of his son Hans to Jonas, but one, that of his nearest and dearest, the wife whose last sad years can hardly fail to interest those who have a care for her husband. Several of her letters have been preserved, all of a formal kind save this, which rings truer and tells more of Katie than anything else. It makes us regret that her other letters to her husband and son Hans have all perished. The occasion of Katie's writing to her sister was to promise her help to her sister's son, Florian von Bora, who was enabled to continue his studies at Wittenberg by a pension given him by Henry Hilbrand von Einsiedel: —

CATHARINE LUTHER TO CHRISTINA VON BORA

WITTENBERG, April 2, 1546.

Grace and peace in God the Father of our Lord Jesus Christ. Kind, dear sister! I can easily believe that you have hearty sympathy with me and my poor children. Who would not be sorrowful and mourn for so noble a man as was my dear lord, who much served not only one city or a single land but the whole world? Truly I am so distressed that I cannot tell my great heart sorrow to any one, and hardly know what to think or how I feel. I cannot eat nor drink, neither can I sleep. If I had had a principality and an empire, it would never have cost me so much pain to lose them as I have now that our Lord God has taken from me, and not from me only, but from the whole world, this dear and precious man. When I think of it, God knows that for sorrow and weeping I can neither speak nor dictate this letter; you yourself, dear sister, have experienced a similar sorrow.

As to your son, my dear nephew, I will gladly do what I can. If he only has the opportunity I fully expect that he will study with all diligence and not spend his precious, noble youth uselessly and in vain. But if he must spend a little more in his studies, or needs other and more books now that he has begun to study law, you must know yourself, dear sister, that I cannot buy him such books. And he should have a little greater consideration, so that he can return what he receives to him, who, as you write, is going to give your son, my nephew, a yearly stipend. Thus he could remain at his studies and more easily obtain his object. But about what I can do for him I will further consult and decide when my brother Hans von Bora comes to see me. God bless you.

CATHARINE VON BORA, Dr. Martin Luther's widow.

In the same year that Luther died the great storm which had so often blown over before, burst, and ruined his family, his sovereign, and for the moment almost appeared to sweep away the Church he had founded. In the Schmalkaldic war, Germany first experienced the horrors of a religious conflict. Duke Maurice of Saxony, lured on by the bait of the electoral hat worn by his cousin, promised him in case of victory, made an alliance with the Emperor and attacked the League of Schmalkalden. John Frederic was defeated by Charles V in the battle of Mühlberg, April 24, 1547, wounded and captured. Philip of Hesse was soon after taken by treachery, and both princes were kept in painful durance for five years. The title of elector, with Wittenberg and half the lands of John Frederic, were transferred to Maurice.

Our present interest in the war is chiefly as it concerned Katie. She fled to Magdeburg in November, 1546, and had hardly returned before she was obliged to flee again to Brunswick, returning to Wittenberg in July, 1547. Although the town had been given to Maurice, the inhabitants were left undisturbed in their religion.

Katie's property, much damaged by the war, was completely ruined by the lawsuits instituted by the unfriendly Chancellor Brück during the captivity of the Elector. Luther had left a considerable property, estimated by him at nine thousand gulden in real estate and one thousand in personal property, minus a few hundreds of debt, an estate roughly equivalent to one hundred thousand dollars to-day. The income from this estate was scarcely one hundred gulden per annum, besides which Katie might expect another hundred in pensions from the Elector and the King of Denmark. The former, however, was unable to pay the pension he had given, but even thus Katie might have lived well but for the fact that her husband's dislike of lawyers induced him to dispense with their services in drawing up his will. The chancellor was therefore able to break the will and have guardians appointed both for Katie and the children. Luther's widow was a woman of no common energy and gained all the contested points both as to the guardians appointed and as to the use made of the property. She did so, however, at the cost of what was left of her fortune, and was obliged to earn her own bread by taking boarders in the Black Cloister.

Thus she lived until, in the autumn of 1552, she was again obliged to leave Wittenberg, this time on account of the plague. The horse shied, and in jumping out of the wagon Katie fell heavily in a pool of water. The mishap brought on an illness, of which she died, after three months of agony, on December 20. She was buried the next day in the church at Torgau far from her husband's side.

APPENDIX

APPENDIX

I

CHRONOLOGICAL TABLES

I. Luther's Life

1483 November 10, born at Eisleben.

1484 to 1497 at Mansfeld where his father is a miner.

1497 to 1498 at school of the Nullbrüder (Brothers of the Common Life) at Magdeburg.

1498–1501 at St. George's school at Eisenach ; with Frau Cotta.

1501 about May, matriculates at the University of Erfurt.

1502 takes the degree of bachelor of arts.

1505 takes the degree of master of arts.

1505 July 12, enters the Augustinian monastery at Erfurt.

1507 spring, ordained priest. First mass May 2.

1508 about November called to teach Aristotle's Ethics at the University of Wittenberg (founded 1502).

1509 March 9, takes the degree of *baccalaureus ad biblia*.

1509 autumn, called to teach Lombard's Sentences at Erfurt.

1510 (or 1511) October to 1511 (or 1512) February, journey to Rome ; the month of December spent in the city.

1511 summer, returns to Wittenberg to lecture on the Bible.

1512 October 18 takes the degree of doctor of theology.

1515 May, elected district vicar of his order.

1517 October 31, posts the Ninety-five Theses on indulgences on the door of the Castle Church at Wittenberg.

1518 October 12, 13, and 14, interview with Cardinal Cajetan at Augsburg.

1519 January 4 and 5 (or 5 and 6) interview with Miltitz at Altenburg.

1519 July 4–14, debate with John Eck at Leipsic.

1520 June 15, Leo X signs the bull Exsurge Domine threatening to excommunicate Luther within 60 days.

1520 August, publication of The Address to the Christian Nobility of the German Nation on the Improvement of the Christian Estate.

1520 October, publication of the work On the Babylonian Captivity of the Church.

1520 November, publication of the tract On the Freedom of a Christian Man.

1520 December 10, Luther burns the Pope's bull and the Canon Law.

1521 April 17 and 18, Luther appears before the Emperor and Diet at Worms.

1521 May 4 to 1522 March 1, at the Wartburg in hiding.

1525 May, writes Against the thievish murderous Hordes of Peasants.

1525 June 13 marries Catharine von Bora (born at Lippendorf, January 29, 1499; enters Nimbschen Cistercian Cloister 1508 (or 1509); takes the veil October 8, 1515; leaves the cloister April 4–5, 1523).

1526 June 7, Hans Luther born.

1527 July, severe illness of Luther.

1527 (?) *Ein Feste Burg.*

1527 December 10, Elizabeth Luther born.

1528 August 3, Elizabeth Luther dies.

1529 May 4, Magdalene Luther born.

1529 October 2, conference at Marburg with Zwingli and other theologians.

1530 April 23 to October 4, at Feste Coburg during the Diet of Augsburg.

1530 May 29, Luther's father dies.

1531 June 30, Luther's mother dies.

1531 November 9, Martin Luther born.

1532 February 4, the Black Cloister deeded to Luther and his heirs.

1532 Completion of the translation of the Bible (begun 1521).

1533 January 28, Paul Luther born.

1534 December 17, Margaret Luther born.

1535 November 7, the papal legate Vergerio comes to Wittenberg and has a conference with Luther.

1536 May 29, the Wittenberg Concordia signed by Luther and the leaders of the German Zwinglians.

1537 February, Luther goes to the Congress of Schmalkalden, but becoming very ill with the stone, is forced to leave.

1537 February 27, Luther's First Will.

1539 May, Luther goes to Leipsic to inaugurate the Reformation in Albertine Saxony.

1539 December 10, Luther signs the "Confessional Counsel" giving Philip of Hesse permission to take a second wife.

1540 January and February, Catharine Luther very ill.

1540 July, Luther at the conference at Eisenach.

1542 January 6, Luther's Second Will.

1542 September 20, Magdalene Luther dies.

1546 February 18, Luther dies at Eisleben.

1552 December 20, Catharine Luther dies.

II. Popes

1503–1513 Julius II.

1513–1521 December 1, Leo X.

1522–1523 September 14, Adrian VI.

1523–1534 September, Clement VII.

1534–1549 Paul III.

III. Emperors

1493–1519 January 19, Maximilian.

1519–1555 Charles V (elected June, 1519; crowned October 23, 1520).

IV. Electors of Saxony (Ernestine Branch)

1487–1525 May, Frederic the Wise.

1525–1532 August, John the Steadfast.

1532–1547 John Frederic the Magnanimous; lived as Duke of Saxony till 1554.

V. Dukes of Saxony (Albertine Branch)

1485–1500 Albert.

1500–1539 April 17, George the Bearded.

1539–1541 August, Henry the Pious.

1541–1546 Maurice, made Elector 1546, and lived till 1553.

VI. Landgrave of Hesse

1508–1567 Philip the Magnanimous (born 1504, declared of age 1517).

VII. Important Events in German History

1485 August 25, Treaty of Leipsic dividing Saxony into two parts, Electoral or Ernestine and Ducal or Albertine.

1521 Diet of Worms. May 26, Edict of Worms signed, dated May 8.

1523 Revolt of the Knights under Sickingen, quelled at Landstuhl, May 7.

1524 Diet of Nuremberg.

1524-1525 Peasants' War, suppressed in the north at Frankenhausen in May.

1525 Conversion of Prussia.

1525 Victory of Charles V over Francis I at Pavia, February 24.

1526 League of Torgau formed between Philip of Hesse and John of Saxony, May 4.

1526 Diet and Recess of Spires, June and July.

1527 Sack of Rome by imperial troops, May 6.

1529 Diet of Spires opened February 26. Recess of Spires April 12. Protest of the Lutheran princes, April 25.

1530 Diet of Augsburg. June 15, arrival of Emperor. June 25, "Augsburg Confession" read. November 19, publication of the Recess of Augsburg in an Imperial Edict.

1531 Election of Ferdinand as King of the Romans, January.

1531 Battle of Cappel, in which Zurich is defeated and Zwingli slain, October 11.

1532 Diet of Ratisbon.

1532 July, Peace of Nuremberg between Catholics and Protestants.

1534 Anabaptist rising in Münster.

1534 Restoration of Duke Ulrich of Württemberg by Philip of Hesse.

1537 Congress of the allies at Schmalkalden, February.

1539 February to April, Congress of Frankfort, negotiations with the Emperor, and Treaty of Frankfort signed April 19.

1539 Reformation of Ducal Saxony under Henry the Pious, May.

1540 Religious conference of Hagenau, June.

1541 Religious conference of Worms, January.

1541 Diet and religious conference at Ratisbon, April to July.

1541 Reformation of Halle.

1542 Diets of Spires and Nuremberg.

1542 War of the Schmalkaldic League with Brunswick, whose duke, Henry, is expelled.

1543 Diet of Nuremberg.

1544 Diet of Spires.

1545 Diet of Worms.

1545 Opening of Council of Trent.

1546 Diet of Ratisbon.

1546 Outbreak of Schmalkaldic War.

1547 Battle of Mühlberg April 24; John Frederic captured and Maurice of Albertine Saxony given the electorate and some of his lands.

II

BIBLIOGRAPHY

General Bibliography

A complete bibliography of books on Luther would include more than two thousand books and perhaps as many articles in periodicals. Most of these are now useless. The following bibliography does not pretend to anything like completeness. I intend to give only the sources in the best editions and the most valuable books on general phases of Luther's life and times.

I. Bibliographies

Fabritius: Centifolium Lutheranum.

E. G. Vogel: Bibliotheca biographica Lutherana. 1851.

British Museum Catalogue. Volume on Luther printed separately. 1894.

Hinrich: Bücherlexicon. Annual, 1750 ff.

Jahresberichte der Geschichtswissenschaften. Annual.

Zeitschrift für Kirchengeschichte. Gotha. Quarterly bibliographies to December, 1909. (With the number March 1910 the bibliographies are discontinued.)

Cambridge Modern History. Vol. ii (London, 1904), pp. 728 ff.

Catalogues of the Bibliotheca Theologica of the collection of Wm. Jackson, issued by Harrasowitz. Leipsic. 1910.

E. Weller: Repertorium typographicum. Nördlingen. 1864. 1874. 1885.

Bibliotheca Lindesiana. Catalogue of 1500 tracts by Luther and his contemporaries, 1511–1598. Privately printed. 1903.

II. Unpublished Sources

Very little of importance that is known is unpublished. The Colloquia Serotina is a manuscript in the royal library at Gotha, containing table-talk from Lauterbach's notes, of the years 1536, 1537, and 1539. A diplomatically correct copy of this was made by J. K. Seidemann, who intended to print it, but died before he could do so. I have read his copy, now in the possession of Professor Kawerau of Berlin. As some extracts from it had been published by E. Kroker

(Luther's Tischreden in der Mathesischen Sammlung, p. 357 ff.),
and as some of the sayings had been taken into Lauterbach's table-
talk (edited by Bindseil, 1863–66), there was very little new in this
manuscript. But cf. p. 466.

I have read a portion of the Commentary on Romans in Luther's
manuscript; this, however, has recently been published.

I have obtained photographs of the original manuscripts of several
letters (at the Berlin Royal Library and elsewhere). From these fac-
similes corrections on the originals can often be made; the most important are on Luther's letter of April 17, 1521, for which see
p. 472. Material on Luther from English libraries hitherto unpublished is published by me in Zeitschrift für Kirchengeschichte,
February, 1911.

On the yet unpublished material on Luther, which is coming out in
the Weimar edition, see:

Koffmane: Die handschriftliche Ueberlieferung von Werken D. M.
Luthers. Liegnitz. 1907.

Other documents follow in this Appendix.

III. LUTHER'S WORKS

Luther's sämtliche Werke, kritische Ausgabe. Weimar. 1883 ff. As
yet have appeared volumes i–ix, x, part i, half i, parts ii and iii, xi–xvi,
xvii, part i, xviii–xx, xxiii–xxx, xxxii–xxxiv, xxxvi, xxxvii, xli, and
(unnumbered) Deutsche Bibel, volumes i and ii. This edition, with
thorough critical work, good introductions, and much new material,
surpasses all others. It is not, unfortunately, quite complete, even as
far as it goes, that is to about 1532. The letters, to be edited by
Professor Kawerau, may be expected to appear when the edition by
Enders and Kawerau is finished; the table-talk, which has been entrusted to Dr. E. Kroker, will occupy six volumes, of which the first
may be expected in 1911.

Dr. M. Luthers Sämtliche Werke. Erlangen. 1826–1886.
German works, 67 volumes (i–xx and xxiv–xxvi in the second
edition).
Latin works, 33 volumes, numbered.
Commentary on Galatians, 3 volumes.
Opera latina varii argumenti, 7 volumes.
Luthers Sämtliche Werke, herausgegeben von J. G. Walch. Halle.
1740–1753. The Latin works are here translated into German. A
second edition of Walch, much improved, has been recently issued by
the Concordia Verlag of St. Louis.

Luthers Werke. Berlin. 1903. 10 volumes. This is a selection edited by the best scholars with good text and introductions.

N. B. I cite from the Weimar edition as far as complete; after that from the Berlin or Erlangen editions.

Besides the collections of Luther's works, the following supplements must be used : —

Drews : Disputationen Dr. M. Luther's. Göttingen. 2 vols. 1895–6.

Ficker : Luthers Vorlesung über den Römerbrief. Strassburg. 1908.

Buchwald : Ungedruckte Predigten D. M. Luthers, 1537–1540. Leipzig. 1906 (1905).

Buchwald : Luthers Predigten zu Dessau, Juli 1534. Leipzig. 1909.

Very many of Luther's works have been translated into English, as may be seen by the catalogue of the British Museum. The most important are : —

De libertate christiani. The Liberty of a Christian Man. Cum privilegio regali. Imprynted at the sonne by me John Byddell. (London. Between 1530 and 1544.)

A Commentarie of Dr. Martin Luther upon the Epistle of S. Paul to the Galathians, first collected and gathered word for word out of his preaching (1535) and now out of Latine . . . faithfully translated into English. T. Vautroullier. London. 1575 (often reprinted).

M. Luther's Preface to the Epistle to the Romans. Translated by W. W. Woodcock. (1575–94.)

Special and chosen sermons of D. M. Luther. Englished by W. G. (Gace) T. Vautroullier. London. 1578. (Thirty-four sermons, often reprinted.)

A right comfortable Treatise conteining sundrye pointes of consolation for them that labour and are laden. . . . Englished by W. Gace. T. Vautroullier. London. 1580. (This is a translation of Luther's Tesseradecas.)

Martin Luther's Colloquia Mensalia, or his last Divine Discourses at his table. . . . Translated out of the High Dutch by Captain Henry Bell. London. 1652 (often reprinted).

On the Bondage of the Will, by Martin Luther. Translated by H. Cole. London. 1823.

Select Works of Martin Luther, an offering to the Church of God in these "last days." Translated by H. Cole. London. 1826. (This contains, besides some minor works and selections, versions of The

Liberty of a Christian Man, The Tesseradecas, On Good Works,
Commentary on the first Twenty-two Psalms.)

Luther's Primary Works, together with his shorter and longer
catechisms, translated by H. Wace and C. A. Buchheim. London.
1896. (Besides the catechisms this contains: The Ninety-five Theses,
The Address to the German Nobility on the Improvement of the
Christian Estate, On the Babylonian Captivity of the Church, and
The Liberty of a Christian Man.)

Standard edition of Luther's Works, translated by J. N. Lenker.
Minneapolis. 1903 ff. As yet have appeared eight volumes containing
the Church Postil, Epistle Sermons, Commentary on the first twenty-
two Psalms, Commentary on Jude and Peter, and The Catechetical
Writings.

The Letters of Martin Luther. Selected and translated by Margaret
A. Currie. London. 1908.

IV. Letters

(A) To February 1540

Dr. Martin Luther's Briefwechsel, bearbeitet von Dr. E. L.
Enders und Dr. G. Kawerau. 12 volumes. 1884–1910. This edition
of the letters is not complete, even as far as it goes. For supplements,
see Appendix II. The German letters are not printed, but only regis-
tered by Enders and Kawerau, and for their text reference is made to
the Erlangen edition of the Works (see above), volumes 53–56.

(B) From February 1540 to February 1546

W. M. L. de Wette: Luthers Briefe. 5 volumes. Berlin. 1825–8.
De Wette–Seidemann: Sixth volume. Berlin. 1856.

Seidemann: Lutherbriefe. Dresden. 1859.

C. A. H. Burkhardt: Dr. Martin Luther's Briefwechsel. Leipzig.
1866.

M. Lenz: Briefwechsel des Landgrafen Philipp mit Bucer. Vol. i.
Leipzig. 1880.

M. Lenz: Nachlese zum Briefwechsel des Landgrafen Philipp mit
Luther und Melanchthon. Zeitschrift für Kirchengeschichte, iv (1881),
133 ff.

T. Kolde: Analecta Lutherana. Gotha. 1883.

Tschackert: Zum Luthers Briefwechsel. Zeitschrift für Kirchengeschichte, xi (1889), 290 ff.

F. Gundlach: Nachträge zum Briefwechsel des Landgrafen Philipp
mit Luther und Melanchthon. Schriften des Vereins für hessische
Geschichte, xxviii. Cassel. 1904.

C. A. H. Burkhardt : Zum ungedruckten Briefwechsel der Reformatoren, besonders Luthers. Archiv für Reformationsgeschichte, no.
xiv. 1907.

V. TABLE-TALK

H. Wrampelmeyer : Tagebuch über Dr. Martin Luther geführet
von Dr. Conrad Cordatus. Halle. 1885.

H. Wrampelmeyer : Tischreden Dr. M. Luthers aus einer Sammlung des C. Cordatus. In Festschrift des königlichen Gymnasiums zu
Clausthal. 1905.

J. K. Seidemann, in Sächsische Kirchen- und Schulblätter 1876–
1877, publishes some of Dietrich's notes.

W. Preger : Luthers Tischreden aus den Jahren 1531 und 1532
nach den Aufzeichnungen von J. Schlaginhaufen. Leipzig. 1888.

E. Kroker : Luthers Tischreden in der Mathesischen Sammlung.
Leipzig. 1903.

E. Kroker : Rörers Handschriftbände und Luthers Tischreden. In
Archiv für Reformationsgeschichte. 1908, pp. 337 ff. ; 1910, pp. 56 ff.

J. K. Seidemann : Lauterbach's Tagebuch auf das Jahr 1538.
Dresden. 1872.

H. E. Bindseil : D. Martini Lutheri Colloquia. . . . Lemgoviae
et Detmoldiae. 3 vols. 1863–1866.

K. E. Förstemann und H. E. Bindseil : Luthers Tischreden. 4
vols. Berlin. 1844–1848.

Lösche : Analecta Lutherana et Melanthonia. Gotha. 1892.

Corpus Reformatorum, xx, 519–608.

(The Table-Talk will be published in six volumes in the Weimar
edition : the first volume, expected in 1911, will be devoted to Dietrich's notes.)

The Table-Talk has been twice translated, from Aurifaber.

H. Bell : Dr. Martin Luther's Colloquia mensalia, or his last Divine Discourses at his Table. London. 1652.

W. Hazlitt : Luther's Table Talk. London. 1848.

VI. COLLECTIONS OF SOURCES

Balan : Monumenta reformationis Lutheranae. Regensburg. 1884.

O. Clemen : Flugschriften aus der Reformationszeit. Halle. 1904 ff.

O. Clemen : Briefe aus der Reformationszeit. Zeitschrift f. Kirchengeschichte, xxxi (1910), 1 and 2.

P. S. Allen : Letters of 1500–1530. English Historical Review,
xxii (1907), 740 ff.

W. Friedensburg : Zum Briefwechsel der katholischen Gelehrter.,

Zeitschrift f. Kirchengeschichte, xviii, 106 ff., 283 ff., 420 ff., 596 ff. ; xix, 231 ff., 473 ff.; xx, 242 ff., 500 ff.; xxi, 537 ff.; xxiii, 110 ff., 438 ff.

Piiper : Primitiae pontificiae. Theologorum neerlandicorum disputationes contra Lutherum, ab 1519 usque ad 1526. Hagae-Com. 1905.

O. Schade : Satiren und Pasquille aus der Reformationszeit. 3 vols. 2d ed. Hanover. 1863.

Aleander, see Bibliography to Chapter x.

Briefwechsel des Beatus Rhenanus, ed. A. Horawitz und K. Hartfelder. Leipzig. 1886.

Briefwechsel der Brüder Ambrosius und Thomas Blaurer. 1509–1548. Ed. T. Schiess. 2 vols. Frieburg i. Br. 1908, 1910.

Briefwechsel Dr. J. Bugenhagen, ed. O. Vogt. 1888.

Calvini opera, ed. G. Baum, E. Cunitz, E. Reuss, in Corpus Reformatorum. Vols. xxi-lxxxvii. Brunswick and Berlin. 1861-1900.

J. Cochlaeus : Commentaria de actis et scriptis M. Lutheri 1517–46. Apud St. Victorem prope Moguntiam. 1549. (I use copy in Bibliothèque Nationale, Paris, D 1447.)

Albrecht Dürer's schriftlicher Nachlass, ed. E. Heidrich. Berlin. 1908.

Briefe von H. Emser, J. Cochlaeus, J. Mensing und P. Rauch an die Fürsten Johann und Georg und die Fürstin Margarete von Anhalt. Ed. O. Clemen. Münster i. W. 1907.

Erasmus, see bibliography to Chapter xviii.

Epistolae obscurorum virorum, ed. Stokes. London. 1909.

Georg Helt's Briefwechsel, ed. O. Clemen. Leipzig. 1907.

Briefwechsel des Landgrafen Philipps mit Bucer, ed. M. Lenz. 3 vols. 1880-91.

Hutten, see bibliography to Chapter vii.

Briefwechsel des Justus Jonas, ed. G. Kawerau. 2 vols. Halle. 1884-5.

J. Kessler : Sabbata. Chronik der Jahre 1523-39, ed. E. Egli und Schoch St. Gallen. 1902.

Hartmuth von Kronbergs Schriften, ed. E. Kück. Halle. 1899.

J. Mathesius' Ausgewählte Werke, ed. G. Lösche, Prague. 1896-8. Historien von des Ehrwirdigen. . . . M. Luthers Anfang, Lehr, Leben und Sterben. Band iii.

Melanchthon, see bibliography to Chapter vii. Melanchthon's Vita Lutheri, Corpus Reformatorum, vi, 155, and xx, 430.

Der Briefwechsel des Mutianus Rufus, ed. C. Krause, Kassel. 1885.

Der Briefwechsel des Conradus Mutianus, ed. K. Gillert. 2 vols. Halle. 1890.

F. Myconius : Historia reformationis 1517-42, ed. Cyprian. Leipzig. 1718.

Bilibaldi Pirckheimeri opera, ed. Goldast. Frankfort. 1610.

K. Rück: Pirckheimeri De Bello Elvetico. Munich. 1895 (with Pirckheimer's autobiography).

(Dr. Reicke of Nuremberg and Dr. Reimann of Berlin are planning to edit Pirckheimer's correspondence.)

Die Handschiftliche Geschichte M. Ratzebergers, ed. C. S. Neudecker. Jena. 1850.

Reuchlin, see bibliography to Chapters II and IV.

Briefe an Stephan Roth, ed. Buchwald. Archiv für Geschichte d. deut. Buchhandels. 1893.

Akten und Briefe zur Kirchenpolitik Herzogs von Sachsen, ed. F. Gess. Tome i, 1517–1524. Leipzig. 1905.

Schwenckfeld, see bibliography to Chapter XXXVII.

G. Spalatin: Annales reformationis, ed. Cyprian. Leipzig. 1718.

Spalatins historischer Nachlass, ed. Neudecker und Preller. Vol. i. Jena. 1851.

Spalatiniana, ed. G. Bierbig. Theolog. St. und Kr. 1907, Heft iv; 1908, Hefte i, ii.

Staupitz, see bibliography to Chapters II and IV.

Christoph Scheurl's Briefbuch, ed. von F. von Soden und J. K. F. Knaake. 2 vols. Potsdam. 1867, 1872.

Vadianische Briefsammlung. 5 parts and 5 supplements. hg. von Arbenz und Wartmann. St. Gallen. 1890 ff.

Zwingli, see bibliography to Chapters XXI and XXII.

Die symbolichen Bücher der evangelischelutherischen Kirche. Besorgt von J. T. Müller und T. Kolde. Güterloh. 1907.

F. Küch: Politisches Archiv des Landgrafen Philipps von Hessen. (Publicationen aus k. preus. Staatsarchiven, vols. 78, 85.) Leipzig. 1904 ff. 2 vols.

Deutche Reichstagsakten unter Karl V. Herausg. von A. Kluckhohn und A. Wrede. München. 1893 ff.

Nuntiaturberichte aus Deutschland nebst ergänzenden aktenstücken, herausg. durch die k. preus. hist. Institut zu Rom. Theil I, 1533–59. Gotha. 1892 ff. (As yet have appeared 12 volumes.)

VII. Recent Lives of Luther

J. Köstlin: Martin Luther. 5th edition by G. Kawerau. Berlin. 1903.

T. Kolde: Martin Luther. Gotha. 2 vols. 1884–1893.

A. Hausrath: Luthers Leben. 1904.

A. E. Berger: Martin Luther in kulturgeschichtlicher Darstellung. Berlin. Vol. i (to 1525). 1895. Vol. ii (to 1532). 1898.

M. Lenz: Martin Luther. 3d edition. Berlin. 1897.

C. Beard : Martin Luther and the Reformation in Germany until the close of the Diet of Worms. London. 1889.

H. Denifle : Luther und Lutherthum in der ersten Entwickelung. I. Hauptband. I. Abteilung 2d edition. Mainz. 1904. (Concerned chiefly with Luther's work on Monastic Vows.) II. Abteilung. 2d edition by A. M. Weiss. 1906. (Concerned mainly with Luther's development till 1517.) I. Ergänzungsband. Die abendländischen Schriftausleger bis Luther über Justitia Dei und Justificatio. 1905.

A. M. Weiss : Luther und Lutherthum. II. Ergänzungsband. Lutherpsychologie. 1906. II. Hauptband. 1909.

A. C. McGiffert, in the Century Magazine, beginning December, 1910.

VIII. Histories of the Time

Cambridge Modern History. Vol. ii. The Reformation. London. 1904.

T. M. Lindsay : A History of the Reformation. Edinburgh. Vol. i, Germany. 1906. Vol. ii, Lands beyond Germany. 1907.

L. Pastor : Geschichte der Päpste. Vol. iv (1513–1534), pt. i. 1906. Pt. ii. 1907. Vol. v (1534–1549). 1909. English translation, edited by Ralph Kerr. London. 1908 ff. Vols. vii–x.

T. Kolde : Friedrich der Weise. 1881.

G. Mentz : Johann Friedrich. 3 vols. Jena. 1903–1909.

J. Janssen : Geschichte des deutschen Volkes seit dem Ausgange des Mittelalters. Vols. i–iii. 17th and 18th editions by Pastor. 1897 ff. English translation. 14 volumes. London.

L. Häusser : Geschichte des Zeitalters der Reformation. 1517–1648. 3d edition. 1903. In Onken's series.

L. von Ranke : Deutsche Geschichte im Zeitalter der Reformation. Vols. i–vi. Leipzig. 1894.

F. von Bezold : Geschichte der deutschen Reformation. Berlin. 1890.

M. Creighton : History of Papacy during period of Reformation. 5 vols. London. 1887–94 (vols. i, ii, in new ed. 1892).

P. Schaff : History of the Christian Church. Vol. vi, The German Reformation (1517–1530). New York. 1888.

F. Thudichum : Die deutsche Reformation (1517–1537). 2 vols. Leipsic. 1909. (Anabaptist point of view.)

T. Brieger : Die Reformation. Weltgeschichte, ed. Pflug-Hartung. Neuzeit. Vol. i. 1909.

W. Möller : Lehrbuch der Kirchengeschichte. Vol. iii. Reformation und Gegenreformation. 3d ed. Bearbeitet von G. Kawerau. Tübingen. 1907. English translation of the second edition by J. H. Freese. London and New York. 1900. 3 vols.

IX. Miscellaneous Works

H. Böhmer: Luther im Lichte der neueren Forschung. 1st ed. Leipzig. 1906. 2d ed. Leipzig. 1910. (Each edition has material not in the other.)

W. Braun: Lutherstudien und ihre Bedeutung für die Gegenwart. Neue kirchliche Zeitung, xx (1909), v, p. 329.

O. Clemen: Beiträge zur Reformationsgeschichte aus der Zwickauer Ratschulbibliothek. 3 parts. Berlin. 1903.

Eckhart: Luther im Urtheil berühmter Männer. 1908.

Hunziger: Lutherstudien. Leipzig. 1906.

Horst Sephan: Luther in den Wandlungen seiner Kirche. Giessen. 1907.

W. Walther: Lutherophilus. Halle. 1893.

W. Walther: Für Luther wider Rom. Halle. 1906.

W. Walther: Zur Werthung der deutschen Reformation. Leipzig. 1909.

D. Erdmann: Luther und die Hohenzollern. Breslau. 1883.

P. Zimmermann: Der Streit Wolf Hornungs mit Kurfürst Joachim I von Brandenburg und Luthers Beteiligung an demselben. Ztsch. f. preussiche Geschichts- und Landeskunde, xx, 310.

G. Bayer: Johann Brenz. Stuttgart. 1899.

Baum: Capito und Butzer. Eberfeld. 1860.

E. Armstrong: The Emperor Charles V. 2 vols. London. 2d ed. 1910.

Flechsig: Cranachstudien, pt. i. Berlin. 1900.

W. Reindell: Luther, Crotus und Hutten. Marburg. 1890.

N. Paulus: Die deutschen Dominikaner im Kampfe gegen Luther. 1518–1563. (Erläuterungen und Ergänzungen zu Janssens Geschichte d. deut. Volkes. hg. von L. Pastor.) Freiburg i. B. 1903.

P. Mosen: H. Emser. 1890.

G. Kawerau: H. Emser. 1898.

G. Kawerau: Caspar Güttel. Halle. 1882.

W. Vogler: Hartmuth von Kronberg. Halle. 1897.

N. Paulus: Der Augustiner Bartholomäus Arnoldi von Usingen, Luthers Lehrer und Gegner. Strassburgische Theolog. Studien. i, pt. iii. Strassburg and Freiburg. 1893.

D. Erdmann: Luther und seine Beziehungen zu Schlesien.

Bossert: Luther und Wittenberg. Ludwigsburg. 1883.

X. Works of Reference

Realencyclopädie für protestantische Theologie und Kirche, ed. Herzog und Hauck. 3d ed. 22 vols. 1896–1909. (Supplementary volume announced for 1912.)

Kirchenlexicon, ed. Wetzer und Weltes. Freiburg i. B. 1883 ff.

Dictionnaire de la Théologie Catholique. Paris. 1903 ff.

Die Religion in Geschichte und Gegenwart. Handwörterbuch in Gemeinverständlicher Darstellung, ed. H. Gunkel, O. Scheel und F. M. Schiele. Tübingen. 1910 ff.

Dictionnaire d'Histoire et de Géographie Ecclésiastique, ed. Baudrillart. Vogt et Ronzies. Paris. 1909 ff.

The New Schaff-Herzog Encyclopædia of Religious Knowledge, ed. S. M. Jackson. New York and London. 1908 ff. Vols. i–viii. On Luther, vii, 69–79.

Allgemeine deutsche Biographie. 1844 ff.

Grimm : Deutsches Wörterbuch. Complete to " Sprechen," 10 vols.

D. Sanders : Deutsches Wörterbuch. 3 vols.

Dietz : Wörterbuch zu Luthers Schriften, pt. i. 1876.

Du Cange : Glossarium mediae et infimae latinitatis. Several editions.

SPECIAL BIBLIOGRAPHIES

CHAPTER I. CHILDHOOD AND STUDENT LIFE. 1483–1505

Sources :

Chiefly Luther's table-talk and other reminiscences in his works ; e. g., that about his spiritual director in the monastery. Weimar, xxx, iii, 530.

Monographs :

O. Clemen : Beiträge zu Reformationsgeschichte. Heft. ii. Berlin. 1903.

Grossler : Luthers Taufort. Mansfelder Blätter, xvii, 179.

Kampschulte : Die Universität Erfurt. 2 vols. Trier. 1858–60.

Krumhaar : Nullbrüder. Evangel. Kirchenzeitung. 1882. p. 442.

G. Oergel : Vom jungen Luther. Erfurt. 1899.

W. Möllenberg : Luthers Vater. Zts. des Harzvereins. xxxix, 169. 1907.

E. Schaumkell : Der Kultus der heiligen Anna. Freiburg. 1893.

Document :

The following account of the plague at Erfurt in 1505 is taken from an excessively rare book in the British Museum Print Room. Cf. Panzer : Annales typographici, vi, 495.

De Recessu Studentum ex Erphordio tempore pestilentiae. Eobani Hessi Francobergii carmen heroicum. Erfurt. 1506. 4°.

Tempus erat iam laeta Ceres adoleverat arvis;
Sole sub ardenti lunata falce Colonus
Venerat agrestis segetes incidere, vites
Frondebant, iam silva leves porrexerat umbras,
Floruit omnis ager, campi sylvaeque potentes
Et laeti arboreis cantum sparsere volucres
Frondibus argutum; repetunt arbusta Cicadae
Et nova transpicuis arrident gramina rivis.
Laeta per integrum radierunt gaudia mundum,
Quidquid erat laetum fuit exultatque per orbem.
Annus erat post quinque decem quoque saecula quintus
Postque virginea deus exiit aeditus alvo;
Tranquilla stetit infoelix Erphordia pace
Tempore non illo foelix velut esse solebat
Antea loetiferi quisquis infausta veneni
Sparsit in egregios flammantia tela Minervae
Cultores. Stygio pestis suffusa furore
Iamiam Sesseo totam madefecerat urbem
Sanguine mortiferas populus effudit et atrox
Viroso vomit ore faces et corpora diris
Suspicit hulceribus, virusque effudit in omnes
Vipereum multi licuit sperare salutem
Cum semel affixa est lateri laetalis harundo
Una lege ruunt cuncti iuvenesque senesque
Innocuam rabies adeo grassatur in urbem
Laetiferae pestis, Danaos non tanta peremit
Impietas altae vastantes moenia Troiae
Dum pater abductam repetit Chriseida Calchas
Urbs luget tetri sanie polluta veneni
Ante suos obeunt nati nataeque parentes
Et patris moriens spectat crudelia natus
Funera, nec propriam cognoscit filia matrem.
Exoritur miseranda lues, it rumor ad aedes
Palladis, et quosdam rabies haec inficit ex hiis
Quos miseri quondam ad studium misere parentes
Inficit, et tristi languencia corda veterno
Obtenebat, ferit incautos, volat ocyor Euro.
Haec fera nunc illos iaculo nunc percutit illos
Nec metuit quenquam quantumvis doctus ad arma
Pallados exurgat, furit, aestuat, inficit, aufert
Corpora, ut esuriens lupus inter ovilia plena
Imbelles obtruncat oves nec exit ab illis,
Nec praedae absistit donec non traxerit omnes
Mortis ad exitium, fera non secus illa cruentis
Aestuat hulceribus. Magnae domus alta Minervae
Moeret, et ingentes morientum sydera planctus
Accipiunt; ipso sedet alti culmine Pallas
Tegminis et peplo faciem velatur. Nephandas

Conqueritur caedes ac tristia fata suorum.
At Cytharam posuit moestam crinitus Apollo
Calliopeque, fugit Nymphis comitata latinis.
Conquerimur cuncti quos docta Erphordia quondam
Fovit et electos gremio suscepit aperto,
Vota precesque deo ferimus juvenesque senesque,
Aerea vasa sonant; Sanctae qua virginis aedes
Tres celebres Mariae tollunt ad sydera turres
Atque aliis quibus hec urbs est celeberrima templis
Atria clauduntur portae; *nigris capita alta Cucullis* [1]
Velantur juvenum ; superest spes nulla salutis,
Iamque ubi desperata salus, ubi nulla precantes
Vota juvant, ubi mors vitae dominatur et omnes
Lege ruunt Pauli, nec erat mens certa morandi,
Effugimus dum quisque potest, dum vita superstes
Cuique sua est quos preteriit furor ille cruentus;
Effugimus; *iuvat ire procul, patriosque penates*
Visere, et externas studiis renovarier urbes
Palladiis, multas quarum iam fama per annos
Delituit, fugiunt una omnes mente magistri
Quisque suos repetunt lares, unaque studentes
Quisque suum sequimur per daevia longa magistrum
Quorum aliquos memorare libet.

(Here follows a passage on two of the dead, Laurence Usingen and
a certain Lupambulus.)

Paulatim tetros Erphordia docta furores
Post multas tandem caedes evasit et aestus.
Candida mox iterum ventis dare vela paramus
Assuetam fatis petituri hortantibus urbem.
Urbs luget commota novae formidine famae.
O quales gemitus nostri peperere recessus,
Quas lachrymas quales miserunt lumina fletus,
Tristia quae nostros abitus odere. . . .

This brilliant picture of the very plague which drove the students
into the monastery and to distant parts is followed by another poem
hardly less interesting : De Pugna Studentium Erphordiensium cum
quibusdam conjuratis nebulonibus. Eobani Hessi Francobergii Carmen. 1506. This tells of a town and gown row which arose from a
student drinking-bout. It was doubtless just such an affray as Luther
says he sometimes saw in his student days. Cf. Buchwald: Ungedruckte Predigten, p. 521.

[1] The poet got one too many feet in this verse.

CHAPTERS II AND IV. LUTHER'S DEVELOPMENT. 1505–1517

A. Sources of Luther's thought in the schoolmen and fathers, in various editions

(For the editions used by Luther, cf. Weimar, ix, 1)

Augustine (works best known to Luther were: De Trinitate, De Civitate Dei). Migne: Patrologia latina, xxxii–xlvii.

G. Biel: Collectorium super quattuor libris sententiarum. Tübingen. 1501.

William of Occam: Super quattuor libris sententiarum annotationes. Lyons. 1475. (Id. Ghent. 1495.)

Id. Political works, ed. Goldast: Monarchia (13 vols. 1614). Vol. ii.

Peter Lombard: Sententiae.

Gerson et d'Ailli, ed. Ellis Dupin. Antwerp. 1706.

Monographs:

J. Altensteig: Lexicon Theologicum. Venice. 1583.

Prantl: Geschichte der Logik im Abendlande, iii and iv.

H. Hermelink: Die theologische Facultät in Tübingen vor der Reformation. Tübingen. 1906.

De Wulf: Histoire de la philosophie médiévale. Paris. 1905.

Rashdall: History of the Universities of the Middle Ages. Oxford. 1895. On Nominalism and Occam, ii, 535 ff.; on Erfurt, ii, 242 ff.

B. Mysticism

Sources:

Theologia Deutsch. Hg. von L. Mandel (Quellensch. zur Geschichte des Protestantismus, Heft 7). Leipzig. 1907.

Theologia Teutsch. sine loco. 1526. (Bodleian Library. Tract. Luth. 46 (22).)

Monographs:

H. Hering: Die Mystik Luthers. Leipzig. 1879.

Cohrs' articles Tauler and Theologia Deutsch in Realencyclopädie, xix.

C. Luther's early writings

Marginal notes on Augustine, Lombard's Sentences, Tauler, &c. Weimar, ix.

Dictata super Psalterium, 1513–16. Weimar, iii and iv.

Luthers Vorlesung über den Römerbrief. Hg. von Ficker. Leipzig. 1908.

Lectures on Judges. Weimar, iv, 529.

Lectures on Galatians. Weimar, ii, 436.

Sermons. Weimar, iv, 587.

Disputatio de theologia scolastica. Weimar, i, 221.

Monographs:

K. Benrath : Luther im Kloster 1505–25. Halle. 1905.

H. Böhmer : Luther im Lichte der neueren Forschung. 2d ed. Leipzig. 1910. Chapter I.

W. Braun : Die Bedeutung der Konkupizenz in Luthers Leben und Lehre. Berlin. 1908.

H. Denifle : Luther und Lutherthum. Vol. ii. 2d ed. Mainz. 1906.

A. W. Hunzinger : Lutherstudien. Heft i. Leipzig. 1906.

A. Jundt : La Développement de la pensée religieuse de Luther jusqu'en 1517. Paris. 1907.

K. Holl : Die Rechtfertigungslehre in Luthers Vorlesung über den Römerbrief. Zts. für Theologie und Kirche. 1910. Heft iv, 245–291.

H. Mandel : Die scholastische Rechtfertigungslehre, ihre Bedeutung für Luthers Entwickelung. Greifswald. 1906.

W. Stange : Luthers Entwickelung. Neue kirchliche Zts. xvii (1906), 661.

O. Scheel : Die Entwickelung Luthers bis zum Abschluss der Vorlesung über den Römerbrief. Schriften des Vereins f. Reformationsgeschichte, no. 100. 1910.

D. Wittenberg

Sources:

Förstemann : Album Academiae Vitebergensis. Leipzig. 1841.

Id. Liber Decanorum facultatis theologiae Academiae Vitebergensis. 1850.

J. Köstlin : Baccalaurei und Magistri der Wittenberg. phil. Facultät. 4 Hefte. 1887–91.

Muther : Die Wittenberger Universitäts und Facultätsstatuten der Jahr 1508. Halle. 1867.

Monographs:

Haussleiter : Die Universität Wittenberg vor dem Eintritt Luthers. Leipzig. 1903.

J. Köstlin : Friedrich der Weise und die Schlosskirche zu Wittenberg. 1892.

K. Schmidt : Wittenberg unter Friedrich dem Weisen. 1877.

E. The Reuchlin trial

Epistolae Obscurorum Virorum ed. Böcking. Leipzig. 1864–70.
Epistolae Obscurorum Virorum, ed. Stokes, with an English translation. London. 1910.
Johann Reuchlins Briefwechsel, ed. L. Geiger. Tübingen. 1875.

Monographs:

Böcking and Stokes, introductions.

F. The Augustinians and Staupitz

Sources:

Staupitzens sämtliche Werke, ed. Knaake. Vol. i. 1867.

Monographs:

T. Kolde: Die deutschen Augustiner Congregationen und J. von Staupitz. Gotha. 1879.

T. Kolde: Das religiöse Leben in Erfurt beim Ausgang des Mittelalters. Sch. d. Vereins für Reformationgesch. xiv. 1908.

O. Clemen, Staupitz, in Realencyclop. xviii.

G. Spalatin. (See general bibliography for sources.)

G. Bierbig: G. Spalatin und sein Verhältnis zu Luther bis 1524.
. . . Halle. 1906.

Kolde, article on Spalatin in Realencyclop. xviii.

CHAPTER III. ROME

A. Hausrath : M. Luthers Romfahrt. Berlin. 1894.

Türk : Luthers Romfahrt. Meissen. 1897.

Th. Elze : Luthers Reise nach Rom. Berlin. 1899.

N. Paulus, in Historisches Jahrbuch. 1891, 314 ff. ; 1901, p. 110 ff. ; 1904, p. 72 ff. In Historische-politische Blätter (1909), vol. cxlii, p. 738 ff.

G. Kawerau, in Deutsch-evangel. Blätter. 1901, p. 79 ff.

O. Clemen : Beiträge zur Reformationsgeschichte, iii, 89.

K. Todt: in Preussische Jahrbücher, 117, 479 ff.

F. M. Nichols: Mirabilia Urbis Romae. London. 1905.

On the Florentine Hospitals, Baedeker's Northern Italy, and P. Monnier : Le Quattrocento (Paris, 1908), ii, 170.

CHAPTERS V AND IX. THE INDULGENCE CONTROVERSY. 1517-20

A. The Theory of Indulgences

Sources :

Alexander of Hales : Summa theologiae, cap. iv.

Thomas Aquinas : Summa theologiae. Supplementum tertiae partis. Quaestiones 25-27.

Köhler : Documente zum Ablassstreit von 1517. Tübingen. 1900.

Albert, Archbishop of Mayence : Instructio summaria pro sub-commissariis. Enders : Luthers Briefwechsel, i, 116. (Extracts.)

Monographs :

Brieger : Das Wesen des Ablasses am Ausgange des Mittelalters. Leipzig. 1897.

Dieckhoff : Der Ablassstreit. Gotha. 1886.

A. Gottlob : Kreuzablass und Almosenablass. Stuttgart. 1906.

Id. Ablassentwickelung und Ablassinhalt im elften Jahrhundert. Stuttgart. 1907.

G. Kawerau : "Sobald das Geld im Kasten klingt." Barmen, 1890.

H. C. Lea : A History of Auricular Confession and Indulgence in the Latin Church. 3 vols. Philadelphia. 1896. Vol. iii, chapter iii, pp. 372-413.

N. Paulus : Johann Tetzel, der Ablassprediger. Mainz. 1899.

N. Paulus : Die Anfänge des Ablasses. Zts. für katolische Theologie 1909. Heft ii.

Id. id. Historische Jahrbücher. 1909. Heft i.

B. Luther's attack on indulgences

Sources.

W. Köhler : Luther's 95 Thesen samt deinen Resolutionen, sowie die Gegenschriften von Wimpina-Tetzel, Eck und Prierias, und die Antworten Luthers darauf. Leipzig. 1903.

The Ninety-five Theses (with facsimile). Weimar, i, 223.

Resolutiones disputationis de virtute indulgentiarum. Weimar, i, 522.

Acta Augustana. Weimar, ii, 6.

Unterricht auf etliche Artikel. Weimar, ii, 69.

A. Corsio : Il Cardinale Caetano e la Riforma. Cividale. 1902. Cajetan on Indulgences, p. 215 ; Luther at Augsburg, pp. 291-332.

C. *Process against Luther at Rome*

Sources and monographs:

Böhmer : Luther im Lichte der neueren Forschung. 2d ed. Leipzig. 1910. Chapter iii.

B. Fritsche : Die päpstliche Politik und die deutsche Kaiserwahl in 1519. Burg. 1909.

P. Kalkoff : Forschungen zu Luthers römischen Prozess. Rom. 1905.

P. Kalkoff : Die Beziehungen der Hohenzollern zur Kurie unter dem Einfluss der lutherischen Frage. Rom. 1906.

P. Kalkoff : Ablass und Reliquienverehrung an der Schlosskirche in Wittenberg. Gotha. 1907.

P. Kalkoff : W. Capito im Dienste des Erzbischof Albrecht von Mainz. Berlin. 1907.

P. Kalkoff : Cardinal Cajetan auf dem Augsburger Reichstage 1518. Quellen & Forschungen aus Ital. Archiven. x, 226–30. Rome, 1907.

Möller-Kawerau : Kirchengeschichte (1907), iii, 15 ff.

K. Müller : Luthers römischer Prozess. Zts. f. Kirchengeschichte. 1903. xxiv, 46.

L. Pastor : Geschichte der Päpste. iv, pt. i (1906), chapters vii and viii.

A. Schulte : Luthers Prozess. Quellen und Forschungen . . . vi, pp. 32, 174, 374.

A. Schulte : Die Fugger in Rom 1495–1523. 2 vols. Leipzig. 1904.

P. Kalkoff : Zu Luthers römischen Prozess. Zeitsch. f. Kirchenges. xxxi (1910), pp. 48–65, pp. 368–414.

W. Friedensburg : Eine ungedruckte Depesche Aleanders. (To Leo X, September 20–23, 1520.) Quellen und Forschungen aus Ital. Archiven, i, 150–3.

In the Harvard Library there is a collection of Luther tracts of the years 1518–20, catalogue number Nor. 2100, # x 64–93. This is annotated in a sixteenth century hand, wrongly said to be Luther's, but which is really that of one of his contemporaries, as is proved by notes referring to the years 1552 and 1556, by two references to a journey to Rome in 1516–17, and by many other allusions contradicting the known facts of Luther's life. One note, however, is of such interest that it may be given here as new evidence on Tetzel's sermons. In one of the tracts, Luther's Answer to Prierias, we read these words (p. E. iii) : " Dicunt praecones : Si haberes unam tunicam vendere deberes, ut venias redimeres, nec hoc potenti suadent, ubi quis necessario primo modo non habuerit, tum alicunde mutuet, aut mendicet, etiam si sit uxor." In the margin is written this note : " Verissima sunt ista. Namque et ego audivi tales praecones a Johanni Tizel anno domini 1516."

D. The Bull Exsurge Domine, and its burning. 1520.

Burning of the bull. Weimar, vii, 184.

J. Agricolas neuer Bericht über Luthers Verbrennung der Bann-bulle. Sitzungsber. d. k. preuss. Akad. d. Wissenschaften. 1907. v, 1–8. (Cf. O. Clemen, Theolog. St. und Kritiken. 1908. 460–469, and 1909, p. 158, and G. Kawerau, ibid. 1908, p. 587 f.)

Der Bericht des H. Scultetus über Luthers Verbrennung der Bann-bulle. Quellen und Forschungen aus Italienischen Archiven, i, 320. Rom. 1898.

Luther : Von den neuen Eckischen Bullen und Lügen. Weimar, vi, 579.

Id. Adversus execrabilem Antichristi bullam. Weimar, vi, 595.

Assertio omnium articulorum M. Lutheri per bullam Leonis X no-vissimam damnatorum. Weimar, vii, 94.

Oblatio sive Protestatio. Weimar, vi, 474.

Bulla decimi Leonis contra errores Martini Lutheri et sequacium, ed. Ulrich von Hutte. s. l. e. a. (1520). Bodleian Library Quarto B 9 Th. Seld. (The Bull Exsurge Domine.)

Bull Exsurge Domine, also edited by J. D. Mansi ; Sacrorum Con-ciliorum Nova et Amplissima Collectio, vol. xxxii (Paris, 1902), p. 1049.

CHAPTER VI. THE LEIPSIC DEBATE. 1519.

The debate. Weimar, ii, 254, with historical introduction.

O. Seitz : Der authentische Text des Leipziger Gesprächs zwischen A. Karlstadt, J. Eck und M. Luther. Berlin. 1903.

Gess : Akten und Briefe zur Kirchenpolitik Herzog Georgs von Sachsen. Leipzig. 1905. Tom. i.

T. Brieger : Einziges über die Leipziger Disputation. Leipzig. 1909. Die Leipziger Disputation, " Wartburg," viii, 30 (1908).

E. Schäfer : Luther als Kirchenhistoriker. Güterloh. 1897.

W. Köhler : Luther und die Kirchengeschichte. (To 1521.) Er-langen. 1900.

Mosellanus' account of the Leipsic debate, and of Luther's appear-ance, in a letter to J. Pflug, ed. Jortin : Life of Erasmus. 2 vols. Lon-don. 1758–1760. Vol. ii, pp. 353–8.

L. Enders : Luther und Emser. 2 vols. Halle. 1890–92.

Corpus Reformatorum, i, 87.

Chapter VII. The Patriot

Melanchthon:

Melanchthon's works and letters, mostly in Corpus Reformatorum, vols. i–xxviii, ed. by Bretschneider & Bindseil. Halle. 1834 ff.

Bindseil : Ph. Melanchthonis epistolae &c. quae in Corpore Reformatorum desiderantur. 1874.

Supplementa Melanchthonis. Ed. Clemen, Müller & al. Leipzig. Vol. i. 1910. Vol. ii. 1911.

G. Krüger : P. Melanchthon. Leipzig. 1906.

Article " Melanchthon " in Realencyclopädie, xiii, with authorities.

R. Seeburg : Die Stellung Melanchthons in der Geschichte der Kirche und Wissenschaft. Erlangen. 1897.

F. Loofs, in Theolog. Stud. u. Kritik. 1897, p. 641.

G. Kawerau, ibid., p. 668.

G. Mix : Luther und Melanchthon in ihrer gegenseitigen Beurteilung. In Theol. Stud. u. Kritik. 1901, p. 449 ff.

G. Kawerau : Luther und Melanchthon, in Deutsch-evangel. Blätter, 1903, p. 29, and 1906, p. 179.

On the influence of Huss :

Köhler : Luther und die Kirchengeschichte. Erlangen. 1900.

On Hutten and the Nationalists :

Meltzer : Luther als deutscher Mann. 1905.

Strauss : Ulrich von Hutten. 2 vols. 2d edition. Leipzig. 1874.

Hutten's works, ed. by Böcking. 5 vols. Leipsic. 1859–64.

Szamaltolski : Ulrich von Hutten. Quellen und Forschungen zur Sprach- und Kulturgeschichte der Germanischen Völker. Heft 67. 1891.

Chapter VIII

The Address to the German Nobility, The Babylonian Captivity of the Church, and The Freedom of a Christian Man

Operationes in Psalmos, 1519–21. Weimar, v.

Explanation of Dr. Martin Luther of certain articles in his sermon on the sacrament. Weimar, vi, 78.

Tesseradecas consolatoria. Weimar, vi, 99.

Of Good Works. Weimar, vi, 203.

To the Christian Nobility of the German Nation on the Improvement of the Christian Estate. Weimar, vi, 405 (with historical introduction, ibid. 381).

Prelude on the Babylonian Captivity of the Church. Weimar, vi, 497 (with historical introduction, ibid.).

On the Liberty of a Christian Man. Weimar, vii, 49 (with introduction, ibid. 1).

Wace and Buchheim : Luther's Primary Works. London. 1896.

W. E. Köhler : Luther's Schrift an den christlichen Adel deutscher Nation im Spiegel der Kultur- und Zeitgeschichte. Halle. 1895.

Benrath : "An den christlichen Adel " von M. Luther. 1884.

CHAPTER X. THE DIET OF WORMS. 1521
Sources :

A. Wrede : Deutsche Reichstagsakten unter Karl V. 1896. Luther's speeches at Worms, here ii, no. 79 ff., and Weimar, vii, 814 ff.

Magnum Bullarium Romanum. Luxemburg. 1727. The Bull Decet Romanorum Pontificem (commonly called Decet Pontificem Romanum), i, 614 f.

T. Brieger : Aleander und Luther, 1521. Gotha. 1884.

P. Kalkoff : Die Depeschen des Nuntius Aleander vom Wormser Reichstage. 1521. 2d ed. Halle. 1897.

P. Kalkoff : Nachtrag zur Korrespondenz Aleanders wahrend seiner ersten Nuntiatur in Deutschland 1520–22. Zt. für Kirchengesch. xxxv. 1904.

" Dr. Martin Luther's Passion," ed. Schade : Satiren und Pasquille, i, no. 11.

J. Paquier : Lettres familières de Jérôme Aléandre 1510–40. Paris. 1909.

P. Kalkoff : Depeschen und Berichte über Luther vom Wormser Reichstage 1521. Halle. 1898.

T. Haase : Ein Lutherbrief und ein Lutherbild. Leipziger illustrierte Zeitung, August 31, 1889. P. 220. (Facsimile of Luther's letter to Cuspinian. Same printed by Preserved Smith : Notes on Luther's Letters, Amer. Journal of Theol. April, 1910.)

E. Heidrich : Albrecht Dürer's schriftlicher Nachlass. Berlin. 1908. pp. 95 ff.

Holzinger : Ein Ulmer Bericht von Luther in Worms. Theolog. Stud. u. Kritiken. 1907. pp. 45 ff.

Monographs :

A. Hausrath : Aleander und Luther. Berlin. 1897.

P. Kalkoff : Aleander gegen Luther. Leipzig. 1908.

P. Kalkoff : W. Capito im Dienste Erzbischof Albrechts von Mainz. Berlin. 1907.

T. Kolde : Der Reichsherold Kaspar Sturm. Ar. Ref-Ges. iv, 117. 1904.

P. Meissner : "Ohne Hörner und Zähne." Ibid. iii, 321. 1904.

Schubert : Luther im Worms. Theolog. Rundschau, ii, 369.

E. Armstrong: The Emperor Charles V. 2 vols. London. 2d ed. 1910.

B. Gebbhardt: Die Gravamina der deut. Nation gegen des römischen Hof. Breslau. 1884.

E. Gossart: Charles V. Bruxelles. 1910. At Worms, pp. 175–199.

A. Wrede: Das Datum des Wormser Edicts. Historische Zeitschrift, lxxvi. 449.

Note on the words: "Here I stand, I can do no other, God help me." These words, traditionally the close of Luther's speech on April 18, appear in this form and order first in the Wittenberg edition of Luther's works, published under his supervision 1545. In a different order they are given in an account printed at Wittenberg while Luther was at the Wartburg. In his own account the closing words are simply: "God help me. Amen"; and other narratives by eye-witnesses give similar but not identical words. It is very possible that the traditional words are the right ones, as the first account is confessedly simply a summary and not an exact reproduction of the speech. But after all, it makes little difference in an estimate of Luther whether he said them or not; the fact remains that he *did* stand there and that he *could* do no other. Cf. Reichstagsakten, pp. 555 f, note, and K. Müller, in Festschrift für Kleinert. 1908.

Note on the condemnation of Luther's writings by the University of Paris. On July 17, 1520, the Sorbonne received a letter from the Elector Frederic asking for an opinion on Luther's doctrines. They referred the question to J. Berthélemi and Noel Béda, who reported their judgment at sittings on September 15 and November 17. The formal condemnation of the university was dated April 15, 1521. (For first edition: Determinatio Facultatis Parisiensis super Doctrina Lutheri, cf. Renouard: Bibliographie des œuvres de Josse Bade Ascensius. 3 vols. Paris. 1908. ii, 402. Reprinted by Du Boulay: Historia Universitatis Parisiensis (1665–73) vi. 116–127). On April 22 the Sorbonne considered what answer to give Frederic, and drafted letters to him and the Emperor, April 24. The latter was submitted to the King, whose adviser, William Petit, defended Luther. Cf. L. Delisle: La Faculté de Théologie a Paris. Notices et Extraits des MSS de la Bibliothèque Nationale (1899) xxxvi, 325 ff., 354.

Note on Luther's pictures. The only good ones are by Lucas Cranach; even the death-mask, now at Halle, being altered, and therefore unreliable. The only genuine pictures by Lucas Cranach the elder are the following: —

1. Copper engraving of 1520. Luther as monk.

2. Copper engraving of March, 1521 (cf. Enders, iii, 107). Luther as monk, profile.

3. Oil painting (somewhat damaged) in Leipsic City Library. Luther as Junker Jorg. December, 1521. This also in engraving.

4. Oil painting, original probably in Wittenberg, Luther house. Luther at his marriage, June, 1525.

5. Oil painting of 1526, in private gallery of Frau Richard von Kaufmann, Berlin. Probably taken from no. 4.

The numerous portraits of later years in German and Italian galleries are by Lucas' son Hans, or the much inferior artists of Cranach's large studio. Something of the old, stout, embittered Luther may be in them, but they cannot be compared with the pictures by Lucas. Cf. Flechsig : Cranachstudien. Pt. 1. Berlin. 1900. pp. 257 ff. I have myself examined all the genuine Cranachs and many other portraits of Luther, and, as far as a layman may, confirmed the expert opinion of Flechsig.

An opinion has been advanced that Luther was the original of one figure in Giorgione's Concert, in which case Giorgione would have had to see him during the trip to Italy (1510). So P. Schaff : History of the Christian Church, vi, 130. The idea is far-fetched and untenable. It goes back a long way. The Duke of Shrewsbury wrote in his journal November 10, 1701, that in the Prince's apartments at Florence he saw " a picture of Calvin and Luther drawn by Giorgione ; they have a woman drawn between them, I suppose to laugh at them. But it is a good piece. Calvin especially seems to have a sensible, thinking countenance." MSS of the Duke of Buccleuch and Queensbury. London. 1903. II, ii, p. 756. Giorgione died in 1511 ; Calvin was born 1509.

Chapter XI. The Wartburg

J. Luther : Die Beziehungen Dr. Martin Luthers zur Wartburg und Koburg. Berlin. 1900.

Postilla. Weimar, x, pt. 1, half i. The continuation of these in 1525 and 1527 will appear in Weimar, xxi and xxii.

Bossert in Theolog. Studien und Kritiken, 1897, pp. 271 ff., and W. Köhler, in Zeitschrift f. Wissenschaftliche Theologie, 1898, pp. 588 ff.

Luther : Wider den falsch genannten geistlichen Stand. Weimar, x, pt. ii, p. 93.

De Votis Monasticis. Weimar, viii, 564.

Scheel : " De votis monasticis," in Berlin edition (1903). Supplementary volumes 1 and 2.

Denifle: Luther und Lutherthum. 1 Hauptband, 1 Abteilung. Mainz. 1904, passim.

N. Paulus: Zu Luthers Schrift über die Mönchsgelübde, in Historische Jahrbücher, 1906, p. 487 ff.

On the New Testament, see chapter on Luther's Bible.

W. Oncken: Martin Luther in the Wartburg. "Die Wartburg," English translation. Berlin. 1907. pp. 263–272.

CHAPTERS XII AND XIII. THE WITTENBERG REVOLUTION

G. Kawerau: Luthers Rückkehr von der Wartburg, Deutsche Litteratur-Zeitung. 1893. Col. 1582.

Von Bezold, in Zeitschrift für Kirchengeschichte (1900), xx, 168 ff.

G. Kawerau: Luthers Rückkehr von der Wartburg. Halle. 1902.

H. Barge: Andreas Bodenstein von Carlstadt. 2 vols. Leipsic. 1904, 1905.

H. Barge, in Historische Zeitschrift, xcix, 256. (1907.)

H. Barge, in Historische Vierteljahrsschrift, ii, 193 ff. and 296 ff. (1908.)

H. Barge: Gemeindechristenthum in Wittenberg und Orlamünde. Leipsic. 1909.

K. Müller: Luther und Karlstadt. Tübingen. 1907.

N. Müller: Die Wittenberger Bewegung von 1521 und 1522. Seven articles in Archiv f. Reformationsgeschichte. 1909, pp. 161 ff., 261 ff., 385 ff. 1910, pp. 133 ff., 233 ff., 353 ff. 1911, pp. 1 ff.

Luther and the Swiss students at Jena, from

J. Kessler: Sabbata. Published by the Historische Verein des St. Gallen. (St. Gallen, 1902.) pp. 76 ff.

P. Wappler: Thomas Münzer in Zwickau und die Zwickauer Propheten. 1908.

Luther's Warning to all Christians to keep themselves from Tumult. Weimar, viii, 670.

Against the Heavenly Prophets of Images and the Sacrament. Weimar, xviii, 37 ff.

Eight Sermons in Lent (March 9–16, 1522). Weimar, x, pt. ii, 1 ff.

H. Lietzmann: Kleine Text für theologische. . . . Vorlesungen. . . . 1902 ff. Bonn. No. xxi. Die Wittenberger und Leisniger Kastenordnungen 1522–23.

CHAPTER XIV. THE PEASANTS' REVOLT. 1525

This is naturally not a bibliography of the Peasants' War (such may be found in Cambridge Modern History, ii (1904), pp. 752 ff. and Schapiro, 154 ff.), but only of Luther's relation to it. It may be men-

tioned, however, that a full collection of sources is to be edited by
O. Merx in three volumes. (One chapter by this author has appeared
in Festschrift zum Gedächtniss Philipps des Grossmütigen. Kassel.
1904. pp. 259–333.)

Besides the histories of Janssen, Bezold, Lamprecht, etc., may be
mentioned the following special works : —

E. B. Bax : Social Side of the Reformation in Germany. 3 vols.
London. 1894.

Götze : Die Artikel der Bauern 1525, in Hist. Vierteljahrsschrift,
iv (1901) and v (1902).

Stolze : Der deutsche Bauernkrieg. Halle. 1907.

J. S. Schapiro : Social Reform and the Reformation (Columbia
University Studies, xxxiv, no. ii). New York. 1909.

Lietzmann : Kleine Texte. . . . Bonn. 1902 ff. nos. l–li. Urkunden
zur Geschichte des Bauernkrieges und der Wiedertäufer. Ed.
Böhmer.

Exhortation to Peace on the Twelve Articles. Weimar, xviii, 279.

Letter on the hard Pamphlet against the Peasants. Weimar, xviii,
375.

Chapters XV, XXXII. The Luther Family

Albrecht Thoma : Katharina von Bora. Berlin. 1900.

E. Kroker : Katharina von Bora. Leipzig. 1906.

Luther's Sermon on Marriage. Weimar, xvii, 12.

Letter to Reissenbusch. Weimar, xviii, 270.

P. A. Kirsch : Melanchthons Brief an Camerarius über Luthers
Heirat vom 16 Juni. 1525 [with incorrect translation]. Mainz. 1900.

W. Meyer : Lauterbachs und Aurifabers Sammlungen der Tischreden Luthers. Abhandlungen d. k. Geselschaft der Wissenschaften zu
Göttingen. Phil. Hist. Klasse. N. F. Bd. i, no. ii. 1897.

Preserved Smith : Luther's Table Talk, a Critical Study. Columbia University Studies. xxvi, no. ii. New York. 1907.

Chapter XVI. Private Life. 1522–1530

On the University :

G. Bauch : Die Einführung des Hebräischen in Wittenberg, in
Montaschrift für Geschichte des Judenthums, Jahrgang 48. p. 22 ff.

G. Bauch : Wittenberg und die Scholastik, in Neues Archiv für
Sächsische Geschichte. 1897. pp. 295 ff.

E. Haupt : Was unsere Universitäten der Gründung der Universität Wittenberg danken. Halle. 1902.

On Luther's diseases, cf. below, Chapter XXXIX.

On the Erection and Maintenance of Schools. Weimar, xv, 1 ff.

Whether one may flee from the Plague. Weimar, xxiii, 323 ff.

Sermons of 1527. Weimar, xxiii, passage quoted p. 689.

Sermons of 1528. Weimar, xxvii.

Sermons of 1528-9. Weimar, xxviii.

Sermons of 1529-1530. Weimar, xxix.

Sermons on Exodus. Weimar, xvi; passage quoted p. 301.

Sermons on Genesis 1527. Weimar, xxiv.

Lectures on Titus, Philemon, and Isaiah. Sermons on Leviticus and Numbers. Weimar, xxv.

Lectures on Ecclesiastes. Weimar, xx, 1 ff.

Sermons of 1526. Weimar, xx, 204 ff.

Lectures on 1 John. Weimar, xx, 592 ff.

Lectures on Minor Prophets. Weimar, xiii.

Lectures on 2 Peter, Jude, Genesis, Deuteronomy. Weimar, xiv.

Sermons of 1530. Weimar, xxxii.

Sermons on John 6-8 (October 1530-1532). Weimar, xxxiii.

Sermons of 1531. Weimar, xxxiv.

CHAPTER XVII. LUTHER AND HENRY VIII

J. S. Brewer, J. Gairdner, R. H. Brodie: Letters and papers, foreign and domestic, of the reign of Henry VIII. London. 1862. . . .

Bergenroth, Gayangos and Hume: Calendar of letters, dispatches and state papers preserved in the archives of Simancas. . . . London. 1862. . . .

R. Brown : State papers . . . preserved in the archives of Venice. . . . London. 1867. . . .

Luther : Contra Henricum Angliae regem. Weimar, x, pt. ii, 175.

Id. Auf den Titel des Königs zu Engelland Lästerschrift. Weimar, xxiii, 17.

Assertio Septem Sacramentorum. I have used an edition without year or place, in the Bibliothèque Nationale at Paris, catalogue number D 5839.

Epistola Martini Lutheri ad Henricum VIII . . . et Responsio dicti invictissimi Angliae et Franciae regis. . . . Dresden. 1527.

A copy of the letters wherein the most redoubted . . . Henry VIII made answer unto a certain letter of Martin Luther. s. l. et a. (Appendix to More's Apology). Bodleian Library Crynes 863.

W. W. Rockwell : Die Doppelehe des Landgraf Philip von Hessen. Marburg. 1904. pp. 202-309.

W. Walther: Heinrich VIII von England und Luther. Rostock. 1908.

J. P. Collier: History of English Dramatic Poetry, i, 108 (on the revel of November 9, 1527). Cf. J. A. Froude: History of England (1875) i, 74–76.

Preserved Smith: Luther and Henry VIII, English Historical Review, no. c. October, 1910.

G. Mentz: Johann Friedrich, ii. Jena. 1908.

G. Mentz: Die Wittenberger Artikel von 1536. Leipzig. 1905.

Assertio Septem Sacramentorum . . . reëdited by L. O'Donovan. New York. 1908.

Henrici VIII contra Lutherum ejusque haeresim, epistola ad Saxoniae Duces. Spicilegium Romanum (1840), iii, 741–50.

Cambridge History of English Literature, vol. v, part i (1910), p. 114, states that John Ritwise, master of St. Paul's School, was responsible for the play of November 9, 1527.

Better readings of Luther's letter to Cromwell, 1536, together with a letter of Jonas to Cromwell of the same date, will be found in my article in the Zeitschrift für Kirchengeschichte, February, 1911. An interesting unpublished source, is: Henrici VIII . . . contra Germanorum opiniones de utraque specie, de missa privata et de conjugio sacerdotorum. Collected by Cuthbert Tunstall and revised by Henry, apparently in 1536. Corpus Christi College, Cambridge, England, MS 109, 1.

On the burning of Luther's works at St. Paul's, Sanuto's Diaries, xxx, 314 ff., 342.

Edicts against Luther in England, Wilkins: Concilia Magnae Britanniae et Hiberniae (1737), iii, 689, 690, 693, 711, 720, 737.

CHAPTER XVIII. LUTHER AND ERASMUS

Erasmi opera omnia, ed. J. Clericus. Lugduni Batavorum. 1703–6.

Erasmi Axiomata, in Luther's Werke, Erlangen, v, 238 ff.

Acta Academiae Lovaniensis, ibid. iv, 308.

Consilium cujusdam . . . , in Zwinglii opera, ed. Schuler & Schulthess, i, 1.

De libero arbitrio Diatribe sive collatio, Clericus, x, pt. i, 1215.

Id. ed John von Walther. Quellenschriften zur Geschichte des Protestantismus. xxiii. 1909.

Hyperaspistes . . . Clericus, x, pt. ii. 1249 ff.

Luther: De servo arbitrio. Weimar, xviii, 551.

Responsio Lutheriana ad condemnationem doctrinalem per magistros Lovanienses et Colonienses. Weimar, vi, 3.

Horawitz : Erasmus und Martin Lipsius. Wien. 1882.

Opus epistolarum Erasmi. The most complete edition is that in Clericus, iii ; a better edition is now in course of publication : by P. S. Allen, 2 vols., Oxford 1906, 1910, which has as yet only the letters before July, 1517. Additional letters in :

J. Förstemann und O. Günther : Briefe an Erasmus. Leipzig. 1904.

L. K. Enthoven : Briefe an Erasmus. Strassburg. 1906.

More light may also be expected from the Bibliotheca Erasmiana, now in course of publication at Ghent : Listes sommaires, 1893 ; Adagia, 1897 ; Annotationes &c., 1900 ; Apophtegmata, 1901 ; Colloquia, 3 vols. 1903–7.

An allusion to Erasmus in 1532, in the preface to Bugenhagen's edition of Athanasius against Idolatry. Weimar, xxx, iii, 531.

Besides the lives of Erasmus by R. B. Drummond (1872), Durand de Laur (1872), J. A. Froude (1895) and E. Emerton (1900), I have consulted the following special treatises : —

H. Hermelink : Die religiösen Reformbestrebungen des deutschen Humanismus. Tübingen. 1907.

Humbertclaude : Érasme et Luther, leur polémique sur le libre arbitre. Paris. 1909.

P. Kalkoff : W. Capito im Dienste des Erzbishof Albrecht von Mainz. Berlin. 1908.

P. Kalkoff : Die Vermittlungspolitik des Erasmus und sein Anteil an den Flugschriften der ersten Reformationszeit. Archiv für Reformationsgeschichte, i (1903).

G. Kawerau : Luther und Erasmus. Deutsch-evangel. Blätter. 1906, p. 12.

F. Lezius : Zur Characteristik des religiösen Standpunkts des Erasmus. Gütersloh. 1895.

A. Meyer : Étude critique sur les relations d'Érasme et de Luther. Paris. 1909.

M. Richter : Desiderius Erasmus und seine Stellung zu Luther. Leipzig. 1907.

K. Zickendraht : Der Streit zwischen Erasmus und Luther über die Willensfreiheit. Leipzig. 1909.

P. Kalkoff : Erasmus, W. Nesen und N. von Herzogenbusch im Kampfe mit den Löwener Theologen. Zwingli's Werke, ed. Egli, Finsler und Köhler, vol. vii (1910), pp. 402–420.

Article " Erasmus," by Mark Pattison and P. S. Allen, in Encyclopædia Britannica, 11th edition (1910–11), ix, 727.

Chapters XIX, XXIV. German Politics

A. *Luther's Political Theory*

Sources:

Luther: Of Civil Authority and how far it is to be obeyed. Weimar, xi, 229.

Luther: Whether Soldiers can be in a state of Grace. Weimar, xix, 616.

Monographs:

N. Paulus: Luther und die Todesstrafe für Ketzer. Hist.-pol. Blätte. vol. cxlv, pp. 177–189, and 243–255.

E. Brandenburg: Luthers Anschauen vom Staat und Gesellschaft, Schriften d. Vereins f. Reformationsgesch. Halle. 1901.

L. Cardauns: Die Lehre vom Widerstandsrecht des Volkes. Bonn. 1903. (Page 125, remarks that Luther followed closely Augustine: Contra Faustum Manichaeum.)

P. Drews: Entsprach das Staatskirchenthum dem Ideale Luthers? Tübingen. 1908.

W. A. Dunning: Political Theory from Luther to Montesquieu. New York. 1905. pp. 1 ff.

P. Wappler: Inquisition und Ketzerprozess zu Zwickau. Leipzig. 1908.

E. Ehrhardt: La notion du droit naturel chez Luther. (Études de théologie et d'histoire, pp. 285 ff.) Montauban. 1901.

G. Jäger: Politische Ideen Luthers und ihr Einfluss auf die innere Entwickelung Deutschlands. Preussische Jahrbücher. 1903.

F. G. Ward: Darstellung und Würdigung der Ansichten Luthers vom Staat und seinen Wirtschaftlichen Aufgaben. Conrad's Sammlung nationalökon. Abhandlungen, xxi. Jena. 1898.

G. von Schulthess-Rechberg: Luther, Zwingli und Calvin in ihren Ansichten über das Verhältnis von Staat und Kirche. Aarau. 1910.

L. H. Warren: The Political Theories of Martin Luther. New York. 1910.

Max Weber: two articles in Archiv für sociale Gesetzgebung und Statistik. 1905. xx, xxi.

K. Müller: Kirche, Gemeinde und Obrigkeit nach Luther. Tübingen. 1910.

B. *Politics*

Sources:

A. Wrede: Deutsche Reichstagsakten unter Karl V. Vol. iii. 1901.

F. Gess: Akten und Briefe zur Kirchenpolitik Herzog Georgs von Sachsen. Bd. i, 1517–24. Leipzig. 1905.

Luther: Of Secret and Stolen Letters. Weimar, xxx, pt. ii, pp. 1 ff.

Luther: On the Turkish War. Weimar, ibid., pp. 81 ff.

Warning to his dear Germans. Weimar xxx, iii, 252.

Commentary on the putative Imperial Edict. Weimar xxx, iii, 321 ff.

Histories :

Cambridge Modern History, ii, chapters 5 and 6.

Pastor: Geschichte der Päpste, iv, pt. ii, pp. 76 ff.

Monographs :

R. Kübel: Ein Jahr aus Luthers Leben (1525). 1883.

T. Brieger: Der Speirer Reichstag von 1526 und die religiöse Frage der Zeit. Leipzig. 1909 (Review by W. Friedensburg, Arch. f. Reformationsgesch. 1910, pp. 93 ff.).

T. Kolde: Friedrich der Weise und die Anfänge der Reformation. Erlangen. 1881.

A. Krencker: Friedrich der Weise von Sachsen beim Beginn der Reformation. 1906.

J. Becker: Kurfürst Johann von Sachsen und seine Beziehungen zu Luther. Leipzig. 1890, 1905. 2 v.

G. Mentz: Johann Friedrich der Grossmütige. Jena. 3 v. 1903, 1908. (I refer especially to ii, 8 and 27.)

H. Schwartz: Landgraf Philipp von Hessen und die Päckischen Händel. 1884.

Ehses: Landgraf Philipp von Hessen und Otto von Pack. 1886.

O. Winkelmann: Der Schmalkaldische Band, 1530–2. 1892.

P. Wappler: Die Stellung Kursachsens und des Landgraf Philipps von Hessen zur Täuferbewegung. Münster i. W. 1910.

CHAPTER XX. CHURCH BUILDING

1. *Church Building.*

German Mass. Weimar, xix, 44 ff.

Deutsche Litaner und Latina Litania correcta (1529). Weimar, xxx, iii, 1 ff.

Instruction for the Visitors of Saxony. Weimar, xxvi, 174 ff.

The Abomination of Private Masses. Weimar, xviii, 8 ff.

Ein Traubüchlein für die einfältigen Pfarrherrn (1529). Weimar, xxx, iii, 43.

Luther: Von Ordnung Gottesdiensts, Taufbüchlein, Formula Missae et communionis. Bonn. 1909.

K. Rieker: Die rechtliche Stellung d. Evangel. Kirche Deutschlands. Leipzig. 1893.

E. Sehling: Die evangelischen Kirchenordnungen des 16. Jahrhunderts. Leipzig. 1906 ff. As yet 3 volumes.

2. Songs.

Songs, Erlangen, vol. lvi. Better edited in Lietzmann: Kleine Texte, &c. 1902 ff. nos. xxiv, xxv.

J. Wagener, in Monatschrift f. Gottesdienst und kirchliche Kunst. iv (1899), pp. 7 ff. J. Adam: Ein Feste Burg, ibid. xiv (1909), pp. 6–9.

Zelle: Das älteste lutherische Hausgesangbuch. (Göttingen. 1903.)

E. Achelis: Die Entstehungszeit von Luthers geistlichen Lieder. Marburg. 1883.

J. Linke: Wann wurde das Lutherlied "Ein Feste Burg" verfasst? Leipzig. 1886.

F. Spitta: "Ein Feste Burg ist unser Gott." Göttingen. 1905.

G. Kawerau: Neue Forschungen über Luther's Lieder, in Deutsch-evangelischen Blätter, 1906. Heft 5, pp. 314 ff.

J. Raubenstrauch: Luther und die kirchliche Musik in Sachsen bis auf 1610. Leipzig. 1906.

Dr. Zelle: Die Singweisen der ältesten evangel. Lieder. Berlin. 1899, 1900.

3. Catechisms.

Catechisms and catechistical writings. Weimar, xxx, pt. 1.

F. Cohrs: Die evangelischen Katechismusversuche vor Luthers Enchiridion. 3 Hefte. Berlin. 1901–1907.

K. Knoke: D. M. Luthers kleiner Katechismus nach die ältesten Ausgaben in hochdeutscher, niederdeutscher und lateinischer Sprachen. Halle. 1904.

O. Albrecht: Neue Katechismusstudien. In Theolog. Stud. u. Kritik. 1909. pp. 592 ff.

Dictionnaire de Théologie Catholique. (Paris, 1903 ff.) Article Catéchismes, in vol. ii.

Der kleine Katechismus D. Martin Luthers nach der Ausgabe von Jahre 1536. Facsimile Neudruck von O. Albrecht. Halle. 1905.

M. Savoye: Étude historique sur la formation des catéchismes de Luther. Paris. 1901.

CHAPTERS XXI, XXII. ZWINGLI AND THE DIET OF
AUGSBURG

Ulrichi Zwinglii opera, ed. Schuler und Schulthess. 8 vols. Zurich 1528–42. Letters, vols. vii, viii.

Ulrich Zwinglis Werke, ed. Egli, Finster und Köhler. (Corpus Reformatorum, vols. 88 ff.) Zurich. 1904 ff. Now out, vols. i, ii, iii.

Vadianische Briefsammlung, part iv, and Briefwechsel der Blaurer, vol. i (see general bibliography).

Oecolampadii et Zwinglii epistolarum libri quattuor. Basle. 1536. pp. 24 ff.

E. Egli: Schweizerische Reformationsgeschichte. Band i. 1519–25. Zurich 1910.

Article on Zwingli by Egli and Stähelin. Realencyclopädie, xxi.

Eight contemporary accounts of the Marburg Colloquy are published in Weimar, xxx, iii, 94 ff.

Luther: Dass diese Worte Christi " Das ist mien Leib " noch feststehen. Weimar, xxiii, 38.

Luther: Vom Abendmahl Christi (Grosses) Bekenntnis. Weimar, xxvi, 241.

Fr. Gräbke: Die Konstruktion der Abendmahlslehre Luthers. 1907.

Article Abendmahlslehre, in Religion in Geschichte und Gegenwart. i, 2092–2112.

Schirrmacher: Briefe und Akten zur Geschichte des Religionsgespräches zu Marburg 1529 und des Reichstages zu Augsburg. 1530. Gotha. 1876.

G. Berbig: Acta Comiciorum Augustae. Halle. 1907.

H. von Schubert: Bekenntnisbildung und Religionspolitik 1529–30. Gotha. 1910.

Müller: Die Bekenntnissschriften der reformierten Kirche. Leipzig. 1903.

Article on Marburg Colloquy by Kolde, Realencyclopädie, xii.

Tschackert: Die Augsburgische Konfession. Leipzig. 1901.

Luther: Warnung zu den Geistlichen zu Augsburg. Weimar, xxx, pt. ii, 237.

J. Luther: Dr. M. Luthers Beziehungen zur Wartburg und Feste Coburg. Berlin. 1900.

CHAPTER XXIII. THE GERMAN BIBLE

Weimar edition: Deutsche Bibel, vols. i and ii.

Preussische Hauptbibelgesellschaft: Luthers Vorrede zur heiligen Schrift. Berlin. 1883.

W. Walther: Luthers Bibelübersetzung kein Plagiat. Erlangen and Leipsic. 1891.

G. Kcyssncr: Die drei Psalterarbeitungen Luthers von 1524, 1528, und 1531. Meiningen. 1890.

Scheel: Luthers Stellung zur heiligen Schrift. Tübingen and Leipsic. 1902.

Luther's Letter on Translation. Weimar, xxx, p. 632.

Realencyclopädie, article Bibelübersetzung, Deutsch. vol. iii, pp. 59 ff.

P. Pietsch: Martin Luther und die hochdeutsche Schriftsprache. 1883.

Das Neue Testament. Facsimile of 1st ed., Sept., 1522, ed. Köstlin. Berlin. 1883.

O. Ritsche: Dogmengeschichte des Protestantismus. Vol. i. Leipzig. 1908. Prolegomena. Biblicismus und Traditionalismus in der altprotestantischen Theologie.

Sir H. H. Howarth: The Biblical Canon according to Luther, Zwingli, Lefèvre and Calvin. Journal of Theological Studies. ix (1908), 188–230.

Luther's marginal notes on his Bible. Werke. Walch, ix, 1774–1821.

O. Reichert: Martin Luthers deutsche Bibel. Tübingen. 1910.

Preserved Smith: The Methods of Reformation Interpreters of the Bible. In the Biblical World (Chicago). 1911.

R. Kuhn: Verhältnis der Decemberbibel zur Septemberbibel. Mit einem Anhange über J. Langes Matthaeusübersetzung. Dissertation. Greifswald. 1901.

Note. It is impossible to credit the testimony of Carlstadt that Luther believed the epistle of James to be a forgery of St. Jerome. Barge: Carlstadt (1905), i, 197.

Chapter XXV. The Church Militant

E. Fabian: Der Streit Luther mit dem Zwickauer Rate im Jahre 1531. (Mitteilungen des Altertumsvereins für Zwickau. viii.) 1905.

The Antinomian quarrel:

G. Kawerau: J. Agricola von Eisleben. Berlin. 1881.

Disputations against Antinomians, ed. Drews (Leipzig. 1895–96), pp. 246 ff., 334 ff., 611 ff.

On Luther and Melanchthon, cf. supra, Chapter VII.

Chapter XXVI. The Wittenberg Agreeement

Wittenberger Konkordie, article in Realencyc. xxi, 384.

Vadianische Briefsammlung Part iv and Briefwechsel der Blaurer, vol. i. (See general bibliography.)

G. Anrich: Die Strassburger Reformation nach ihrer religiösen Eigenart und ihrer Bedeutung für die Gesamtprotestantismus. Die Christliche Welt. 1905. Nos. xxv, xxvi, xxvii.

Chapter XXVII. Relations with France, England, etc.

G. Mentz: Johann Friedrich. (Jena 1903–1908.) Vol. ii, chapter 4.

Fr. Hülsse: Der Streit Kardinal Albrechts mit dem Kurfürst Johann Friedrich von Sachsen um die magdeburgische Burggraf. Magdeburg. 1887.

L. Cardauns: Zur Kirchenpolitik Herzog Georgs von Sachsen. Rome. 1907. (Quellen und Forschungen aus Italienischen Archiven.) Vol. x, pp. 101–51.

Redlich: Kardinal Albrecht und das Neue Stift. 1900.

Luther and Albert. Weimar, xxx, iii, 400–1.

The Sermon against which Duke George's son complained. Weimar, xxxvii, 577. Nov. 1, 1534.

Wider den Meuchler zu Dresden. Weimar, xxx, part iii, pp. 413–71.

Chapter XXVIII. The League of Schmalkalden

The visit of Vergerio :

Bindseil: Lutheri Colloquia (Lemgovioe et Detmoldiae. 1863–66). Vol. iii, p. 89.

W. Friedensburg: Nuntiaturberichte aus Deutschland, vol. i (Gotha, 1892), p. 538. Vergerio's letter to his friend Ricalcati.

Corpus Reformatorum, vol. ii, col. 987.

Luther's Articles on the Donation of Constantine, 1537. In Werke (Berlin, 1903), vol. i, p. 182.

Pastor : Geschichte der Päpste, v (1909), 49–50.

Schmalkalden :

Luther: Of the Council and Church. Werke (Berlin, 1903), vol. ii, p. 1 ff.

Schmalkaldic Articles, ibid., vol. iii, p. 35 ff.

K. Thieme: Luther's Testament wider Rom in seinen Schmalkaldischen Artikeln. Leipzig. 1900.

Pastor, v, 64–65.

Chapter XXIX. Character and Habits

G. Kawerau : Vom kranken Luther, in Deutsch-evangelische Blätter, vol. xxix (1904), p. 303 ff.

W. Ebstein : Martin Luther's Krankheiten. Stuttgart. 1908.

H. Böhmer : Luther im Lichte der neueren Forschung. 2d ed. Leipzig. 1910. Chapter iv.

H. P. Denifle : Luther und Lutherthum. I. Hauptband. 2d ed. 2 parts. Mainz. 1905–1906.

W. Walther : Für Luther wider Rom. Halle. 1906.

H. Grisar : Der " gute Trunk " in den Lutheranklagen. In Histor. Jahrbücher, vol. xxvi (1905), p. 479 ff.

The anecdote on Luther's mending his trousers is taken from the unpublished source, Colloquia Serotina, Blatt 103. See above, general bibliography. The section is found in somewhat similar form, though without the date, in Bindseil, vol. ii, p. 126.

Chapter XXX. At Work

Sermons (apart from the Postilla). Erlangen, vols. xvi–xx. A selection of edifying passages from the sermons, Berlin, vols. vi and vii.

Luther's Disputationen 1535–1546, edited by Drews. Göttingen. 1895–96.

Böhmer : Luther im Lichte der neueren Forschung. Leipzig. 1910. Chapters iv and v.

Loofs : Luthers Stellung z. Mittelalter u. z. Neuzeit. Halle. 1907.

P. Kleinert : Luthers Verhältnis z. Wissenschaft und ihrer Lehre. Berlin. 1883.

Sermons 1533–34. Weimar, xxxvii.

Sermons 1535–36. Weimar, xli.

G. Buchwald : M. Luthers Predigten im Juli 1534 zu Dessau, zum erstenmal herausgegeben. Leipsic. 1909.

G. Buchwald : Luthers Predigten 1537–1540. Halle. 1906 (1905).

Chapter XXXI. Religion and Culture

O. G. Schmidt : Luthers Bekanntschaft mit den römischen Klassikern. 1883.

Schäfer : Luther als Kirchenhistoriker. 1897.

W. Köhler : Luther und die Kirchengeschichte. Gütersloh. 1900.

Schmidt : Faust und Luther, in Sitzungsberichte d. k. Preuss. Akad. d. Wissenschaften zu Berlin. 1896. pp. 568 ff.

Xanthippus : Gute alte deutsche Sprüche, in Preuss. Jahrbücher.
Vol. lxxxv. July, August, September 1896. pp. 149 ff., 344 ff., 503 ff.

P. Curtis : Luther's variations in sentence arrangement from the
modern literary usage. . . . New Haven. 1910.

A. Götze : Volkskundliches bei Luther. Weimar. 1909.

Note on Luther's Theology. This biography does not aim to deal
with Luther's theology per se, any more than a life of Darwin would
necessarily involve a thorough investigation of evolution. The best
works on the subject are :

J. Köstlin : Luthers Theologie in ihrer geschichtlichen Entwickelung
und ihrem inneren Zusammenhang. 2d ed. Stuttgart. 1901.

W. Herrmann : Der Verkehr des Christen mit Gott im Anschluss an
Luther dargestellt. 3d ed. Stuttgart. 1896.

J. Gottschick, articles in Zeitschrift f. Theologie und Kirche, 1897,
p. 352 ; 1898, p. 406 ; 1903, p. 349 ff.

K. Thieme : Die sittliche Triebkraft des Glaubens. Eine Untersu-
chung zu Luthers Theologie. Leipsic. 1895.

R. A. Lipsius : Luthers Lehre von der Busse. Brunswick. 1892.

A. Galley : Die Busslehre Luthers. Gütersloh. 1900.

E. Fischer : Zur Geschichte der evangel. Beichte. (to 1523). 2
parts. Leipsic. 1902, 1903.

K. Jäger : Luthers religiöses Interesse an seiner Lehre von der
Realpräsenz. Giessen. 1900.

Graebke : Die Construction der Abendmahlslehre Luthers. Leipsic.
1908.

M. Staub : Das Verhältnis der menschlichen Willensfreiheit zur
Gotteslehre bei Luther und Zwingli. Zurich. 1894.

J. Göttschick : Luthers Anschauungen vom christlichen Gottesdienst
und seine tatsächliche Reform desselben. Giessen. 1887.

J. Hans : Der protestantische Kultus. 1890.

K. Eger : Die Anschauungen Luthers vom Beruf. Giessen. 1900.

H. Stephan : Luther in den Wandlungen seiner Kirche. Giessen.
1907.

O. Ritschl : Dogmengeschichte des Protestantismus. Vol. i. Leipzig.
1908.

Loofs : Leitfaden zum Studium der Dogmengeschichte. 4th ed.
1906.

A. Harnack : History of Dogma, translated from the third German
edition by N. Buchanan. Boston. 1900. Vol. vii, pp. 168–274.

A. Harnack : Dogmengeschichte. 4th edition. Tübingen. 1909–10.
Vol. iii, chapter v. Die Ausgänge des Dogmas in Protestantismus.
pp. 808–902.

H. Wace : Principles of the Reformation. London. 1910.

Paul Lehfeldt : Luthers Verhältnis zu Kunst und Künstlern. Berlin.
1892.

On Luther's copy of Homer (Aldus. 1517) given to Melanchthon in
1519, cf. my article in Zeitschrift für Kirchengeschichte, February,
1911.

Chapter XXXIII. Domestic Economy

Note on the price of wheat. Luther's statements are so startling that
they seem to require some support. The average price of wheat in
England for the half century 1451–1500 was six shillings and two
pence a quarter, or nine pence half-penny a bushel. (Rogers.) Cf.
further : —

Conrad, and Lexis, articles in Conrad's Handwörterbuch der Staats-
wissenschaften. Jena. 1900. iv, pp. 277, 323.

Th. Rogers : A History of Agriculture and Prices in England. Oxford. 1882. Vol. iii, 1401–1582.

K. Lamprecht : Deutsches Wirtsshaftsleben im Mittelalter. 3 vols.
Leipzig. 1885–86.

L. Keller : Zur Geschichte der Preisbewegung in Deutschland
wahrend 1466–1525. Jahrbücher für Nationalökonomie und Statistik
xxxiv.

G. Wiebe : Zur Geschichte der Preisrevolution in xvi and xvii
Jahrhunderten. Leipzig. 1895.

J. A. Froude : History of England (1875), i, p. 21. Many interesting prices. Wheat is said to average 10 pence the bushel in the
16th century, the lowest price mentioned 2 pence 1 farthing. Froude
reckons general purchasing power of money as twelve times as great
then.

Note on Luther's house. The Black Cloister is still shown at Wittenberg, the interior preserved as it was in Luther's day. The exterior
has since been stuccoed ; it was formerly of brick. In front of the
house, between it and the street, has been built the Augusteum, used
as a theological seminary.

Chapter XXXIV. The Bigamy of Philip of Hesse

M. Lenz : Briefwechsel Philipps des Grossmütigen mit Bucer.
Vol. i. 1880.

W. W. Rockwell : Die Doppelehe des Landgrafen Philipp von
Hessen. Marburg. 1904.

Brieger : Luther und die Nebenehe des Landgrafen Philipps von
Hessen. In Preussische Jahrbücher (1909), pp. 35 ff.

Brieger : Luther und die Nebenehe des Landgrafen Philipp.
Zeits. f. Kirchengeschichte, xxix (1908), p. 174 ff.

OX: 11-27-84

Thursday at 3 PM, we are
requested to be in the
personnel Conf. Rm. for
a meeting.

    Our replacements have
been enformed of the same.

                    Steve

                    Herbie

G. Sodeur : Luther und die Lüge. Leipzig. 1904.

F. Küch : Politisches Archiv des Landgrafen Philipp von Hessen. Vol. i. Leipzig. 1904. Vol. ii. 1910.

Luthers Briefwechsel, ed. Enders und Kawerau, xii, 319–328.

Philipp der Grossmütige. Beiträge zur Geschichte seines Lebens und seiner Zeit. Hg. von Hist. Verein f. d. Grossherzogthum Hessen. Marburg. 1904.

Chapter XXXV. Protestant and Catholic

Wider Hans Wurst. Berlin, iv, 257 ff.

Against the Papacy at Rome. Ibid. 122 ff.

C. Wendeler : M. Luthers Bilderpolemik gegen das Papsthum von 1545. In Archiv f. Lit.–Geschichte, xiv, p. 17 ff.

Mitzschke : M. Luther, Naumburg a. S. und die Reformation. Naumburg. 1885.

O. Albrecht, in Theol. Stud. u. Kritiken. 1904. pp. 32 ff.

F. Roth ; Der offizielle Bericht der von den Evangelischen zum Regensburger Gespräch Verordneten (1542). A. R. G. Vol. xx, 1908, p. 378 ff.

S. Cardanus : Zur Geschichte der kirchlichen Unions- u. Reformbestrebungen 1538–1542. Rom. 1910.

K. Bauer : Luther und der Papst. Schriften des Vereins für Reformationsgeschichte, no. c (1910), pp. 231–273.

Satires against Henry of Brunswick, Schade, op. cit. i, Nr. viii–xiii.

A. Korte : Die Konzilspolitik Karls V in den Jahren 1538–43. Schriften des Vereins für Reformationsgeschichte, no. lxxxv. 1905.

Pastor : Geschichte der Päpste, v, 253–347.

Chapter XXXVI. Lutheran and Sacramentarian

J. Haussleiter : Die geschichtliche Grundlage der letzen Unterredung Luthers und Melanchthons im Abendmahlstreit. 1546. Leipsic. 1899. This, and the fact that Luther directed Rörer to omit some of his sharpest sayings against Zwingli in the first volume of his German works (1545), has been made the ground for supposing that he was ready to smooth over the old quarrel before his death. The letters quoted above disprove this.

Other sources, Vadianische Briefsammlung, part v, and Briefwechsel der Blaurer, vol. ii. (See general bibliography.)

Schwenckfeld's works are now being edited in the Corpus Schwenckfeldianorum, of which one volume has appeared.

Disputatio de divinitate et humanitate Christi (Against Schwenckfeld). Ed. Drews: Disputationen, p. 585 ff.

On Luther's attitude to the Anabaptists in general: —

P. Wappler: Die Stellung Kursachsens und des Landgrafen
Philipp von Hessen zur Täuferbewegung. Münster. 1910. (Reforma-
tionsgeschichtliche Studien und Texte, no. xiii–xiv.)

CHAPTER XXXVII. DEATH

Kawerau: Briefwechsel des Justus Jonas (Halle, 1885), vol. ii,
p. 177 ff.

F. Roth: Der offizielle Bericht der von den Evangelischen zum
Regensburger Gespräch Verordneten. In Archiv für Reformationsgeschichte, no. xx (1908), pp. 378 ff.

Cochlaeus: Commentaria de actis et scriptis M. Lutheri. 1549.
Appendix, account of John Landau, apothecary of Mansfeld. It is on
this account that the proof of the stroke of apoplexy rests. It seems
to me that the proof is somewhat doubtful.

P. Majunke: Luthers Lebensende. Mainz. 1890.

M. Honef: Der Selbstmord Luthers geschichtlich erwiesen.
München. (No year.)

G. Claudin: La mort de Luther. Noisy-Le-Sec. 1895.

N. Paulus: Luthers Lebensende. Freiburg. 1898.

A contemporary account of Luther's death and burial, written in
a copy of his Sommerpostille (1554) by an eye-witness, probably
John Albrecht, in whose house he died, has just been discovered in
the library of the Lutheran Theological Seminary at Mt. Airy, Penn-
sylvania. It has been published by A. Spaet, in the Lutheran Church
Review, April, 1910, vol. xxix, no. ii (Philadelphia, 1910), pp. 313–
325.

III

DOCUMENTS

THE last edition of Luther's letters, that of Enders and Kawerau, complete at present to February, 1540, does not contain all the known letters. I have decided to print three which are not easily found, and to register the others, as far as known to me, which are missing in this edition.

I. LUTHER TO GERARD LISTRIUS, AT ZWOLLE [1]

WITTENBERG, July 30 (1520).

[H. C. Rogge : Een onuitgegeven Brief van Dr. Martin Luther. Archief voor Nederlandsche Kerkgeschiedenis, vii, ii (1898), p. 204.]

Martinus Lutherus Augustiniensis Gerardo Listrio, rectori Swollis.

Salutem. Accepi literas tuas, vir eruditissime, magna cum voluptate, placuitque pater hic Johannes et quidquid nobiscum contulit, atque tales invenisset nos quales et tua et illius opinio praesumpsit. Quod ad me attinet scio quam michi curta supellex. Plurimum superat fama virtutem. Philippus vero felicissime theologizat professus pro tyrocinio suo Paulum ad Ro.[2] quingentis fere auditoribus, vero incredibile successu. Deus proficiat quod incepit, et hoc vasculo suo quod futurum brevi confido, ut theologiam purissimam in fonte suo bibat orbis Christianus.

Arbitror in mille annis sacras literas non ea sinceritate et luce fuisse tractatas proximumque esse donum eius apostolico seculo. Nostrum erit, ne ingrati simus, Deo rem suam acceptam referre et commendare. Ego meos hos annos infelicibus bellis perdidi mallemque meos labores in universum interire ne quid obessent puriori theologiae vel melioribus ingeniis, quanquam hodie sine cede et sanguine philosophor, ita me meum fatum rapit, quidquid enim est malarum bestiarum me unum petit, omnes ex me lauream querunt et palmam.

---

[1] On Listrius, rector of the School of the Brethren of the Common Life at Zwolle from 1516 to 1521, see Rogge, op. cit. pp. 206–220.

[2] Melanchthon was at this time lecturing on the Romans, the work which afterwards became the foundation of his celebrated Loci Communes. Cf. O. Clemen : Supplementa Melanchthoniana, i (1910), 1 ff.

Utinam ego fuero David sanguinem fundens, Philippus autem Salomon pace regnans. Amen.

Ceterum omnia referet hic, quem misisti, Johannes, qui si minus vestrae expectationi satisfaceret, culpa vestra esto, qui de nobis temere super id, quod non nobis est, cogitastis. Roma adhuc spirat minas et cedes in me ; sed contempno. Germania enim sapere coepit et hipocrisim papistarum intelligit. En queso nomine meo resaluta optimos viros omnes, qui per te me salutarunt. Psalterium ad psalmum XVIII deduxi virossimo [1] commentario cepitque me penitentia explicandi eius non propter laborem, sed quod res iste minime sunt vulgares et paucissimorum captui accomode necdum statui ultrum mitti oporteat et faciliora tractantia ; perfectorum enim cibus est. Vale mi Gerarde, in Domino. Wittenberge die 3 Kalendas Augusti.

II. Luther to John Cuspinian, at Vienna

Worms, April 17, 1521

(This letter is very badly printed in Enders, iii, 122. A facsimile of the original at Vienna was published by Haase in Leipziger Illustrierte Zeitung, August 31, 1889, from which I print it here.)

Salutem.[2] Frater carnis tuae, Cuspiniane celeberrime, facile mihi persuasit, ut e medio isto tumultu ad te auderem scribere, cum antea ob nominis tui celebritatem optarim tibi familiariter notus esse. Suscipe ergo me in tuorum album, ut vera esse comprobem quae frater tuus mihi de te [3] tam pleno ore cantavit.

Hac hora coram Caesare et Senatu [4] Romano constiti interrogatus, an libros meos revocare velim. Ubi respondi, libros quidem esse meos, caeterum quid de revocatione sentiam,[5] cras dicturum, petita et data mihi non amplius spatii et temporis ad deliberandum parte. Verum ne apicem quidem revocabo in aeternum,[6] Christo quidem propitio. Vale mi Cuspiniane charissime. Wormatiae, f. 4. p. Quasimodogeniti [7] 1521.

---

[1] Perhaps for "verbosissimo." Luther's Operationes in Psalmos, being his lectures on Psalms i–xxi, for the year 1519–21, appeared in 1521. Weimar Edition, vol. v.

[2] Instead of "Salutem. Frater carnis tuae," Enders has "Charitas tua."

[3] Enders omits "de te."

[4] Enders: "fratre."

[5] Enders: "statuam."

[6] Enders: "iterum." Luther writes the word here according to his custom "inaeternum."

[7] In his haste Luther makes a mistake in the date. Cf. Enders, iii, 123.

III. John Feige, Chancellor of Hesse, to Luther

(*Worms? April, 1521?*)

(This fragment is published by Dr. Gundlach, Festschrift zum Gedächtnis Philipps von Hessen, Cassel 1904, p. 64, with the date "perhaps March 3, 1521." The concept is in Feige's hand. The date must be too early, as the book mentioned, Ennarationes Epistolarum et Evangeliorum . . . D. M. Lutheri, appeared at Wittenberg March 7, 1521 (Enders, iii, 94), and it would have taken some time for the letter of Luther to have reached Feige after that. I suggest that Luther took some copies of the book with him to Worms, and while there, coming into communication with Philipp of Hesse (supra, p. 224), sent his old school friend Feige one of them.)

Gratia domini nostri Jhesu Christi cum omnibus nobis amen. Accepi literulas tuas, Martine doctissime, verum quas scribas te misisse enarrationes in S. evangelistas non accepi, interrogatusque tabellio se eas non habere respondit, tibi vero non minores habeo gratias quum si eas accepissem, tametsi me talibus tuis dignari lucubrationibus opus non fuisset, quum propter laborum multitudinem sacris michi literis incumbere raro liceat. . . .

IV. Lutheri Epistola gratulatoria super inventione et editione lucubrationum J. Tauleri . . .

(Edited by O. Clemen: Johann Pupper von Goch. He places it in 1521, but it is probably later (1523–1529). Cf. Theolog. Stud. und Kritiken. 1900. p. 135.)

V. Dr. John Rühel, Councillor of Mansfeld, to Luther, May 21, 1525

(A fragment of this letter is in Enders, v, 177. The whole is published by Kawerau, Schriften des Vereins für Reformationsgesch, no. c, pp. 338–340.)

Narrates the captivity of Münzer, the execution of seven priests at Heldrungen, the spoils taken at Frankenhausen. Asks Luther for details of the death of Frederic the Wise. Begs him to write to Albert of Mayence to induce him to change his spiritual for a temporal estate.

VI. Dr. John Rühel to Luther, May 26, 1525

(Fragment in Enders, v, 180; the whole published by Kawerau, ibid. pp. 340–342.)

Sends Münzer's recantation. Tells of the surrender of Mühlhausen May 24, and of Münzer's conveyance thither, and the interview between him and Philipp of Hesse.

VII. LUTHER TO LAMBERTUS HEMERTUS, JUNE 12, 1527

(Zeits. f. Kirchengesch. xviii, 231.)

VIII. PHILIPP OF HESSE TO CHANCELLOR BRÜCK AND LUTHER. SHORTLY BEFORE SEPTEMBER 22, 1531

(Gundlach, loc. cit., No. 2, p. 64.)

On the embassy from Henry VIII requesting the opinion of Luther on his divorce. (Answered, Enders, ix, 105. Further see my article, Luther and Henry VIII, English Historical Review, no. c. 1910.)

IX. LUTHER AND OTHERS TO JOHN, ELECTOR OF SAXONY. END OF APRIL OR BEGINNING OF MAY, 1532

(Burkhardt: Zum Briefwechsel der Reformatoren, Archiv für Reformationsgesch. no. xiv (1907), p. 184. Contents only given.)

X. LUTHER, JONAS AND MELANCHTHON TO JOHN FREDERIC, ELECTOR OF SAXONY. BEGINNING OF SEPTEMBER, 1532

(Ibid. p. 185.)

XI. ELECTOR JOHN FREDERIC TO LUTHER AND OTHERS. OCTOBER 22, 1533

(Ibid. p. 186.)

XII. ELECTOR JOHN FREDERIC TO LUTHER. NOVEMBER 15, 1533

(Ibid. p. 186 ff.)

XIII. ELECTOR JOHN FREDERIC TO LUTHER. DECEMBER 21, 1534

(Mentz: Johann Friedrich. Jena. 3 vols. 1903–1908. Vol. iii, Supplement, no. 1.)

Inquires about a sermon of Luther's (against Duke George) delivered on All Saints Day (November 1).

XIV. B. KNOR TO LUTHER AND JONAS. MAY 22, 1535

(Burkhardt, loc. cit., p. 188.)

On Church visitation.

XV. LUTHER, JONAS AND BUGENHAGEN TO JOHN FREDERIC. APRIL 5, 1536

(Ibid. p. 190.)

XVI. Luther's and Bugenhagen's certificate to J. Pogan.
June 11, 1536

(Ibid. p. 191.)

In the Boston Public Library there is a book with what is apparently an autograph of Luther. Epistolae sancti Hieronymi. (Colophon) Lugdunum-Jacobus Saccon. 1518. The autograph consists of a quotation from Gerson: "In floreno litis non est obolus caritatis. Gerson." It is well known that Luther had a low opinion of Jerome.

INDEX

INDEX

The Riverside Press
CAMBRIDGE . MASSACHUSETTS
U . S . A